FLASH FLAHERTY

FLASH FLAHERTY

Tales from a Film Seminar

Edited by **SCOTT MACDONALD**
and **PATRICIA R. ZIMMERMANN**
with **JULIA TULKE**

INDIANA UNIVERSITY PRESS

This book is a publication of

Indiana University Press
Office of Scholarly Publishing
Herman B Wells Library 350
1320 East 10th Street
Bloomington, Indiana 47405 USA

iupress.org

Manufactured in the
United States of America

Library of Congress Cataloging-in-Publication
Data

Names: MacDonald, Scott, 1942-editor. |
    Zimmermann, Patricia Rodden,
    editor. | Tulke, Julia, other.
Title: Flash Flaherty : tales from a film
    seminar / edited by Scott
    MacDonald and Patricia R. Zimmermann ;
    with Julia Tulke.
Description: Bloomington : Indiana
    University Press, 2021. | Includes index.
Identifiers: LCCN 2020039741 (print) |
    LCCN 2020039742 (ebook) | ISBN
    9780253053985 (hardback) | ISBN
    9780253053992 (ebook)
Subjects: LCSH: Flaherty (Organization) |
    Flaherty Seminar. | Independent
    films—Production and direction. |
    Independent films—History and criticism.
Classification: LCC PN1993.43.F43 F53 2021
    (print) | LCC PN1993.43.F43
    (ebook) | DDC 791.4306073—dc23
LC record available at https://lccn.loc.
    gov/2020039741
LC ebook record available at https://lccn.loc.
    gov/2020039742

1 2 3 4 5   26 25 24 23 22 21

Contents

Preface   *xiii*

Acknowledgments   *xv*

Introduction   1

1 | Sheafe Satterthwaite, Frances in
Her Inglenook   7

2 | Jonas Mekas, A Screening of
Flaming Creatures in Vermont   10

3 | Jay Ruby, The Aborted
Indigenous Seminar   13

4 | Amalie R. Rothschild, I Was Taken
Seriously as a Filmmaker   17

5 | Nadine Covert, Reminiscences
of Flaherty   21

6 | Linda Lilienfeld, Notes on the
Flaherty Seminar   24

7 | Deirdre Boyle, Video Slowly Emerges
at the Flaherty Seminar   28

8 | Juan Mandelbaum, Forty Years   32

9 | Patricia R. Zimmermann,
Get Out Your Shovel   36

10 | Lucy Kostelanetz, Godmothers,
Godfathers, and an Organization with a Soul   40

11 | Bruce Jenkins, Bordering on Fiction   44

12 | Richard Herskowitz,
My First Few Flahertys   48

13 | Ann Michel and Phil Wilde,
Video Projection at the Flaherty   52

14 | Michael Grillo,
A Medievalist's Projection   56

15 | Lynne Sachs, Refractions   60

16 | Tony Buba, Taking the Plunge   64

17 | Linda Blackaby and Tony Gittens,
Media Matters and Meteor Showers   68

18 | Jeffrey Skoller, Thirty Years Later   73

19 | Helen De Michiel, The Flaherty in 1986   78

20 | Louis Massiah, The One
Who Names You   82

21 | Philip Mallory Jones, Sparks 86

22 | Timothy Murray,
On the Road to Flaherty 91

23 | Su Friedrich, One Lake and
Two Kerfuffles 95

24 | Scott MacDonald,
Without Anesthesia 99

25 | Mark Geiger, In Over My Head 103

26 | Patti Bruck, Simply Put 105

27 | Stacey Steers, The Flaherty Laboratory 109

28 | Margarita De La Vega Hurtado,
Practical Difficulties and Different Locations 112

29 | Ayoka Chenzira, At the Table 116

30 | Andrei Zagdansky, Notes from
the 1990 Flaherty Seminar 121

31 | Steven Montgomery,
Overcoming Contempt 125

32 | Laura U. Marks, The Scent of Places 129

33 | Aviva Weintraub, Folders 133

34 | Ken Jacobs, The To-Do Over
XCXHXEXRXRXIXEXSX 137

35 | Portia Cobb, Points of Departure   141

36 | Jason Livingston, Many Moons   145

37 | Kathy Geritz, Programming the 2000
Flaherty Seminar   149

38 | Sami van Ingen, Coming of Age at
the Flaherty   152

39 | Marlina Gonzalez, Flaherty 1995   156

40 | Ayisha Abraham,
Aurora, Bangalore, Mysore   160

41 | Grace An, Beginnings/Endings   164

42 | Dorothea Braemer, Talking   169

43 | Ulises A. Mejias, Recovering
Lost Memories   173

44 | Thomas W. Bohn, I Never Met
Robert Flaherty   176

45 | Jacqueline Goss, Tendon Stretches   179

46 | Dan Streible, Up All Night   183

47 | Tan Pin Pin, The Art of
Asking Questions   187

48 | Alyce Myatt, Indelible Marks   191

49 | Erika Mijlin, An Unruly Endeavor   195

50 | Vicky Funari, Familiar and Strange   199

51 | Brian L. Frye, How I Learned to
Stop Worrying and Love the Flaherty   203

52 | Ed Halter and Matt Wolf, Remembering   207

53 | Chi-hui Yang, A Radical Openness   212

54 | Simon Tarr, Flaherty Reflections   216

55 | Lucius Barre, Flaherty Replaces Cannes   220

56 | Howard Weinberg, Film vs. TV:
Flaherty & INPUT   224

57 | John Gianvito, I Remember
Being Profoundly Moved and Inspired   228

58 | Ilisa Barbash, Five Reflections in
Search of the Flaherty's Zeitgeist   232

59 | Sam Gregory, "Witnessing" and
Witnessing at the Flaherty   236

60 | Carlos A. Gutiérrez, I Drank
the Kool-Aid   240

61 | Joanna Raczyńska,
Four Flaherty Seminars   243

62 | Roger Hallas, Critical Humility   247

63 | Jean-Marie Teno, Long Walks   251

64 | Andrés Di Tella, Breaking All the
Ordered Surfaces 255

65 | Leandro Katz, *Un banquete* at Claremont 259

66 | Amir Muhammad, The Sound of
White People Talking 263

67 | John Knecht, The Flaherty Finds a
New Home at Colgate University 267

68 | Jim Supanick, Stranger Comes to Town 271

69 | Dale Hudson, Patty Sent Me 275

70 | Shannon Kelley,
Tilting, Torquing, and
Shuffling between Dimensions 279

71 | Jason Fox, Returning to the
Scene of the Crime 283

72 | Amalia Córdova, Indigenous
Media Detonations 287

73 | John Muse, Forgetting Flaherty 291

74 | Marit Kathryn Corneil, Breathing
through the Screen 295

75 | Richard Shpuntoff, The Act of
Seeing Attentively 299

76 | Frances Guerin, From Colgate
University to the Central African Republic 303

77 | Dagmar Kamlah, A Virus and a Mission   307

78 | Paweł Wojtasik, I Didn't Know
What I Was Doing   311

79 | Dayong Zhao, Scents   315

80 | Josetxo Cerdán, My Own
Private *Rayuela*   319

81 | Karin Chien, Reverberations and
Amplifications   324

82 | Caroline Martel, *Dans mon imaginaire*   328

83 | Susana de Sousa Dias,
From Doc's Kingdom to
the Brotherhood of the Crystal Skull   332

84 | David Gracon, Homecoming   336

85 | Joel Neville Anderson, My First Flaherty   340

86 | Bo Wang, Everyone Recommended It   344

87 | Gabriela Monroy and Caspar Stracke,
Turning the Outside in Again   348

88 | Ohad Landesman, The Tactile
Unconscious   352

89 | Alberto Zambenedetti, Small Victories   356

90 | Eli Horwatt, What the
Flaherty Taught   360

91 | Hend F. Alawadhi, Certain Voices
Were Painfully Missing   364

92 | Ekrem Serdar,
Learning Things, Losing Things   368

93 | Jonathan Marlow, Time Travels   372

94 | Roy Grundmann, A Cinema
that Breathes   376

95 | Lina Žigelytė,
Grass, Rocks, Water   380

96 | Jiangtao (Harry) Gu, Not Exactly a
House of Prayer   384

97 | Greg de Cuir Jr., Speaking
Nearby Flaherty   388

98 | Sheafe Satterthwaite, No Longer
an Odd Voice at the Flaherty   391

99 | John Bruce, Uncertain Expeditions   395

100 | Anocha Suwichakornpong,
In That Silence   399

101 | Scott MacDonald,
Alas, the Logo!   403

102 | Patricia R. Zimmermann,
Seeing Bill Sloan, 1928–2017   407

Index   411

Preface

Soon after our earlier book on the Robert Flaherty Film Seminar, *The Flaherty: Decades in the Cause of Independent Cinema*, was published (in 2017) by Indiana University Press, we realized that our work was not complete.

For *The Flaherty*, we had spent years working to provide two kinds of institutional history: a standard, chronologically organized, carefully researched overview of the organization during its sixty-plus years and various stages of development, and a panorama of crucial and revealing instances of the "big-group" discussions that have become the stuff of Flaherty legend. Our book braided together these two kinds of history in order to provide a sense of the complex nature of this unusual institution, among the oldest continuously running nonprofit institutions in the world dedicated to independent cinema.

Once *The Flaherty* was published, we realized that a crucial dimension of the seminar's history was not evident in that book. We had not represented, in any direct way, what *the Flaherty experience* had been for the thousands of Flaherty seminarians who had attended the seminar. This period starts from the founding of the Flaherty in 1955, when Frances Flaherty convened a small gathering of film aficionados at the Flaherty farm in Dummerston, Vermont, to explore and learn from what she understood as Robert Flaherty's approach to filmmaking. It has continued into the present, when close to two hundred filmmakers, video artists, new media practitioners, theorists, film critics and historians, librarians, distributors, funders, programmers, cinema students, and cineastes come together at Colgate University to experience a weeklong series of screenings and formal discussions, with informal conversations among newcomers and longtime Flaherty veterans percolating on the edges.

At the 2017 Flaherty seminar, where *The Flaherty* was launched, we began hearing responses to the book, from newcomers and longtime seminarians, from those who saw themselves represented in the book, and from those who were disappointed at not being represented. We soon realized that some of the Flaherty veterans responding to our work could be convinced to put into writing their memories, their thoughts and feelings, and their sense of how their experiences at the seminar came to affect their personal and professional lives later on. That many of these veterans had made significant contributions to media culture in the United States and abroad suggested that their stories might provide some sense of how a particular organization impacts both individuals and media ecologies over the decades.

The first result was the *Flaherty Stories* blog, then available at the Ithaca College website (managed by Patricia R. Zimmermann, a veteran blogger). Once the blog began publishing Flaherty stories, others with stories to share began submitting them to us. We quickly realized that short lyrical creative nonfiction essays worked best for this project and continued to approach potential writers, asking that they write approximately a thousand words about particular Flaherty events that had been important to them.

Originally we had imagined that a few seminarians might want to share their experiences and reflections with us and with others who had, or had not, been to the Flaherty. We were surprised when blog postings continued to arrive on a regular basis from Flaherty veterans far and wide. By the time we had published several dozen, and with others on the way, we knew that these previously untold stories could—perhaps should—become a companion to *The Flaherty: Decades in the Cause of Independent Cinema*.

The thought that *Flaherty Stories* could become a book raised obvious questions. Did the data-saturated world really need another book about the Flaherty seminar? Did cinema and screen studies scholarship and the independent media world need a book about seminar participants' responses to the Flaherty experience? And did *we* need to be involved in still another Flaherty history project?

Ultimately, the answer seemed obvious. For us and for many of our colleagues, independent cinema in its various articulations has been a lifelong fascination and an ongoing education. We have spent much of our lives sharing our excitement and respect for the accomplishments of independent filmmakers and media artists with our students. And we have long recognized that our access to this major dimension of cinema and media history has been contingent on organizations that, over the long haul, have made it possible for us to explore this field, think and write about it, and utilize it in our teaching. Of course, the Flaherty is one of these organizations—and we realized that we could and should continue to learn from the ongoing impacts of its multilayered and serpentine history.

Acknowledgments

Flash Flaherty: Tales from a Film Seminar started out as a blog; we wanted to expand the conversation around the institutional histories elaborated in our book *The Flaherty: Decades in the Cause of Independent Cinema* into social media. The *Flaherty Stories* blog gradually transformed into something larger: a first-person, oral-history mosaic of the voices of some of the myriad people who have attended the seminar and who wanted to process and reflect on their experiences from their personal perspectives and locations across international film and media ecologies.

Our first thanks go to all of our storytellers. They contributed time, thought, research, and writing to our project. They were generous in sharing their Flaherty stories and patient with our queries and with the back-and-forth of our structural and fine-line editing of their pieces.

Several colleagues helped us to find contributors and cajole them into writing stories. For their advocacy and their suggestions, we thank Karin Chien, Margarita De La Vega Hurtado, Richard Herskowitz, Ann Michel, and Phil Wilde. Special thanks to Steve Montgomery, who, for the eighteen-month duration of this project, acted for all intents and purposes like our agent and ambassador. He suggested names. He reached out to the Flaherty community. He found writers. He sent emails and cards encouraging our efforts.

We also thank Elizabeth Wijaya for her translation work on Dayong Zhao's Flaherty story.

Julia Tulke was our research assistant extraordinaire. She wrangled the various forms and permissions and organized the headshots of the writers.

An Ithaca College Provost's Small Grant and a Roy H. Park School of Communications James B. Pendleton Research Grant supported the final stages of manuscript preparation. Hamilton College provided Scott MacDonald with time away from teaching to help see the manuscript to the finish line. Thanks, too, to Yvonne Schick at Hamilton College's Print Shop.

We particularly extend our gratitude to our editor at Indiana University Press, Janice Frisch, who supported this unusual project and immediately understood that it would work as a companion to our earlier book. We have valued her collegiality and her vision of what film and media books can be and what they can do. We also thank Allison Blair Chaplin, our current editor, who took over the project in its final stages with such generosity. Special thanks to Malin Wahlberg and Janet Walker for their valuable feedback on the manuscript.

So much of this book owes its origins to the upstate and central New York State region, where we both have lived and worked for decades. A place of hills, lakes, colleges, and vibrant media practices, it has been the primary host of the Flaherty since the late 1970s. It also is a place of hidden culinary delights. Therefore, we end our acknowledgments with a special thank-you to Red Chili Restaurant in Syracuse, the halfway point between our homes in Ithaca and Utica, where we schemed about the book while savoring Szechuan cuisine.

FLASH FLAHERTY

INTRODUCTION

AS IT BECAME CLEAR TO us, in the wake of the publication of *The Flaherty: Decades in the Cause of Independent Cinema*, that many Flaherty seminar veterans had stories they were interested in telling, we decided that a collection of short writings by these veterans would not only help embody the impact of the Flaherty on those who have attended the semi nar but also demonstrate some of the obvious, as well as some of the often invisible, impacts of a crucial media arts organization on the wide world of cinema and media and on modern culture in general. Although attendance at the Flaherty is small compared to major film festivals and theatrical exhibition venues, the seminar's influence on how our field considers nonfiction cinema and media has been enormous.

We quickly realized that in order to be efficient in dealing with what would now be chapters of a book, we needed to create some minimal guidelines for the storytellers. Almost unconsciously we had developed an editorial procedure for working with the stories so that we and the storytellers could be sure that the published renderings of their Flaherty experiences were accurate, informative, and readable—first on the *Flaherty Stories* blog and subsequently in the book. We asked contributors to do their best to keep their postings to a thousand words and to allow us the opportunity to shape and fine-tune what they sent us, when that seemed necessary, to insure both the book's scholarly value and its clarity and accessibility for the nonspecialist reader.

During the subsequent months, when each story was submitted (along with a short biography and a photograph of the writer), Zimmermann would query the writer about details, ambiguities, and statements requiring more elaboration. Then, once the writer had responded, the resulting draft of the story was forwarded to MacDonald for fine-tuning and sometimes assistance with structuring and further clarification—often producing further drafts. Once each writer had signed off on a final version of a Flaherty story, it was posted to the blog and distributed by us and by the writers across various social media platforms, which often generated further comments, debate, and engagement—and sometimes instigated additional stories. New pieces were placed with the earlier stories in a quickly accumulating file for the book that soon we were calling *Flash Flaherty: Tales from a Film Seminar*.

By the end of a year of working with the *Flaherty Stories* blog and as further stories continued to be submitted, we began to face the challenge of how the increasing dozens of Flaherty tales might be organized within a book. Two factors influenced our decisions in structuring *Flash Flaherty*.

First, from the beginning, we were quite clear in our communications with prospective storytellers that the *Flaherty Stories* blog project and the *Flash Flaherty* book were not meant as public relations activities or testimonials for the Flaherty seminar. The seminar organization itself has had nothing directly to do with our project. We mounted this project as scholars interested in histories from below and in the histories of nonprofit media organizations.

We have always understood that a good many of those who attend the Flaherty seminar, either as filmmaker guests or as tuition-paying seminarians or Flaherty fellows, do not have a wonderful experience or even an experience they find interesting, useful, or memorable. And of course, not all of those who have had negative experiences are interested in writing about them—the seminar may seem to them, in retrospect, merely a badly spent week. But we have always been clear that each Flaherty story can take any position in regard to the seminar or the writer's own experience of it and become part of our project.

Second, we agreed that we would not become involved in trying to make a selection of the "best" Flaherty stories. When we were sure that each story that had come through the submission, query, fact-checking, and editing process was an honest rendering of what the storyteller considered a meaningful experience and that the story was informative and readable, it became part of *Flaherty Stories*, then *Flash Flaherty*.

The decision that the collected pieces from the *Flaherty Stories* blog would be a book also presented us with a further challenge. How could we be sure that, insofar as possible, the collection would speak to the long history of the Flaherty and the range of experiences individuals have had at the seminars?

We hoped that *Flash Flaherty* could, at least to some degree, address the considerable diversity of the particular seminars from one year to the next as programmed by individual or collaborating curators from many nations and many kinds of curating experience. We hoped it could address the wide diversity in age, background, ethnicity, and national origin of those who have attended the seminars and/or have been filmmaker guests. And we hoped that our collected stories would reflect the fact that over the decades, the Flaherty has attracted some of the same people over and over, although in most every edition, a substantial number of seminar attendees are what the Flaherty organization dubs *first-timers*. Especially in recent years, first-timers have qualified for grants from several foundations and academic institutions that sponsor their attendance, a mixture that has added to the diversity of class, racial, gender, and national identity backgrounds of Flaherty participants.

Different eras of the seminar have incorporated differences in American society at large and, in particular, changes in American and international academe. During the earliest years of the Flaherty, there was virtually no way to study cinema in any organized academic context. In those days, the Flaherty functioned as an elite, private educational organization serving accomplished filmmakers, programmers, and passionate cineastes. As Cinema Studies and later Cinema and Media Studies gained a foothold in higher education, then became an increasingly substantial field of study, the seminar began to attract college and university professors and their students. This sector imported ways of thinking and speaking about cinema that were rather different from the ways in which nonacademic cineastes, programmers, and moving-image artists had communicated during earlier eras.

And finally, more fully than any other institution we are aware of, the Flaherty has often brought together partisans of what until very recently seemed to be two distinct dimensions of independent cinema: the various forms of documentary and the various types of what has usually been called *avant-garde cinema*. Indeed, it has long been an assumption among aficionados of avant-garde filmmaking that the Flaherty is hostile to cinematic experiment, though from its beginnings the seminar has hosted many established avant-garde film artists. It is true that the Flaherty audience can seem resistant to avant-garde work (after all, most showcases for avant-garde film self-select for aficionados), but seminarians have been known to direct their vitriol, sometimes inexplicably, at instances of virtually all forms of cinema and media.

In the later stages of our process, we reached out to individuals, including a variety of Flaherty "casualties," whose negative experiences seemed sure to produce stories that could add variety and nuance to the reader's experience of exploring the book. We were not as successful in this quest as we would have liked to have been. Some wounded veterans were not interested in revisiting their experiences—Peter Watkins, for example, who visited the Flaherty with *The Journey* (1987) in 1987, and Dominic Gagnon, whose *of the North* was shown amid much controversy in 2017. Others had passed away by the time we were working on the project.

When biologists want to learn about what insects and other invertebrates are living in a field of tall grasses, they often do what's called "sweep netting": they use a net (sometimes with a canvas bag) at the end of a stick. They sweep the net through the grass and see what the random stroke has captured. *Flash Flaherty* is an oral history of the Robert Flaherty Film Seminar; our sweep net was the set of rules we sent to Flaherty veterans when we agreed to do our second book on the seminar. Our question was, who will respond by sending us a personal essay about some aspect of their experience of the Flaherty no longer than one thousand words? Whether the 102 Flaherty stories included here constitute a random sample of the thousands of people who have attended one or more seminars over the Flaherty's sixty-five-plus years, we do not know. What we do know is that these storytellers were willing to take time out of their lives not only to write their essays but to work with us, sometimes over a period of months, to refine the essays for publication here.

It should be mentioned here that in several instances, Flaherty veterans who had had what they felt were negative experiences at the seminar revisited these experiences in their own ways. In the third part of his *Lost Lost Lost* (1976), Jonas Mekas revisits a guerilla art invasion of the 1964 seminar in Vermont during which Mekas, Ken Jacobs, and several friends arrived with 16mm prints of Jack Smith's pioneering queer film, *Flaming Creatures* (1963), and Jacobs's own *Blonde Cobra* (1963), a portrait of Smith. In *Lost Lost Lost*, we see Mekas and Jacobs, having been rejected by the seminar, sleeping outside in the cool night (an allusion to *Nanook of the North*) and the next morning commemorating the event by posing as the monks of cinema and doing some ritual filmmaking. *Lost Lost Lost* was widely seen in avant-garde circles, and its depiction of the Flaherty seemed to argue the seminar's hostility to modern avant-garde filmmaking. Mekas would revisit the event in his *A Dance with Fred Astaire* (New York: Anthology, 2017) and has made his memories, now at several decades' remove, available to *Flash Flaherty*.

Film and video artist George Kuchar, who passed away in 2011, was invited to the 1996 seminar, "Landscape and Place," programmed by Ruth Bradley, Kathy High, and Loretta Todd, to show several of his *Weather Diaries* videos focused on his annual trips to Tornado Alley in Oklahoma during tornado season to experience passing tornados (that sometimes literally scared the shit out of him). The sudden close-up of a turd in a toilet in *Weather Diary 1* (1986) created consternation among grossed-out viewers, a response that confirmed the filmmaker's suspicion of the seminar. Kuchar would soon produce a video docudrama, *Vermin of the Vortex* (1996), which used footage taken during the 1996 seminar in order to make clear what seems to have been for him an entirely negative experience, especially in contrast to that year's Chicago Underground Film Festival, where Kuchar was celebrated.

Deciding on a final structure for the hundred-plus stories included in *Flash Flaherty* involved several considerations. Most obviously, we realized that no matter how carefully a scholar may organize a collection of short essays, each by a different writer, in an attempt to create an implicit narrative that progresses in a recognizable trajectory from introduction to final chapter, few if any readers will access these tales in this way. This has been especially obvious to us, given our commitment to nearly equal-length, very brief stories—what these days have come to be called *flash nonfiction*, drawing on flash fiction collections such as *Flash Fiction Forward* (2006) by James Thomas and Robert Shapard. The flash nonfiction genre uses a short-form, first-person, creative nonfiction approach that crystalizes through condensed storytelling, rich details, revelatory turning points, and reflection. It mines the spaces between memoir, journalism, and lyricism.

Though we begin *Flash Flaherty* with a story by Sheafe Satterthwaite, who was witness to several of the earliest Flaherty gatherings held in a barn at the Flaherty farm and continued to attend the seminar off and on for over fifty years, this is not meant to signal a subsequent structure that needs to be read in any particular chronological or ideological order. Indeed, since all the Flaherty stories were written during a period of two years, chronology did not at first seem a useful structural option, particularly since the pieces usually focused on Flaherty experiences from previous, often long-ago years—and sometimes on several seminar experiences during different decades. Nor did the ideologies evident in the wide variety of Flaherty tales suggest any particular intellectual trajectory or unity. For a time we considered following the lead of Argentine novelist Julio Cortázar (*Rayuela/Hopscotch*, 1963) and of William Burroughs and Brion Gyson (*The Nova Trilogy*, aka *The Cut-Up Trilogy*, 1960s), who experimented with randomly organized narratives. And certainly one of the ways to read *Flash Flaherty* is to approach the stories randomly, according to one's instincts. For these readers, *Flash Flaherty* can be understood as a tweaked randomness.

In the end, we decided on a chronological scheme that would foreground, for those who read the stories in order, a clearer sense of the ongoing evolution of the seminar. The stories are organized in the order of the years during which the individual storytellers first attended the Flaherty, no matter if their stories focus on their original experiences with the seminar, on later experiences, or on events that occurred before they attended (the only exceptions to this chronology are the final four stories). For us, *Flash Flaherty: Tales from a Film Seminar* is a companion to *The Flaherty: Decades in the Cause of Independent Cinema*, and its approach to chronology provides a different way of accessing and expanding on the braided history recounted in that volume.

It will be obvious that *Flash Flaherty* was a collaborative project. Like *The Flaherty*, it was produced by two scholars working in collaboration—in this instance a nearly continual collaboration over several years. But it also required the collaboration of each of the storytellers with the two of us. We are deeply grateful for their patience and persistence.

While it would be absurd to compare our efforts here to the remarkable work of Svetlana Alexievich, whose oral histories document horrific traumas that occurred in the wake of the Chernobyl nuclear disaster and during World War II, reading Alexievich has allowed us to imagine that a plethora of memories of individuals who have experienced the complex impacts of a particular institution devoted to reality-based cinema might be as valuable as the more conventional scholarly approach we used in our earlier book. We hope *Flash Flaherty* will be as useful for readers as working with the storytellers has been for our understanding of the Flaherty's contributions to film culture during the past sixty years. Together, *The Flaherty: Decades in the Cause of Independent Cinema* and *Flash Flaherty: Tales from a Film Seminar* are a gesture of respect and gratitude for what the seminar has meant to us and to our teaching and scholarship.

1

FRANCES IN HER INGLENOOK

Sheafe Satterthwaite

SHEAFE SATTERTHWAITE taught landscape history and design, which he studied at Harvard University under John Brinckerhoff Jackson, at Williams College for more than forty years. As a young man, he attended some of the earliest Flaherty Film Seminars, sometimes working as a gofer. He is one of the few remaining veterans of the seminars that convened at Robert and Frances Flaherty's Black Mountain Farm. Over the following decades, he became one of the most recognizable and perceptive contributors to the Flaherty big-group discussions.

Why, when I think of the early (1957?) Flaherty seminar where I worked as an eighteen-year-old gofer, do I indelibly envision Frances Flaherty sitting high above the main floor of the barn, beside Sam Ogden's chimney, looking down on the proceedings—while also being separate from them?

Curious, too, is how she tended, I believe, to be present at most screenings of her husband's work whenever she had occasion to be present, as was true at her home, which was what the Dummerston setting for the seminar was—otherwise known as Black Mountain Farm, very much a hillside location, possibly deserted when the menfolk went off to war in the 1940s.

Figure 1.1. Photograph by Kenny Hersey.

(I don't know this factually in Frances's instance, but I do know that by 1957, there had been well over a century of hillside farm abandonment in Vermont and other New England uplands.)

I do know, both at the University of Virginia, where I founded a film society (Moving Images) around 1958 and where she appeared (and just how was that trip from Vermont financed?), and at Williams College (where I once hosted her), that she would sit through whatever Flaherty film was being screened, even though she must have seen these works hundreds of times. Could it be that tending to Bob's work, *caring* for his work, was an act of devotion, even a religious observance, say like Holy Communion, to be celebrated or practiced again and again?

So I don't have a sense of Frances's being down on the main floor of her barn, which housed both the screening/discussion room and (was it?) two larger bedrooms on the south side—the left side, as the building was entered from the east. There must have been a bathroom, but I don't recall it.

Confusing now to me, some sixty years later: Was there a projection booth? There must have been, but do I now also recall David Flaherty, Bob's brother, threading 16mm projectors out in the open room?

Also, when Satyajit Ray's *Pather Panchali* (1955) was screened that summer (and he himself was present as that seminar's featured guest), surely no 16mm print existed, and just how was 35mm handled, presumably with two projectors?

Of significance in the main screening room was a grand piano. Included within the large coterie of summering artists and scholars among whom the Flahertys had settled in southern Vermont was Rudolf Serkin, who usually played at the early seminars. But I don't recall his doing so when I was there. Of course, my gofer role did cause me to be away from the property on errands to neighboring Brattleboro and elsewhere, wielding Frances's coupe car with a rumble seat (why the Flahertys, or why *she*, with such a car?).

But back to the aerie: Frances up there alone in her high-elevation inglenook. It was a balcony seat of a sort. I never recall anyone else being up there with her, and I don't know if I myself ever went up.

And I should say, it was always difficult, however often in her later years I saw Frances, mostly in Dummerston, to know what she was thinking. There was, about her (at least for me), an air of superiority, and maybe that air has wafted through subsequent seminars over the years: *here is film that, on the whole, is not blockbuster, that is the work of individuals more than companies, that may be somewhat outside the mainstream of box office successes, that is somehow special and to be savored by only the cognoscenti or self-appointed.*

I also see Frances up there, hawklike. Always my sense was that some people discussing Bob's work did not know the truth as she and Bob himself knew it, and she would silently correct them.

Excellent examples of this "correcting" mode are documented in the remarkable *Louisiana Story Study Film* (1960), made years back at the University of Minnesota (and, stupidly, never shown at any of the many seminars I attended—since it is so very helpful to understanding the Flaherty approach). How often in that film does she correct Bob's cameraman, Ricky Leacock, by saying, "You know," as if the cameraman did not know!

2

A SCREENING OF *FLAMING CREATURES* IN VERMONT

Jonas Mekas

JONAS MEKAS (1922–2019) was a crucial figure in the independent film world for nearly seventy years. The prime mover behind the New York Film-Makers' Cooperative, Anthology Film Archives, and the journal *Film Culture,* Mekas brought attention to a broad range of independent cinema through his writing for the *Village Voice* and the *Soho Weekly News.* A poet, then writer-on-film and filmmaker, Mekas produced many films and has had considerable influence on independent filmmakers across the world. Major films include *The Brig* (1964), *Walden* (1969), *Reminiscences of a Journey to Lithuania* (1972), and *Lost Lost Lost* (1976), in which Mekas documents a visit he, Ken Jacobs, and others made to the 1964 Flaherty to show Jack Smith's *Flaming Creatures* (1964); "rejected by the seminar," they sleep outside and perform a ritual to film art in the cold morning.

I do not remember how it really came about, but it happened that in 1964, the Robert Flaherty Film Seminar that took place in Vermont every year had invited me to come and screen Jack Smith's film *Flaming Creatures* (1964) as a special event of the seminar. Earlier that year, I had been arrested in New York for screening it. So I figured they wanted to find out what the fuss was all about. I agreed to come.

Our little gang consisted of Barbara Rubin, her friend Debbie, and Ken and Flo Jacobs—both of whom were also arrested that same evening

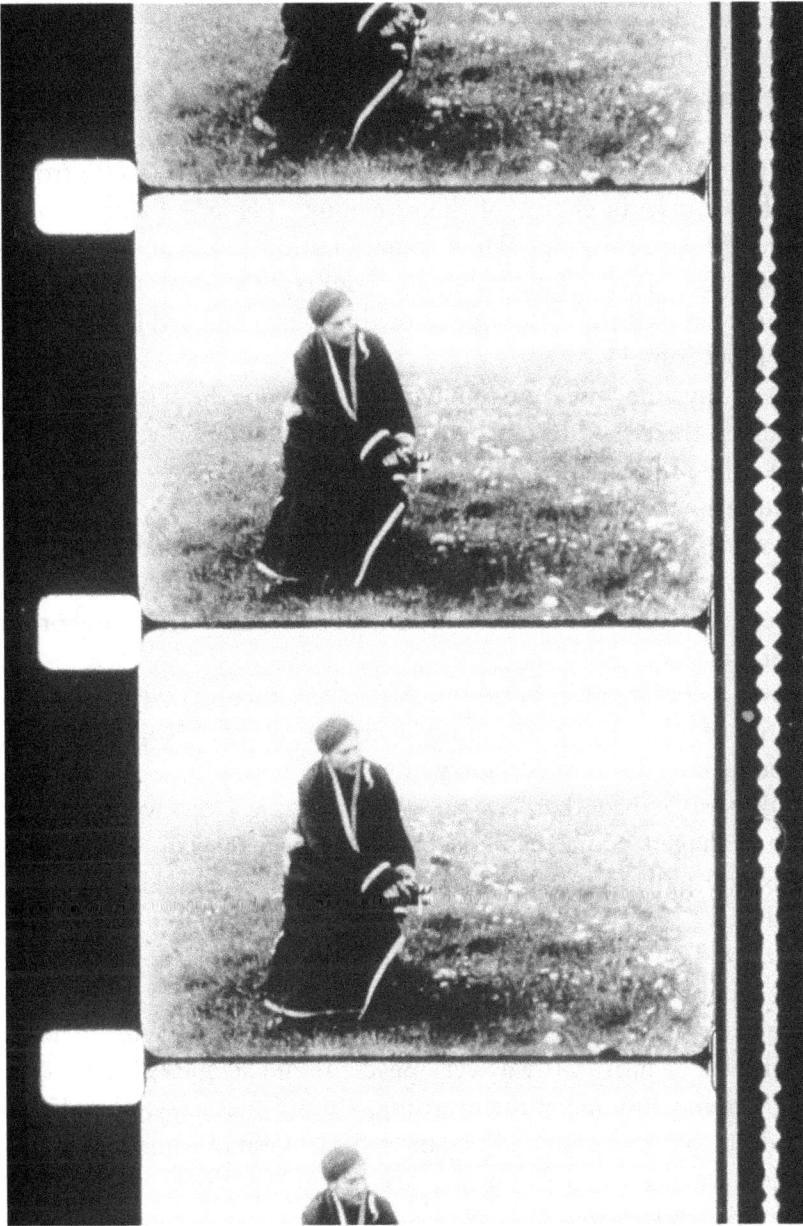

Figure 2.1.

with me. We drove to Brattleboro, Vermont, with a print of *Flaming Creatures*.

The screening was announced for 10:30 p.m. As New York City folks, we thought that was a perfectly good time for closing an evening with a movie.

We arrived on time—actually half an hour early. We drove into the seminar grounds and were a little bit surprised to find it totally empty. As we were wandering about, someone came to us from the half darkness. I recognized the man; it was Louis Marcorelles, my good friend from *Le Monde*, Paris. "Where is everybody?" I asked. "They are sleeping," said Marcorelles.

At that point, a young man appeared from the dark and introduced himself as a man in charge of the screenings. He asked us not to be so loud, people were sleeping. "How come?" I said. "What about the show?"

So the guy says, "This being the country, the sleeping time at the seminar is ten o'clock." "But our screening was scheduled for ten-thirty," I say. "How come?"

"Oh," says the guy. "We told everybody about the screening. We put it in the ten-thirty slot because of the controversial nature of the movie. We have the projectionist ready for you."

"But we have nobody here to see it," I say.

"I want to see it," said Marcorelles. "I came specially for it from Paris."

"Let's screen it!" we all said enthusiastically. And so we did. For Louis Marcorelles.

It was a cold night in Vermont. After the screening, we were ready to crash. So we asked our host to take us to our rooms. "No," says the guy. "All rooms have been filled. Sorry guys."

"OK, sorry to hear that," we said. "We'll be OK. Don't worry about us."

We managed. Some of us slept in our beat-up van. I slept among brooms and pails in an abandoned open country truck I found on the grounds.

No, we didn't sleep well that night.

We all got up early.

We were surprised to see a Vermont morning emerge over the land-scape. It was beautiful. It was very peaceful and serene. We stood there, still half asleep, looking at the morning, almost in ecstasy. Then Ken and I pulled out our cameras and began to film. We had to do it, we had to film; we were filled with the ecstasy of cinema. We felt we were the monks of the Order of Cinema.

Then we got into our beat-up van and began our journey back to New York. We looked at the seminar houses. Everybody was still sleeping. We thought we had a most perfect screening. We drove singing, happy, as the day was opening around us, a beautiful Vermont day.

[Thanks to Jonas Mekas for permission to reprint this piece, which originally appeared in *A Dance with Fred Astaire* (2017): 261–262.]

3

THE ABORTED INDIGENOUS SEMINAR

Jay Ruby

JAY RUBY, Emeritus Professor from Temple University, has been exploring the relationship between cultures and pictures for the past forty years and is considered one of the founders of visual anthropology. His research interests revolve around the application of anthropological insights to the production and comprehension of photographs, film, and television and ethnographies of American cultures. He has conducted fieldwork in Southern California; the Sudan; Utah; Juniata County, Pennsylvania; Oak Park, Illinois; and Malibu, California. The results have been published in ten books, over one hundred articles, and several films.

In 1991, Faye Ginsburg proposed a Flaherty Film Seminar that was devoted to films produced by indigenous filmmakers.

She submitted the proposal to the International Film Seminar (IFS) board, the organization that at that time ran the annual Robert Flaherty Film Seminar, and it was approved. Both Faye and I were serving as board members.

Shortly after obtaining approval, Faye asked me to co-program the seminar. I agreed. We met with Tom Johnson, IFS president at the time. He approved the idea.

Shortly after that, IFS sent out a press release announcing the seminar and an open call for films, and Faye and I began a list of potential films

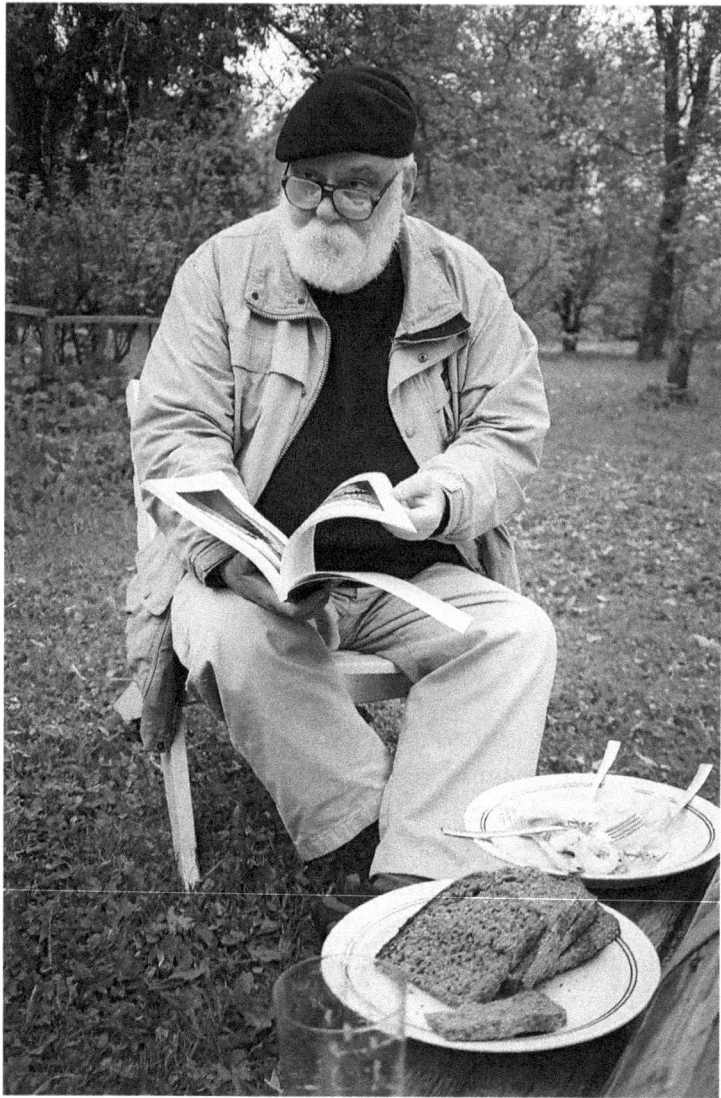

Figure 3.1.

we already knew. As far as I was aware, Faye was the most knowledgeable person on indigenous filmmaking in the country.

Soon thereafter, two board members circulated a memo via fax to other board members. I never received a copy.

Apparently, Pearl Bowser, a programmer, and Louis Massiah, a film-maker, objected to having two white academics organize the seminar. They felt this perpetuated the domination of the West over underrepresented minorities. They felt the seminar should be programmed by an indigenous person or at least co-programmed by Ginsburg and an indigenous programmer.

The board discussed the problem. If a meeting was called, I never received an invitation.

Evidently, the board supported Bowser and Massiah's objections. In addition, the question of cost was raised. Someone suggested that transporting the indigenous filmmakers, some from a great distance, was beyond the budget the organization had allotted for the seminar.

It is unclear why the issue raised by Bowser and Massiah and the question of excessive costs had not been discussed when Faye's proposal was under consideration.

I learned of these matters when Faye called me. She had come to feel that the situation was hopeless and that her only option was to resign as programmer. I agreed and did the same.

No other board member or the president or executive secretary showed me the courtesy of calling me to discuss the situation. As the old cliché goes, I knew when I was not wanted, so I resigned as a trustee. I never again attended a Flaherty seminar.

It is crucial to remember that the Bowser/Massiah memo provided no names of qualified programmers from indigenous communities, nor, so far as I know, did any board member or the president or executive secretary offer such suggestions.

No one asked Faye, me, or anyone else for a list of names. The reason for this is simple: at the time, there were, so far as any of us knew, no indigenous programmers. The board's new demand simply displayed a lack of knowledge of this field. While their stance appeared to be ideologically correct, it resulted in a demand impossible to meet.

The Bowser/Massiah memo made impossible what might have been possible: the mounting of an indigenous seminar where the growing number of Native American filmmakers like Larry Littlebird might have had a chance to meet people who could have helped them find a wider public for their work, as well as an opportunity to get to know other indigenous filmmakers. To my knowledge, in the subsequent decades, the Flaherty has never been able to produce such a seminar.

During this time in the late 1980s and early 1990s, anthropologists were wrestling with what was called "the crisis of representation." Both Faye and I had published articles that dealt with the profound problem of who has the right to represent another.

I'm fairly certain that none of the people involved with IFS were aware of how thoroughly these issues were being discussed in anthropology and in other scholarly fields.

Had we been allowed to program the seminar, there could have been useful discussions about how to deal with the thorny question of who gets to program whom and whether the only way to correct the wrongs of the past was to restrict the programming of events like the Flaherty seminar to programmers from the same community as the filmmakers whose films are being shown.

It is also difficult for me to understand why Massiah and Bowser waited to voice their concerns until an announcement of the seminar was publicly circulated. This embarrassed the Flaherty organization and damaged its reputation.

Had they expressed their reservations at the meeting where Ginsburg's proposal was discussed, a decision could have been made in private, thus avoiding the negative public impact of the memo.

The indigenous seminar could have been postponed, or the board could have acknowledged the lack of experienced programmers among the underrepresented. It could have tried to develop some sort of apprentice program where people from these communities could acquire the experience needed to be film programmers.

This was an unfortunate episode in the history of the seminar. It could easily have been avoided. I have never understood why it was not.

4

I WAS TAKEN SERIOUSLY AS A FILMMAKER

Amalie R. Rothschild

AMALIE R. ROTHSCHILD is an award-winning filmmaker and photographer noted for her documentaries about social issues as revealed through the lives of people in the arts and for her music photographs from the Fillmore East, Woodstock, Isle of Wight, and other seminal rock events from 1968 to 1974. She is cofounder of New Day Films and author of *Live at the Fillmore East: A Photographic Memoir.* Her fine art limited-edition prints show in many exhibitions internationally. While based professionally in New York City, since 1983, she has lived seven to eight months of the year in Italy.

I don't recall who saw it, but my first film *Woo Who? May Wilson* (1970) was selected for the 1970 Flaherty Film Seminar. I finished it in 1969; it was my New York University MFA thesis. Thrilled to find out about the seminar, I was honored to be invited.

That first seminar was a revelation. I met filmmaking peers and important people in the nontheatrical New York film world. I was taken seriously as a filmmaker.

The seminar gave me confidence to keep on making films. Edith Zornow, a Flaherty programmer (1965, 1967), was there. She selected my film for the 1970 New York Film Festival, a huge career boost.

Figure 4.1.

Between 1970 and 1981, I attended nearly every seminar, either as an invited filmmaker (1970, 1971, 1972, 1975, 1981) or as a participant. I missed 1980 due to the final editing on my Willard Van Dyke film, *Conversations with Willard Van Dyke* (1981), screened the following year.

During those years, the Flaherty was the single most important event for me; it opened me to creative possibilities. The contacts I made and the seminar's open forum for impassioned argument invigorated, empowered, and fed my soul. I began advocating for others to attend "summer camp for filmmakers."

The 1970s were amazing years for independent social-change filmmaking. Documentaries chronicled civil rights, the Vietnam War, and the developing women's movement. For the first time, both the National Endowment for the Arts and the National Endowment for the Humanities, both established in 1965, awarded grants supporting all kinds of filmmakers. The newly formed American Film Institute also dispensed grants. These institutions were recognizing young producer/directors, especially people of color and women.

The 1971 seminar was transformative. It gave birth to New Day Films and the First International Festival of Women's Films, held in New York City in 1972. That summer, I was producing *It Happens to Us* (1971) with an all-woman crew. My sound person, Angie Parnicky, had gone to college with Julia Reichert and Jim Klein. She told them about my film and told me to see their *Growing Up Female* (1971)—and that year Julia and Jim were seminar guests.

Willard Van Dyke programmed excellent political films: *Millhouse: A White Comedy* (1971) by Emile de Antonio, *The Selling of the Pentagon* (1971) by Peter Davis, *The Murder of Fred Hampton* (1971) by Mike Gray and Howard Alk, *Sad Song of Yellow Skin* (1970) by Michael Rubbo, *One P.M.* (1971) by D. A. Pennebaker and Jean-Luc Godard, and *Interviews with My Lai Veterans* (1971) by Joseph Strick.

Eight women directors presented films. These included *The Woman's Film* (1971) by Judy Smith, Louise Alaimo, Ellen Sorrin, *Mosori Monika* (1970) by Chick Strand, *Wanda* (1970) by Barbara Loden, Julia and Jim's *Growing Up Female: As Six Become One* (1971), and my own almost-never-seen *The Center* (1970). The heated discussions around the women's films led a group of women to gather for a breakfast meeting where, among other things, we organized the screening committee for the 1972 First Women's International Film Festival.

After the seminar, Julia and Jim came to New York City. They moved in with my boyfriend (later my first husband) and me for five months. That fall, Julia and I served on the screening committee for the Women's Film Festival, which met in my loft.

That's where we both saw Liane Brandon's *Anything You Want to Be* (1971). Julia and Jim had already started distributing *Growing Up Female* themselves. We joined forces. We felt that if you believed in your film, the other half of your job was to get people to see it. Julia went to Boston to convince Liane to join us to form New Day Films. While living with us, Julia shared with me that she had had an abortion. I filmed her story, which ended up in my film *It Happens to Us*, shown at the 1972 seminar.

At the 1976 seminar, Susan Seidelman showed her fictional short, *And You Act Like One Too* (1976), about an unfaithful wife and a hitchhiker. During the discussion, Willard Van Dyke lobbed a negative comment. I disagreed completely, taking great umbrage. I raised my hand, stood up, and refuted him in what I hoped was an evenhanded yet forceful way. I stopped short of calling him a chauvinist pig.

I was nervous. No one ever stood up to Willard. Later, he told me my comments had made him think about his knee-jerk reaction. He admitted I was right and he was wrong. Although I didn't realize it then, that exchange marked the beginning of his respect for me, and it led me to direct his biography, *Conversations with Willard Van Dyke*, which I began shooting in 1977.

Between 1975 and 1980, I served on the board of International Film Seminars (IFS) (the name on the original Flaherty charter). In 1976, I prompted IFS to collaborate with the Educational Film Library Association (EFLA), headed by longtime Flahertyite Nadine Covert, and the Association of Independent Video and Filmmakers (AIVF), of which I was a founding board member. Drawing on our pioneering experiences with New Day Films, we organized the first conference on independent film distribution. Afterward, through AIVF, we published the first self-distribution guide.

For me, the Flaherty's greatest achievement is being a forum for filmmakers and professional film users to come together. It makes room for the debate and ferment that ignite critical thinking. At Flaherty, I met lifelong friends and mentors. Without it, I never would have entered the orbits of Nadine Covert, John Katz, Austin Lamont, Grant Munro, William Sloan, Willard Van Dyke, Barbara Van Dyke, and Sol Worth.

Without the affirmation and intellectual support from the people I met at the seminars, I'm not sure I would have continued on a social-issue filmmaking path.

Thanks to the seminar, New Day Films, a cooperative of 160-plus social-issue filmmakers, has flourished, now distributing nearly 400 titles.

5

REMINISCENCES OF FLAHERTY

Nadine Covert

NADINE COVERT is a consultant and specialist in visual arts media. From 1984 until 1998, she worked for the Program for Art on Film, a joint venture of the J. Paul Getty Trust and the Metropolitan Museum of Art, where she developed and managed the Art on Screen Database. She has been a juror for international festivals of films on art. From 1972 until 1984, she served as Executive Director of the Educational Film Library Association (EFLA), where she also functioned as Director of the EFLA-sponsored American Film Festival—the major documentary competition in the United States at that time. She was the New York Delegate to the Montreal International Festival of Films on Art (FIFA) from 1996 to 2015. Since 2011, she has been a contributing editor to the *Cuban Art News* website.

I first heard about the Flaherty seminar when I enrolled in D. Marie Grieco's Nonprint Media in Libraries course at the Columbia University School of Library Service, either in the fall of 1968 or the spring of 1969. D. Marie shared with us Frances Flaherty's eclectic and inspiring reading list and told us about the seminar that Frances had launched in the 1950s.

Later, I was hired by the New York Public Library and had the life-changing opportunity to work as an assistant librarian with Bill Sloan

Figure 5.1.

in the now-legendary Donnell Film Library. Bill was a very supportive and generous mentor, and he encouraged me to attend the Flaherty seminar.

What an incredible experience for a young professional just entering the film field! Where else would you be able to share meals and informal conversation with such luminaries as Erik Barnouw, Willard Van Dyke, Joris Ivens, William Greaves, D. A. Pennebaker, Emile de Antonio, Dušan Makavejev, and so many other talented filmmakers?

Bill Sloan was invited to program the 1972 seminar, and he asked me to co-program with him. We spent an entire year screening hundreds of films to select those that we thought would make an interesting and provocative program.

At that time, the seminar was not programmed around a theme; it was strictly the programmers' choices. Because recent seminars had emphasized current events and social-issue documentaries, we made a conscious decision to seek variety. We included fiction films, documentaries, experimental/avant-garde films, early classics, and recent releases.

The filmmakers themselves were ethnically varied: black, Latino, Asian; some were already famous, and others were promising newcomers. Included were films from Africa, Brazil, Canada, England, France, Germany, Japan, Mexico, and Yugoslavia, as well as the United States.

In addition to a short film by Senegalese director Ousmane Sembène, we chose other films by black filmmakers, including several early works by documentarian St. Clair Bourne, and short films by Stan Lathan (who went on to direct films in Hollywood and for television), as well as now-classic dramas by Oscar Michaux (1884–1951) and Clarence Muse (1889–1979).

Latino filmmakers were represented by Joaquim Pedro de Andrade (Brazil), Miguel Littin (Chile), and Jaime Barrios (Chile/United States). We showed Yasujiro Ozu's classic *The End of Summer* (1961) and several documentaries by Japanese television director Yasuko Ichioka. Other women filmmakers whose works we presented included Liane Brandon, Abigail Child, Martha Coolidge, Nancy Graves, Sarah Kernochan, Amalie Rothschild, and Claudia Weill.

Among the experimental/avant-garde works were short films by celebrated Canadian director David Rimmer, a selection of unforgettable shorts by Yugoslav director Vlatko Gilic, and Canadian animator Ryan Larkin's Oscar-nominated *Walking* (1968).

We were privileged to have a number of special guests that year, including French director Marcel Ophuls, who presented his outstanding documentary *The Sorrow and the Pity* (1969), as well as Les Blank (*The Blues Accordin' to Lightnin' Hopkins*, 1968, and *Spend It All*, 1971), Saul Landau (*Qué hacer!*, 1971), Ken Loach (*Family Life*, 1971), Jonas Mekas (*Reminiscences of a Journey to Lithuania*, 1972), and Fred Wiseman (*Essene*, 1972). George Stoney presented an evening of videotapes.

In subsequent years, I attended many other Flaherty seminars, met other excellent filmmakers, and made numerous friends there. But the seminar I had the privilege of co-programming with Bill Sloan was a high point of my career.

6

NOTES ON THE FLAHERTY SEMINAR

Linda Lilienfeld

LINDA LILIENFELD is Creator and Director of Let's Talk About Water (LTAW). Linda has over thirty-five years of experience as a film and picture researcher, specializing in science and history, on projects ranging from PBS documentaries to museum exhibitions and books. For the past ten years, she has served as a research assistant to Peggy Parsons, Curator of the Film Program at the National Gallery of Art in Washington, DC. She has been a member of the steering committee and prescreening committee for the International Water and Film Events. In 1992, Linda was inspired to create the LTAW project while working on an exhibit on global warming at the American Museum of Natural History in New York City.

Part One

Dear Flaherty Seminar:
    I love you!
    I love you!
    I love you!
    There, I've said it.

Who am I? And why do I feel that way? I will try to be brief—though I rarely am!

My name is Linda Lilienfeld.

Figure 6.1. Image courtesy of Global Institute for Water Security, University of Saskatchewan.

Years ago, I started to work with Peggy Parsons at the National Gallery of Art film program in Washington, DC. This allows me to travel to film archives around the world, where material has not been digitized, and look at all kinds of films. The National Gallery of Art shows a sampler of each year's Flaherty program.

In 1992, I worked on an exhibit about climate change for the American Museum of Natural History in New York City. The companion book was written by Andy Revkin. It was so compelling that it changed the course of my life. Climate change: what the f—k was that? I mean, I'm from Brooklyn, what do I know about plants and animals?

But I realized it was a very important and complex subject.

So I started a project known as Let's Talk About Water (http://www .letstalkaboutwater.com), where I bring scientists together in a panel discussion after a film showing connected to water and do my best to instigate a dynamic interaction with the audience. I try to get the scientists to speak more simply and clearly and let people feel comfortable to ask "stupid" questions—there are no stupid questions. I try to make it fun. I work with the Consortium of Universities for the Advancement of Hydrologic Science (CUAHSI, http://cuahsi.org). We do events all over the world.

Water knits it all together and is a great point of entry for conversation about climate change.

Part Two

So, why do I love the Flaherty seminar?

Years ago, a colleague of mine, who is very reticent, had just come back from the Flaherty (whatever that was!). He told me it was a week-long seminar where people watched film together morning, noon, and night. After each program, they would talk about it as a group and continue talking over dinner and into the wee hours of the morning. They argued, fought, and agreed. They deepened each other's insight into the films—and in some cases changed each other's opinions of the film.

Each year, when we would meet after a "Flaherty," he could not stop talking—this person who barely said a word!

So he invited me to attend a Flaherty in 1976. Now, in 2017, I have attended between twenty-five to thirty seminars. How crazy is that?

My first time speaking to the group was utterly terrifying. I was clammy and hyperventilating. But I said my piece. When I'd finally made public contact with the group, the experience deepened.

What is more amazing is how sad I was when it ended and I had to leave the Flaherty family and reenter real life.

Afterward my mind kept racing. It was hard to talk to friends who had not been at the Flaherty.

Shards of images continued to flash through my mind, along with connections between the films, the genius of the programmer, why one film sat near another in the sequence, the way those interconnections opened deep reflective thinking about beauty, love, conflict, process, change. And what the filmmakers, who also attended the Flaherty, had had to say.

The smorgasbord of films and ideas upon which we feasted would express a visual idea so compelling as to be breathtaking. I wanted that feast again and again.

The idea of leaving the real world behind, watching films all day long, spending time with wonderfully bright people to *think*, *talk*, and *reflect* about life—the good, the bad, and the ugly—is just so gratifying, challenging, and fulfilling.

The programmer has complete freedom—no censorship—to program what she or he wants. But we never know what it will be until the actual show.

No preconception. What is that? *Rare!* In today's world, everyone knows too much about everything before experiencing it.

Currently, we are housed on the beautiful and welcoming campus of Colgate University in Hamilton, New York. Due to excellent administration of the event, we glide seamlessly between dorm rooms, not-so-bad cafeteria meals, walks to the screening room, breaks, discussion, happy hour . . . We float through the magic as film upon film, day after day, unspools and chat after chat washes over us.

As a group, you become one big organism (which in fact we all really are). You pass people in the hallway. You might never directly talk with them and yet somehow you miss them when it is over. It is the way they said hello or the fact you met at various intervals in a mysteriously synchronous way. At the Flaherty, I've also made friends for life.

But the most amazing effect is how the Flaherty experience enriches my real life and my work—especially my work.

One of the most important challenges of our time is why people are in denial about climate change. How can it be that scientists, geoscientists in particular and hydrologists especially, know so much—and we know so little. How can anyone call climate change a hoax?

I think the problem and the solution is communication between scientists and the public, with universities as the conduit.

I took what I absorbed from the Flaherty and created the Let's Talk About Water project.

I serve as moderator in many of the panels or as a consultant to the host university team. But I strive over and over again to recreate the life, the light, the warmth, the energy, the conflict, the resolution, the clarity that I have experienced at the Flaherty.

The process of the Flaherty gives me confidence to work against the grain of the quiet, reserved scientific community and to push them gently into the Flaherty way.

We try to convey the power of an image, the many ways it can be read, and the ability to open minds with information, experience, context, and emotion to help us communicate our way out of oblivion.

Thank you, dear Flaherty seminar. As I said at the beginning, I love you.

7

VIDEO SLOWLY EMERGES AT THE FLAHERTY SEMINAR

Deirdre Boyle

DEIRDRE BOYLE is Associate Professor in the School of Media Studies at The New School in New York. She is author of *Video Classics: A Guide to Video Art and Documentary Tapes* (1986) and *Subject to Change: Guerrilla Television Revisited* (1998), as well as numerous essays and reviews for *Cineaste, Film Quarterly, Frameworks, Millennium Film Journal, Short Film Studies,* and other journals. She is former Director of the Graduate Certificate in Documentary Studies at The New School. Her most recent book is *Rithy Panh: Ferryman of Memory,* on the work of the Cambodian filmmaker and genocide survivor.

I attended my first Flaherty seminar at Pine Manor Junior College in 1977. That was forty years ago! It was a momentous event for me for many reasons. Part of it had to do with something no one could have foreseen: a film community known for its often-heated debates came together in mourning over the sudden and unexpected death of one of its much-loved participants, Sol Worth.

Still in shock, I soon discovered that the women's movement was still being hotly debated at Flaherty: gender politics challenged the power dynamics of discussions, which surfaced most conspicuously around the work of Swiss filmmaker Alain Tanner. I remember it well because I cut my teeth as a media critic by summoning my courage to take Tanner to

Figure 7.1.

task for his cavalier representation of women in his films. Laughed down by some audience members, I persisted with my critique, winning Tanner's fury and my self-confidence in speaking up for women's voices.

Not surprisingly, given all that was going on that year, no one challenged the conspicuous absence of video at the seminar. This upstart, unprofessional medium was dismissed by an old guard who considered film the only medium worth looking at; video didn't even rate a debate.

If memory serves, it took the seminar's most revered elder statesman to overturn resistance to screening video. In 1982, Erik Barnouw programmed what was for many of us our most memorable Flaherty seminar at Camp Topridge in the Adirondacks. It was a glorious site that had once been the summer home of Marjorie Merriweather Post, owner of General

Foods and long reputed to be the wealthiest woman in the United States. Ms. Post also owned Mar-a-Lago in Palm Beach, Florida, which was later purchased by you-know-who.

Post considered Camp Topridge a "rustic" retreat situated on 300 acres in God's country. It contained numerous buildings, including a Russian *dacha* that proved essential to this story. Topridge was a stunning location for the seminar; the main lodge featured a huge, circular, windowed room surrounded by sofas and a plethora of animal trophies mounted along the walls. Post-screening discussions looked out over a sparkling lake, and each day, fabulous meals were prepared by students at a local culinary school.

Arguably the best thing about the place, though, was the *dacha*, a charming Russian cottage dedicated to screening video. Several large-screen monitors were scattered in the vaulted but cozy central hall, where videotapes by Daniel Reeves (*Smothering Dreams*, 1980), Edin Vélez (*Meta Mayan*, 1981), and Minneapolis public TV producers Deanna Kamiel, Ken Robbins, and Tom Adair were shown. Passionate discussions about the relationship of video to television and the documentary tradition were conducted there.

I do not know what it took for Erik to persuade International Film Seminars (IFS) naysayers to give video a chance, but whether it was the spectacular sunsets on the lake, the superb dinners, or the eerie stag antlers on the walls, video arrived at Flaherty with panache and seemed to please most everyone; video was no longer an oddity at Flaherty but a partner with film.

The following year, tapes by video artists and documentary activists like Bill Viola (*Hatsu Yume,*1981; *Chott el-Djerid,* 1979; *Ancient of Days,* 1979–1981), Skip Blumberg (*Pick Up Your Feet: The Double Dutch Show,* 1981), and Paper Tiger Television were shown. Emboldened by the success of single-channel tapes, Flaherty programmer D. Marie Grieco boldly decided to present the first video installation in 1984. Bill Stephens, one of the first African American video artists to be featured at the Whitney Museum in New York, showed *Belief Sandwich, Relief Gauntlet* (1981), which proved challenging to stage. Cornell University was not equipped to handle an outdoor display like this, but the seminar's adept technical staff pulled it off.

Bill Stephens was not the only video practitioner that year; also featured were works by Michelle Parkerson (*Gotta Make This Journey: Sweet Honey and the Rock,* 1983), Ed Emshwiller (*Sunstone,* 1979), Cecilia Condit (*Possibly in Michigan,* 1983), Max Almy (*Perfect Leader,* 1983*)*, and Dan Reeves (*Amida,* 1983). The inclusion of innovative work by so many talented video makers made it clear that video had become a seminar staple.

More tapes were featured the following year by artists like Louis Hock (*The Mexican Tapes: A Chronicle of a Life Outside the Law,* 1986), David Schulman (*The Race Against Prime Time*, 1985), and Kirby Dick (*Private Practices,* 1986). Soon, any differentiation between work shot on film or tape receded, and all those doubts raised about the video medium and its professionals subsided.

Today, a generation that calls everything *film* probably knows little about the battles that once raged between film purists and video iconoclasts determined to defend the distinctive features of this outlier electronic medium. I suppose this struggle to include analog video at the seminar seems strange today. But it took leadership from influential figures like Erik Barnouw and George Stoney to usher reluctant trustees and snooty filmmakers to accept the new medium called video as part of the Flaherty.

Once I stepped down as an IFS trustee, I attended far fewer seminars, but I did travel to Riga, Latvia, in 1990 for a terrific cross-cultural seminar where the audience was surprised less by media than by the clash of confused expectations about *the Other*. The Americans expected the Soviets to make political films like Vertov, and the Soviets thought the Americans would offer up "heroes" like Flaherty.

Instead of a cozy capitalist *dacha*, we enjoyed the generous appointments of a spa retreat for Soviet artists. No one was particularly interested in video, especially since the Soviet filmmakers were just beginning to use portable 16mm cameras instead of 35mm. Asked to introduce guerrilla television to colleagues who knew nothing about video, I got nowhere fast: we hadn't understood that our new friends were just beginning to experiment with their brand of cinéma vérité.

Several decades later and back in the states, I decided to see what was happening at the Flaherty seminar. I attended the 2009 seminar at Colgate University, which was brilliantly programmed by Irina Leimbacher. I was delighted to see the sophisticated presentation now given to video installations. Amar Kanwar's multichannel work was beautifully installed on several walls in a room of its own where participants could spend as much time as they wished to fully appreciate it. The seminar had come a long way in recognizing the seriousness and artistic excellence of the now *digital* medium of video.

Looking back over all this time, I am pleased to have been a participant and witness to the early days of video at the seminar and to have known many of the people—video makers, programmers, technicians, trustees, and seminar participants—who helped this history unfold. Many of them are gone now, and I am honored to bear witness to their varied contributions to making the seminar new-media friendly, inclusive, and illuminating to this day.

8

FORTY YEARS

Juan Mandelbaum

JUAN MANDELBAUM is a director and producer. His work has been broadcast from *Sesame Street* to *Independent Lens* and screened at the Museum of Modern Art, Centre Georges Pompidou, Boston Museum of Fine Arts, and Pacific Film Archive. He directed *Caetano in Bahia* (1994), *Ringl and Pit* (1995), and *A New World of Music* (1995). His film *Our Disappeared/Nuestros Desaparecidos* (2008), about people he knew who were disappeared during the 1970s Argentine dictatorship, played in over thirty international festivals. He produced the PBS series *Americas*. He was consulting producer on *Chavela* (2017), which chronicled the legendary singer Chavela Vargas and premiered at the 2017 Berlin International Film Festival.

My first connection with the Flaherty seminar was not auspicious.

In 1977, I came from Argentina to the United States to study under Sol Worth at the Annenberg School of Communications at the University of Pennsylvania.

At the first class, we learned Sol had passed away the week before at something called the Flaherty seminar. The school was in shock.

I took the Documentary Film Lab under two of Sol's PhD students, Bob Aibel and George Custen, who became good friends. Bob programmed a series with many films he'd seen at Flaherty. He insisted I go. I finally made it in 1980.

Figure 8.1.

John Katz programmed an impressive film lineup ranging from feature films such as Robert M. Young's *Alambrista* (1977) and Anne-Clair Poirier's *Mourir à Tue-Tête (Scream from Silence,* 1979) to animations by Doris Chase, Emily Hubley, and Derek Lamb to Les Blank's *Garlic Is as Good as Ten Mothers* (1980). Les sold T-shirts for the film out of a leather suitcase. I still have mine.

I was hooked.

In 1981, the seminar traveled to the University of California San Diego at La Jolla, where it was programmed by Stan Lawder. The Pacific Ocean setting was heavenly, but the programming reflected unease about the nuclear arms race under President Reagan.

That year also brought classics like Ed Pincus's *Diaries (1971–1976)* (c.1980), which opened a new way to explore personal relationships. The highlight for me was the 16mm double-system presentation of Les Blank's work-in-progress, *Werner Herzog in Peru,* on the making of *Fitzcarraldo* (1982). Les was open to reactions in a very fruitful post-screening discussion. This project became *Burden of Dreams* (1982), a better film than *Fitzcarraldo.*

The food at this seminar was less than stellar. On the second day, I wrangled a few people to go down the hill for lunch at a nudist beach. A few days later, what began as a trickle of people had become a crowd.

The 1982 seminar was held at Camp Topridge in the Adirondacks, programmed by the legendary Erik Barnouw. Camp Topridge was one of Marjorie Merriweather Post's homes. Screenings happened in the vast living room adorned with trophy heads.

Nineteen eighty-two was the height of nuclear war fears. I was honored Erik showed my short, *Button, Button: A Dream of Nuclear War* (1982). For many years, I shared my films with Erik. He sent back lovely cards with thoughtful reactions.

Other nuclear war films included the recently restored *Atomic Café* (1982) and Tom Johnson and Lance Bird's *No Place to Hide* (1983). Both made masterful use of archival footage. Video appeared with Daniel Reeves's brilliant *Smothering Dreams* (1981) and Edin Vélez *Meta Mayan II* (1981).

Bill Sloan, then the film librarian at the Museum of Modern Art, invited me to join the Board of Trustees. The invitation was a great honor. I was one of the youngest trustees—the others had links to Frances Flaherty and the first seminars. Board meetings were held in Vermont at the hilltop home of Paul and Dorothy Olson. Paul was a kind, gracious attorney who ran everything by the book. Dorothy made a killer pumpkin soup.

The 1986 seminar featured the great Brazilian Eduardo Coutinho, Ross McElwee, Richard Gordon, Carma Hinton, and Henry Hampton. Their work showed the power of documentary to enlighten the human condition. Henry brought *Eyes on the Prize* (1987), a soon-to-be-released groundbreaking history of the civil rights movement. He piloted his small plane to the seminar; I picked him up at a nearby airport. The discussions, which missed the point of the series' achievement, bemused him.

In 1995, Richard Herskowitz tricked me. He suggested I follow him as president. He said, "It's no big deal, doesn't take much time."

As copresident and then president, I weathered tough times on the financial side and around struggles to make the organization more inclusive. Tom Johnson and Patti Bruck stepped forward to save the seminar, providing crucial financial support through family foundations.

In 1998, thanks to funding provided by longtime friend of the seminar Steve Scheuer, we presented an additional seminar in Israel, programmed by Bobby Abrash and Linda Blackaby. Ricky Leacock and George Stoney presented their work and gave classes at Tel Aviv University.

We tried to include Palestinian filmmakers, a great challenge. Our Israeli partners said, "We invited them, they didn't come." Daoud Kuttab, producer of a local version of *Sesame Street*, did come. The polarization became evident during an explosive discussion of Amos Gitai's *House in Jerusalem* (1998). A film professor accused Amos of being a traitor for daring to explore Palestinian past-home ownership.

During the wrap-up, our local partner, Dani Waxman, said, "You showed us how to do it, now we have to do it." Years later, I found out that Dani and other documentarians had gathered every year for four years and even published the proceedings!

The 2010 seminar coincided with the soccer World Cup. Fans of Mexico, Argentina, and Spain fulfilled their obligation to watch their countries' matches. Alas, a few screenings were missed.

The seminar leaves lasting memories. Taking a leak alongside Raoul Peck while I gushed over his masterful *L'Homme sur les Quais* (*The Man on the Shore*, 1993). The gracious Johann Van der Keuken and his observational films. Walking to lunch with Marlon Riggs after being blown away by *Tongues Untied* (1989). Catching up about mutual Cambridge friends on the lovely Lake Cayuga dock with Mira Nair. Discovering the work of Ulrike Ottinger and finding out we shared a great friend, Ellen Auerbach, the subject of my film *Ringl and Pit* (1995).

The most successful seminars mix realist docs, experimental, and animation to explore the human condition and provoke emotional responses. I fear the Flaherty's humanist tradition is slipping away to favor the latest formalist fads.

Extraordinary documentaries such as Giancarlo Rossi's *Fuocoammare* (*Fire at Sea*, 2016), on the immigration crisis in the Mediterranean, don't seem to have a chance of a seminar screening now. I hope future programmers will keep in mind the Flaherty's humanist origins.

9

GET OUT YOUR SHOVEL

Patricia R. Zimmermann

PATRICIA R. ZIMMERMANN is Professor of Screen Studies and Codirector of the Finger Lakes Environmental Film Festival at Ithaca College in New York. She is author and editor of numerous books, including *Thinking Through Digital Media: Transnational Environments and Locative Places* (2015, with Dale Hudson), *Open-Spaces: Openings, Closings, and Thresholds of International Public Media* (2016), *The Flaherty: Decades in the Cause of Independent Film* (2017, with Scott MacDonald), *Open Space New Media Documentary: A Toolkit for Theory and Practice* (2018, with Helen De Michiel), and *Documentary Across Platforms: Reverse Engineering Media, Place, and Politics* (2019).

"I bet you thought I was dead!"

At my first breakfast at the 1980 Flaherty seminar at Wells College in central New York, I picked at overcooked scrambled eggs and burnt wheat toast. I had sat down at the only open seat at a table with two gray-haired gentlemen.

Sheepishly, I introduced myself. One man offered he was George Stoney, who I knew as the community media and Challenge for Change legend.

The other, the one who thought I figured he was dead, identified himself as Erik Barnouw.

Figure 9.1.

I blurted out that I had just read his books on documentary and the history of broadcasting to prepare for my PhD qualifying exams at the University of Wisconsin–Madison. That's when he chortled the statement above. He was seventy-two.

I had received what was then called a grant-in-aid to attend the seminar programmed by documentary scholar John Stuart Katz, a film professor at York University in Toronto. This Flaherty was the first film event I'd ever attended on the East Coast. Madison friends insisted I was insane to go just two weeks before my exams.

When I signed in, Barbara Van Dyke, the Flaherty seminar's executive director, greeted me with a hug. I wondered if she was related to Willard Van Dyke, the legendary filmmaker from the radical film group Nykino and eventual head of film at the Museum of Modern Art.

At the opening reception, I'd gravitated to a huddle of twenty-somethings like me. I connected with Ruth Bradley, a PhD student at the University of Michigan who later became editor of *Wide Angle*, director of the Athens Film and Video Festival, and a longtime friend and collaborator.

At that first breakfast, I froze. I was sitting at a table at 7:30 a.m. with two men who had, in my neophyte assessment, changed documentary history.

When they kindly probed about my in-progress dissertation on the history of amateur film, I blurted out that I felt overwhelmed by mountains of unknown material. Erik smiled. He said, "Never be intimidated. Just get out your shovel and keep digging."

In graduate school, I'd read and battled about documentary, then a marginalized area in film studies. The abstractions of Bateson, Fanon, Foucault, Habermas, Marxism, psychoanalysis, and critical historiography drowned my soul—and my clarity.

At that Flaherty, independent film was front and center. A practice, a theory, a history, a community, the Flaherty redefined the documentary community as a seething cauldron of obsessed partisans and gutted my preconceptions about documentary and independent film.

I watched American regional independent narrative cinema like *Alambrista* (1977), *Gal Young 'Un* (1979), and *Heartland* (1979).

Observational documentaries such as *Garlic Is as Good as Ten Mothers* (1980), *Faces of November* (1964), *N!ai, the Story of a !Kung Woman* (1980), and *Scenes from Childhood* (1980) were jammed against archival works such as *The War at Home* (1979), *The Trials of Alger Hiss* (1980), and *America Lost and Found* (1974).

Experimental documentaries like *D.O.A.* (1980) and *Poto and Cabengo* (1980) jolted me. For the first time, I experienced how documentary, programmed with experimental films by Warren Bass, Dana Hodgson, Emily Hubley, and Caroline Leaf could propel new conceptual thinking.

The French Canadian documentary/narrative film *Mourir à tue-tête* (1979) scraped away my feminist documentary theories. The film chronicled a rape with daring self-reflexivity. Anne Claire Poirier, the militant feminist director from the National Film Board of Canada, was present. In the campus pub, I crammed into a booth with her and three other young women, enthralled.

I could not figure out if the seminar was radical, liberal, or conservative. I had never attended any media event so focused on long discussions, intense debates, and entanglements between observational, archival, expository, personal, ethnographic, and hybrid documentary, narrative film, experimental work, and animation.

The participants featured filmmakers from every genre, as well as anthropologists, art world types, broadcasters, cinematographers, commercial media workers, distributors, elderly cineastes, exhibitors, film scholars, graduate students, librarians, journalists, marketers, and producers. Their combustions torched something inside me about the urgency of independent media that I'd not felt as a PhD student.

I was utterly intimidated. The seminar experience catapulted me into verbal paralysis.

Discussions cascaded like ferocious waterfalls of anger, debates, histories, ideas, and positions. I listened from the back of the room, jumbled up with anxieties, awe, critique, disdain, engagement, fascination, frustration. I uttered one incoherent, overly theoretical, tortured statement. I filled a spiral notebook with notes.

Here, documentary was not about theories but about aesthetics, debates, histories, people, politics, and high stakes. Documentary and experimental film felt confusing, embodied, pulsing, significant. Devotees possessed feverish intensities.

Walking to a screening, I bumped into visual anthropologist Jay Ruby. His sharp mind terrified me. He knew exactly what he thought about every film. Back then I criticized *Nanook of the North* (1922) as racist and colonialist, a position I later gutted after reading Jay's reassessment of the film as an early collaborative ethnographic film.

At lunch, I met Bill Sloan, the librarian for the Museum of Modern Art, who spoke generously about the short experimental works.

I met film librarian D. Marie Grieco. Before a screening, she whispered two revelations to me. First, Frances Flaherty, not Robert, inaugurated the seminars, but film history had erased her. Second, Barbara *was* Willard's ex-wife, and she, too, had been expunged from film history.

I realized that *Frances* Flaherty had built a place where young people like me could talk to legends like Erik—and George, D. Marie, Jay, and Anne Claire . . .

At the end of that seminar, Erik Barnouw offered the closing benediction. He performed this at every seminar he attended.

Erik recounted a story about a seminar acolyte who asked French filmmaker Chris Marker how he created such complex editing. Marker replied, "I get lost."

Smiling, Erik commanded all of us: "Now get lost."

10

GODMOTHERS, GODFATHERS, AND
AN ORGANIZATION WITH A SOUL

Lucy Kostelanetz

LUCY KOSTELANETZ is a filmmaker. She has directed two documentary features: *Sonia* (2007), about the Russian avant-garde painter
Sofia Dymshitz-Tolstaya, and *We Don't Wanna Make You Dance*
(2013), about a white funk band named Miller, Miller, Miller &
Sloan. Her previous work includes two award-winning films for
children, *Rebeka Goes Down the Slide* (1986) and *Rebeka Goes
to China* (1992). Her most recent project is a film about her uncle,
orchestra conductor Andre Kostelanetz, entitled *Andre Kostelanetz:
His Journey.*

My first encounter with Robert Flaherty was in 1962, the spring of
my first year at Bennington College.

Totally by chance, I happened to see a handwritten announcement on
a chalkboard on the stairs going to the top floor of the commons saying
that Frances Flaherty would be screening Robert's films. I had never heard
of Flaherty. But something compelled me to go.

The following fall, I wrote to Arnold Eagle, who had worked with
Flaherty on *Louisiana Story* (1948), inquiring about an internship. I
never heard back from Mr. Eagle. But years later, in the 1980s, I became
his student at The New School, taking courses in 16mm production and
subsequently using his studio as a place to work.

Figure 10.1. Photograph by Saskia Kahn.

One day, when he was cleaning out his files, Arnold happened to find my letter. It stated that Frances had screened Flaherty's *Man of Aran* (1934) and *Louisiana Story*. I sort of remember her doing it in two visits. In any event, I'd been blown away. I'd never seen anything like these films.

After college, I embarked on a career as an arts administrator. I worked primarily for the New York State Council on the Arts (NYSCA). My last position there was as deputy director for what was then called the Division of Communication and Visual Arts, where I supervised funding for film and media organizations.

Although I loved being part of something I believed in, I'd always wanted to work on the creative side of film and media. So I left NYSCA in 1981. Fortunately, by 1982, I found the Flaherty seminar. I was hooked forever.

My first Flaherty was in 1982 at Topridge in the Adirondack Mountains in northern New York State. The film and media historian Erik Barnouw programmed it. Barbara Van Dyke was helming the organization as executive director and coordinator of the seminar. The projectionist was Murray Van Dyke. Located deep in the woods on a lake, with its many historic buildings intact, Topridge was the former "rustic" retreat of Marjorie Merriweather Post.

At this seminar I felt such gratitude to find a community of people with whom I shared goals, dreams, and mission. And, as an aspiring filmmaker, I found this seminar experience and the many, many more to follow extremely helpful in giving me the courage to pursue my own creative path.

As I became more and more familiar with the organization and its people, I discovered what I would call Flaherty godmothers and godfathers, people who came almost every year.

As I said at his recent memorial, Bill Sloan was one of these treasured people. He first attended the seminar in 1964, which means he knew Frances Flaherty. He programmed his first seminar in 1972 with Nadine Covert and another one in 1975 with Barbara Van Dyke, then worked solo to put together the 1979 seminar.

When I read the program Bill Sloan created with Nadine in 1972, I know I would have been totally blown away. They showed *The Sorrow and the Pity* (1969). Does that mean Marcel Ophuls was actually there? They showed a film by Yasujirō Ozu, several films by Claudia Weill and Eli Noyes, and of all things, *Greed* (1924) by Erik Von Stroheim. They also screened many titles by filmmakers I'm sorry to say I do not know.

My overall impression of their program is one of great variety and richness. I understand from Patricia R. Zimmermann and Scott MacDonald's recent book about the history of Flaherty (*The Flaherty: Decades in the Cause of Independent Cinema*), as well as from Nadine herself, that variety was something they worked hard to accomplish and promote as a programming goal.

Bill served on the Flaherty Board of Trustees and as its president from 1974 to 1977. I believe he continued on the board over subsequent years in various capacities. He established Bill's Bar. To this day, it persists. The best conversations about film take place at that makeshift bar.

As I look through the various seminar programs during those years, I regret I was not there. The 1970s seem like the Flaherty's golden age of film programming.

I served on the Flaherty Board twice, once in the 1980s and again in the late 1990s. For two years (2000–2001), I was president. Like most nonprofits during both those periods, Flaherty was working to transition into a more professional and stable organization. A lot of our focus centered on a need for an office and a paid director, first part-time and eventually full-time.

There were, of course, a number of rocky years along the way, but Flaherty always seemed to bounce back stronger than before. I've come to think of the Flaherty as an organization with a soul. It never lost its reason for being.

I attribute this clarity of purpose to the Flaherty "godparents": Erik Barnouw, Jack Churchill, Nadine Covert, Tom Johnson, Dorothy Olson, Paul Olson, Bill Sloan, George Stoney, Barbara Van Dyke, and many others. With their unique charismatic presence, these godmothers and godfathers operated as spiritual guides to film and media. Forgive me if I wax too metaphysical.

After taking a break for a few years, I came back to the Flaherty for its sixtieth anniversary in 2015. I was hooked again and have returned several times. I'm astounded by the community of people that the seminar attracts, a group that has become more and more international. The word is out; this year the seminar sold out in less than twenty-four hours!

I'm proud of all the time I contributed to help the Flaherty develop and flourish. I see my work for the organization as a chance to give back some of the good the seminar has given me through the decades.

A Flaherty godparent passed away in 2017 at age ninety-nine: Dorothy Olson, a journalist, arts administrator, former Flaherty trustee, and mentor to many in the film and media world. In my last conversation with her, she talked about never forgetting and never recovering from seeing *The Sorrow and the Pity* at that 1972 Flaherty.

The Flaherty is an organization with a soul. It always seems to find a way to continue and, I like to think, evolve.

11

BORDERING ON FICTION

Bruce Jenkins

BRUCE JENKINS is Professor of Film, Video, New Media, and Animation at the School of the Art Institute of Chicago (SAIC). Prior to SAIC, he was the Stanley Cavell Curator at the Harvard Film Archive. He served as Curator of Film/Video for many years at the Walker Art Center, Minneapolis. He has authored *Gordon Matta-Clark: Conical Intersect* (2011) and edited *On the Camera Arts and Consecutive Matters: The Writings of Hollis Frampton* (2009). His writing has appeared in *Aperture, Artforum, Millennium Film Journal,* and *October.* He coauthored the second volume of the catalogue raisonné for the films of Andy Warhol.

Back in the early 1980s, I was working for Gerald O'Grady at what was then called Media Study/Buffalo, a regional media arts center. For six years, I served as the film programmer there, organizing series that ranged from programs of classic narrative cinema and the various new waves to contemporary independent and avant-garde films.

The roster of visiting filmmakers who came to screen and discuss their work ranged from feature-film directors, such as Chantal Akerman, Jonathan Demme, and Wim Wenders, to key figures in the avant-garde, such as James Benning, Valie Export, and Yvonne Rainer, to influential documentary filmmakers, such as Richard Leacock, Marcel Ophuls, and D. A. Pennebaker.

Figure 11.1.

During that period, I became involved in a pair of collaborative projects with Melinda Ward, then director of the Film/Video Department at the Walker Art Center in Minneapolis. One of these involved organizing and curating a touring film series titled *The American New Wave: 1958–1967*, which premiered in January 1983 at the Sundance Film Festival.

The project began during a period of growing interest in alternatives to Hollywood movies and commercial television. It was designed to showcase films from an earlier generation of American independent filmmakers active in the late 1950s and early to mid-1960s. Makers of that period, such as John Cassavetes, Shirley Clarke, Robert Frank, and Jonas Mekas, were attempting to create a new form of feature filmmaking that paralleled the new waves emerging in Europe. The National Endowment for the Arts funded this touring program, which was shown across the United States at film archives, media centers, museums, and universities.

The second project initiated with Melinda was programming the Robert Flaherty Film Seminar in the summer of 1983. Our partner in both undertakings was Bill Horrigan, my close colleague from the graduate program in cinema studies at Northwestern University and then Melinda's assistant.

At the time, Melinda and Bill were also actively engaged in the creation of the PBS series *Alive from Off Center*, which focused on contemporary performing and media artists whose works were too experimental for the more established PBS series *Live from Lincoln Center*. *Alive* gave television viewers their first encounters with artists such as the musician and performance artist Laurie Anderson, storyteller Spalding Gray, photographer William Wegman, and dancer and choreographer Trisha Brown.

When we were invited to program that year's seminar, there was no titled concept for the week, as was Flaherty's practice at the time. This said, for each day, we devised screenings that revolved around a particular theme, even if that theme sometimes shifted meaning in the course of moving from morning to afternoon to evening sessions.

Our first full day was devoted to the theme of youth. We started in the morning with a Paper Tiger Television program that critiqued *Seventeen* magazine, continued with three compelling new nonfiction films about young people—Bill Jersey's *Children of Violence* (1982), Josh Hanig's *Coming of Age* (1982), and Joel DeMott and Jeff Kreines's *Seventeen* (1980)—and ended with William Farley's *Citizen* (1982), a lively portrait of a group of young West Coast performance artists roaming the streets of San Francisco.

Another daily focus probed the heritage of radical politics within the history of nonfiction filmmaking. The program initiated this theme with a morning screening of Chris Marker's short experimental video *Guerre et révolution* (1977). It continued with two feature films, Leo Hurwitz's two-part feature *Dialogue with a Woman Departed* (1980) and James Klein and Julia Reichert's *Seeing Red* (1983).

Had Melinda and I given that year's seminar a name, it might have been something on the order of "bordering on fiction." This concept was perhaps best exemplified by the boundary-blurring practice of our main guest, Filipino filmmaker Kidlat Tahimik, who had directed *Perfumed Nightmare* (1977). He used his appearance at the seminar to share his newer features, *Turumba* (1982) and *Who Invented the Yo-yo?/Who Invented the Moon Buggy?* (1980–1981). Because this reflexivity was conducive to comedy, much of Kidlat's work involved a level of playfulness not typically associated with nonfiction filmmaking.

No less forceful in their hybridity were films like Jill Godmilow's *Far from Poland* (1984) (shown as a work in progress) and Trinh T. Minh-ha's *Reassemblage* (1982). Michelle Citron's *What You Take for Granted* (1983) provoked heated debate among seminar participants. This explicitly feminist film focused on the growing relationship between two women, a blue-collar worker and a professional. Their story was intercut with a series of fictionalized interviews with other working women, based on actual interviews. For some participants, this hybrid form seemed to undermine valued tenets of nonfiction filmmaking. For others, it represented a significant innovation for the field.

In many ways, this mode of organizing programs around thematic conceits emerged as an offshoot of our own professional endeavors. We were all programmers or, as we eventually came to be called in the 1990s, curators. The thematic bent, then, was more aligned with the art world, which was somewhat different from either the academic or production communities at Flaherty. Rather than focusing on explicating or producing individual works, the curator's role is to organize ensembles of work for exhibition around authorial or thematic subjects. Such exhibition is intended to elicit relationships among works in order to signal historical movements or reveal contemporary trends. It was this perspective that Melinda, Bill, and I brought to the Flaherty programming that year.

To this day, I remain deeply indebted to those programmers who came before me and who each spent a lifetime devoted to screening and advancing the work of avant-garde artists, documentary directors, and independent filmmakers. Amos and Marcia Vogel, founders of the seminal Cinema 16; Ulrich Gregor, who founded and programmed the Forum section of the Berlinale for many years; Adrienne Mancia, the mainstay for me at the Museum of Modern Art; and Edith Kramer, the heart and soul of the Pacific Film Archive, define this group of dedicated cinephiles.

12

MY FIRST FEW FLAHERTYS

Richard Herskowitz

RICHARD HERSKOWITZ is Artistic and Executive Director of the Ashland Independent Film Festival in Oregon. He was Artistic Director of the Houston Cinema Arts Festival and also Director of Cinema Pacific at the University of Oregon. From 1994 to 2008, he was Director of the Virginia Film Festival. He ran the Cornell Cinema media arts center, presenting over five hundred films annually from 1982 to 1994, and served as Film and Video Curator at the Herbert F. Johnson Museum of Art in Ithaca, New York. He has served as President of the Flaherty Film Seminar and chaired its Fiftieth Anniversary Committee.

Patty Zimmermann led me to my first Flaherty seminar in 1983, and I led Scott MacDonald to his first in 1987.

Patty and I were close friends in grad school at University of Wisconsin–Madison when she had her Flaherty initiation in 1980. A year or so later, she moved away for a teaching job in Ithaca, where she lobbied a nearby search committee to hire me to run Cornell Cinema.

Now that I was in central New York, earning a salary, I was finally able to experience the Flaherty seminar for myself. I still cannot believe the range of artists whose work I experienced at the 1983 seminar, in what still feels like the most expansive film viewing week of my life: Bill

Figure 12.1.

Viola, Kidlat Tahimik, Julia Reichert, Trinh T. Minh-ha, Joel DeMott, Jeff Kreines, Beth and Scott B, Danny Lyon, Paper Tiger TV, and more.

Looking back, I realize that Patty and I were pretty immature and snarky, particularly toward the old timers' reverence for seminar ancestors and traditions. D. Marie Grieco and Barbara Van Dyke talked reverentially about the seminar's late founder, Frances Flaherty, spouse and champion of Robert and a neglected visionary herself. I'll never forget the moment D. Marie got up in front of the seminar, in that bizarre Camp Topridge lodge (filled with mounted animal heads) we used as a screening room. She announced that she had received a call from Frances, who sent us good wishes. Patty and I gave each other a look you might translate as *Get me away from this nutty cult!*, not realizing that there was a Flaherty daughter named Frances who had, in fact, phoned D. Marie (Frances H. Flaherty died in 1972).

Patty and I joined in the fierce questioning of Skip Blumberg after the screening of a video we thought exploited the workers it depicted. We were inflamed way beyond what the video deserved. Because it was midweek at the seminar, there was pent-up energy and frustration from earlier discussions (it used to be theorized that a midweek guest was inevitably sacrificed to this bad energy; when Peter Watkins got it during my 1987 seminar, as Scott may remember, he was in the Wells College chapel in front of a mounted crucifix).

After the Blumberg auto-da-fé, Patty and I took a rowboat out onto the nearby Adirondack lake. We paddled and raged until we were calm. (Just recently, Patty emailed me and asked, "Remember the rowboat?"). We came back subdued but soon learned that Skip Blumberg had taken off, distressed by his experience.

I'm still mortified by this and by the memory of a few other attacks in which I played a role. These attacks, I should say, were rare and vastly outnumbered by enthusiastic responses but have become legendary and symbolic to many who, understandably appalled, have stayed away from the Flaherty.

One of those incidents is the Peter Watkins discussion mentioned above. In 1987, the first Flaherty seminar I programmed, I had originally wanted to show excerpts from the fourteen-hour film *The Journey* (1987) and tried to persuade Watkins to allow this. He insisted on screening it all. He was a filmmaker I revered, so I concurred, unwittingly sending him to his midweek crucifixion.

Twelve years later, at a Flaherty seminar I programmed at Duke, I told David Williams that I wanted to show his trilogy of films on his elderly friend Lillian in reverse chronological order. I knew that after people saw the insight and sensitivity of the final film, *Thirteen* (1997), they would be intrigued by the films that led up to it.

David insisted on my showing the films chronologically—and he was the filmmaker. As it turned out, several African American attendees found his portrait of Lillian in the first film (*Lillian*, 1993, shown smack in the middle of the week) to be stereotypical and hurtful. The discussion that followed wounded him deeply. Quite a few people then skipped *Thirteen*.

I'm more assertive now about conveying my programming instincts and challenging an artist's wishes when I sense how a film will be best received.

Finally, there was the 1992 explosion following Ken Jacobs's performance of his Nervous System piece, *XCXHXEXRXRXIXEXSX* (in various versions beginning in 1980). Jacobs's Nervous System involves two linked analytic 16mm projectors, mediated by a propeller device, that can show images at various speeds and in various formations, backward and forward, side by side, or in superimposition, which Scott presented (with my encouragement) at the seminar he co-programmed. I chaired the discussion. That intense, painful session is well-documented in Patty and Scott's book *The Flaherty: Decades in the Cause of Independent Cinema.* You get a sense of how the discussion turned around and how the critics were chastened after Ken stormed out of the room.

You do not, however, get a sense of the affirming late-night conversation a few of us had with Ken or the following day's exhilarating screening and discussion of Ken's *Two Wrenching Departures* (Nervous System performance, in various versions from 1989), both of which sent Ken off on a high.

Like Scott, I also came to feel that the Flaherty's immediate post-film discussions were often frustrating and not nearly as illuminating as the mealtime and late-night conversations that flowed between the films and big-group discussions, unrecorded.

13

VIDEO PROJECTION AT THE FLAHERTY

Ann Michel and Phil Wilde

ANN MICHEL is founder, president, and co-owner of Insights International, a production firm specializing in science and educational online, TV, and theatrical events. She has also served as President of the Robert Flaherty Film Seminars. PHILIP WILDE is vice president and co-owner of Insights International. Their documentary *Reversing Oblivion* (2017), about recovered Jewish identity, lost land, and abandoned property in Poland, toured the international festival circuit.

In 1984, the Robert Flaherty Film Seminar made its way to Cornell University. Richard Herskowitz, who was then the director of Cornell Cinema, maneuvered to get it there.

Well known in Ithaca, Richard and his wife, Jill, mounted memorable Halloween costume parties. One party was "Come as Your Parents." Ann channeled her mother, dressing as a super dreadnought. At another party, "Come as Your Art," a woman draped Tampax dipped in blue water around her neck and asserted she was in her "Blue Period."

So when Richard appeared at our Cornell University office and asked if we could help him screen video for a crowd of rabid cinephiles, it sounded like fun. We had never heard of the Flaherty.

At the time, we had an office on the fifth floor of Statler Hall, home of Cornell's famous School of Hotel Administration. To get to our office,

Figure 13.1.

you had to push through a set of heavy red doors adorned in white paint with the words *Research and Development*.

The office buzzed with gear and gearheads. Cables, cameras, distribution amps, microphones, mixers, and television monitors crowded the space—everything needed for the creation and display of half-inch and three-quarter-inch video. The IBM PC had just been released, and the Mac was released that year.

For the video sessions at that year's seminar, Richard had access to a basement classroom in Cornell's dreary psychology building, not far from the Cornell Cinema theater, where films were screened during the Flaherty week.

We pushed the classroom's chair-desks into the four corners and dragged in four twenty-five-inch monitors, eighty-pounders on tall racks. We draped the floor with cables. The monster monitors did not match, and they made the room hot. For video presentations, twenty to twenty-five people crowded closely around each monitor. Back then, fewer than eighty people attended the seminar.

We showed Meredith Monk's *Ellis Island* (1981) that week. Showing video to a large group in the early 1980s wasn't always easy, but her video and the way that we showed it were a success. We were now part of the projection team.

That week, we met experimental collage filmmaker Bruce Conner, who screened *A Movie* (1958), *Ten Second Film* (1965), *Permian Strata* (1969), and *Mongoloid* (1978). At the time, we had no idea who any of these people were!

Lovable, formidable, old-school tyrant, film librarian D. Marie Grieco programmed that year. She showed a plethora of short films and videos, constantly rearranging the program on the fly. When his screening times were changed, Bruce Conner had a meltdown on Phil's shoulder.

In 1985, curator and historian Deac Rossell was the programmer. The Flaherty had found a new home at Wells College, about thirty miles north of Ithaca. We had full use of their lovely old grande dame theater, with its thrust stage, generous apron, and orchestra and balcony seating.

Gorgeous nineteenth-century three-story windows graced both walls of the theater. We used many fifty-foot rolls of black garden plastic to ensure the blackout needed for projection during daylight hours. It was August, and with air circulation cut off, the theater was hot. Sometimes, we brought in factory-size fans and battled their noise. Wells College sits on the shores of Cayuga Lake, one of the narrow, forty-mile-long Finger Lakes in central New York. The swimming was excellent, and lounging on the dock, between or after screenings, offered daily relief from the heat.

The projection booth at Wells housed two finicky carbon-arc 35mm projectors (the same projectors William Randolph Hearst had installed in his castle), gamely manned by projectionist Michael Grillo, who had worked with us at that original Cornell seminar. The 16mm projectors were ancient too, and it was a continual battle to keep them working. We supplied the growing mountain of video playback decks in formats such as Betacam, Betacam SP, PAL, SECAM, three-quarter-inch, Hi-8, VHS, Super-VHS, then later, DVCAM, mini-DV, and DVD. At some point, we rented a theatrical sound system for the week.

Eventually, we teamed up with Richard Herskowitz to share a Sony multi-standard video projector. The Flaherty used it for one week in the summer. Cornell Cinema used it and stored it for the rest of the year.

In 1986, seminar programmers Tony Gittens and Linda Blackaby screened plenty of video, an important turning point for the seminar. Very politely, they provided us with a long list of shorts to screen, with almost no time for preparation. We balked. They discovered that we were unpaid help. In time, we arrived at an understanding with the Flaherty about how to plan the video screenings, and our role came to include a stipend, plus food and a dormitory room.

By 1987, the Flaherty seminar experience had become our summer camp, and in 1994, Jason Livingston, then a Cornell University student, joined our team.

For us, one of the most memorable events was video artist and experimental musician Steina Vasulka's outdoor walk-through installation, a total surprise for seminarians as they left the theater that night in 1996. We'd set four video projectors on their sides, turning them ninety degrees or more so images of waterfalls ran sideways and geysers shot downward. We used bedsheets for screens to create both front- and rear-screen projection effects that combined with the shadows of passersby. Miraculously, the summer rains stayed away that night.

For both of us, the Flaherty has meant much more than just the films and the formal discussions about them. Even at our first Flaherty, we noticed that there was plenty of time to meet people and discuss almost any aspect of our art, our careers, and our lives with people who soon were to become lifelong friends.

Later, when Phil, as a member of the board of trustees, helped organize and administer the Flaherty seminar in Israel, the people of Kfar Blum, our host kibbutz, understood the Flaherty's informal *gemutlicheit* and embraced it immediately. This was something that Ann encouraged when she became president of the board.

We remember swimming in Cayuga Lake with George Stoney; sitting on the terrace late into the evening with Eric Barnouw; helping Bill Sloan keep up with the early rush for drinks at Bill's bar, even before it became "Bill's Bar"; convincing Frannie Flaherty, Robert and Frances's daughter, to stay up and dance to some pretty good rock and roll; and realizing that the delightful woman we'd just had lunch with was Meredith Monk—knowing that we'd be showing *Ellis Island* the next afternoon and confident that it would look really good!

14

A MEDIEVALIST'S PROJECTION

Michael Grillo

MICHAEL GRILLO is an art historian at the University of Maine. He researches the semiotics of fourteenth-century Italian paintings and teaches a variety of courses covering the Medieval and Renaissance periods. His recent publications include "Dissolving the Frame: Phenomenology and Index in Trecento Painting" and "Illuminated Architecture: The Influence of Manuscripts on the Palatine Chapel." Having grown up in a movie projection booth and spurred on by his interests in fourteenth-century narration, he went on to research and teach film theory and history. He teaches an annual documentary course centered on the Camden International Film Festival in Maine.

Working as the film projectionist for the Flaherty Film Seminars in the 1980s and early 1990s positioned me in the wonderfully dualistic role of distanced observer and full participant.

The job kept me occupied for endless hours each day, as I worked to keep balky equipment running smoothly and make sure that everything the programmer had scheduled would screen properly.

But projecting also gave me ample time to observe the seminar as a detached observer.

As a medievalist art historian, my interest in film was not the all-in level of engagement of most everyone else who attended the seminars:

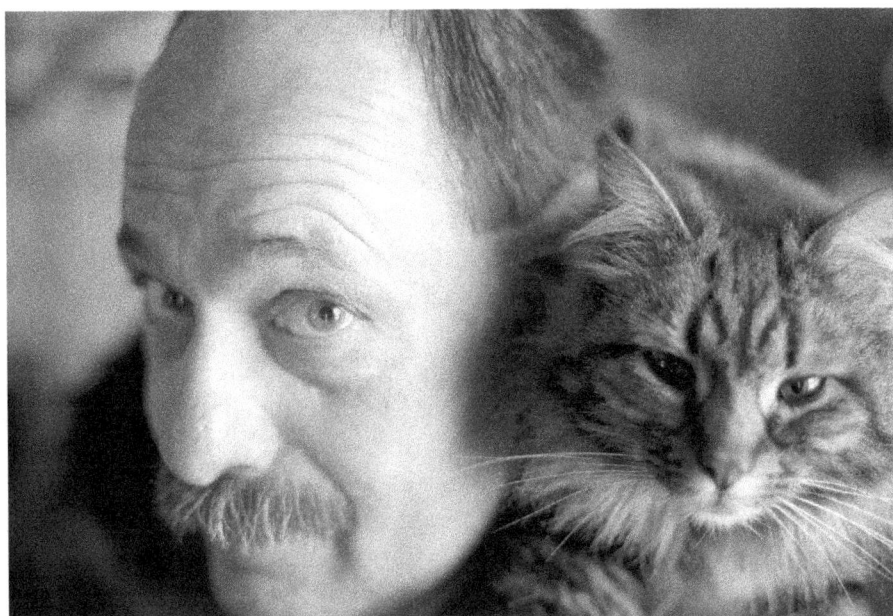

Figure 14.1.

professional filmmakers and archivists, film scholars, and critics. But my interests in critical theory bridged my medieval focus and film interests. Documentary professionals put theory into practice and irresistibly drew me in. For the Flaherty week, I could be a *mediavalist*.

Each year, the filmmakers initially knew me as *the projectionist*.

As I think back, the booth looked like a steampunk tableaux. With its carbon-arc housings and ancient Simplex E-7 projectors, the Wells College projection booth's vintage equipment created a snapshot of a passing era.

With intense protectiveness, filmmakers handed over their films. The rough-looking equipment concerned them. Frequently, the films we screened had come directly from postproduction, sometimes before prints had been made.

They worried about how the equipment might affect their films, but their cautious apprehension stemmed more deeply from their concern about how such a diverse crowd of professionals would receive their work. The rapidly evolving technologies in the decades of the late twentieth century shadow and inform the parallel evolution of evolving film theory.

The intellectual challenges to modernism in the generations influenced by Michel Foucault and Jean Baudrillard tested theoretical underpinnings. Film and photography's ideological origins embodied modernisms derived from the Renaissance era and the technological advancements of the Industrial Age.

For documentarians in the 1980s and 1990s, the bulkhead separating documentary from fiction was becoming far more permeable. New challenges to the norms set off alarms but also offered new artistic and intellectual opportunities, which, coupled with feminist, LBGTQ, ethnic, and postcolonialist studies, made for wonderfully rich screenings. As someone who had grown up under the projection booth model, both literally and figuratively, I was interested in the discussions. These interdisciplinary postmodern currents roiled my field of Late Medieval History of Art.

The projection booth model has the advantages of the shared audience experience, which forms the core of the Flaherty, along with traditional documentary and early film studies. But like the Simplexes, the projection booth speaks to an earlier era, when a single source provided the vision for a mass audience, an act of ideological colonization.

The term *documentary*, after all, stems from the Ciceronian term *docere*. In its original usage in *De Oratore*, it means to teach, to guide, or to lead, which was totally compatible with the modernist use of education as a means of creating a rational social unity. Through the illusion of experiential witnessing framed to create a rational argument, documentaries sought to educate their audiences. *The Man with a Movie Camera* (1929) and other experimental documentaries proved the exception.

As the Flaherty seminar progressively embraced experimental forms, it ended up questioning that model more and more, opening up to a multiplicity of coexisting perspectives to create a web of histories rather than any single restrictive tradition.

What most excited me was exactly those moments that tested out fresh critical approaches in a relatively conservative genre. Unlike studying fourteenth-century painting, where explorative methodologies run the risk of treating artworks in a manner not relevant to their contexts, documentary film offered an environment where many filmmakers embraced new ideological groundings in their films. This made the critical language circulating around them feel exactly appropriate.

While the art world offers various venues for dialogues between practice and theory, none do so with the focused alacrity, diversity, immediacy, and intensity that the Flaherty offered each year I was there. Discussions in the 1980s and 1990s with a savvy film community about the films of Sadie Benning, Tony Buba, Su Friedrich, Jean-Pierre Gorin, John Porter, and Marlon Riggs underscored the intellectual change we were participating in. In retrospect, we hacked out a crucible for the ensuing digital era, which philosophically grew out from both critical theory and broadening media-making practices.

The Flaherty was a microcosm of larger cultural currents. It served as a place of experimentation where a broadening documentary community could question the premises of the genre, its media, and their cultural roles.

While the projection booth model certainly still has some purpose, it now operates in a wider field of multiple smaller screens, participatory interactive digital narratives, and sensory immersive technologies, inspiring the future potentials for documentary.

Those years in the booth and at intensive seminar discussions continue to shape my scholarly research. I keep asking how an ever-evolving critical theory drives technological changes and how both can galvanize a socially responsible and diverse cultural engagement.

15

REFRACTIONS

Lynne Sachs

LYNNE SACHS makes films, installations, performances, and web projects. Between 1994 and 2006, she produced essay films in Bosnia, Israel, Italy, Germany, and Vietnam. Her recent hybrid work combines nonfiction, experimental, and fiction modes. Her twenty-five films have screened at the Images Festival, MoMA, New York Film Festival, Sundance Film Festival, Walker Art Center, the Whitney Museum of American Art, and Wexner Center for the Arts, with retrospectives at the Buenos Aires International Festival of Independent Cinema, the China Women's Film Festival, and the Festival International Nuevo Cine in Havana. A 2014 Guggenheim Fellow, she teaches part-time in the Art Department at Princeton University. More information is available at http://www.lynnesachs.com.

I was twenty-three years old when I attended my first Flaherty seminar as a fellow in 1984. I'd never taken a cinema studies class. I was just beginning to figure out how film could become the place to bring together my love for art and politics.

With hindsight in my pocket, I can see that meeting the artists and scholars that programmer D. Marie Grieco convened that summer was one of my life's most influential experiences.

Collage-cinema genius Bruce Conner showed his work. I saw Conner's *A Movie* (1958), *Cosmic Ray* (1969), and *Crossroads* (1976). Scholar

Figure 15.1.

VèVè Clark presented her newly published book *The Legend of Maya Deren, Vol. 1, Part 1: Signatures (1917–1942)*, a monumental collection of Deren's writings. And I saw Deren's *Ritual in Transfigured Time* (1946) and *A Study in Choreography for the Camera: Out-takes* (1945). I was hooked. Forever changed.

The next year, I moved to San Francisco and began a one-year internship with Bruce. We drove around in his convertible looking for Geiger counters to measure the radioactivity under his home. In his basement studio, I listened to his stories about the 1960s and 1970s art scene and growing up in Kansas, while he re-spliced his films for preservation—work I was supposed to be doing.

In 1989, Flaherty programmer Pearl Bowser invited me to screen my then-recent San Francisco State University graduate thesis film, *Sermons and Sacred Pictures: The Life and Work of Reverend L. O. Taylor* (1989). I was grateful for—and surprised by—her invitation to be part of a Flaherty seminar comprised almost entirely of African American and African filmmakers.

As a high school student in Memphis, Tennessee, I had seen Reverend Taylor's 16mm film archive of black urban life. Eight years later, I returned to my hometown to reconnect with this complicated, racially traumatized city in a new way, through his images and by talking to the people who knew him.

Making *Sermons and Sacred Pictures* was an intense, intimate, revealing experience. I spent two months walking around neighborhoods I barely knew. I asked questions about Taylor and myself. This was my first brush with making a film about a person's life experience outside my own.

Reverend Taylor was a filmmaker I admired like none other. He shot from the inside out, a black minister filming his *own* community with his *own* Bolex with the intention of screening these films *for the people who were in them*.

I tried to deal with my own presence as filmmaker. I resisted filming my face. I always made it clear that I was the one listening and filming, hiding and exposed, in ways that only cinema makes possible. I spent a lot of time talking about this issue with my professors Trinh T. Minh-ha (who was also a Flaherty guest artist that year) and Peggy Ahwesh.

I'd had very little experience discussing my film with an audience. Film scholar Teshome Gabriel, the facilitator for that day at Flaherty, was extraordinarily supportive of the film and me. Filmmakers Marlon Riggs and Zeinabu irene Davis, my Brown University college friend, were both there. Many of us at that seminar remained deeply connected. During the 1991 Gulf War, about twenty of us reconvened on a charter flight to Burkina Faso, where we attended the Pan-African Film Festival of Ouagadougou (FESPACO).

But screening *Sermons* at that Flaherty also brought a new awareness and self-consciousness. Some seminarians reacted to my depiction of a black man's life from my perspective as a white woman with a mixture of skepticism and enthusiasm. (Just before I wrote this piece, I was in touch with filmmaker Ayoka Chenzira, who attended that 1989 seminar and has written poignantly about her own feelings about these issues in her Flaherty story.)

In 2000, I returned to the Flaherty. Programmer Kathy Geritz had asked me to facilitate several post-screening discussions of Tran T. Kim-Trang's *Blindness Series* (1992–2000): five videos exploring blindness as a metaphor.

For weeks, I threw myself into Tran's work, watching each video many times. I took scrupulous notes. Her films are difficult in the best way: aggressive, casual, complex, discursive, irrepressible, nuanced, refined . . . The seminar divided between those transfixed by her cerebral magic and those insulted by her opaque point of view, her aggressive editing, and her comfort with what some might consider vulgar.

Consumed by Tran's work, I wrote a letter about the videos to my hero of all things female and body, French feminist theorist Hélène Cixous. It was published as "Letter to Hélène Cixous" in *More than Meets the Eye: The Videos of Tran T. Kim-Trang*, edited by Jesse Lerner, Trang Tran, and Holly Willis, and published via Scalar, a free, open source publishing platform.

In 2011, I attended Dan Streible's Sonic Truth seminar as a participant. I was struggling with the editing of my hybrid documentary *Your Day Is My Night* (2013), convinced that by attending the seminar, I'd discover editing strategies to help me climb out of what I considered the disaster of my film. I saw important work by legendary filmmakers Les Blank and George Stoney, both of whom died not long after. Yet no work at that seminar sparked me.

Two years later, I returned for Pablo de Ocampo's History Is What's Happening seminar. It featured astonishing films by the audacious Canadian maker Jean-Paul Kelly and by the cerebral British collective, The Otolith Group. That year, I finally realized how to take notes at the Flaherty. After every screening, I now write about the films on the right side of my journal, then I write new ideas about my own projects on the left.

In 2018, I returned again. Programmers Kevin Jerome Everson, a filmmaker, and Greg de Cuir Jr., a curator, reclaimed the commitment to presenting the work of African and African American filmmakers that I had witnessed in 1989. They presented an awe-inspiring collection of films by experimental makers Karimah Ashadu (Nigeria), Ephraim Asili, Christopher Harris, Kitso Lynn Lelliott (South Africa), and Cauleen Smith. Revelations filled both sides of my journal.

16

TAKING THE PLUNGE

Tony Buba

Tony Buba has produced over thirty films, including four features that explore working-class issues, since 1976. Buba began his career with *The Braddock Chronicles* (1972–1985), a dozen short documentary portraits of the stubborn signs of life in a dying mill town. Buba's films have played at Anthology Film Archives, Berlin, the Museum of Modern Art, Sundance Film Festival, Toronto International Film Festival, the Whitney Museum of American Art, and more than one hundred museums and universities. He has received fellowships from the Guggenheim Foundation, National Endowment for the Arts, and the Rockefeller Foundation. His work has won many awards; in 1985 Buba was named Pennsylvania Media Artist of the Year.

It will be thirty years ago this August that my first feature film, *Lightning Over Braddock: A Rustbowl Fantasy* (1988), led off the Flaherty seminar at Wells College on the banks of Cayuga Lake in central New York State.

For years, I'd wanted to go to the seminar but never seemed to have the time. I was doing freelance work in Pittsburgh and working for George Romero on feature films. I was also making my own films. Because I paid for these films out of pocket, I could not afford to lose a paycheck. However, in 1985, I received a Guggenheim Fellowship, so I could relax a bit.

Figure 16.1. Tony Buba and his wife Jan McMannis on the set of his film "Ghosts of Amistad: In the Footsteps of the Rebels."

In graduate school at Ohio University, I'd heard a lot about the Flaherty and about the notorious "Flaherty moments" from visiting filmmakers and other guests who came to the Athens Film Festival. And for years, two Philadelphia friends—programmer Linda Blackaby and filmmaker Louis Massiah—encouraged me to go.

So, in 1985, I took the plunge.

I'd heard about how grueling and tiring the week would be, but I thought, *how tough can it be to watch films and listen to filmmakers all day long?*

I had judged film festivals. At the Ann Arbor Film Festival, Ruth Bradley made the jury look at every film in competition all the way through the credits. I remember viewing Ed Pincus's *Diaries* (c.1980) at the Athens Film Festival in one sitting.

So I thought I was prepared.

I was not.

The week started off fine. People I knew were there: Emily Calmer, who had just taken over the Athens Film Festival; Manny Kirchheimer; Linda Blackaby. I got to meet other filmmakers, like George Stoney, and programmers, like Bill Sloan from the Museum of Modern Art, who I knew by reputation. The seminar even screened a film by David

Sutherland that I'd done some audio and assistant camera work on: *Paul Cadmus: Enfant Terrible at 80* (1984).

Like I said, I thought I was prepared. But it wasn't even mid-week before I was getting exhausted. The seminar was unrelenting, with films, discussions, then more films, and more discussions, from 8:00 or 9:00 a.m. until late at night. Around midnight, a bar operated by Bill Sloan would magically pop up. People would party until 2:00 or 3:00 a.m., then run down to the dock and plunge into the lake for a swim, go to bed, and be ready to go in the morning.

I'm a lightweight. I was never much of drinker, so I joined the group that liked to go outside and get a smoke, if you know what I mean. The only problem was *the munchies*. There was nowhere to go to get anything to eat. One night, we raided the school cafeteria. We ended up repeating this subversive activity on several occasions.

We were in the town of Aurora, but I still don't know if the *town* of Aurora really exists. I never saw it. I just saw Wells College and the lake. And I only *saw* the lake; I never went in for a swim. I didn't have a bathing suit.

At the beginning of the week, Manny Kirchheimer screened *We Were So Beloved* (1985). The film was good, and so was Manny. Manny answered the hard and insightful questions honestly. He was never defensive.

I saw a lot of films. Some I liked, some I didn't. Some got me questioning why the film had even been made, but the discussions after the films were always interesting.

The days blur, but I do remember that a film about the Amish was the last to be screened before lunch on a Wednesday or a Thursday. For some reason, the Amish and Mennonites were hot film topics in the mid-to-late 1980s. The film was OK, though not my type.

Over lunch, everybody started talking about the film. There was a definite buzz, and it wasn't about the ice cream missing from the cafeteria. The discussions were drilling into the use of telephoto lenses in the film.

We went back into the theater.

The moderator called the producer and director to the stage. Then it began: a barrage of questions about the use of long lenses. Had the filmmakers obtained permission to film the people in these shots? How many Amish knew they were being filmed? The audience aggressively questioned the integrity of the filmmakers.

Finally, the producer admitted that some of the people in the film did not know they were being filmed. Then he said (I'm still not sure if he was upset and heckling the audience or if he was telling the truth) he was negotiating with McDonald's because they wanted to use some of his footage in one of their hamburger commercials. You can imagine the audience response. I now knew what a "Flaherty moment" was.

That seminar reinforced my belief that the filmmaker's intentions when making a film do not matter. What's important is how the audience reads the film.

I left the Flaherty inspired.

Within days of returning home, I made a five-minute silent film, *Braddock Food Bank* (1985), based on some discussions that had taken place at the Flaherty. It screened at the 1986 seminar.

So now we're back to 1988. *Lightning Over Braddock*, the film I was working on when I went to the Flaherty in 1985, is finished. I'm getting ready to screen it, and I'm nervous because I have no idea how the audience will respond.

It was so hot that night that the projectionist had to stop the film several times so the projector could cool off. Maybe I caught a break because the projector was stopping and starting or because it was the first film screened. For whatever reason, the audience response was positive. There was no Flaherty moment.

August 1988 turned out to be a great month for me: I screened at Flaherty; I got married to Jan; and I got into the Toronto International Film Festival, thanks to Debra Zimmerman, who'd shared *Lightning Over Braddock* with Kay Armitage.

When we got married, the justice of the peace had said, "The family that goes to Flaherty together, stays together." In 2015, I returned, with Jan, to the Flaherty.

The seminar felt a little different at Colgate University. Some people did not stay the whole week. There was an actual town you could walk to if you did not want to go to a screening. But the intensity was still there. It was just as exhausting, maybe more so because of our age.

The next time I go to the Flaherty, I will bring my bathing suit. And before I come home, I will go to Wells College, take a plunge into Cayuga Lake, and see if Aurora really exists.

17

MEDIA MATTERS AND METEOR SHOWERS

Linda Blackaby and Tony Gittens

In 1975, LINDA BLACKABY founded the Neighborhood Film/Video Project, a Philadelphia media arts center, adding the Philadelphia Festival of World Cinema in 1992. She was Director of Programming for the San Francisco Film Society/San Francisco International Film Festival (2001–2009), Program Consultant and then Program Director for the San Francisco International Asian American Film Festival (1997–2002), and programmer for several other festivals. She has served on the boards of International Film Seminars, Independent Television Service, Philadelphia's WYBE channel 35, The Film Fund, and Cine Information. Currently, she is Program Consultant to the Washington, DC, International Film Festival, CAAM-Fest, and LUNAFEST, and is the Princess Grace Foundation–USA Film Chair. ANTHONY (TONY) GITTENS is Founder and Director of the Washington, DC, International Film Festival. He has served as Executive Director of the Washington, DC, Commission on the Arts and Humanities, the District of Columbia's cultural office. His major recognitions include Knight in the Order of Arts and Letters, French Ministry of Culture and Communications; the Mayor's Award for Excellence in Service to the Arts; Professor Emeritus of the University of the District of Columbia; and Public Humanist of the Year by the Humanities Council of Washington. The *Eyes on the Prize* (1987–1990) Public Television series profiled him for his contributions to the civil rights movement.

Figure 17.1.

The 1986 Flaherty Film Seminar at Wells College in Aurora, NY, stands nearly equidistant between the first Flaherty seminar in 1955 and the present.

The 1986 Flaherty pivoted the seminar to align with exciting new contributions to documentary filmmaking.

The powerful social and political movements of the 1960s and 1970s increased access to filmmaking for women and people of color. The African American civil rights movement crested with the murder of Dr. Martin Luther King Jr. in 1968 and the resulting civil unrest in major urban areas. Black Power reflected black self-identification and a more militant stance. Resistance to the unpopular US war in Vietnam, especially on college campuses, took demonstrations into the streets to burn compulsory draft cards. Women became more self-assured, refusing subservient and unequal treatment. These upheavals fostered emerging voices, new stories, innovative forms, and fresh perspectives. Filmmakers began to explore identity issues and challenge accepted social mores.

The films we programmed in 1986 reflected the issues of the times: life in the developing world, the long struggles in the United States against racism and for equal rights, the experience of searching for roots, the long reverberations of dictatorship in Brazil, and the indigenous, immigrant, LGBTQ, and other communities that had rarely been heard from before in documentary or highlighted at the Flaherty.

As community-based media organizers and film programmers, we had been deeply involved with creating platforms to showcase politically engaged work. We brought our background and commitment to using film to the Flaherty seminar. We wanted to curate new voices into a meaningful, cogent program.

Esme Dick, executive director of International Film Seminars, the organization that presents the Flaherty seminar, invited Tony to program the 1986 seminar. At the time, Tony was a Flaherty board member and professor in the Learning Resources Division of the University of the District of Columbia in Washington, DC. He also founded and directed the university's Black Film Institute.

"Everyone else on the board has programmed the seminar, and you should have a turn," noted Esme. Tony was the first person of color to program the weeklong seminar.

Tony invited his longtime colleague and Flaherty attendee, Linda Blackaby, to co-program with him. At the time, Linda was director of the Neighborhood Film/Video Project of International House in Philadelphia. We collaborated to conceptualize and mount the program.

Frances Flaherty's principles of non-preconception and exploration guided us.

The traditional seminar structure consists of screenings and discussions. For filmmakers and media workers, the Flaherty seminar offers a special experience, a movie camp filled with film watching and discussion by day, socializing and more discussion by night. Spectacular meteor showers over Lake Cayuga illuminated some of the nighttime discussions.

We wanted to create an inclusive and diverse seminar experience where filmmakers, films, and participants represented many ethnic, racial, gender, class, and sexual orientations.

We wove identity politics and independent cinema with countercultural and alternative views of social issues. We connected some of the new ways video, TV, and public media addressed the audience and innovated new storytelling methods and structures.

Most importantly, we brought rising star filmmakers of color to Wells College to present and discuss their work: Henry Hampton (with a preview of his American epic public television series on the civil rights movement, *Eyes on the Prize*, 1987–1990), Mira Nair (*Mississippi Masala*, 1991; *India Cabaret*, 1985; *Monsoon Wedding*, 2001; *Queen of Katwe*, 2016), and Trinh T. Minh-ha with *Naked Spaces: Living is Round* (1985).

Native American video artist Victor Masayesva insisted that his *Itam Hakim Hopiit* (1984) be screened without subtitles in order to assert the dominance of Hopi, his indigenous language.

LGBT filmmakers presented their work. Peter Adair came with his and Rob Epstein's *The AIDS Show* (1986). Richard Fung showed his more theoretical *Orientations* (1986). Andrea Weiss and Greta Schiller screened their *International Sweethearts of Rhythm* (1986). Lucy Winer and Paula de Koenigsberg brought *Rate It X* (1986).

We also invited international filmmakers who worked in different styles of documentary and experimental film.

The great Brazilian documentarian Eduardo Coutinho screened one of his first feature-length works, *A Man Marked for Death/Twenty Years Later* (1984). Ghanaian filmmaker King Ampaw showed *Kukurantumi: The Road to Accra* (1983), one of sub-Saharan Africa's first feature-length films. Taieb Louhichi from Tunisia presented *Shadow of the Earth* (1982). Chilean Jaime Barrios offered a work he codirected with Gaston Ancelovici, *Memories of an Everyday War* (1986). And we screened French expat Jean-Pierre Gorin's *Routine Pleasures* (1986)

The seminar also highlighted US indie films. Carma Hinton and Richard Gordon came with *To Taste a Hundred Herbs* (1984), the third film in their landmark trilogy chronicling rural China. Lisa Hsia attended with *Made in China: A Search for Roots* (1985). Tony Buba screened *Braddock Food Bank* (1985). Indie feature films included Keva Rosenfeld's *All American High* (1986), Ross McElwee's groundbreaking and hilarious *Sherman's March* (1986), and John Hansen's *Troubled Waters* (1986).

We enjoyed programming shorts by Jim Blashfield, Cathy Edwards, Jan Krawitz, Dean Parisot, Joanna Priestly, and Osamu Tezuka.

Our seminar was the first to embrace video as a format equal to film. Rather than relegating video works to a sidebar, we deliberately presented them in the theater space.

We showcased Marina Abramovic, Jon Alpert and Downtown Community Television (DCTV), Helen De Michiel, Joan Logue, Victor Masayesva, Daniel Reeves, and Jeffrey Skoller. Karen Ranucci brought the video collection *Latin American TV*, and Martha Wallner presented Paper Tiger TV's *Central America Comes to Middle America* (1985–1986).

Since our 1986 seminar, the seminar has regularly featured works by filmmakers of color.

In 1987, the year after our seminar, Tony founded the Washington, DC, International Film Festival, now in its thirty-second year. He also served as executive director of the Washington, DC, Commission on the Arts and Humanities.

In 1992, Linda founded the Philadelphia Festival of World Cinema. She co-programmed the 1998 Flaherty seminar with Barbara (Bobbie) Abrash. Later, she was program director of the San Francisco Film Festival.

Looking back, it feels as if the most powerful meteor showers of the 1986 seminar were in the screenings, discussions, and participants' reflections where alternatives to dominant cultural narratives from independent and international media artists lit up the media scene.

18

THIRTY YEARS LATER

Jeffrey Skoller

JEFFREY SKOLLER's films, video, and photography have been exhibited internationally at the Pacific Film Archive; Museum of the Moving Image; J. Paul Getty Museum; Whitney Museum; P.S. 1; Yerba Buena Center for the Arts; the Robert Flaherty Film Seminar; Arsenal Kino, Berlin; Mannheim Film Festival; Latin American Film Festival, Havana; and National Film Theatre, London. His essays on experimental film and video have appeared in *Film Quarterly*, *Discourse*, *Representations*, *Afterimage*, *Animation: An Interdisciplinary Journal*, *World Records*, *Cinematograph*, and other journals. His books include *Shadows, Specters, Shards: Making History in Avant-Garde Film* (2005) and *POSTWAR: The Films of Daniel Eisenberg* (2010). He teaches in the Department of Film and Media at University of California, Berkeley.

For those of us who came up in the often-parochial world of 1970s and 1980s experimental film, the American social documentary seemed like a sedimented form. Its clichéd ideas about political film were disconnected from theoretical discourses and fertile experimental practices.

For us, it was the avant-garde's materialist, anti-illusionist rethinking about film form that continued the promise of a radical cinema that could transform political consciousness. We were steeped in Peter Wollen's "Two Avant-Gardes," Fernando Solanas's "Third Cinema," Julio García

Figure 18.1.

Espinosa's "The Imperfect Cinema," and the American avant-garde's explosive aesthetics. We ardently tried to practice a politically radical cinema with experiment and invention at the center.

Back then, we could never have imagined that our concerns about perception, representation, and the materiality of the medium could ever find a place at the legendary Flaherty Film Seminar, viewed by many as the home of the American social documentary.

So, in 1986, I was surprised to be invited to show my new work, *Nicaragua: Hear-Say/See-Here* (1986). An hour-long essay, the film chronicles my travels through revolutionary Nicaragua during the height of the Contra War.

Influenced by Straub/Huillet, Trinh T. Minh-ha, and Peter Hutton, *Nicaragua: Hear-Say/See-Here* elaborated an earnest attempt to make a personal image and text film, shot with a hand-cranked Bolex. My goal was a committed political advocacy work, integrating the formal problems of representation and the subjectivities of the filmmaker exploring daily in the midst of US aggression against Nicaragua.

This essay film form is common today. But in 1986, attacks from Flaherty seminar attendees came fast and hard: "Who are you to talk about my own impressions and feelings in the face of dying Nicaraguans?" "Why would you make a film that would be difficult for viewers to sit through?"

I was stunned to see my contemplative experiment in an experimental activist medium transformed into one of the seminar's bad objects. I slinked out.

Seminarians pummeled Trinh T. Minh-ha, Jaime Barrios, and Robert Gardner with moral outrage, confirming my sense that the politics of form had no place at Flaherty. I did not return for thirty years.

Gradually, I started to hear about a new generation of curators, such as Kathy Geritz, Ed Halter, Irina Leimbacher, Susan Oxtoby, Gabriela Monroy, and Casper Stracke, who were broadening Flaherty programming with formal and aesthetic exploration. They blurred the lines between experimental, personal film and social documentary. The Flaherty had a new buzz as *the* place where experimentation beyond social documentary was championed.

Then, in 2015, I heard that Laura U. Marks, the brilliant theorist of experimental media who had just published a book on contemporary experimental cinema from the Arabic-speaking world, was the programmer. I thought it might be time to check back in.

Her program, The Scent of Places, featured no conventional social-issue documentary! Instead, it focused on the ephemeral, textural, and affective experiences of cinema and place. She presented extraordinary works I had never seen by Mounira Al Solh (Lebanon), Hassan Khan (Egypt), Tariq Teguia (Algeria/Greece), and Laila Shereen Sakr (Egypt/USA), who worked beyond social documentary. Their aesthetic engaged invisible histories, affective forces, and the textures of ordinary lives.

Two years later, in 2017, I had to go see the adventurous Portuguese curator Nuno Lisboa's programming. In Future Remains, he presented a wide range of cinematic strategies with extraordinarily diverse forms and geographies that he claimed created an archive of gestures for an uncertain future. I had never seen the formally experimental works of Filipa César and Dominic Gagnon. I took a deep dive into the ever-prolific Kevin Jerome Everson's extraordinarily important work and admired again Trinh T. Minh-ha's historic films.

In 2018, I had to return for The Necessary Image, co-programmed by filmmaker Kevin Jerome Everson and scholar Greg De Cuir Jr., the most radical departure from realist documentary forms I had experienced at Flaherty. The invited filmmakers and the attendees seemed uncharacteristically diverse for Flaherty.

Their program featured both single-screen and expanded gallery installations. It emphasized complex formalist work by nonwhite experimental filmmakers from Africa, Asia, and the United States.

I saw pieces by Ephraim Asili, Christopher Harris, Sky Hopinka, Beatriz Santiago Muñoz, and Cauleen Smith. I listened to the filmmakers talk to each other. They created a dense critical mass that demanded rethinking American avant-garde cinema history as white and European. I was astonished to see Christopher Harris's *still/here* (2001) finally received in a nonfiction context and understood as important.

The intersections of Nigerian/British artist Karimah Ashadu, South African installation artist and scholar Kitso Lynn Lelliott, and Thai filmmaker Anocha Suwichakornpong suggested strong cultural differences in subject positions and modes of production.

The atmosphere was electric. The highly politicized forms ranged across the lyrical, poetic, structural, surreal. I asked myself, what were the formal histories and traditions of these works? The political urgency and commitment to new forms of these nonwhite fimmakers' works was extraordinary. The most challenging works embodied the cutting edge of twenty-first-century experimental cinema.

Yet, unfocused conflicted responses and the lack of a common language to speak about aesthetic form remain pervasive at Flaherty.

In 2015, Hassan Kahn and his extraordinary *Blind Ambition* (2012) were attacked for incomprehensibility. Nearly forty years after presenting *Reassemblage* (1982) at the seminar, Trinh T. Minh-ha was still accused by 2017's attendees of bad cinematic technique and criticized for her refusal of identity.

In 2017, the discussion of Canadian Dominique Gagnon's *of the North* (2015) included sanctimonious denunciations of the film, and some accused Gagnon of racism, expressing outrage that the film was even shown. There was little discussion about what this problematic work exposes about emerging technologies, database representation, privacy, and the ethics of found-footage films.

In 2018, Nigerian/British artist Karimah Ashadu's films became bad objects. She was criticized for refusing to discuss her personal relationships to her Nigerian subjects. Many accused her of empty formalism and exploitation, negating what she had done. She insisted the focus be on her work. A haze of easy moralism hung over the discussions.

At times, a collective swoon of sanctimony drenched the discussions about experimental films. Accusations of bad technique, lack of context, positive representation, and a privileging of structure and aesthetics over political engagement often smothered dialogue about experimental films.

Is this inevitable? Is it possible to structure more constructive and meaningful discussions?

The Flaherty seminar has become one of the film world's most valuable contexts for complex and emerging radical media practices.

Perhaps the Flaherty Film Seminar should be renamed the Flaherty Laboratory, in order to emphasize its experimental nature and to recognize that filmmakers are not simply seers, but also experimenters, explorers, inventors. Trying, failing, and sometimes failing better . . .

19

THE FLAHERTY IN 1986

Helen De Michiel

HELEN DE MICHIEL is a filmmaker, writer, and community designer based in Berkeley, California. Her documentary projects include the work in progress *Knocking on Doors, Lunch Love Community* (2015), *The Gender Chip Project* (2004), *Turn Here Sweet Corn* (1990), the dramatic feature *Tarantella* (1994), and many other shorts and media installations. She is author, with Patricia R. Zimmermann, of *Open Space New Media Documentary: A Toolkit for Theory and Practice* (2018).

The year was 1986. I was planning to be married in October. The AIDS epidemic was spreading, and ACT UP was forming during the second term of the Reagan presidency.

I was working for *Alive from Off Center*, the pioneering public television show that we created and produced in St. Paul, Minnesota. The National Endowment for Arts (NEA) funded artists and regional arts organizations and awarded media production fellowships. I cooked my way through dinner parties with the *Silver Palate Cookbook*.

Video was a new medium at the Flaherty Film Seminar. In June, I was invited by programmers Linda Blackaby and Tony Gittins to present my performance video art piece, *And One And One And One* (1986) at the Wells College seminar.

Figure 19.1.

After the screening, the projectionist approached me in the hallway. He was neither a young guy nor an old curmudgeon. He looked like a man who enjoyed tinkering in the darkness, with light flickering on celluloid as it worked its way through a film projector, sprocket sounds ticking smoothly. He said to me in total seriousness, "Why was your video so poorly shot?"

I saw Mira Nair talking in a phone booth over in the hallway corner. I giggled nervously, which became a petulant squint, the only response I could muster at the moment. I said, "I have no idea what you are getting at. We shot the piece exactly like we wanted." He said, "I wasn't sure why they picked something like that for the Flaherty."

I hated the shame and second-guessing that welled up as I walked away, not getting in the last word. Any trust and confidence I had built up in my abilities as a media maker were evaporating. Who else was thinking that same thing? Why did it matter so much to me? And worse: Could I face the possibility that I was an impostor and failed artist?

Later on that day, I watched *Forest of Bliss* (1986), the deeply observed ethnographic documentary by Robert Gardner. When the audience gathered to discuss the film, the laconic filmmaker joined us for a Q and A session along with his moderator. People asked some factual questions about his production craft.

Then, like a small spark igniting a fire, someone made a comment questioning the filmmaker's right to film death ceremonies along the Benares River in India. One by one, others joined in to interrogate and criticize the film's right to exist and be shown publicly.

I was shocked listening to these speakers who were standing up to offer arguments for why this study was politically and aesthetically offensive. I do not remember whether Gardner engaged in the debate. He was the patrician stoic, who simply endured this apparently not unusual Flaherty ritual. Later, I heard the rumor that he'd immediately left the seminar, flying away in his own airplane.

Thirty-one years later, I look back at the 1986 program that Linda and Tony curated, containing so many new voices, forms, and styles. This banquet of works on film and video confronted power dynamics across cultural and political boundaries and pointed far beyond the constricted lanes that had been allowed to documentary in previous years.

Participants in the seminar came as connoisseurs with decided opinions and an eagerness to discern, comment, argue, and debate this new proliferation of directions across the media arts. This was a unique Flaherty game that could not be played either in academe or in the cinematic marketplace.

At the 1986 seminar, I watched the power of programming unfold over the hours of a day and across the length of a week.

In documentary filmmaking, I record, organize, and create narratives that reckon with a life, a situation, or the puzzle of events. Contrasting this and that fragment, I stitch together a story from sensations, impressions, and lucky breaks.

During the seminar, it was impossible not to realize that programming itself is the electric current and under-recognized art that gives actual, real-world context and significance to the works being presented and defines them historically beyond simple crowd-pleasing judgments.

When the curators shape a Flaherty program, they choose films and other media-based works to trigger dialogue—with the self, with the community, and across global boundaries. In this hothouse environment, the dialogue grows intense, willful, hurtful, ridiculous, needless, and engaged.

The curators hold the power to direct the force of this experience, uncomfortable or enlightening as it may be. Our films are only elements in this larger performance that the Flaherty seminar incites. What is good? Why should we take this film seriously? How does an artist make choices in the face of real and present challenges?

Documentary carves out a space for a sensory-directed philosophical inquiry. How does this practice influence the way a culture organizes and makes stories out of the chaos of living in this world?

It was during that Flaherty seminar in 1986 that I confronted these kinds of questions that were pushing my own creative process forward. After my encounter there, I realized that it would be impossible to make pleasing an audience my goal, as much as it might be pleasant and rewarding and as much as I might have liked to.

I reckoned that my documentary practice would have to aspire to connect globally, remain intensely local and community-oriented, and still hold its own as an individual act of creative expression. Occasionally, my projects have reached bits and pieces of that goal.

But more importantly, early in my development as an artist, the Flaherty seminar gave me the framework in which to realize that this aspiration could be real, and it has always been worth the struggle.

20

THE ONE WHO NAMES YOU

Louis Massiah

Louis Massiah is a documentary filmmaker and the Founder/Director of Scribe Video Center in Philadelphia. He has received a MacArthur Fellowship (1996–2001), two Rockefeller/Tribeca fellowships, and a Pew Fellowship in the Arts. His award-winning documentaries, *The Bombing of Osage Avenue* (1986), *W. E. B. Du Bois—A Biography in Four Voices* (1996), two films for the *Eyes on the Prize II* series (1990), and *A is for Anarchist, B is for Brown* (2002), have been broadcast on PBS and screened worldwide. In 2011, the National Park Service's President's House historic site commissioned him to create a five-channel permanent video installation. In 2018, the Museum of Black Civilizations in Dakar, Senegal, selected forty-three films Massiah produced at Scribe Video Center for exhibition.

My early awareness of the Robert Flaherty Film Seminar is intertwined with conversations during the 1980s with the programmer, filmmaker, and archivist Pearl Bowser.

Pearl was the one who encouraged me to attend the seminar and provided the rationale that made it inevitable for me to pay the registration fee and make the five-hour drive from Philadelphia to Wells College in Aurora, New York. She offered the persuasive syllogism, "You're a

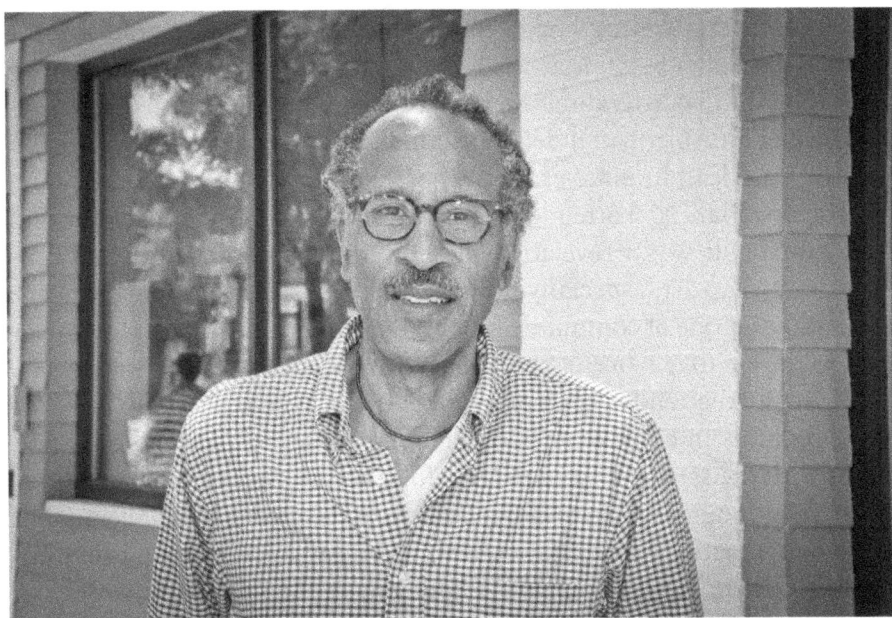

Figure 20.1. Photograph by Conrad Louis-Charles.

filmmaker. Filmmakers need to meet other filmmakers and talk about their work. You need to attend."

The first sentence was a declarative creation of fact: *You're a film-maker*, something I hadn't quite had the courage to say to myself. The second sentence, *Filmmakers need to meet other filmmakers and talk about their work*, was an introduction to a protocol that I hadn't really thought much about before. *You need to attend* is typical of Pearl—a call to action.

Pearl was the one who first named many of us cultural workers, who created definitions for our roles in the community: "Greaves [William] is a conductor." "Ayoka [Chenzira] is an engineer." "Miles [Bill] is an historian." "Toni [Cade Bambara] is a strategist." "Henry [Hampton] is an admiral."

I had just turned thirty and had been working as a producer at a public television station in Philadelphia, producing witness-based documentaries on social and cultural issues as well as multi-camera studio shows. But even though I'd been making documentaries, some of which were broadcast nationally, I hadn't labeled myself a filmmaker. That was Pearl's name for me. My self-definition had been *someone who works in public television*.

The Flaherty seminar had been referenced when I was a grad student in the Film/Video Section at MIT, a documentary film program. But I never thought that attending the Flaherty seminar was part of the essential work of an American independent filmmaker, or more specifically an African American filmmaker, until those conversations with Pearl.

The first Flaherty I attended was programmed by Linda Blackaby and Tony Gittens. It was a revelation. It showed me the impact of film programming as an art, especially how the selection and sequencing of work operates as a mode of communication. Programming the seminar is analogous to the creative work of the deejay: it is a dance with the audience.

Though I'd attended screening series before, the Flaherty experience of seeing films in context with other films for seven very full days and nights with the same group of people, followed by peer-to-peer conversation, brought new understanding not only to the work I was seeing, but to my own practice. Conversations over meals and drinks with programmers like Cheryl Chisholm, who helped create the African Film Society in Atlanta, and MoMA programmers Mary Lea Bandy, Sally Berger, and Bill Sloan made clear to me that programming is an art.

Seeing the films of Trinh T. Minh-ha and the reaction and debate surrounding her work demonstrated that cinema was as rigorous and as rich an investigative and analytical tool as the written essay.

Presenting my own work at Flaherty added another layer to my relationship to the seminar. In 1987, Richard Herskowitz invited me to screen *The Bombing of Osage Avenue* (1986), a film I made with Toni Cade Bambara. That experience led to important new collaborations for me.

At those early seminars, I saw breakthrough films by Canadian filmmakers John Greyson and Richard Fung, who had an ease of storytelling not yet reflected in US queer cinema. And I found the critiques launched by film and media scholars like Patricia Zimmermann and Scott MacDonald to be important and deeply appreciated their multileveled analyses of aesthetics, class, economics, ethics, politics, and technologies.

In 1989, a confluence of forces led to a Flaherty that had an enormous impact in the US independent media community. B. Ruby Rich, who was then the program officer for film and media at the New York State Council on the Arts (a primary funder of the Flaherty), articulated a need for institutions supported by public funds to reflect the diversity of the public and not replicate class, gender, heteronormative, and racial power structures. She compelled the Flaherty to expand beyond its 1950s and early 1960s roots as an elite East Coast club for white men and (occasionally) their spouses.

That year, Pearl Bowser, a Flaherty board member, was chosen as co-programmer with Grant Munro, a producer at the National Film Board of Canada. Their programming palette included a mixture of African and African-diasporic films, new works from Latin America, Chicano films and queer cinema, as well as Glasnost documentary and Canadian animation.

Pearl also saw to it that film studies scholars and cultural theorists of color, such as Toni Cade Bambara, Manthia Diawara, and Teshome Gabriel, attended. Pearl's invitees created a critical mass of film theorists who could expand the discussion and analysis of film so that films made by filmmakers of color, women, and those locked out of the academy and mainstream culture might be analyzed within the context of the communities that created them.

Word of Pearl and Grant's curation attracted a new and diverse cadre of filmmakers to the seminar in addition to curated guests, including the Palestinian filmmaker Alia Arasoughly and Ethiopian filmmaker Salem Mekuria. That seminar also allowed me to experience Lourdes Portillo's extraordinary *La Ofrenda* (1989).

Pearl invited me to screen *Power!*, a work in progress I had directed with Terry Rockefeller for *Eyes on the Prize II* (1988). She also invited Henry Hampton, the creator and executive producer of the *Eyes* series, to present a mini-retrospective of his works. *Eyes II* posed more challenges to the white attendees with its more complex issues of black self-determination, ongoing Northern struggles, the Black Panthers, and community control. That seminar also had an impact on works that were finished in its direct aftermath, including Marlon Riggs's *Tongues Untied* (1989).

Pearl intervened in the traditional structures of the Flaherty. For Pearl, I think this was not just about getting people of color to the table, but about building a new kind of place to gather and explore new ways of seeing and relating to the works shown and to each other.

21

SPARKS

Philip Mallory Jones

PHILIP MALLORY JONES's media art and storytelling span five decades and include animation, books, digital graphics, interactive game/VR/AR immersive environments, museum/gallery installation, performance, photography, prints, sculpture, video, and writing. The Ford Foundation, Rockefeller Foundation, National Endowment for the Arts, Smithsonian Institutions, and American Film Institute have supported his work. He has worked and exhibited in the Caribbean, Central America, West and Southern Africa, India, the South Pacific, and Europe. He was the Batza Distinguished Scholar in Art and Art History at Colgate University. He produced *Bronzeville Etudes & Riffs* (2018 image/text book) and *Dateline: Bronzeville* (2017 book/game design/photographs).

It is my experience, encompassing three seminars, that there is always an "ignition moment." Around the midpoint of the weeklong seminar, there is a spark, and the atmosphere changes. Q and A sessions that had been generally pleasant discussions over the first several days are by midweek becoming decidedly more edgy in atmosphere and exchange—and louder. Then, the ignition moment arrives! Weary, bleary, and a bit cranky, participants get to their more pointed critiques, and ideological perspectives become clearer. The ignition moment is palpable. It releases tension in the room. Someone says something, and it's as if a window opens and

Figure 21.1.

fresh air washes in. It gives permission to engage. The ignition moment is also a function of the intentionality of the program sequence and viewing regimen, which are central to the seminar psyche. The participants are at the mercy of the programmers. It's an adventure . . . a journey.

1987—Wells College—Richard Herskowitz, Programmer

The central presentation of the seminar at Wells College, 1987, was the Peter Watkins opus on the most critical crisis facing humanity past/present/future: *The Journey* (parts 1–19). The fourteen-and-a-half-hour film, in global and microscopic perspectives, explains the threat that the nuclear industry poses to the persistence of life on Earth. The nineteen parts were screened before Watkins's Q and A session.

The seminar had already passed the ignition moment regarding the twin tyrannies of *The Journey*. The first tyranny was the structure of each episode and the series. Each episode was relentless in its compositional and narrative repetition, imprinting intervals on our minds that would then trigger certain thoughts—Watkins's thoughts. These eye/earworms became running jokes between screenings, small acts of rebellion and/or coping.

The second tyranny was that of compulsory attendance at the morning, afternoon, and evening screenings. I don't think it should be different and fully agree with the approach that everyone sees everything, together. But, it's a beating.

In this context, the surreal and disturbing melodrama (Q and A) involving Peter Watkins, following the final episode of *The Journey*, transpired. Watkins was accompanied by an entourage of acolytes, who sat on the floor around him, and proceeded to lecture the seminar on the unassailable priority and correctness of his vision and work. There were several severe and uncomplimentary critiques of the *Journey* and offended/indignant denunciations in response from Watkins. A particularly impassioned comment came from a Palestinian filmmaker who contended that, at that moment, people were dying in occupied Palestine.

Eventually Watkins had had enough, and he departed the seminar early, in a huff.

And then there was happy hour!

1989—Wells College—Pearl Bowser, Grant Munro, Programmers

One night, Bill Sloan, head of the Circulating Library at the Museum of Modern Art, invited me to tend bar with him, a distinct privilege and pleasure. Bill's presence behind the bar was the stuff of Flaherty seminar lore. He radiated joy in being there. If you weren't smiling when you walked in, you would be after Bill served you a beer. Bill and I got into a rhythm, a choreography of bodies, cups, and cans in that cramped space, with the noise, the dozen faces shouting at you to be heard, some smiling. "What's in a. . . ?" Focus. Immersion in the tumult, and Bill is the eye of the storm. Then it's over. The swirling throng of bodies and voices thins and recedes. People wave as they drift out of the hall. The shared satisfaction of the storm weathered, the job well done.

Twenty-nine years later, I smile and weep at the memory of sharing Bill's delight in that cacophonous madhouse.

1999—Duke University—Richard Herskowitz and Orlando Bagwell, Programmers

The featured presenter at Duke University in 1999 was David Williams, who was present for the screening of four films: *Lillian* (1993), *Nina*

Split in Two (1988), *Thirteen* (1997), and *Inner World of Aphasia: The Thirteen* (1998).

Several issues were raised during the discussion of the films. The portrayal of a middle-aged, poor African American woman was not credible to me or to others who had firsthand experience with middle-aged, poor African American women who were raising their child's child. Lillian and her granddaughter came across as the romanticized fantasy of a young, middle-class white man. Each of David's films had similar problems. And David's insistence that since his films were "character-driven," he was absolved of the requirement that a film must still tell a coherent story, or that the character must be credible, persuaded none of us. Among the most strident in this critique was Ricky Leacock.

David refused to embrace, accept, or even consider the voices of experience and perspective.

By the closing session, the collective animosity toward Williams and his work was high. His opening remarks were a brief rebuke of the seminar participants for being unfair to him. David invoked Roger Ebert's praise for his films as validation, as if Ebert knew anything about middle-aged, poor black women who were raising their child's child! Then Richard asked for comments. No response. Silence in the hall. Something needed to happen. I rose to speak, having no idea what I was going to say. My thought was, *What would Ellis say?*

Ellis B. Haizlip was a friend and mentor. When I knew him, he was programming events at the Schomberg Library, among many other things. He called himself *The Archivist*. Ellis was a visionary of the African diaspora, catalyst and instigator, collector, world traveler, impresario extraordinaire. His critique was piercing, cutting to the essence. Zero bullshit.

To David and that silent gathering, I spoke about the point of being at the Flaherty seminar and the responsibilities of presenters and participants to engage and learn. For presenters, the seminar affords extraordinary opportunities. Among these is the chance to develop one's appreciation and management of critique. When one presents work in public, one must be willing to take the heat that may result. Critique helps clarify the vision and thickens the skin.

I said to David that he shouldn't miss this opportunity to grow in his vision and craft, just because his work is challenged and his feelings are hurt. One either steps up to the level of rigor demanded by the seminar or enrolls in Big Rig Driver School (which I've considered more than once!). People around me nodded in affirmation and appreciation.

I said that at this moment, a thousand years of experience and insight are present in this hall.

Later at lunch, several participants remarked that they had appreciated my comments; one said she'd wept. Suddenly George Stoney, the legend of community media and someone who had been attending the Flaherty seminar since forever, was standing in front of me. He shook my hand and said that I had said something important. I had to sit down; tears ran down my face. George Stoney had just said that *I* had said something important! I thought, *Thank you, Ellis!*

Later, as we were all departing the Duke campus, David approached, shook my hand, and thanked me for my remarks.

22

ON THE ROAD TO FLAHERTY

Timothy Murray

TIMOTHY MURRAY is Director of the Cornell Council for the Arts (CCA), Professor of Comparative Literature and English, and Curator of the Rose Goldsen Archive of New Media Art, Cornell University. He curated the 2018 CCA Biennial. His many books on visual studies and digital culture theory include *Medium Philosophicum: Thinking Art Electronically* (2019); *Critical Essays on Xu Bing's Background Stories* (2016); *Digital Baroque: New Media Art and Cinematic Folds* (2008); *Zonas de Contacto* (1999); *Drama Trauma: Specters of Race and Sexuality in Performance, Video, and Art* (1997); and *Like a Film: Ideological Fantasy on Screen, Camera, and Canvas* (1993).

At first, there was something furtive in my relation to the Flaherty.

I first remember excited drives up Cayuga Lake to crash the seminar during its years at Wells College. Those journeys up the lake from Ithaca usually ended in a welcoming embrace with Patricia Zimmermann or Richard Herskowitz before I was secreted into the rooms where the magic was happening.

This was a period when we Ithacans were actively promoting cinema's embrace of video, installation, theory, and the diversification of Flaherty's guest media makers and audiences. Our local activation was done through Cornell Cinema, the Experimental Television Center, and

Figure 22.1.

public television and with colleagues at Ithaca College and Cornell University. We expanded on what we were seeing through readings of theory and prolonged, urgent discussions about diversifying cinema from the ground up and across the board—from makers and audiences to spaces and formats. There was a charge in the air that we couldn't contain.

Similarly, each summer up Cayuga Lake, the Flaherty was as much about process as about works of cinematic art, and it brought together a rather raucous band of screen folks whose work, discourse, and passion took cinematics to an expanded level of duration. For me, the seminar calls to mind the wild extensions of cinematic time and space, inside and beyond the theater—including discourse carried on long after screenings and formal discussions, during outdoor projections and experimental installations, and into late-night conversations down at the Lake Cayuga docks. And throughout the rest of each year, Flaherty continued to percolate, producing innovative artwork and thinking.

No instance of Flaherty programming made as strong an impact on my curating, teaching, and theorizing as the 1990 seminar that brought together inventive feminist works by Su Friedrich, Vanalyne Green, Kathy High, Indu Krishnan, and Janice Tanaka, along with searing works on the duration of life itself by queer makers facing the horrors of AIDS: *DiAna's Hair Ego: AIDS Info Upfront* (Ellen Spiro, 1989) and *Paris Is Burning* (Jennie Livingston, 1990), both echoing the programming, two years earlier, of work by the heroic Marlon Riggs.

For many of us who grew up as the first generation of American media scholars and theoreticians, the intensity of Flaherty programming channeled our teaching and writing throughout the 1990s and brought history and theory in contact with the demands of gender, sexual, racial, and economic difference.

Then there was the year when Patricia Zimmermann and Michelle Materre took Flaherty on the road to Ithaca College for a condensed seminar, Exploration in Memory and Modernity. For me, the "Flaherty on the Road" initiative meant further expansions of Flaherty time and space via the electronic highway. This was an exciting and contentious time for cinema, as digital media promised to open cinema up to new global experimentation and online audiences while also transforming the ontology of film itself.

Several of us who were concerned with broadening the seminar's efforts at social inclusion as well as its commitment to the electronic arts seized on the invitation offered by Zimmermann and Materre to mark these transformations. My contribution was a Digital Salon programmed in conjunction with screenings by Leah Gilliam, Alex Rivera, and Reggie Woolery—exciting young artists who were blending the analog and the digital within provocative reflections on race and sexuality. What a gift it was to have the promise of new media introduced to Flaherty by these brave artists for whom the magic of digital archives and production enhanced their ability to better represent their cultural histories and contemporary challenges.

The Digital Salon I programmed focused on exposing the thrill of global interconnectivity evident in the work of Shu Lea Cheang, Constance DeJong, Per Eide Spjeld, Guillermo Gomez-Peña, Antoni Muntadas, Tony Oursler, Roberto Sifuentes, Stephen Vitiello, and Adrianne Wortzel.

The Digital Salon expanded the Flaherty beyond its cinematic walls by featuring interactive works by artists who embraced the new nimble tools of digitality for their potential in dismantling the history of restrictive cinematic identifications and enabling broader participation across various spaces of presentation and reception. The Digital Salon drove the Flaherty beyond central New York and down the electronic highway.

Yet, somehow the Flaherty never left Ithaca. During and after the Digital Salon, I began to think about the cultural necessity of finding a way to archive these innovative works created for CD-ROM and the internet. The result was my founding in 2002 of the Rose Goldsen Archive of New Media Art in the Cornell Library. Named after the pioneering Cornell media sociologist, the Goldsen Archive now houses many of the titles and artists introduced by Flaherty and challenges the new threat to artistic duration posed by planned digital obsolescence.

The Goldsen Archive is home to repositories of work produced in conjunction with the New York State Council on the Arts (NYSCA) Electronic Media and Film program, with Rockefeller grants and the Renew Media grants in New Media Art, along with central New York's cherished Experimental Television Center, where so many Flaherty video titles were produced. Over the years, the Goldsen has grown into one of the world's leading digital repositories of individual artist portfolios and large institutional collections. While some of its more than 10,000 digital images, 4,000 artworks, and twenty archival collections can be accessed online (http://goldsen.library.cornell.edu), most are readily accessible on location in Cornell's Division of Rare and Manuscript Collections. Indeed, the Goldsen's recent exhibition, *Signal to Code: 50 Years of Media Art in the Goldsen Archive* (http://rmc.library.cornell.edu/signaltocode/), serves as an archival marker of the social and conceptual inventiveness of Flaherty's expansion of the boundaries of cinema.

The Goldsen collections now entice users to take an excited drive along the electronic highway and back to Ithaca, where the critical legacy of Flaherty and its video and new media artists now cohabit together.

23

ONE LAKE AND TWO KERFUFFLES

Su Friedrich

SU FRIEDRICH has been making films and videos since 1978. These works have been featured in twenty-one retrospectives at major museums and film festivals, including the Museum of Modern Art, the Whitney Museum, Anthology Film Archives, and the National Film Theater in London. Her films have been widely screened at film festivals, universities, and art centers and have been extensively written about. They have won numerous awards, including the Grand Prix for *Sink or Swim* (1990) at the Melbourne International Film Festival. Her DVD collection is distributed by Outcast Films. She teaches video production at Princeton University.

Attending the Flaherty four times over a span of many years has been really valuable, really exhausting, really fun, really instructive, and sometimes (really) aggravating.

Full disclosure: for financial reasons, I've only attended on the four occasions when films of mine were showing. Needless to say, it would be great to attend in other years so that I could see a lot of films and interact with many interesting people, but also because there wouldn't be the pressure to be *on*.

I attended my first Flaherty in 1987 with *The Ties That Bind* (1984) and *Damned If You Don't* (1987), when Richard Herskowitz was the programmer. I was thrilled to be invited and even happier when I arrived

Figure 23.1.

at Wells College and saw that lake. Oh, that lake! After hours of watching filmsfilmsfilmsfilms and then talkingtalkingtalkingtalking, it was sheer bliss to jump off the dock into the beautiful water of Cayuga Lake.

I was impressed by the quality of the films and the discussions, although it was back in the day and there was a little too much of *This doesn't follow the acceptable rules of what a documentary should be* coming from the old guard. And although those remarks were tedious, they weren't surprising: Richard, with his wealth of knowledge about experimental film, had decided to break the box open, to bring works (like mine and many others) that weren't obeying the rules about how to make a "proper" documentary. It was an excellent move on his part that helped to open up Flaherty in ways that are still reverberating, and which he did even more aggressively (I use that adverb as a compliment) when programming the 1999 Flaherty with Orlando Bagwell.

I don't recall being chastised for breaking those rules but was astonished to be told by a *woman* during the discussion about *Damned If You Don't* that it "wasn't yet time" for films to be showing the female nude. She cited Laura Mulvey's famous and influential analysis of the male gaze, while I pointed out that I was a female doing the gazing, and a lesbian at that!

Three years later, in 1990, I was extremely fortunate to be invited to the special Flaherty seminar held in Riga, Latvia, where I screened *The Ties That Bind*. This one was programmed by Richard Herskowitz, Raul

Zaritsky, Ivars Seleckis, and Abraham Kalzkins and was structured so that half the group were Americans and half were from the Soviet Union (which dissolved a year later).

It would take many pages to describe that experience; suffice it to say that it was one of the highlights of my forty years as a filmmaker. There was no lake this time; instead, we swam in a lot of good vodka.

The very funny/ironic/preposterous/predictable aspect of the seminar was that the Americans kept oohing over the fact that the Soviet filmmakers had access to shoot in 35mm and were making films that often relied on visually and intellectually wonderful metaphors (since they couldn't speak openly about political or social issues), while the Soviets did the same amount of oohing over our ability to shoot down and dirty anywhere we wanted and to speak so openly about our political and social concerns.

One thing I will always feel grateful for was the chance to spend so much time with Marlon Riggs, who died just a few years later from complications related to AIDS.

The third opportunity came in 1998, when Barbara Abrash and Linda Blackaby invited me to show *Hide and Seek* (1996). I don't have any memory of the responses to the film, but it might have been problematic, since half of *Hide and Seek* is narrative—though by then there was more acceptance of, and interest in, the ways that one could problematize documentary or simply use it as one part of a film that also drew on other genres.

What I do remember is that they invited Hirokazu Kore-eda to show the documentary *Without Memory* (1996) and his second feature narrative, *After Life* (1998). Both films were revelatory, in so many ways, and have had a lasting impact on me. I was also delighted to discover the work of Ning Ying, especially *On the Beat* (1996).

Most recently, in 2012, Josetxo Cerdán included three of my films in his Open Wounds seminar: *The Odds of Recovery* (2002), *The Head of a Pin* (2004), and *Gut Renovation* (2012), a feature documentary about the destruction of my neighborhood in Brooklyn.

Aside from a kerfuffle during the discussion about *Gut Renovation* with a filmmaker who felt that what I was doing was "wrong" in some way (I guess in comparison with what I had done earlier on; maybe I'm supposed to keep remaking *Sink or Swim* (1990) for the rest of my life?), it was another great experience.

It seems that each Flaherty introduces me to one filmmaker's work that particularly blows my mind. In this case, it was the work of Laila Pakalnina, and I wasn't the only attendee who fell head over heels for her work.

But speaking of kerfuffles, that's a known and remarkable aspect of the seminar. One can't (proverbially) lock a hundred-plus people in a room all day, every day for a week without there being an explosion halfway through. I recall that during my first or second time at the Flaherty, the filmmakers who had done *Atomic Café* (1992) presented a work in progress about animal rights. It seemed to me that they'd done solid research and had an impressive array of archival material to illustrate each of the themes they were planning to cover, just as they had had with *Atomic Café*. But some attendees went ballistic, accusing them of insensitivity to the issue.

Usually during these blowups, people step in to defend the filmmaker(s), who are understandably in a certain amount of shock. I don't recall whether I defended them or their film, though I might have, because I tend to jump into a fight. I do hope that I did. The Flaherty is an environment in which it's presumed that serious conversations will take place about the effectiveness of a film, and any filmmaker who presents their work should be prepared and should allow that to happen. But this other thing? Nah. . . .

But aside from that annual funkiness, the Flaherty is remarkable. I feel grateful for all that I've learned when attending and for the filmmakers, scholars, and programmers I first befriended at the seminar and with whom I have kept in touch during the many years since.

24

WITHOUT ANESTHESIA

Scott MacDonald

SCOTT MACDONALD has written/edited many books on independent cinema, most recently *Avant-Doc: Intersections of Documentary and Avant Garde Film* (Oxford, 2015), *Binghamton Babylon: Voices from the Cinema Department (a nonfiction novel)* (2015), *The Flaherty: Decades in the Cause of Independent Cinema* (with Patricia R. Zimmermann; 2017), and *The Sublimity of Document: Cinema as Diorama (Avant-Doc 2)* (2019). He has programmed independent films for the Museum of Modern Art (MoMA), San Francisco Museum of Modern Art (SFMoMA), Harvard Film Archive, Film Forum, the Flaherty Film Seminar, the Brakhage Symposium, the Beauborg, Thomas Cole National Historic Site . . . and everywhere he has taught. Currently, he teaches film history and directs Cinema and Media Studies at Hamilton College.

I arrived at Wells College in August of 1987 of two minds.

For fifteen years, I'd been passionately interested in what has been called, variously, "avant-garde film," "experimental film," "underground film"—and had heard legendary tales of how the Flaherty seminar chewed up avant-garde filmmakers. Jonas Mekas and Ken Jacobs had apparently attempted to crash the 1963 Flaherty to screen Jack Smith's *Flaming Creatures* (1963) and Jacobs's own *Blonde Cobra* (1963), an event Mekas later documented in *Lost Lost Lost* (1976). To Mekas and Jacobs, the

Figure 24.1.

Flaherty seemed the tired past, not the creative present—an organization and an annual event in need of an intervention.

On the other hand, I'd agreed to be present at the seminar as one of the representatives of Peter Watkins's epic media critique, *The Journey* (1987), which had premiered at Berlin the previous winter. I was proud of the work I had done, along with hundreds of collaborators, on *The Journey*—and excited that Richard Herskowitz (at the time program director at Cornell Cinema) had decided to show all fourteen and a half hours of the film, much of it outside normal screening hours for the Flaherty. This was to be an intervention into conventional media time, including the media time of Flaherty seminarians.

I registered to attend the whole week, saw a few acquaintances, made some new ones—and kept telling myself that it would be fun to discuss the visionary Watkins film with seminarians on Wednesday evening.

Visionary? The process of making *The Journey* was meant to model a new kind of political organization: an international, nonhierarchical network of people around the world committed to social justice and environmental sanity and interested in using the grassroots production of media as a way of learning about the world and acting progressively within it. Ideally, the network created in the production of the film would continue to expand beyond the film, perhaps by using the film (remember, this was before the internet). Watkins had circled the earth three times between 1984 and 1987 to establish grassroots production units in twelve countries, to talk with locally organized crews, and finally to shoot the film.

I told myself I was not at all nervous about the upcoming discussion.

Then, that Wednesday morning, I woke up with large welts covering my body. I'd never had them before and have never had them since.

The discussion with Watkins (and several others who had worked on *The Journey*) turned out to be a legendary "trashing" of a film/filmmaker (the discussion is included in *The Flaherty: Decades in the Cause of Independent Cinema*). The film had more than tested the patience of many seminarians, and they were happy to vent their frustrations.

In the end, I was disappointed with the response to what I thought was a remarkable project and, later on, saddened to realize that my having worked to bring Watkins to the seminar had seriously damaged my relationship with him.

I'm not sorry *The Journey* was presented at the Flaherty; it deserved to be shown and resonated well with the other films Herskowitz had programmed (by Su Friedrich, Yervant Gianikian and Angela Ricci Lucchi, John Greyson, Alfred Guzzetti, Johan van der Keuken, Ilan Ziv . . .). But looking back on that discussion, I do have regrets.

The Journey is focused on the fact that, around the world, serious global issues were almost never a topic around the family dinner table (not sure the "family dinner table" still exists!). Watkins was interested in demonstrating how conventionally organized families avoided discussing serious issues together. I remember Patricia Zimmermann directing a question to me in particular—something like "Do you think the film might be stronger if it included an unconventional family, like say a lesbian couple?" I should have said, "Well, the focus here is on the dangerous anti-educational, anti-political habits of what traditional culture considers 'normal' families." Instead, I remember saying something (I no longer remember exactly what) that I felt would ingratiate me with Patty and others who felt her question was pertinent.

I believe the final comment to Watkins was by a woman who identified herself as a former clinical psychologist: "I'm not being mean when I say this, just brutally real—please understand that. I liken your film to radical surgery with a rusty knife without anesthesia." She went on to explain that there was no way her students could be expected to sit through the film.

Watkins said, "I'm sorry. I can't respond to your comment." But I continue to wish *I'd* said, "If you honestly believe you were not 'being mean' with your comment, I'm afraid you're not clear on what *being mean* means!" Or perhaps, "I see why you're a *former* clinical psychologist!"—though actually being a smart-ass never works out for me.

I returned to the Flaherty the following year, partly because I felt I might need to continue to defend *The Journey* (I was correct)—and as had been true the year before, I continued to see films of considerable interest, to meet new filmmakers, and to develop new relationships.

The irony is that, though I've found it fascinating to transcribe and edit many of the big-group Flaherty discussions—first, for a special issue of *Wide Angle* (vol. 17, nos. 1–4), bravely published by longtime Flahertyite and then-editor Ruth Bradley, and years later for *The Flaherty: Decades in the Cause of Independent Cinema*—I've never liked the seminar model of discussing a film immediately after seeing it and with the filmmaker present. I'm rarely clear, immediately after a film, about what I think, nor am I interested in hearing others' off-the-cuff reactions.

I attended the Flaherty regularly for many years, but my relationship with the seminars has always felt tentative—perhaps a residue of my experience with *The Journey*. I guess I've never quite forgiven that group of seminarians for not having a sense of humor about how their own impatience with the Watkins epic (a film meant to be a conscious intervention within the regular, predictable, comfortable schedules of those who see it, including "media-savvy" audiences like those at "Flaherty summer film camp") was, in fact, the essence of what *The Journey* was about.

25

IN OVER MY HEAD

Mark Geiger

MARK GEIGER is the founder of Geiger Guitars, where he builds custom stringed instruments. An Ithaca College Cinema and Photography alum, he was engaged for many years in set construction at Paramount Pictures before turning to custom instrument making. He can be reached at geigerguitars@earthlink.net.

I was a townie and former carpenter who was a cinema and photography student at Ithaca College in upstate New York.

In 1987, I was privileged to be one of the first undergraduate students to attend the Flaherty seminar on an internship.

I was encouraged to apply and delighted to be accepted. I enjoyed meeting filmmakers and scholars from around the world. I enjoyed seeing films I would never have been able to see otherwise.

I have two very vivid memories of the Flaherty.

One is the screening of *The Journey* (1987) by Peter Watkins, and the other is a discussion of *The Bombing of Osage Avenue* (1986) by Louis Massiah.

I'll start with the latter.

It's the story of the police bombing of a house controlled by MOVE that engulfed an entire block in the Cobbs Creek area of West Philadelphia.

During the discussion, a British man made comments about how police in the United States used excessive force as a matter of course, which struck me as much as the film did. My immediate gut reaction was

Figure 25.1.

to think of the official British response to the conflict in Northern Ireland. My takeaway was that we all seemed to be myopic about our own state of affairs.

Unfortunately, I was a little too timid and unsure of myself to speak up.

I also give a lot of credit to Richard Herskowitz, as well as Peter Watkins and Scott MacDonald, for screening Watkins's fourteen-hour epic, *The Journey* (1987).

While I did indeed consider it a marathon, I'm glad I watched the whole film.

I even turned my name badge over and drew a "?" to mimic the ending of each segment of *The Journey*.

At that 1987 Flaherty seminar, I had the rather schizophrenic reaction of being simultaneously in over my head and at home.

26

SIMPLY PUT

Patti Bruck

PATTI BRUCK is a filmmaker and educator. Her award-winning documentary and experimental films have screened at festivals internationally. From 1990 to 2014, she taught film and video production at the University of Colorado, Boulder. She has served on the Black Maria Film Festival selection committee and on granting panels for the Colorado Council on the Arts, the National Endowment for the Arts, and the Pennsylvania Arts Council. She has also served on the Boulder Arts Commission and is currently Selection Committee and Programming Adviser for the Boulder International Film Festival. She was President of the Robert Flaherty Film Seminar from 2002 to 2010.

I harbor a secret I rarely express: I often dread going to the Flaherty.

The long travel from Boulder, the inevitable delays connecting through Chicago O'Hare, and the first few nights of small talk and awkward discussions are not inviting.

Yet, the Flaherty seminar has changed my life twice.

In the mid-1980s, I was the program coordinator for the Western States Regional Media Arts Fellowship at the Rocky Mountain Film Center in Boulder, Colorado.

The Film Center had received a MacArthur Foundation grant to program a Learning Channel film series called *The Independents*. The first

Figure 26.1.

programmer was documentary video scholar Deirdre Boyle. Because my film education had centered on experimental work, I was unfamiliar with documentaries beyond the well-known theatrical releases.

I had many conversations with Deirdre. When I wanted to know more about the works she programmed, she commanded, "You should go to the Flaherty!"

A year later, film scholar Patricia Zimmermann, in Boulder for summer research, stopped by my office. During our conversation, she insisted, "You should go to the Flaherty!"

A flyer arrived at our office several months later announcing the upcoming 1987 Flaherty seminar, entitled The Media Construction of Identity and programmed by Richard Herskowitz. By this time, I was a graduate student studying for my MFA in Integrated Media Arts at the

University of Colorado. The Flaherty theme matched my interests. I was granted a fellowship to attend.

Shy and intimidated, I walked into the opening reception at Wells College in Aurora, New York, where scholars, programmers, and filmmakers had gathered into groups for conversations about film.

I spotted Patricia. She introduced me to a welcoming circle of her friends: Sally Berger, John Columbus, Richard Herskowitz, Scott MacDonald, David Tafler, and Raul Zaritsky. They remain among my dearest friends.

Richard programmed a mind-boggling number of short and feature films, including Alan Berliner's *The Family Album* (1986), Ilan Ziv's *Consuming Hunger* (1987), John Akomfrah's *Handsworth Songs* (1987), Darcus Howe's *Unfinished Revolution* (1986), from the Channel 4 *Bandung File* series (1985–1991), and John Greyson's *Moscow Does Not Believe in Queers* (1986). Each night we viewed episodes of Peter Watkins's epic, multipart, antinuclear media critique, *The Journey* (1987), often until 2:00 a.m.

Each film created an argument with the one that preceded it.

Yervant Gianikian and Angela Ricci Lucchi's *From the Pole to the Equator* (1987) and the works by John Akomfrah and the Black Audio Film Collective resonated with me. Some pieces were revolutionary. All challenged mainstream documentaries and cultural stereotypes.

The Dutch experimental documentary filmmaker Johann van der Keuken was the featured filmmaker, an éminence grise. What began as a contentious confrontation between Johann and participants over what were seen as his insensitive depictions of cultural rituals gradually evolved into affection and delight as his spirit and films charmed participants. As his humanitarian approach to diverse cultures became clear, the heated challenges evaporated.

During those years, the seminar included fewer than a hundred attendees. Affinities developed. Discussions spilled from the seminar discussion room into the dining room, where large tables encouraged expansive exchanges that no one wanted to leave.

The following fall, armed with a multitude of new ideas and discourses, I returned to graduate school, where questions about radical feminism and *the Other* were boiling up. I felt a new confidence leading discussions, and by the time I graduated, my reputation for sophistication about current political dialogues in media production had convinced the University of Colorado to hire me to teach video, then film production.

Over the last three decades of my attending the Flaherty seminar, I've jumped naked into the lake with friends. I've watched the northern lights with video artist Marlon Riggs. I've stretched out on the lawn to watch shooting stars with film scholar Scott MacDonald. I've taken splendid drives from New Jersey to central New York with John Columbus. And I've taken long, mind-opening walks with Pacific Film Archive curator Kathy Geritz.

And I've marveled at the documentary films of Kazakhstan filmmaker Sergey Dvortsevoy and been challenged by the unnerving Pavel Medvedev, maker of *Vacations in November* (2002). I've witnessed angry confrontations with Austrian documentarian Michael Glawogger about his *Workingman's Death* (2005), and I've listened to queer experimental filmmaker Kenneth Anger's marvelous stories and to participants raging over a surprise screening of the video of Daniel Pearl's beheading.

Every seminar has been different, yet somehow the same.

In 2000, the Flaherty changed my life a second time. I was invited to join the board of trustees—an honor. Eventually, I became Flaherty board president, serving for nine years.

During my first years on the board, the organization was in tumult. Personnel disruptions and waning income threatened the Flaherty's existence. Yet many board members refused to give up the ship. I am forever grateful to Margarita De La Vega Hurtado, who assumed the role of executive director in 2002. Her generous warmth, grace, and courage transformed the position and revived the seminar

Over the decades, the Flaherty has changed. The number of participants has nearly doubled, and as a result, the discussions have tended to lose the satisfying sense of a true seminar experience. The higher registration cost inhibits participants' return. Cell phones and social media lure people away from mealtime discussions. The Flaherty's reputation as an immersive retreat may now be more illusory than real.

Yet, at the end of each Flaherty week, the demanding schedule, difficult films, and complex discussions generate a crisis that breaks down barriers and resistance to new ideas.

Although exhausted and ready for the safety of home, I always know I've refound my tribe.

The Flaherty is more than the films, the programmer, and even the organization. It sustains an increasingly rare opportunity for face-to-face interchange. For one week, participants come together with a yearning for a richer understanding and connection to film culture, and that yearning is rewarded.

The Flaherty is also the community we want and need. These days, it's hard to find. During the Flaherty week, different layers of our intimacy with cinema, and with each other, gradually unfold.

The Flaherty: I came for the films. I come back for the community.

27

THE FLAHERTY LABORATORY

Stacey Steers

STACEY STEERS is known for her process-driven, labor-intensive animated films composed of thousands of handmade works on paper. Her recent work employs images appropriated from early cinematic sources from which she constructs original, lyrical narratives. Her films have screened extensively throughout the United States and abroad and have received numerous awards. She is the recipient of major grants from the John Simon Guggenheim Foundation, the Creative Capital Foundation, and the American Film Institute.

I first attended the Flaherty seminar in 1988.

My dear friend, feminist experimental filmmaker Patti Bruck, had returned from the previous year's event feeling transformed. The distance from Colorado to upstate New York was long and challenging travel, but Patti's conviction about the power of the Flaherty seminar convinced me. And off I went with her to Wells College in central New York.

As a person living in relatively isolated Boulder, the impact of the weeklong seminar of films and conversation with people deeply committed to film and filmmaking as an art of the highest order was exceptionally profound for me. Though we have a strong film community in Boulder, there are seldom resources to bring international artists and their work for screenings. The Flaherty focuses on exactly that kind of

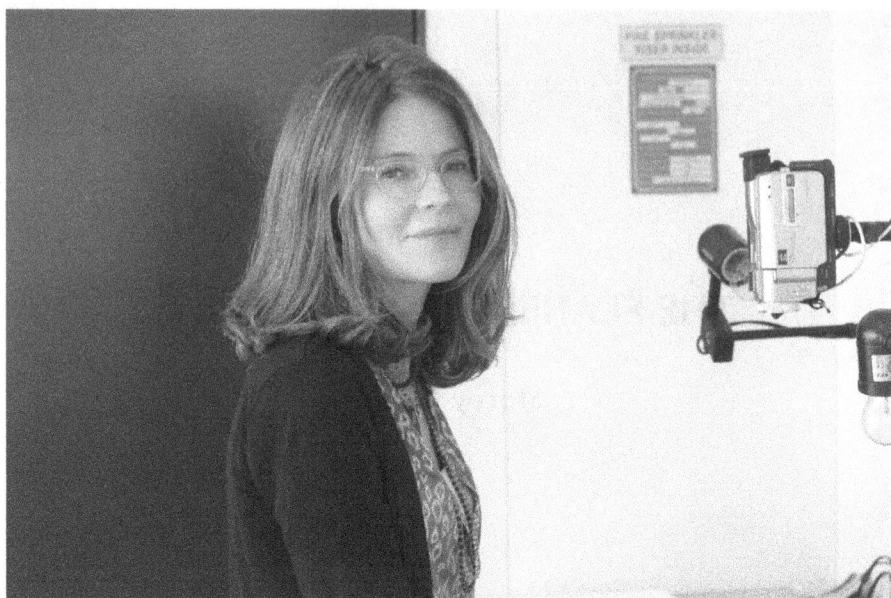

Figure 27.1.

programming. The artists they bring are almost always centrally involved in conversations about the nature of image making.

Because I had young children at home, it was some years before I could start to attend regularly. Finally, in 1999, I went to the seminar at Duke University programmed by Richard Herskowitz and Orlando Bagwell. I've missed very few since.

I consider the Flaherty seminar a laboratory for trendsetting, cutting-edge thinkers whose medium of interest is media. This group includes the programmers, seminar participants, and, of course, the presenting filmmakers.

I've often marveled at how the Flaherty's various programmers continue to bring work that engages the larger cultural conversation around media art. Whether I respond to the work I see or not (and I sometimes *do not* respond at all), I am challenged to engage with the various articulations of cinema. With a kind of clairvoyance, the seminar programmers point toward new concerns and emerging developments. It is as if they have a crystal ball illuminating the future of critical dialogue in the field.

The works I have seen at Flaherty seminars across the decades stay with me. The screenings inevitably challenge my assumptions.

I find myself employing the aesthetic and structural strategies I've seen there in my own work.

In 2002, Ed Halter brought a seminar packed with underground work. I found myself dismissive of the limited focus on craft or aesthetics.

Now, what I saw at that seminar has become an established strategy for a certain style of filmmaking I often applaud.

I've also learned important lessons about geopolitics and historical consciousness from witnessing insiders' views of conflict or social unrest that elude most media coverage.

I discovered Jem Cohen's lyrical, understated elegance, Pedro Costa's languorous, intrepid portraits, Michael Glawogger's uncanny journeys, Lisandro Alonso's relentless, visceral portraits of outsiders, Hito Steyerl's incisive wide-ranging feminist media essays, and Laura Huertas Millán's inspired, visually vivid documentaries. The list goes on and on.

I'm an experimental animator working in the surrealist tradition. It may seem strange that I would look to the Flaherty for inspiration, especially given that it is better known for documentary and experimental modes than for animation. However, I've always used my animation work as a platform to think seriously about the world and how to live in it. The Flaherty is an institution founded precisely to excavate that field of inquiry. It offers a perfect place for reflection, a necessity for any legitimate art practice.

Over decades of many Flahertys, I've made myriad friends, including Daniela Alatorre, John Bruce, John Columbus, Margarita De La Vega Hurtado, Kathy Geritz, Richard Herskowitz, and Dennis Lim, to name only a few. The meals shared and the screening-and-discussion-inspired conversations incubate shared experience and deepen these relationships.

Every year, Patti and I still try to go to the Flaherty together. On our way up from New York City, we always stop at Target to pick up mattress covers, small lamps, and fans to make the dorm rooms a bit more comfortable for sleeping. We usually drive with our good friend John Columbus, founder of the Black Maria Film and Video Festival. He, too, has attended the seminar for decades.

It's a physical challenge to watch so many films and sit still for so long. The schedule involves continuous immersion in screenings and curated conversations with the artists. A trip to the bar follows evening screenings, promising the chance to unwind from the day's experiences late into the night. Sleep deprivation and sensory overload are built into the Flaherty.

Each year as I am about to leave for the seminar, I have mixed feelings. I muse on whether this experience is worth the physical challenge.

However, when I receive the email each January announcing registration for the next seminar, I never hesitate. I sign up for another round.

28

PRACTICAL DIFFICULTIES AND DIFFERENT LOCATIONS

Margarita De La Vega Hurtado

Margarita De La Vega Hurtado was Colombia's first woman film critic. She taught at the University of Michigan in Ann Arbor and University of California, Santa Cruz. She was Executive Director of the Robert Flaherty Film Seminar. She has served on the Houston Museum of Fine Arts film committee and the Aurora Picture Show board. She helped to create the Houston Cinema Arts Society, and has served as a board member since 2008. She has presented at film festivals, museums, and universities in the United States, Latin America, Spain, and Germany. She also executive produced the Juan Manuel Echavarría documentary *Requiem N.N.* (2013–2014), screened at the Museum of Modern Art, the Houston Cinema Arts Festival, and festivals worldwide.

I first attended the Flaherty seminar in 1988. Julie Levinson programmed. Since 1960, I had been a film lover.

Growing up in Colombia, I was a Hollywood movie fan. I got involved in a cine club that screened film classics, documentaries, and world cinema.

I worked at the first Cartagena International Film Festival in 1960, where I discovered the French New Wave. An article I wrote about it was published in a national newspaper.

Figure 28.1. © Flaherty / International Film Seminars Inc. Photograph by Theo Rigby.

I got married. I read a lot. I continued to write, about Colombian cinema and the New Latin American cinema. I moved to the United States with my family, had three wonderful children, and went to the University of Michigan in Ann Arbor—home of many active film societies and the Ann Arbor Film Festival—to study film.

I'd heard about the Flaherty seminar from Gabriela Samper, a Colombian filmmaker politically active in the sixties. Somehow, I figured out how to attend and drove from Ann Arbor to Wells College in central New York. I arrived at lunchtime, and someone instructed me to sit at a table, which I did—and discovered that the person sitting next to me was Erik Barnouw, the author of the groundbreaking book *Documentary: A History of the Non-Fiction Film* (1974).

Ruth Bradley, a friend from the American Culture program at Michigan, introduced me to Juan Mandelbaum and Patricia Zimmermann, who have remained close friends.

The Flaherty became an annual ritual where I could see extraordinary films and meet filmmakers and theoreticians. It rippled through my studies, my intellectual development, and my teaching.

My best experiences at the Flaherty were instigated by artists and works that I loved immediately: the Black Audio Film Collective from the United Kingdom, Barbara Hammer, Steina Vasulka, animators from Canada, and African American documentarians.

The Flaherty seminar nurtured my passion for cinema, deepened my cinematic knowledge, and broadened my horizons. Eventually, I presented films and participated in the heated theoretical discussions.

But almost two decades later, I still think about one particular seminar.

In 1999, Richard Herskowitz and Orlando Bagwell programmed Outtakes are History with support from the Film and Video Program (Jane Gaines, in particular) and the Center for International Studies at Duke University, which hosted that seminar.

The seminar featured Ricky Leacock (who analyzed the *Louisiana Story Study Film*, 1999), Johan van der Keuken, Phil Solomon, Artavazd Peleshyan, and a tribute to Henry Hampton, the executive producer of *Eyes on the Prize* (1987–1990). Herskowitz and Bagwell focused on editing and montage with van der Keuken's *Amsterdam Global Village* (1996), Peleshyan's epic films, Sam Pollard's blending of interviews and archival material in Spike Lee's *Four Little Girls* (1997), and Leacock's DV explorations.

However, the new site seemed to generate uncertainty.

I'll never forget the first screening's projection problems. The seminar staff could not mount the right system for van der Keuken's work, despite assumptions that Duke's vast resources would resolve infrastructure challenges. Van der Keuken refused to screen his film. In the end, the programmers substituted a different van der Keuken film.

The next day, David D. Williams presented *Lillian* (1993), which had won a prize at Sundance, and the seminar began to erupt. Williams's feature focused on an African American caretaker of children and adults. The director, a white filmmaker, had made the film in a cinéma vérité style, telling the protagonist's story with nonactors who performed in their homes in an African American community in Richmond, Virginia.

As the discussion began, Ricky Leacock (Flaherty's cameraman for *Louisiana Story*, 1948) jumped up and shouted, "And you brought me all the way from France to watch this shit?" He left immediately.

An agitated discussion ensued.

The seminar participants included a group of African Americans, including Sam Pollard, Louis Massiah, and people from *Eyes on the Prize*. Ricky Leacock's outburst seemed to have offended everyone, and the next day, the atmosphere was combative and loud. David Williams presented two short documentaries. Race and gender debates tore through the discussions.

When Elizabeth Barret showed an unfinished film (*Stranger with a Camera*, 1999), it was met with nasty comments. So the women at the seminar, including film editors Jacquie Jones and Jeanne Jordan, decided to meet together during free time for our own separate discussions.

Artavazd Peleshyan presented his films in this charged atmosphere. Critics and scholars recognized his complex conceptual editing style. Participants praised him. He answered questions, but without revealing much about his technique—while Mrs. Peleshyan sat in the audience, her appearance summoning the Hollywood stereotype of a Russian matron.

Mrs. Peleshyan went shoe shopping with the Russian/Armenian interpreter. When they returned, the interpreter mentioned that Mrs. Peleshyan, ignored by almost everyone at the seminar, had worked as an editor with her husband. During their outing, she had shared their editing methods. This reminded me of Frances Flaherty's collaborations with Robert. Our women's group invited Mrs. Peleshyan to join us.

At this seminar, divisions widened as racial and gender debates became part of every discussion. However, the fragmentation into smaller affinity groups made space for more in-depth conversations about our differences and deepened my understanding of how social and political contexts influence creativity and style.

I ended up using that seminar's contentious debates to program a series focusing on diverse women filmmakers for the University of Michigan's Film and Video Department.

The intensities and destabilizations at that 1999 seminar spurred me to attend the seminar every subsequent year, tossing aside my preconceptions just as I imagine Frances Flaherty would have wanted. And I committed to expanding the presence of Latin American and Latinx filmmakers and participants at the Flaherty.

I remain one of the Flaherty's greatest fans and advocates. I've supported the Flaherty as a participant, a programmer, a board member, an executive director, and a coordinator for the Flaherty fellows.

My week at the Flaherty became my favorite time of the year. I remain addicted.

29

AT THE TABLE

Ayoka Chenzira

AYOKA CHENZIRA is an award-winning pioneer in black independent cinema, experimental media, and interactive digital media arts. She is among the first African American women to write, produce, and direct a 35mm feature film, *Alma's Rainbow* (1993). She is also one of the first female animators with *Hair Piece: a film for nappyheaded people* (1984) and *Zajota and the Boogie Spirit* (1989). Most recently, she directed a season-three episode of Ava DuVernay's *Queen Sugar* for Oprah Winfrey's OWN network. The first African American to earn a PhD in Digital Media from the Georgia Institute of Technology, she currently serves as Division Chair for the Arts at Spelman College.

I said to Pearl: I've been obsessed with figuring out how to create films using the Macintosh 512 computer.

I'm working on this project called *Zajota and the Boogie Spirit* (1989) that uses drawings I run through my printer, which has an infrared light that scans the image and draws it on the screen so that I can animate it.

Pearl says: What's the film about?

I say: It's about how people of the African diaspora have deep connections with each other and can communicate histories and recognizable frameworks despite the impact of colonialism and hundreds of years of separation.

Figure 29.1.

Pearl is silent. She's thinking.

Wanting to connect the dots, I tell her: A few years ago, I traveled alone throughout urban and rural communities in the Gambia, Kenya, Liberia, Mauritania, Sierra Leone, Zaire, and Zimbabwe, exhibiting films by African American filmmakers. In most places, English was the common language. But in rural communities, there was also a cacophony of local languages. I quickly learned it didn't matter that I did not speak any of these languages. Dance and the movement of the body signified common denominators. We spoke through dance. I wanted to understand this process and this connection, so I made a film called *Zajota and the Boogie Spirit*.

Shortly after, author, producer, and curator Pearl Bowser was the guest programmer for the 1989 Robert Flaherty Film Seminar. She invited me to screen my work.

At that time, the Flaherty had run for nearly thirty-five years. It branded itself as the place where forward-thinking filmmakers, historians, educators, and others interested in intellectual discussions around film could gather for a week to view films and engage in discussions and debates about aesthetics, ethics, and praxis.

However, like many in black film circles, I considered Flaherty elitist and unwelcoming to people of color. Despite its view of itself as progressive, what I knew was this: we weren't invited to the table.

At Pearl's invitation, I joined friends and colleagues, including John Akomfrah, Orlando Bagwell, Toni Cade Bambara, Julie Dash, Zeinabu irene Davis, Teshome Gabriel, William Greaves, Philip Mallory Jones, Gaston Kabore, Horace Ove, Lourdes Portillo, Jackie Shearer, Trinh T. Minh-ha, and many more.

I settled in at Wells College, the upstate New York small women's college on Lake Cayuga that housed Flaherty that year.

With a Super 8 camera, I recorded my then nine-year-old daughter, HaJ, playing volleyball with emerging filmmakers who would soon become seminal figures in the field and with established filmmakers who, in a few short years, would no longer be with us. As I write this story, I find myself wanting to go through my unorganized archives to retrieve these images.

Pearl's curatorial vision focused on the cinemas of the African diaspora, much to the surprise of the many white filmmakers, programmers, and scholars who had attended Flaherty for years.

During the 1989 Flaherty, the conversations moved beyond aesthetics, the avant-garde versus documentary, and the language of cinema. The politics of race and representation reared and loomed large and weighty over screenings, discussions, and events.

In addition to Pearl's primary focus on the cinemas of African diaspora, other works were screened. Three white filmmakers—Helen Levitt, Janice Loeb, and James Agee—made *In the Street* (1948). They went to Spanish Harlem with hidden cameras to photograph neighborhood street life, focusing mostly on young children. Some attendees were not comfortable with the film. (As a side note, the film is now listed on the US Library of Congress National Film Registry).

Lynne Sachs's *Sermons and Sacred Pictures* (1989) ignited fiery discussions around race and representation, race and colonialism, anthropological and ethnographic films from the subject's standpoint, and authorship and the ownership of images.

Sermons and Sacred Pictures is about a black Baptist minister, Reverend L. O. Taylor, from Memphis, Tennessee, who preached in the 1930s and 1940s.

The resentment in the room by most of the black filmmakers was palpable. Accusations, questions, and statements were hurled to the stage. Sachs appeared to be caught off guard by interrogations about her right as a white filmmaker to make a film about a black community. After a while, she politely refused to answer these questions.

I remember being angry—but not with Lynne.

For me, the issue was less about a white filmmaker's right to tell a story centered in black culture and more about access, funding, and white privilege.

In the late 1980s, African American filmmakers experienced difficulties securing funding to produce films about their own communities, cultures, and histories. Often, funders did not consider their ideas valuable. Sometimes, it was necessary for a project to be attached to a white producer in order to be considered important.

As someone from a community who found creative and financial support in Europe, I saw how the European seal of approval opened up US funding, as well as a seat at the exhibition table. For me, *Sermons and Sacred Pictures* represented yet another example of white privilege on the home front.

However, this conversation about Sachs's documentary contained more complex layers than who could make a film about whom. Although the post-screening discussion with Sachs was tense, it was Pearl who had invited her.

In the discussion, writer, activist, and filmmaker Toni Cade Bambara foregrounded a different kind of political concern: ancillary programming (which I think was common at Flaherty) seemed to undermine Pearl's curatorial focus. I remember that the audience became quiet after Toni's remarks.

Although Pearl broke ground curating the cinemas of the African diaspora and convincing black filmmakers and scholars from across the globe to attend, other work that seemed at best tangential to her theme was also programmed.

For example, screenings and conversations with Glasnost-era USSR filmmakers Uris Podnieks, Ivars Seleckis, Valery Solomin, and Mark Soosar were mounted, I think, by a Flaherty board member. Grant Munro programmed Canadian animation. Some attendees contended that the seminar had a tradition of programming teams, while others, mostly people of color, countered that these programs hijacked space from Pearl's progressive and transgressive agenda.

The screening of Alexander Korda and Robert Flaherty's *Elephant Boy* (1937) galvanized intense debate. The film is based on a story in Rudyard Kipling's *The Jungle Book* (1894). In some circles, Flaherty is considered the father of documentary film with his *Nanook of the*

North (1922). In others, he is viewed as a colonialist who exploited the Inuit community to stage his fantasies of *the Other*, mixing fact with his desired fiction.

The 1989 Flaherty seminar produced an extraordinary moment in film culture when a marginalized community occupied the center and asserted the power of its history. This community unapologetically called out long-standing myths and injustices about race in cinema.

After Pearl's Flaherty, the organization seemed to recalibrate. It appeared to become more aware that it needed to become more inclusive, not only about who was invited, but also about moving image production, ideologies, and subject/maker relationships previously not considered.

Looking back three decades later, I realize Pearl had invited me to take a seat at the table at a landmark Flaherty seminar and a turning point in international film culture.

30

NOTES FROM THE 1990 FLAHERTY SEMINAR

Andrei Zagdansky

ANDREI ZAGDANSKY was born in Kiev, Ukraine. He received an MFA from Kiev State Theater and Film University. His first feature-length documentary, *Interpretation of Dreams* (1989), was a coproduction of Kiev State Studio and Austrian TV ORF. In 1992, he and his family settled in the United States, where he received an *alien of extraordinary abilities* status. He conceived/directed/edited the feature-length documentaries *Vasya* (2002), *Konstantin and Mouse* (2006), *Orange Winter* (2007), *My Father Evgeni* (2010), *Vagrich and the Black Square* (2015), and *Michail and Daniel* (2017). He currently resides in Fort Lee, New Jersey, with his wife, Tamara, and a Scottish Fold named Ulysses.

It was late September when two quite colorful groups of people descended on the charming resort town of Jūrmala in Soviet-occupied Latvia.

The groups spoke two different languages, and there were just two interpreters to facilitate communication.

One group was Soviet documentary filmmakers and scholars, and the other, American documentary filmmakers and scholars. That was the first and only Soviet-American Robert Flaherty Film Seminar.

Rather than a hotel, we all checked into a sanatorium of the Union of Soviet Composers, a spacious structure just two steps away from a beach

Figure 30.1. © 2018 Alexei Zagdansky.

on the Baltic Sea. This was where Soviet composers were supposed to rest from the daily grind and soak in the musical inspiration carried by the salty Baltic air.

The year was 1990. The Soviet Union would be dead by the end of next year, but few in the world sensed the unforeseeable.

For seven days, we explored each other's films. And, inevitably, we explored each other.

To start, the Americans said a few kind words about Gorbachev. We winced. In turn, the Soviets made a few kind remarks about Ronald Reagan, whose stature for a brief period in the Soviet Union was not unlike that of Simón Bolívar in South America. American filmmaker Steve Roszell then stood up and ripped Reagan apart to the enthusiastic cheering of his fellow Americans.

We all took note and dove back into films.

The screenings began with the obvious and the sacred—*Nanook of the North* (1922) and *The Man with a Movie Camera* (1929)—and progressed to then-current American and perestroika films. Although it seems unbelievable now, most of us so-called Soviets had never seen *Nanook* until that seminar. And most of the Americans had never seen Dziga Vertov's masterpiece.

That September we saw a great number of excellent films. I personally made three major discoveries: *The Thin Blue Line* (1988) by Errol Morris,

The Seasons (1975) by Artavazd Peleshyan, and *Sherman's March* (1986) by Ross McElwee. Of the three filmmakers, only Ross was present. I fell in love with his film and its brave, intricate self-irony.

Michael Moore's blockbuster *Roger and Me* (1989) was also screened. Its showmanship struck me with its chutzpah and subtle card stacking. After the screening, some American filmmakers were quick to explain to the uninitiated that not all aspects of capitalism were as bad as painted in Michael's film. Those were kind and reassuring sentiments.

Another important discovery was *Tongues Untied* (1989) and its gentle, amiable author, Marlon Riggs, who passed away so young.

Our two interpreters were in high demand. Not one of the Americans spoke any Russian. A handful of the Soviets spoke some basic English. Outside of the theater, our professional interactions were rather limited, although everyone generously compensated with hand gestures. We were genuinely interested in understanding each other.

No matter how free-spirited, the Soviets were more or less part of the state system of filmmaking. There were no independent film studios. Everything we did, no matter how subversive (remember perestroika?) was financed by the state. We worked with set budgets and as a rule tight production schedules.

Unlike us, the Americans were truly independent. They often assumed considerable personal and financial risk when they embarked on a project.

To borrow a phrase from *Pulp Fiction* (1994), "the little things" stood out. We shot 35mm stock, whereas the Americans shot mostly 16mm and with a few exceptions, video. None of us Soviets had ever worked with video. *U-Matic* was a word we heard at that seminar. Steve Roszell, who directed the documentary *Writing on Water* (1984) on video, patiently explained U-Matic to all of us. With his thumb and index finger, he had us imagine three-quarter-inch tape. The *U* sounded exotic and foreign, maybe because it reminded us all of a U-boat.

"It took me four years to complete *Sherman's March*," Ross McElwee told me over our evening glass of kefir. I shook my head in awe and disbelief. In 1989, I completed my first feature documentary, *Interpretation of Dreams*, in under ten months. Little did I know that it would take me sixteen years to complete a feature documentary when I relocated to the United States.

My film was rather well received by this binational crowd. No small part of this favorable reception was due to the simple fact that Freud and his books were on the forbidden list in the Soviet Union. Our American friends were just beginning to discover the Soviet realities. "The little things" were very often shocking to them. Impressed with my film, video scholar Deirdre Boyle brought a tape of *Interpretation of Dreams* to

Richard Peña. The next year, he invited me to the New Directors/New Films series. That invitation was a transformative event in my life.

I offer one final memory about that September.

The seminar coincided with the Jewish High Holidays. One day, several American filmmakers expressed interest in visiting the only synagogue in Riga. Some of us Soviets joined them. We arrived in the city. We met a number of old men praying outside the synagogue. One of them asked who we were. I began to explain, of course, in Russian. Then British Israeli scholar and filmmaker Alan Rosenthal asked if they spoke Hebrew. Some did.

We stepped aside and watched Alan and several of these men converse in a once dead and now revived ancient tongue. Two worlds connected without any external help.

In a way, this connection across divides is exactly what happened during that 1990 Flaherty seminar. Half of us did not speak Russian, the other half did not speak English. Certainly, almost none of us spoke Hebrew. But we all spoke film. And we connected. We all got some sense of each other, and maybe even a better sense of the world.

Where this better sense of the world took us all is a whole different story.

P.S. The former Soviet Republic of Latvia is now an independent country and a member of the European Union. The sanatorium that once belonged to the Union of the Soviet Composers has long been converted to luxury condominiums. A three-bedroom apartment currently lists for 650,000 euros. Long live capitalism, I guess . . .

31

OVERCOMING CONTEMPT

Steven Montgomery

STEVEN MONTGOMERY produced and directed the award-winning documentaries *Hobie's Heroes* (1980) and *Morocco: The Past and Present of Djemma el Fna* (1995). Currently, he is a development consultant. He has helped to secure major funding for New York City nonprofits, including the New York Philharmonic, Rosie's Theater Kids (founded by Rosie O'Donnell), and Opportunities for a Better Tomorrow. He is a board adviser for UnionDocs, has served as a trustee on the board of the Flaherty, and is a past president of the New York Film/Video Council.

The Flaherty seminar was legendary in the New York City independent film community when I became a part of it in the early 1980s. People spoke about the seminar reverently.

However, it took me years to find the courage to take the plunge.

I finally signed up for my first seminar in 1991. At lovely Wells College on the shore of Cayuga Lake, the seminar lived up to all my expectations. It fostered serious devotion to film but was also very social and enjoyable.

The cinema of the Arab world shown that year deeply impressed me: *Halfaouine: Boy of the Terraces* (1990, Tunisia) by Asfour Stah; *Omar Gatlato* (1977, Algeria) by Merzak Allouache; *Canticle of the Stones* (1990, Palestine) by Michel Khleifi; and *A Door to the Sky* (1989, Morocco) by Farida Benlyazid. The year before, I had traveled to Morocco

Figure 31.1. Photograph by Hee Quu Cho.

twice, hoping to make a documentary, but the filmmakers' deep commitment to their material, their compelling storytelling, and their expert cinematic techniques taught me more about the Arab world than I had perceived as a traveler.

The founder of the seminar, Frances Flaherty, had described the value of my experience at the Flaherty. Invoking philosophy, she had written about watching films as a means of "learning to see."

An image stays with me from that first seminar. After sitting in the darkened auditorium in the morning, quietly concentrating on what was on the screen, I walked out into the sunshine and down to Lake Cayuga with others from around the country and the world. The seminarians were so friendly; the group spirit, very encouraging. Filmmakers discussed the subjects of their films and how they'd secured funding. Programmers and curators talked about what they were showing. Students, with their great enthusiasms about film, nudged me to recall my own passions for media when I was their age.

However, after such a memorable first Flaherty, I must admit I became disillusioned at subsequent seminars because of what was programmed and what was left out. I felt that Flaherty programmers began to favor poorly made "personal documentaries" and nearly incoherent experimental works on trendy subjects. Films that come to mind: *Mirror Mirror* (1990) by Jan Krawitz, shown in 1993; *Video Letters 1, 2 & 3* (1993) by Yau Ching, shown in 1994; *Self Portrait Post Mortem* (2002) by Louise Bourque, shown in 2004; and *Mutual Analysis* (2004) by Péter Forgács, shown in 2005. In the worst of these films, the filmmakers narrated in gloomy tones and complained about how harsh reality had hurt their sensitive souls.

In an article for *International Documentary* in 1997, I wrote about these works as "Films about Me." I noted they "convey a bitterness toward the world, forever moaning about being victimized by one thing or another." The creators seemed to disdain cinematic techniques. For example, some filmmakers waved a camera around the room and asserted heavy-handed conclusions on complex subjects. The preponderance of these films eclipsed an important documentary tradition, in which directors expressed a large concern for humanity and the world beyond oneself.

In the years leading up to the 2008 financial crisis, works on personal subjects so crowded the Flaherty schedule that almost nothing was programmed about the American economy, the banking and financial industries, or the struggles of people in the workplace. The Flaherty contributed little or nothing to prepare people for the financial crisis or to provide a lens though which to understand it.

Despite this critique, I wish to express my enduring admiration for the Flaherty at its best. At the seminars I've attended, there has always been something extraordinary to see: *Lumumba: Death of a Prophet* (1992) by Raoul Peck in 1993; *Secuestro: The Story of a Kidnapping* (1993) by Camila Motta, also in 1993; and *Symbiopsychotaxiplasm: Take One* by William Greaves (shot in 1968, first version 1971) in 2005, for example.

Many people have tried to describe exactly what makes the Flaherty unique. I've been thinking about this question since my first Flaherty twenty-some years ago. After reading the new book *The Flaherty: Decades in the Cause of Independent Cinema*, which vividly evokes the great times of the seminar over the years and its important discussions, I finally understand how to answer two important questions. How did the organization that presents the seminar endure for over sixty years? Why are busy and sophisticated people like me spending time writing essays on the Flaherty?

Here is my answer. The seminar's structure, designed by Frances Flaherty, is the best forum in the world for enabling us to truly care about cinema in all its forms.

To make my case, I invoke philosophy, as Frances Flaherty did in writing about the origins of the seminar. I'll use terms from the philosophy of

Aesthetic Realism to explain, starting with a description of the contradictory nature of the self who signs up for his or her first Flaherty.

Founded by the American poet and literary critic Eli Siegel, Aesthetic Realism argues that the self is dual—one aspect of a person yearns for a deep experience in life, hoping to be profoundly affected by the world. This experience can obviously occur after seeing a significant work at the Flaherty.

But something can get in the way of this experience, at the Flaherty or at any other film event. Aesthetic Realism contends that another part of the self seeks to remain intact and runs away from expansive, deep feelings. For example, I might see the greatest film of my life at the Flaherty but ten minutes later jokingly ask friends about the latest gossip concerning someone at the seminar. Aesthetic Realism describes this impulse as "contempt" and defines it as "the false importance or glory from the lessening of things not oneself."

In other words, I may love a film and be genuinely moved but stubbornly resist its sway over me by gossiping, making a phone call, or mindlessly checking my email in an effort to regain composure.

Fortunately, the structure of the Flaherty effectively counters this contempt.

After a great work is presented, we discuss it in formal sessions and then again at breakfast, lunch, and dinner. There is no running away from the impact and meaning of a film.

No matter how unsettling the original experience, the seminar allows the film to get inside of us and endure. For me, this is the legacy of the Flaherty.

32

THE SCENT OF PLACES

Laura U. Marks

LAURA U. MARKS works on media art and philosophy with an intercultural focus. Her most recent books are *Hanan al-Cinema: Affections for the Moving Image* (2015) and *Enfoldment and Infinity: An Islamic Genealogy of New Media Art* (2010). She programs experimental media art for venues around the world. She is the Grant Strate Professor in the School for the Contemporary Arts at Simon Fraser University in Vancouver. With Dr. Azadeh Emadi, she is a founding member of the Substantial Motion Research Network, http://www.substantialmotion.org and http://www.sfu.ca/~lmarks.

For years, I'd organized experimental cinema programs from the Arabic-speaking world. Once the Vancouver free newspaper *Metro* joked about my new program: "Did you wake up this morning thinking, gee, I don't have enough Arab experimental cinema in my life? Well this program is for you!"

But most filmmakers from Arab countries told me they really disliked being categorized as Arab. They wanted their works received as cinema, with their own immanent aesthetics and politics. I wanted to find a way to present some of these works at the Flaherty, to allow the audience to appreciate the filmmakers for what they were doing, rather than treat them as spokespeople for the Arab world, fielding questions about Israeli-Palestinian politics, the Syrian war, Hizbollah, the veil, etc.

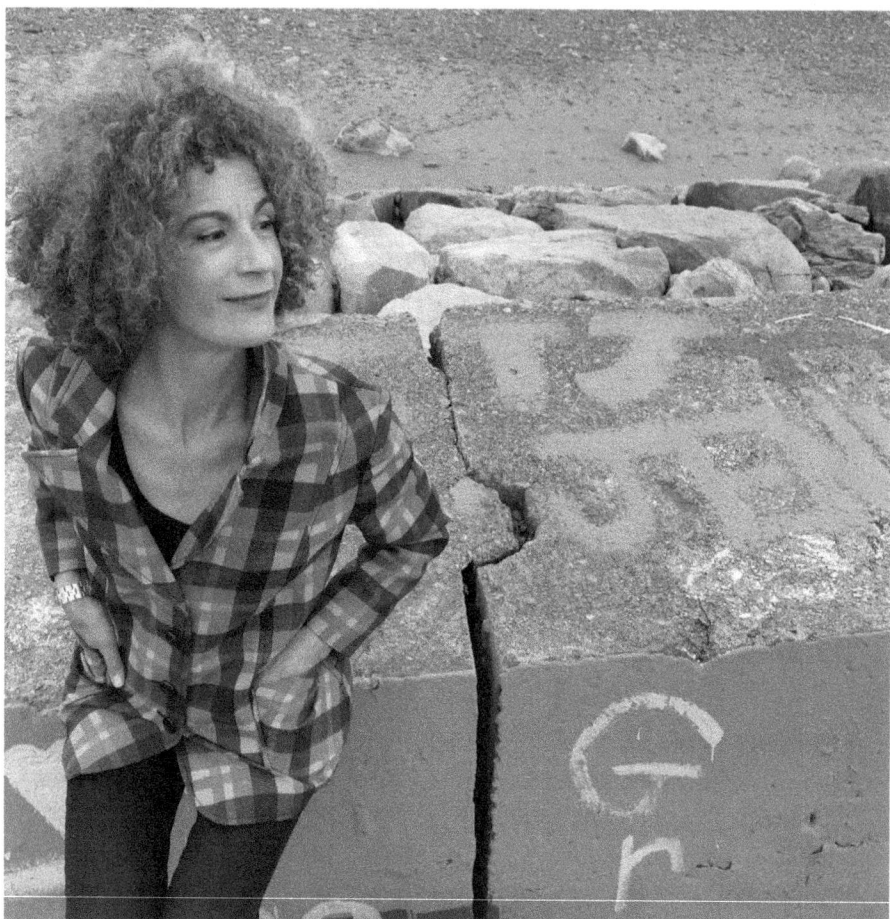

Figure 32.1. Photograph by Richard Coccia.

I promised the filmmakers that the 2015 Flaherty would give their work the most generous and thoughtful reception. I promised they'd get high-quality discussions about the aesthetics and particular qualities of their work. I promised that their films would not be instrumentalized.

I'd attended the Flaherty about eight times—in the 1990s and in 2004 and 2014. By 2014, it seemed that a discursive miasma had settled over the seminar, with a newly procrustean frame of identity politics and cultural sensitivity into which the audience needed the films to fit. Alarmed, I designed an anti-discursive program. It would be about the smart and subtle ways filmmakers render perceptible latent presences—those aspects of the world most delicate and difficult to grasp.

I looked for a suggestive yet noncommittal title that worked in both English and Arabic and would have a nice-sounding English transliteration of the Arabic. I entertained:

Dhawq al-Zaman (Flavor of the Times)

Rihat al-Zaman (Scent of the Times)

Nakhat al-Zaman (Flavors of the Times—Walid Raad's suggestion)

Rihat al-Amkina (The Scent of Places)

Rawaih al-Amkinah (Scents of the Places—Mounira al Solh and
Fadi el Tofeili's suggestion, with a more elegant plural of *scents*)

I find the Arabic word *'atr*, perfume, more inspiring than *riha*, scent. Finally, I settled on The Scent of Places/*'Atr al-Amakin*. The title hints at the ways cinema actualizes evanescent presences.

Designing the program was a struggle, but I was very happy with the final roster.

In 2011, David Pendleton, programmer at the Harvard Film Archive, had given a talk called "Reasons to Believe in This World: The Responsibilities of a Film Programmer" at UC Santa Cruz. Drawing on Walter Benjamin and Pier Paolo Pasolini, he addressed exactly the issue I faced when I programmed the Flaherty.

David said that when programming films from other countries and cultures, it is important that "the image [be] used not instrumentally, not as information, not as communication, but as *expression*." A film does give information about other parts of the world, but this is then turned into expression. The filmmaker's aesthetic intervention "ensure[s] that these images don't turn into pure information; they don't get compressed or instrumentalized."

David's words describe my attempt to "de-Arabize" Arab filmmakers by combining them with other filmmakers with similar interests. After all, expression is also a method of perfume making. Spinoza said that the world is the expression of God.

In my introductory speech, I begged attendees to open themselves to the films Frances Flaherty–style: without preconceptions. I requested that they refrain from talking about politics at the expense of the films. Then I let go of control and stayed in the background.

Many Flaherty audience members appeared to be anxious that a film tick all the correct political boxes—non-racist, queer-friendly, ever so sensitive about colonial power relations—and could not relax until it did. The Arab filmmakers tended to disconcert the seminarians, who felt they could not critique these films. Instead, they directed their umbrage toward the great Ulrike Ottinger's *Under Snow* (2014), a fabulative documentary set in Hokkaido, accusing Ottinger of orientalism. Patricia Zimmermann suggested to me that this mania for correct representation arises from despair, or fear, in economically perilous times.

I programmed on themes, styles, moods, and feelings. For example, the second night's program combined works with striking cinematography that dealt with being compressed in a space. Joana Hadjithomas and Khalil Joreige's fiction film *Ramad/Ashes* (2003): a son returns to Beirut with his father's coffin but without his body, the family's pressure on him, an hours-long Lebanese wake. Tariq Teguia's *Hacla/The Fence* (2003): young men in Algiers talk about the everyday humiliation of unemployment, government repression, and nepotism, which traps them in a vicious circle. Arthur Jafa's *Dreams Are Colder than Death* (2014): framed by shimmering, subtle cinematography, powerful African American speakers argue that blackness is a force of creative resistance that cannot be assimilated.

And on the final morning, I offered a gentle program for hungover people, on documentary performance. Robert Flaherty's *A Night of Storytelling* (1935): an Irish storyteller addresses rapt listeners. Mounira Al Solh's *A Double Burger and Two Metamorphoses . . .* (2011): performing her Arab self for Dutch people, she transforms into various animals. Steve Reinke's *Afternoon, March 22, 1999* (1999): a virtuosic nonfiction video performance in his apartment, waiting for the new millennium.

I wanted my program to work as an affective composition that would gain in complexity over the course of the week. I think I succeeded. When I remember my Flaherty program, I see colors, textures, and scents wafting and moving together in a variety of rhythms. Some resisted the embargo on politics and resented the lack of Important documentaries. One questionnaire respondent dismissed my program as "eye candy." Yet many attendees relaxed and submitted to this drug-like experience, trusting the movies and me. I felt like a silent priestess in some kind of opium cult.

Luckily, the excellent projection capacity at Colgate and the genius of projectionist Gibbs Chapman allowed the lo-fi movies to really shine. We were able to play Arnait Video Collective's ten-minute *Qulliq* (*Oil Lamp*) from 1989, not on the original format of three-quarter-inch U-Matic video, but on the next-best analog video format, Beta SP. In an old-style igloo, Susan Avingaq and Madeline Ivalu (*Before Tomorrow*, 2008) sing about starvation and staying warm as they try to light the stone lamp. Finally, the *qulliq* lights, in a string of flames too bright for the analog video camera to grasp. By seeing the piece in the original medium, the audience could feel the tense focus on that center of light and heat.

David Pendleton attended the 2015 seminar. He'd been chosen to program in 2016. Dear, wise David, who died on November 6, 2017, was beloved by many.

33

FOLDERS

Aviva Weintraub

AVIVA WEINTRAUB is Associate Curator at the Jewish Museum, mounting exhibitions such as Yael Bartana's *Entartete Kunst Lebt* (*Degenerate Art Lives*, 2018–19); Chantal Akerman's *NOW* (2018); *Maya Zack: Living Room* (2011); *Jem Cohen: NYC Weights and Measures* (2011–12); and the ongoing *Television and Beyond* series. She also serves as Director of the New York Jewish Film Festival, copresented by the Jewish Museum and the Film Society of Lincoln Center. She coordinated the New York exhibitions of *Sharon Lockhart | Noa Eshkol* (2012–13); *They Called Me Mayer July: Painted Memories of a Jewish Childhood in Poland before the Holocaust* (2009); and *Isaac Bashevis Singer and the Lower East Side: Photographs by Bruce Davidson* (2007–08).

The first time I attended the Flaherty seminar at Wells College in central New York, I didn't know what to expect.

It was 1991, and I was working at the Jewish Museum in New York City. Started in 1904, the museum, a hub for art and Jewish culture from ancient to contemporary times, was the first of its kind in the United States and is one of the oldest in the world. At the time, I was the archive coordinator there for the museum's National Jewish Archive of Broadcasting.

Figure 33.1. © Jewish Museum, New York; Photograph by Daniel Rodriguez.

I'd studied Yiddish in the Linguistic Department in graduate school from 1986 to 1989. I wrote a thesis about photo books on the so-called last Jews of Eastern Europe.

Wanda Bershen, the well-known programmer who was the museum's film festival director and my supervisor, recommended that I go. We thought that since I worked with television and broadcast material, the seminar could push me a bit further, into film. Wanda thought very highly of the Flaherty.

I'm a somewhat reserved person. When I arrived at Wells, I didn't know anyone and was constantly finding myself in large groups. Though I knew no one there, *everyone* seemed to know Wanda. That made me feel welcome.

Wanda had told me that the seminar's philosophy was to never announce the screening schedule in advance. I was intrigued about having no idea about what I would watch. I think I was a bit relieved that my unstructured time would have some structure. Back then, no one had computers or mobile phones, so time felt different. The screenings happened three times a day, with an occasional optional late-night screening of a film by Robert Flaherty or someone else.

The three-screenings-a-day concept excited me. Growing up in Far Rockaway, Queens, daytime was for outside play, not for TV and movies.

So watching films all day felt like a special treat. Watching a movie while the sun shines remains a guilty pleasure for me.

The board insisted that we attend every screening and discussion. I learned that when everyone immerses themselves in the same films and discussions, rich conversations ensue.

Strong memories from the three seminars I attended in 1991, 1992, and 1993 linger: the theater, shared meals, dorm rooms, swimming in Cayuga Lake, stargazing at night. And people: David Callahan, Graham Leggat, Ann Michel, Steve Montgomery, Bill and Gwen Sloan, and Phil Wilde became close friends and valued colleagues. The Flaherty made it easy to develop these relationships. It was a bucolic setting where no outside obligations intruded. I found myself in groups of people who loved to talk about films, which was thrilling.

I saw works by Sadie Benning, Joe Berlinger, Cheryl Dunye, Kazuo Hara, Raoul Peck, Ela Troyano. Rea Tajiri's *History and Memory* (1991) and Roddy Bogawa's *Some Divine Wind* (1992) touched some deep place in me as they wove personal, family, and world events together.

The discussions got heated over issues of inclusion, gender, and race. I was there the year Ken Jacobs performed *XCXHXEXRXRXIXEXSX* (1980), which led to a now-notorious confrontational moment. His Nervous System apparatus extended an excerpt of an old pornographic film through hand-cranked manipulation. The long performance agitated some. The content upset many women. The argument, hurt feelings, anger, and intensities spanned several days.

At the end of that rancorous seminar, the wonderful Margarita De La Vega Hurtado introduced Paul Leduc's *Barroco* (1989), the closing screening. With its musical exuberance, the film felt like a reward, a nice balance to the bitterness of the week.

My favorite Flaherty experience was William Greaves's *Symbiopsychotaxiplasm: Take One* (1971). I not only admired Greaves's films, but also his warmth, generous spirit, humor, and openness. A scene in the film where the crew rebels against him brought the seminarians to a joyous place.

The Flaherty seminars were valuable for my early career.

First, they created sustaining connections. Before the Flaherty, I simply did not know many festival programmers. David Callahan, Steve Montgomery, and Bill Sloan got me involved in the New York Film and Video Council, which furthered my networking in the film world.

Second, the seminars helped me understand the pleasures of duration and endurance watching. There is nothing like coming into a dark theater, not knowing what you will see or how long you might be there.

Third, the Flaherty taught me to immerse myself in programming as a holistic experience. Binge-watching is common now. But back then I had never spent a full day watching films! Over a week's programming, the films really do start to *speak* to each other. Sharing the same screening experiences with people who grasp references and resonances is priceless. It's an intangible, but essential, lesson about programming: show films that spur an audience to make connections across the films.

An obsessive archivist and saver, I still have my folders with all the film descriptions. Back then, programmers kept files on filmmakers, films, addresses. When I've wanted to program a particular film or filmmaker, I've consulted these folders. Sometimes I simply luxuriate in the nostalgia they evoke.

Almost three decades later, the seminar still impacts my New York Jewish Film Festival programming. Started in 1992 as a joint project between the Jewish Museum and the Film Society of Lincoln Center, it originally focused on Eastern European Jewish life after the fall of the Berlin wall in 1989, which enabled many films on Jewish topics to be created and seen. Now, the festival is international and explores many themes. We program thirty films over two weeks.

We consciously structure a mix of documentary, narrative, and experimental works and a range of early career to established artists. Our programming team is excited when films resonate with content, mood, or tone, enabling our audience to make connections. Flaherty programming has left an imprint on our programming for decades.

34

THE TO-DO OVER *XCXHXEXRXRXIXEXSX*

Ken Jacobs

KEN JACOBS has been producing cinema and cine-performance since 1956. He was at the forefront of the battle against New York State censorship rules when he and Florence Jacobs publicly screened Jack Smith's *Flaming Creatures* (1967). His *Star Spangled to Death* (various versions 1958–1960) and *Tom, Tom, the Piper's Son* (1969, revised 1971) are formative landmarks in what has come to be called *found-footage film* or *recycled cinema*. In the 1970s, he created the Nervous System, a two-projector device that allows him to create a wide range of aesthetic, intellectual, often-visceral effects with recycled footage during feature-length performances. Two Nervous System performances—*Two Wrenching Departures* (from 1989) and *XCXHXEXRXRXIXEXSX* (from 1980)—were presented at the 1992 Flaherty seminar.

Understand, Flo had been arrested by the nice cop after he asked, "What do you think of this movie?"—*Flaming Creatures*—and she answered, "It's beautiful." "You're under arrest," he said. He'd only wanted to hear her say she'd seen it. We were running the Film-Maker's Showcase, she earning five dollars a night selling tickets while I earned ten dollars for managing. Jonas Mekas appeared and insisted that he should also be arrested for booking the film.

Figure 34.1.

Porn could be humane, witty, beautiful. The combo of primitive religion and capitalism could be transcended. Jack Smith (I have his Bible, rewarded to him when a kid for *true believing*) had said to me some years earlier, "I'm strapped." Sexually tied in knots this meant. And that was what was behind the film's emotive force. Within its wit, *Flaming Creatures* is a struggle for air, for freedom. The title indicates the struggle; these are people going to hell with themselves.

I'd been teaching in Binghamton for a number of years by the time of the Flaherty event. The NY arrests would be written about in the local newspapers when I crossed religious Ukrainians by insisting that my silent short *Nissan Ariana Window* (1969), showing Flo pregnant with our daughter, not be shown *after* an operatic feature made in the Ukraine, *Shadows of Our Forgotten Ancestors* (1965). A priest stood up at the start of the projection, calling out parishioners by name and shaming them to leave. One man resisted: "We're parents," he said, "we've all seen this."

The school president's secretary said to me, "This was a nice place until you Jews from New York got here."*

I began speaking at Flaherty about the development in our live Nervous System projections that took it from flat levels—like cutouts arranged in depth—to rounded forms, to *voluptuous* depth illusion. And how this pushed me, for the first time, to want to work with the body. A friend, Ela Troyano, was a film editor for the mafia, and she gave us a handful of 16mm shorts deemed too old to exploit—dumb comedies, but one was extraordinary, and I responded to it as to my first viewing of *Tom, Tom, the Piper's Son* (1905). Filmed outdoors in France around the time of the First World War, it was called *Cherries*. A man meets two women picking cherries from a tree—a nature essay that proved gloriously explicit. Lucky man (in this time of war), and the women are clearly delighted. The performers were not professional actors and were as nakedly present in their persons as was the tree.

I was shouted down. The audience seemed to have missed seeing *Flaming Creatures*. I began cursing, and the talk was cut short. An article followed by Laura U. Marks sometime after, giving her slant on the event. Don't believe it. (*The Independent*, 16, No. 5, December 1992.)

*The priests were miffed at Flo shown pregnant and unclothed, not working at being alluring but considering changes to her body (lactating breasts) and baby clothes. The churches of Binghamton's Ukrainian community had requested a preview when it was learned that a film made in the Ukraine would be shown by the university film club. After the screening, they demanded that the bad short follow the good feature so that congregants could be ushered out before it began.

That priests should determine what anyone sees at a university was not to my liking, and I urged the student-staff of the film society to refuse. Programming the films the way the priests wanted made no sense; the feature was big, loud, and my short was silent, utterly gentle, featuring kittens as much as humans.

After the screening, a few friends of our little daughter (the film was named after her) would see her no more. We received threats over the phone, and I kept a small hammer on me when outside. It continued for weeks, for the semester. The Jew thing wouldn't let up; we were—as Trump would later put it—*infesting* their America. The local papers kissed Ukrainian asses, but a few academics came to our defense. When the academic year ended, we took a year's leave of absence without pay (our yearly income before teaching was $3,500) to mend, unsure we could return. This was the early seventies.

Flaherty brought all this back—no Jew baiting, but the accusation that the good establishment had been sullied. Revulsion against America's murderous BS had fired up a deep and spreading resistance, and *XCXHXEXRXRXIXEXSX* was part of it. Besides being a revolutionary film *as film,* it reflected the hope that the normalizing of sex might come to the rescue of life itself. I reacted badly during the Q and A to the expression *jerk off,* with all its smutty guilt and con-notations of self-contempt. A seventy-five-minute transcendent motion study with that as its aim? Absurd, no?

I respect, even admire, the people on-screen, who had needed the money or were simply obeying pimp orders. Even if so, they got with it, and there's vis-ible enthusiasm for what they do. I liked them then and still do, those doing the necessary "dirty work" for the society. Wasn't it obvious, didn't the music make it clear that this was a deeply felt opus? An interlude of *drumming* made it racist? Was the intellectual left—which I still identify with—as screwed up and as lost to art as the boob right?

When you're called a fascist and intellectual snob for making something new, you split the scene. There's no talking.

35

POINTS OF DEPARTURE

Portia Cobb

PORTIA COBB is Associate Professor in the Department of Film, Video, Animation, and New Genres at the University of Wisconsin–Milwaukee. She is an interdisciplinary artist whose work draws from personal and collective histories and reconstructed memory. It fuses ethnography, personal essay, and folklore. Her documentary work spans moving image, photography, audience participation, and performance. For *Performing Grace* (2016) she created digital photographic essays, field sound recordings, and video to reflect Gullah-Geechee culture in the Low Country South Carolina barrier islands. Her work is inspired by place-bound/rooted identities and engages social justice issues emerging in the preservation of these historical places.

Twenty-six years ago, I presented four videos at the 1992 Flaherty seminar at Wells College in central New York State.

It was my first and only Flaherty seminar. I've never returned and was never invited back.

Kind and empathetic, Marlon Riggs, the black queer filmmaker, had recommended my work to programmers Austin Allen, Ruth Bradley, Scott MacDonald, William Sloan, Jackie Tshaka, and Lise Yasui. I had never worked with Marlon on set, but he invited me to view a rough fine

Figure 35.1. Photograph by Nick Collura.

cut of *Black Is . . . Black Ain't* (1994) and gave me a consultant credit. I began to think of Marlon as a mentor.

I'd completed graduate film school at San Francisco State University. My fourteen-minute essay video, *No Justice, No Peace: Young, Black, Immediate* (1992), chronicled violent police behavior, media representations of young black men in the Bay Area, and the aftermath of the acquittal of the policemen in the Rodney King beating.

That seminar revolved around conditions governing access. I screened *Drive-By Shoot* (1992), *No Justice No Peace*, and *Species in Danger Ed!* (1989).

I also shared a work-in-progress audio-doc performance, *Points of Departure for a Diaspora Dawta!* (1991). It featured exchanges between four women from different points of the African diaspora (United States, United Kingdom, the West Indies, and the US Virgin Islands) sharing stories about exile, forced movement, home, and place. I'd recorded them at a kitchen table, each reading an excerpt from bell hooks's essay, "Home Place: A Site of Resistance." I later developed it into an experiential multimedia installation, *Home Places*, for a University of Wisconsin–Milwaukee (UWM) campus gallery.

I think I presented this work just before Ken Jacobs's Nervous System performance called *XCXHXEXRXRXIXEXSX* (various versions since 1980), but I may be mistaken.

I looked at that film's erratic movement, transfixed. The images were hard to decipher. I did not realize *what* I was seeing. In time, almost everyone seemed as surprised as I was to realize that we had been captivated by performatively looped footage of a found pornographic film of what I remember as women masturbating. Brilliant! But I didn't think so then.

I'd felt angry. I'd felt tricked into watching something offensive. When the lights came on, a lot of side-eye commenced between those sharing similar feelings. Guilt! The feelings of guilt and shame by the spectators were intense, and this had intensified the experience of the film and the discussion afterward.

Over the years, I came to appreciate that experience, and I've recounted that screening many times to my students, other makers, scholars, and academics. This story marks me in the experimental landscape, underscoring my own agency and belonging.

During a short lunch break, film director Camille Billops filled a huge Super Soaker water gun. She slid the water gun under her chair on stage, then glared at *every spectator*, as if to say, "Go ahead, f—k with me!"

Camille's *Finding Christa* (1991, co-made with James Hatch) followed her personal experience as a mother who had surrendered her three-year-old daughter to an adoption agency. The film triggered responses from adoptees and fostered children. One woman became very emotional, describing other screenings during the week that had offended her and other women. Camille was criticized for lacking guilt or remorse. She had come prepared, but nothing jumped off. The Super Soaker remained unused.

Kazuo Hara's *The Emperor's Naked Army Marches On* (1987), the Cheryl Dunye shorts, *She Don't Fade* (1991) and *Janine* (1990), and *Barroco (Baroque)* (1989), a lush feature by director Paul Leduc (Mexico/Cuba/Spain) and presented by scholar Margarita De La Vega Hurtado, stood out for me.

I spent intense time with the most powerful African American women visionaries in film and public TV: Cheryl Fabio Bradford, Mable Haddock, and Jackie Tshaka. I considered them big sister aunties.

I was assigned to room with Mable Haddock, founder of the National Black Programming Consortium (NBPC). Mable asked me to switch rooms so she and Jacquie Jones could be dorm mates. I agreed.

Jacquie was a producer Mable later tapped to lead Black Public Media after her 2005 retirement. They were very close. I learned of Jacquie's death at fifty-two from cancer on January 28, 2018, as I was composing this reflection.

Sitting on the edge of dorm-room bunks, these women smoked cigarettes like champions. A nonsmoker, I suffered through their secondhand smoke to join their wise, candid conversations about the industry, life, and creativity. It was a rite of passage.

I smile remembering several pairs of woman-sized undies hanging to dry in our shared small bathroom. This image evokes unpretentious auspiciousness, familiarity, and these women, my indie foundation and family.

Between screenings, I recorded impromptu interviews with other seminarians with my Hi8 Sony Camcorder. I asked subjects to define *a point of departure,* a concept echoing my own journey. Folks were cooperative and a bit perplexed. I still have that footage.

Last year, I digitized the footage and spotted the young, somewhat reserved, then-emerging video artist Cheryl Dunye. Cheryl's first feature, *Watermelon Woman* (1996), has entered the historical canon of film schools. Recognized by mainstream media, she currently directs episodes of the Oprah Winfrey Network television series *Queen Sugar* (2016–present). Who woulda thunk it?

During the seminar, UWM was courting me. Each day, I received notes from them on a common-area message board. They were negotiating my contract and arranging my move.

Two weeks after the seminar, I relocated from Oakland, California, to Milwaukee and began my career as an assistant professor and director of the Community Media Project at UWM. Twenty-six years and many adventures later, I anticipate retirement in a few years.

My first syllabi heavily reflected themes from that 1992 Flaherty seminar. I introduced students to work from the West Coast, festivals, and the Flaherty. The Midwest was puritanical compared to California. Milwaukee's PBS station had declined to broadcast Marlon's *Tongues Untied* (1989). When I showed it to my class, some students refused to look at the screen or participate in the discussion.

Jacquie Jones's death conjures thoughts of collective and individual embarkations and questions about whether one can ever return to anywhere. Departure and arrival, present and past tense, together. This reflection is circular. Back then, I was in rhythm with others embarking on their own journeys, and I witness similar launchings in my students.

That Flaherty put me among great minds, visionaries, and creative people shaping *our* movement, *our* history.

The Flaherty marked my psyche. Are the others I met there still active, healthy, and productive?

36

MANY MOONS

Jason Livingston

A filmmaker, writer, and programmer, JASON LIVINGSTON has worked with many nonprofits, including Cornell Cinema, the Experimental TV Center, and the Standby Program. He has served on the Flaherty Film Seminar Board of Trustees. His award-winning work has screened widely, including at the International Film Festival Rotterdam, Anthology Film Archives, Austrian Film Museum, and the Vancouver Art Gallery. *Under Foot & Overstory* (2005) is distributed by the Canadian Filmmakers Distribution Centre, and *Lake Affect* (2007) is available through Electronic Arts Intermix as part of the Experimental Television Center DVD boxed set. In 2019 he began pursuing a practice-based PhD with the Department of Media Study at the University at Buffalo, New York.

When *was* my first Flaherty? The prompt seems simple enough.

Was it in 1993? At the time, I was working as a projectionist at Cornell Cinema, then under the direction of Richard Herskowitz.

Richard had his eye on me. He saw that the furthest reaches of cinema enticed me. Did you need someone to push a video cart up the hill through the snow for the Sunday afternoon video art series at the Johnson Museum? Call me. To project the Thursday evening experimental ethnography show? I'm your guy.

Figure 36.1.

As a student of the late Cornell University professor Don Fredericksen, I had taken a shine to Dutch filmmaker Johan van der Keuken. Fredericksen had become a devotee of the filmmaker following Richard's groundbreaking 1987 Flaherty seminar. One day, Richard asked me, "What are you doing this summer? There's something you may want to do."

I'd heard about the Flaherty from both Richard and Don, who loved to tell the story of Joris Ivens and his wife, Marceline, dancing late into the night. Jean Rouch's *Chronique d'un été* (1961) had featured Marceline, a Nagra in her handbag, walking in Paris, reciting moments from her childhood—and thus helping to invent cinéma vérité.

As humidity set in and thunderstorms rolled through the summer of 1993, I'd open the narrow old window by the Cornell Cinema projection booth, as the films I was projecting were running, and crawl out onto the ledge. There, I could see Cayuga Lake curving north. Past that bend lay the Flaherty seminar.

As I drove up the lake to Wells College, I recalled Richard's warning: don't tell anyone in Ithaca or at the Flaherty that you're sneaking in; this is a secret.

I timed my arrival to sit in the back of the auditorium just as the film began. The windows had been blacked out; the wooden seats in the old auditorium creaked. Raoul Peck's *Lumumba* (2000) started. I was spellbound.

I don't remember how long I lingered that day. Richard was glad I'd made it. I'm surprised that in my excitement I didn't pick up a speeding ticket or drive straight into the lake on the way home. This first experience sparked my commitment to the Flaherty.

Even though I crashed it and saw only one film, *was* that my first Flaherty?

In 1994, I joined the seminar staff as assistant projectionist to Michael Grillo, a brilliant art historian who lived in Maine and devoted time each summer to the Wells College 35mm carbon-arc projectors. I handled the 16mm films, although it took a few days to adjust to operating the projection equipment without shaking. Michael exuded patience, and so did Phil Wilde and Annie Michel, the video projectionists. Over cheap beer from Phil's cooler behind the stage, I bonded with them between screenings.

Maybe my first Flaherty happened years later, in 1999 at Duke University, when I attended the seminar as a participant for the first time—and no longer worked in the booth. I looked forward to this seminar with great enthusiasm, arriving at the end of a weeklong road trip, prepared to practice Frances Flaherty's *non-preconception*.

On the first night, Johan van der Keuken—in person!—climbed onto the stage to denounce the technical staff for butchering the projection of his work. As we say these days, *awkward*.

After I saw Warren Sonbert's breathtaking *Noblesse Oblige* (1981), I stood up during the group discussion and proclaimed its montage genius. From the back row of the auditorium, a voice boomed. Legendary direct-cinema filmmaker Ricky Leacock, famous for his honesty, interrupted me to yell out, "You're blind!" Although stunned that an elder had attacked me, I was more stunned by his inability to recognize Sonbert's vision.

For my first Flaherty, I could just as easily choose a year when I fell out of love there or a year when I fell in love. I could name a dozen nights on the dance floor when the sequencing of songs and my complex interactions with people far surpassed anything I'd seen on the screen that day.

I discovered that deejaying the Flaherty is harder than programming the films. When successful, the dance party reaches transcendence.

The last two years I attended have become new firsts. Despite its warts and wounds and boring *enfants terribles*, Nuno Lisboa's Future Remains in 2017 revived the Flaherty for me once again.

Alone in the Adirondack Mountains after that seminar and occasionally ducking out of my tent for a rainy hike, I returned to a question. Why hadn't Nuno screened a Flaherty film, which was considered a seminar programming tradition? A longtime participant had conjectured, "Frances would be rolling in her grave."

But later, upon examining the previous sixty-two years, I found that 2017 did not violate the sacrosanct tradition. In fact, 2017 represented the ninth or tenth time a Flaherty film was not screened.

How easily we mythologize the Flaherty, even those of us with years of experience at the seminar.

Recently, as I was scrolling through the Flaherty seminar's online database and hopping through the years, line by line, a realization occurred to me. Future Remains was exactly the right title for Nuno's program.

Non-preconception suggests the nonlinear. If you embrace the Flaherty's contradictions, you can then work through the ambiguities of non-preconception. In the theater, the future remains unknown, and the past cannot yet be known. Each screening conjures an experiment in seeing anew, with consequences for the past and the future past. The Flaherty extends beyond the seminar week and beyond the films into our lives.

In 2016, David Pendleton programmed the Flaherty around the theme of Play. This became another *first* Flaherty, since for the first time in my life, I felt mortality's pressures, limits, and lightness. I wept multiple times, especially when witnessing the beauty of Portuguese filmmaker Joaquim Pinto's survival-by-camera in films such as *E agora? Lembra-me* (*What Now? Remind Me*, 2013) and *Rabo de Peixe* (*Fish Tail*, 2003).

The moon seemed to appear during each of the films in David's program. It seemed as though he had delicately placed it into each of the works. These moons reminded me that our time on Earth is brief. I drove away from that seminar and called my friends. I told them that I loved them.

37

PROGRAMMING THE 2000 FLAHERTY SEMINAR

Kathy Geritz

KATHY GERITZ is Film Curator at Berkeley Art Museum/Pacific Film Archive, where she curates annual series on experimental cinema and documentary film, as well as programs on historical, international, and contemporary cinema. She served on the Flaherty Film Seminar Board from 2003 to 2008 and the Seminar Advisory Committee since 2009. She was coeditor of *Radical Light: Alternative Film and Video in the Bay Area, 1945–2000* (2010).

I was honored to be invited to program the 2000 Flaherty seminar. I had attended a seminar in 1994, which featured an eye- and mind-opening array of works selected by Somi Roy and, as part of a fortieth anniversary series, by Erik Barnouw and Patricia Zimmermann. That was enough to intimidate me.

Like others before me, I decided that my programming for the seminar would not focus just on documentary but explore nonfiction films.

In addition to documentary, this strategy allowed me to consider animation—including documentary animation—and avant-garde work. I wanted to feature artists working within these different realms whose films looked at the world, history, or social and political issues in radical or innovative ways or explored ideas, even cinema itself, in an experimental or essay form.

Figure 37.1.

The title of my seminar, Essays, Experiments, and Excavations, reflected this conceptualization.

I began by thinking about artists whose work pushed these boundaries, such as Peggy Ahwesh, Zoe Beloff, Harun Farocki, Tran T. Kim-Trang, Abraham Ravett, Chris Sullivan, and Travis Wilkerson,

Once I had confirmed five or six filmmakers, I started to look at relationships between their works. As I did, other filmmakers came to mind, as did earlier, historical films, sometimes suggested directly by a particular film of one of these artists.

I allowed myself the freedom to interweave films by artists of the past—Santiago Alvarez, the Lumière Brothers, Jean Painlevé—with contemporary films. I wanted to create a provocative array of resonances, a challenging dialogue between the films themselves as well as between participants.

It was natural for me to bring my experience programming experimental films at Pacific Film Archive (now BAMPFA) to the Flaherty. There is a lot of creativity in curating programs of experimental shorts but also a lot of pleasure for the audience. They come to understand filmic and intellectual ideas embedded in a work through seeing it in relation to other films. The programming itself can help bring out ideas that an artist is exploring.

Unusual for the Flaherty, the majority of my seminar programs consisted of short films and videos. I relished mixing together works with different stylistic approaches that linked on multiple levels of theme, idea, or mood.

Such juxtapositions create sparks between works, allowing further readings to arise. Today the term *curating* is in common use. But back in 2000, I think it was surprising and stimulating for participants at that Flaherty to see programs of shorts and to understand that somebody carefully *curated* not only each program, but also the overall flow throughout the week of the seminar.

I wanted those attending the seminar to see several pieces by each filmmaker in order to better understand the artist's concerns and aesthetic approach. My goal was to generate a deeper audience engagement. Setting this up over a weeklong seminar can be challenging; even the best-laid plans can go awry.

After a screening that included one of Tran T. Kim-Trang's early videos, someone stood up and attacked her work. The person asserted that Tran's video was little more than an intellectual exercise. She would never show Tran's videos to *her* students.

As the days went by, several of Tran's other videos were screened. Toward the end of the seminar, this same woman, now having viewed many of Tran's works, spoke out again. As I recall, she said, "I have an apology to make," then offered a beautiful tribute to Tran's *Blindness Series* (1992–2006).

These moments of revelation are very particular to the Flaherty seminar, where viewers can immerse themselves in an artist's work over a period of days, hear the invited filmmakers and others speak about cinema, and have time to reflect and reconsider.

38

COMING OF AGE AT THE FLAHERTY

Sami van Ingen

SAMI VAN INGEN is a Finland-based experimental filmmaker, installation artist, curator, and educator. He has made over thirty films probing the act of seeing through deconstructing, manipulating, and rephotographing found footage such as home movies, travelogue scenes, mainstream blockbusters, or archival discoveries. His films have screened at the Edinburgh Film Festival, Image Forum Tokyo, Kurzfilmtage Oberhausen, Bienal de la Imagen en Movimiento in Buenos Aires, National Gallery of Art in Washington, Centre Pompidou, and Anthology Film Archives. He has also published *Moving Shadows: Experimental Film Practices in a Landscape of Change* (2012).

The Wells College campus felt hot, bright, and oddly sterile.

I had just spent time in the south of England shooting my new film about memory and coincidence. With my 16mm Bolex, I'd wandered around Europe, revisiting places I had been and spontaneously reacting to these encounters. It was 1995.

My knowledge of Wells College was as slight as my knowledge of the Flaherty seminar.

I lived in Helsinki, Finland, and knew only two people attending the seminar: Phil Hoffman and Monica Flaherty.

Figure 38.1.

Phil and I had been invited to present our film *Sweep* (1995), which critiqued traditional strategies of representation in documentary films. Monica Flaherty was my grandmother's sister. She would be presenting her own project.

Within the Finnish film scene, *Sweep's* open-ended, self-reflective, radical form had stirred debate. In our film, Phil and I problematize Robert Flaherty's trip to Thunder Bay on his way to film *Nanook of the North* (1922)—when he was thirty-three, the same age as I was when we made *Sweep*. I had no idea if our film would resonate at the Flaherty seminar.

I shared my dormitory room with Riyad Wadia, a filmmaker from India who was the grandson of J. B. H. Wadia, the founder of Wadia

Movietone Studies. Riyad was also one of the first openly gay filmmakers in India. Like me, he was attending the Flaherty for the first time.

Riyad was two years younger than me, but I remember him as a much more mature, dedicated, and knowledgeable filmmaker than I was.

In his post-screening sessions, Riyad discussed his family history and talked about his family's archive of Indian films. He shared his own very personal and touching film, *Fearless: The Hunterwali Story* (1993), about Australian actress and circus artist Mary Ann Evans, a 1930s Hindi cinema action queen who did her own stunts. She was known as Fearless Nadia or Hunterwali.

During the Flaherty week, screenings, common meals, and discussions merged in a flurry of activity and people. I never contributed to the post-screening discussions. Listening to the abstract academic jargon, I felt clueless. Verbose commentators aggressively slashed at my fellow media artists. The discussion petrified me.

Maybe because both of us came from outside the North American academic and filmmaking community, we shared similar impressions of our first Flaherty. We witnessed the slightly hysterical expressions about "Flaherty family" among longtime seminarians, who revealed an awe-inspiring familiarity with each other. It felt like a cult—a friendly and kind-spirited cult.

I felt much less freaked out expressing these observations with Riyad.

My father's family were descendants of Dutch colonials from south India. Riyad's family were Parsees from Bombay. Our shared background but different family histories intensified our connection. After the seminar, we stayed in touch. Sadly, I never met him again in person. He passed away in 2003.

At some point, Monica Flaherty, one of Robert Flaherty's three daughters, presented her *Moana with Sound* (1981).

Monica had spent years creating an atmospheric—and in her words, authentic—soundtrack for her parents' 1926 film *Moana of the South Seas*. Although her 16mm print of *Moana with Sound* was more than ten years old, Monica zealously carried it from screening to screening. She seemed desperate to protect the reel of plastic from loss, damage, and the evil eye.

An awkward discussion followed *Moana*.

Monica was defensive. She aggressively protected the Flaherty legacies. She refused any new readings of the film. I did not imagine that years later I would devote a large part of my life to salvaging and restoring her *Moana with Sound* project.

Philip and I finally screened *Sweep*. I understood very little of *Sweep's* post-screening discussion. Phil answered some questions. The discussion bypassed all our ideas to critically interrogate heroic male road trips in documentary.

On the way out of the theater, I joined Monica for the walk to the discussion room. I was curious for her feedback. I'd shot an entire scene at the Flaherty farm in Vermont. Despite the fact that I was her grand-nephew, Monica had been reluctant to grant permission. She'd had grave concerns about how I might deal with the myths of Robert Flaherty's genius.

Monica and I walked slowly. She was seventy-five at the time. She did not seem to want to comment on our film.

Finally, I asked for her thoughts on *Sweep*. She offered one frosty comment: the credits misspelled her surname. After all my anticipation of a challenging discussion about representations of the exotic, the problems of non-preconception, and our common family heritage, her comment was a downer.

As the week rolled on, I met many serious, dark-clothed people from New York City. They seemed to know everyone. I also met fellow artists dedicated to their causes. All were interesting, insightful, and generous.

Several filmmakers impressed me. Craig Baldwin screened *Sonic Outlaws* (1995), an eruption of powerful media-political energy. For *Spin* (1995), Brian Springer organized weird satellite feeds that caught American presidential candidates and campaign spin doctors off guard.

Slowly but surely, Flaherty seminar traditions sucked me in.

On the last day, I took my Bolex over to the Wells College golf course. I'd enlisted Phil as a stunt person.

With new creative vigor germinated at the seminar, I returned to my work in progress about memory and coincidence. I filmed two rolls of silly golf antics. We sped around the course in the golf cart. One golfer had a black Lab. That beautiful black dog, glistening in the midday central New York sun, kept us company.

I used nearly every frame from those two rolls in the film I titled *Texas Scramble* (1996). Texas Scramble is a particular way for a group of golfers to play together. After each shot, all agree to hit their next ball from the position where one of the golfer's balls has landed. In some odd way, Texas Scramble seems to correlate with how I experienced the 1995 Flaherty seminar.

39

FLAHERTY 1995

Marlina Gonzalez

MARLINA GONZALEZ is a multimedia arts curator and producer using art for social change. She was Exhibition Director for Asian CineVision, Associate Film/Video Curator at the Walker Art Center, and Digital Media/Community Development Program Manager at Intermedia Arts. The Filipina Women's Network named her one of the 100 Most Influential Filipina Women in the United States as an Innovator and Thought Leader. A recipient of the 2012 Joyce Foundation Award (Theater), she codirected (with Meena Natarajan) her play, *Isla Tuliro* ("Island of Confusion"), for Pangea World Theater and Teatro Del Pueblo (Minneapolis) in April 2018.

The Camera Reframed was the first Flaherty seminar with an explicit title and theme.

The idea evolved out of my fascination with what was then called "the information superhighway."

As a child, I witnessed how the emergence of video drastically impacted my father, a documentary filmmaker. He had a business developing 16mm dailies for national broadcasting stations airing the evening news in the Philippines. Video killed my father's film-processing business.

So, reframing the camera, now positioned at the intersection of changing media technologies, seemed a most pressing question. What would happen to analog visual culture?

Figure 39.1. Photograph by Gasket Studios.

Through robust brainstorming and conversations with my cocurator, Bruce Jenkins, The Camera Reframed emerged from my desire to launch into a historical examination of the camera, not merely as instrument of the historical gaze, but *camera as subject*.

We unpacked this idea by curating self-reflexive documentaries, looking for works that interrogated the camera as a vehicle for interpreting, conveying, shaping, even manipulating the histories and stories we tell.

August 1995 also coincided with two very significant historical events: the fiftieth anniversary of the bombing of Hiroshima and Nagasaki and the death of Jerry Garcia of the Grateful Dead.

To commemorate the anniversary of the bombings during the Second World War, I selected Rea Tajiri's *History and Memory* (1991), a video about the internment of American citizens of Japanese descent. Tajiri's title and complex artistic process spoke to how media makers of color create alternative histories.

History and Memory declares a dialectic between what we are taught to remember as a function of control and what we are expected to forget—and therefore what we are forced to hide in safekeeping through memory.

History and Memory opens with representative images of what Tajiri thought was a childhood memory. The black-and-white Library of Congress archival footage of the Japanese American internment camps shows lines of Japanese American families with their suitcases in hand, lining the sidewalks and staring at the camera with perplexed eyes. This footage represents the *permitted institutional memory*.

In contrast, Tajiri reenacted a scene representing what she thought was a memory: a woman (perhaps her) drinking from a water pump in an internment camp. In filming the reenactment, Tajiri realized that this "memory" could not have happened. She was born years after the Japanese American internment. This revealed *personalized memory*: repressed or imagined images of fear, uncertainty, exclusion—images that evoke realities more personally palpable than the institutional footage.

In *History and Memory*, memory resides in the mind's hidden camera. This camera bears the burden of censored history. It identifies what we were told not to see and recreates what we were told to forget.

In August 1995, the death of Jerry Garcia and the emergence of a new mass media represented a second historical congruence.

News of Garcia's death coincided with *the* day and hour that we launched a Flaherty experiment in digital media.

Part of our curatorial intention was to observe the crux of moving-image technology at the time—the emergence of the World Wide Web.

We invited Asian American experimental media artist Shu Lea Cheang to talk about her cybernetic installation, *Bowling Alley* (1995–1996). I had previously curated it for the Walker Art Center in Minneapolis.

The presentation was scheduled for August 9, 1995. The audience would witness Cheang's conversation live digitally onstage and on-screen with her project partners, Kevin Sawad Brooks and Beth Stryker, in another state (no longer sure where they were). Golf ball cameras (the predecessor of today's GoPro) via the internet (an early version of Skype) were used.

The exercise failed.

At the exact time of the presentation, the Ethernet blazed with news announcing the death of Jerry Garcia. And at the moment when our new technology crashed, a new form of mass media emerged. Internet traffic jammed the information superhighway. The connections at Wells College could not accommodate the glut of rapid communication.

Ordinary people dethroned multinational broadcast media. Accidentally, they subverted the message of our Flaherty seminar's theme. The masses decided that Jerry Garcia's death was the most important message to pay attention to.

Importantly, the seminar did not fail to open up opportunities for dialogue and debate between Western and Third World critics and historians about different postcolonial ideas and LGBTQ concepts, as they related to older and new technologies.

Controversy erupted. Many participants vigorously argued that *Nanook of the North* (1922) affirmed the Western gaze and positioned the cinematographer as "redeemer." Flaherty's camera created narrative tropes for a fantasy construction of First Nations and the Third World. Filmmaker and film historian Nick Deocampo (Philippines) asserted that "Third World Camera," in contrast, evidenced and exposed colonial scars.

How the West chooses to see the world and *the Other* drives the rules of storytelling. First Nations, Third World countries, and marginalized cultures within Western cultures become the Other. At the seminar, Cheang, Deocampo, and Tajiri disrupted the imposition of the Western gaze. They took ownership of the camera. They told their stories with their *own* images and likenesses.

Our 1995 Flaherty seminar brought these image makers together into a zone that collapsed the distances and dichotomies between colonizer/colonized, as well as the camera as the gaze and the camera as the object of the gaze. The seminar unpacked the act and the art of looking.

In the decades since the 1995 Flaherty seminar, I've become a multidisciplinary arts curator and artist.

My projects now move beyond the black box theater and the screen and into public spaces. As program manager for Intermedia Arts in Minneapolis, I cocurated *The UnConvention* (summer 2008) with partners in the arts, media, and academia. Steve Dietz, founder of Northern Lights .mn, a Twin Cities–based collaborative interactive media arts organization, conceived this citywide participatory art and media response to the 2008 Republican National Convention in St. Paul.

The UnConventional Gathering Space transformed Intermedia Arts into a cross between an alternative-artist press center and an exhibition venue.

One gallery featured Fang Yu Frank Lin's *Political Science 101*, which simulated an old-fashioned classroom, where a hacked slide projector presented graphs, tables, and pie charts with frequently mentioned words from the presidential election. My curated traveling show, *Instructions for Peace* (2001–present), commissioned artists to construct interactive multimedia installations meant to engage the public toward acts of peace.

With augmented reality (AR), selfies, and DIY culture, my curatorial and artistic work explores moving-image technology's impact on how we view the world and shape stories through our own gaze. My current project, *Living Rooms*, uses AR to reveal the experiences of adoptees, dreamers, immigrants, "mail-order" brides, political asylees, and refugees impacted by Deferred Action for Childhood Arrivals (DACA).

I am not done reframing the camera.

40

AURORA, BANGALORE, MYSORE

Ayisha Abraham

AYISHA ABRAHAM is an installation artist and experimental film-maker. She is currently Dean of the School of Media Arts and Sciences at Srishti Institute of Art, Design, and Technology in Bangalore, India, and a member of the Bengaluru Artists Residency (BAR1). Her work has been shown at numerous international exhibitions, festivals, galleries, and museums in Austria, Brazil, China, Denmark, France, Germany, India, Japan, Norway, Spain, United Kingdom, and the United States. Her films include *Amnesia* (2001); *Straight 8* (2005); *One Way* (2007); *You are Here* (2008); *Enroute or of a Thousand Moons* (2011); *I Saw a God Dance* (2012); and *Through the Gold Mine* (2013).

The year 1995 was one of change. After living in New York for six years, where I'd found my niche, I was moving to Bangalore. I was in my twenties and still finding myself as an artist.

The small artists' collectives in New York had been a strong influence. Originally, I'd been a painter, but conceptual art, critical theory, film, installation, and video art had begun to influence me. I'd become comfortable in New York; Bangalore loomed as an unknown.

I had just exhibited a photographic installation that used my family's nineteenth-century photographs. Found images had seduced me. My

Figure 40.1.

family had lived in Bangalore; they had converted to Christianity. What role did photography and film play in the British colonies?

Before I left for Bangalore, I applied to the Flaherty seminar. The theme that year was The Camera Reframed: Technology and Interpretation. Marlina Gonzalez Tamrong and Bruce Jenkins programmed.

I arrived at Wells College in Aurora, New York, and ventured into the first event. Outside the auditorium perched a few computers, early versions of the Mac SE. They were running CD-ROMs with films from Rick Prelinger's archive.

Rick had hired a pickup truck to collect neglected industrial and advertising reels in small film formats. He invested his own money and time for numerous road trips across America (what a way to see your country!). He rented storage, digitized hundreds of hours of footage with primitive technology, and established an open source digital library. The images he made available spoke like oracles of personal and public pasts, the disintegrating histories of a media-dependent capitalist society, its workplaces and industries.

I was stunned. As I swam in the lake near the college, these reels played in my mind.

Twenty-four years later, Rick's work still profoundly reverberates. At the time, it resonated with my American friends' pioneering, spirited thinking about culture and their confident creation of media paradigms outside established exhibition venues, galleries, museums, and universities.

My own film work evolved from home movie reels I collected in Bangalore and other Indian cities between 2000 and 2008—inspired by Rick. My grandmother had lived in Bangalore, so it was a place of my childhood. My new neighborhood and the city beyond became a landscape to mine for films. Clutching my newborn son on my hip, I walked the streets and talked to aging Anglo Indians of the British cantonment of Bangalore East. Their meandering, enchanting memories of the twentieth century unfolded like an opera.

The excitement of discovery filled my walks. I was a flaneur, a scavenger, and an archaeologist. It was a happy time where voices beckoned to me. Today, I quietly retreat into my own work, teaching, reading, living with animals and plants, and recycling home movies. But I remain thankful for those restless days of searching and discovery.

My first film was *Straight 8* (2005), a compilation of home movies by Tom D'Aguiar, an Anglo Indian whose family had been in India since the early nineteenth century. He spoke with a clipped British accent yet had never traveled outside India. Living among the British in the cantonment deeply influenced his work for the newly instituted telegraph system and his amateur activities. By the 1930s, he was making films. I replayed Tom's deteriorating 8mm reels on my new Eumig projector, my best friend during long nights in my studio, where I projected the films and reshot them on Mini DV tape.

I've now made ten found-footage films and have material for more.

By the early twenty-first century, international information technology (IT) companies were favoring Bangalore. The city dissolved from a retirees' haven with quiet evening walks and amateur passions in books, cars, film, and nature into an unheavenly maze of flyovers, ring roads, and countless vehicles rushing to meet the demands of IT.

Tom's films, and the interview I did with him, triggered my fascination with rewinding the past. His amateur moving images of lakes, forests, and agricultural land spreading throughout the city fascinated me. They delivered a sense of the calm that had preceded the wreckage of demolished old buildings and the new construction sites.

Out of this rubble, a new art scene was emerging in Bangalore. Chennai, Kolkata, and Mumbai were considered the "real cities." Bangalore had been considered dull, a place for amateur activity rather than professional life. After the 1990s, creative people outside the market culture and established institutions of the "real cities" began to move away from these urban centers. In their search for cheaper real estate, community, and space, they found Bangalore, still known for its liberal sensibilities, greenery, and gentleness.

Tom D'Aguiar introduced me to Ram Gopal, a gay dancer born in Bangalore. Ram had contacted Tom years before because Tom had a movie camera and color film: "I've never seen myself in color—please film me." Exquisite despite the crackled emulsion, the amateur footage shows a dancer performing on the rooftop of an old house in the cantonment in the late 1930s—a serendipitous find.

One evening, during the 1995 seminar, the Flaherty served dinner on the lawn. I met Monica Flaherty, who had screened a new print of *Moana* (1926). Later I talked to her nephew, an interesting young filmmaker named Sami. When he learned I was moving to Bangalore, he shared that his father lived close by, in Mysore.

Sami told me that Robert and Frances Flaherty's oldest daughter, Barbara, had married Botha van Ingen, whose family had emigrated from Holland to Ceylon to India. He owned a tea and coffee estate and was a well-known taxidermist (the van Ingen brothers, Dewet, Kruger, Botha, and Joubert, and their company, van Ingen & van Ingen, were known throughout the world for their tiger and leopard head mounts and rugs). Sami's grandfather, Botha, a difficult personality, had a collection of glass negatives Sami had tried to procure.

Years later, when I had extended my search for amateur footage to Mysore and beyond, I finally met Sami's father, Michael van Ingen, living in his rambling old home. Although at the time he had only a very few photographs and films, he shared that photography and filmmaking had been important activities for this family of taxidermists and for Barbara and Botha.

I was amazed that Robert Flaherty's daughter had married a van Ingen decades earlier in Mysore. Barbara van Ingen was prominent in the elite circles of Mysore and Bangalore. As I hunted for small format films and their hidden histories, I discovered that many remembered her.

41

BEGINNINGS/ENDINGS

Grace An

GRACE AN is Associate Professor of Cinema Studies and French at Oberlin College, where she has served as Director of the Cinema Studies program. She has published on directors Olivier Assayas, Chris Marker, and Alain Resnais as well as on actresses including Jane Fonda and Delphine Seyrig. Her teaching and research interests include 1968, the documentary and essay film, militant cinema, and French feminisms. Her current book project is *Disobedient Muse: Delphine Seyrig, Feminism, and The Cinema*.

The Flaherty seminar gave me access and exposure to many of my cinematic, cultural, and intellectual firsts: first viewings of experimental and avant-garde film, a first immersion in documentary and nonfiction, first encounters with militant cinema, film collectives, and microcinemas.

Normally, filmmakers I had studied were usually too lofty or distant to engage with in person. Once the Flaherty came into my life, my timid self worked up the courage to describe my response to Eve Heller's *Glint* (2001) and *Her Glacial Speed* (2002) to the filmmaker herself. This foray rewarded me with the many conversations that followed, both with her and other filmmakers since then. All those conversations, with the murmur of constant revelation and the chorus of dissonant and searching voices, are the foundation of my engagement with the world of film.

Figure 41.1.

My first exposure to the world of the Flaherty seminar occurred in the fall of 1996, three weeks into my first semester of graduate school at Cornell.

I arrived with the intention of specializing in the literature of Francophone North and sub-Saharan Africa. I hadn't even heard of Robert Flaherty. I enrolled in Timothy Murray's film seminar, my first film course ever. I found myself being taken for a trip over the hills across town to Ithaca College, where I met Patricia Zimmermann and made my way through a weekend of Flaherty programming.

Patricia has likened the Flaherty to a "finishing film school" for people like me, who wrote a dissertation on the films of Olivier Assayas, Chris Marker, and Alain Resnais for a French literary studies program at Cornell, when French studies in the United States was just starting to integrate the study of a film in French studies curricula.

Several years later, in June 2004, I accompanied Patricia to the Flaherty seminar at Vassar College to participate in a special fiftieth-anniversary program titled Arctic Requiem, a multivalent performance screening of *Nanook of the North* (1922). This experience served as the other bookend of my PhD, which launched a career as a professor of French *and* cinema studies.

The 2004 seminar began with Michel Brault's *Pour la suite du monde/ For Those Who Will Follow* (1963), which took us to the Lower Arctic region of Canada, where a French Canadian village reconstructed the tradition of a whale hunt. With Richard Leacock present, cinéma vérité and cinéma direct assumed more definition in my brain with more texture and resonance.

I learned about Jennifer Reeves for the first time. I felt honored to be in the presence of Charles Burnett after watching *Killer of Sheep* (1978) with him in the audience. Film history books and theoretical texts absorbed throughout the PhD stayed on the shelves as the seminar brought me up close and personal—and political—with the real people and real stuff of film.

I'll never forget the generosity of Scott MacDonald, who spent an evening reconstructing the critical context of certain interventions that had troubled me that day. I learned about specific histories shared by specific individuals in this community—sometimes harmoniously, sometimes not. It was an important lesson on the importance of thinking about the political *and* social aspects of a problem together. Again, real people with real histories were at stake.

Patricia Zimmermann directed a team of musicians and scholars in an ambitious project titled Arctic Requiem, a production that included a screening of *Nanook of the North* in dialogue, with performances by violinist Ritsu Katsumata and vocalist Louise Mygatt alongside theatrical and lighting effects by Ann Michel and Phil Wilde and contributions by fellow professor Anna Siomopoulos and me.

The fiftieth anniversary of the seminars occasioned something extra for this annual ritual screening of *Nanook*. Patricia paid special homage to the culture of the seminars, with its own history of relationships between the critical and the artistic, as well as between the scholarly and the performative. We invoked Frances Flaherty and infused the experience with our shared feminist sensibility so that it would honor the traditional aspects of *Nanook* and the seminars yet position them through new windows, on different screens, and in new frames. Count this endeavor as yet another first for me and for many seminar participants that year.

Those very real encounters that week led to lifelong commitments that enrich my life every day.

Most importantly, who knew then that I, ensconced in auteurism and French national cinema at the time, would be working today on militant cinema and feminist video collectives in a book project on actress-agitator Delphine Seyrig, who forged new definitions of the political actor and rejected male auteurist cinema in her time?

Many seeds were planted that June, including a meeting with Ulrike Ottinger, whom I visited for a week in Berlin during October 2017, as she was the last filmmaker to work with Seyrig. Pure coincidence? Or testament to a subconscious reservoir of encounters to come?

The Flaherty was such an eye-opening and eye-training experience for me that it took me a full decade to appreciate its imprints on my work and life. It exposed me to avenues beyond the disciplining apparatuses of my fields, and the effects of that week proved both disruptive and edifying.

There would be no more hiding in disciplinary bunkers after the Flaherty, where participants simply did interdisciplinarity without wearing it as a banner, and no one had to call it that because it could be taken for granted by academics and nonacademics alike. How often I've wished that such ease and seamlessness could have characterized what we call interdisciplinarity in the academy.

I later understood that cinema/film studies is a discipline like no other—partly because it was born in the twentieth century and not the nineteenth—but also because its origins are multiple. Ultimately, the Flaherty is about cinema, not cinema studies, and its prehistory and history are all the more complex.

What a gift to take with me to the first of many semesters of a career that has been driven by the motivation to learn and relearn the life practices of empathy, engagement, embodiment, and community. I've been fortunate to work with students who embrace the problematization of what I've called *about-ness* in film, which is less about subjects and more about creating and recognizing them. We learn more from them than about them.

I'll be forever grateful for this Flaherty privilege of seeing anew, according to what Frances Flaherty qualified as *non-preconception*, as we continue to grapple with the ever-evolving relationships between the pragmatic and the utopian, the documentary and the experimental, the indexical and the imaginary, the struggle and the dream.

This "finishing school" was the beginning of so much.

Yet if I've learned anything, it's that there is no single beginning and no single ending to anything. Multiple beginnings and endings—the Flaherty is all that for me.

42

TALKING

Dorothea Braemer

DOROTHEA BRAEMER is an award-winning independent filmmaker and Assistant Professor in the Communication Department at Buffalo State College in Buffalo, New York. She worked at Scribe Video Center, a media arts center dedicated to participatory community-based video in Philadelphia, Pennsylvania. Later, she served as Executive Director at Squeaky Wheel, a media center in Buffalo, New York, that hosts gallery exhibitions, screenings, and other special events year-round, with visiting artists, special workshops, and off-site events. In 2011, she received a Fulbright Award to make a documentary in Brandenburg, Germany. She lives in Buffalo, New York, with her daughter and her husband, Carl Lee.

Going to the Flaherty was a rite of passage.

When I was a graduate student in the MFA program for Film and Media Arts at Temple University in Philadelphia, professors and students talked about it. If you wanted to be become a serious filmmaker, you needed this experience!

In 1996, I journeyed to the Flaherty seminar on my own, taking various trains and buses. I landed at Wells College, a pretty location on Lake Cayuga's shores in the Finger Lakes region of central New York.

I had bought myself a blue, roomy, and comfortable backpack just for the occasion. It made me feel independent and ready for new adventures.

Figure 42.1.

For one week, it was nice to be part of a group and not have to think about what to do next. Someone else decided what we would watch and what we would do after. This predetermined structure freed up a lot of mental space.

It was eye-opening to see what topics were okay to make documentary films about.

In Marlon Fuentes's *Bontoc Eulogy* (1995), people from the Philippines walked through difficult terrain on the way to the World's Fair—all fictionalized. Marina McDougall's *If You Lived Here, You'd Be Home by Now* (1993) was about signs along the road. Ellen Spiro's *Roam Sweet Home* (1996) was an entire film from a dog's point of view. Leighton

Pierce's *50 Feet of String* (1995) featured a piece of string as the main character.

I remember Austin Allen's rumination about space, *Claiming Open Spaces* (1995), and Alanis Obomsawin's *Kanehsatake: 270 Years of Resistance* (1993), an intense documentary about indigenous people in Canada. Elizabeth Barret's work in progress, *Stranger with a Camera* (2000), left a lasting impression. It dealt thoughtfully with the quintessential documentary dilemma of an outsider making films about the suffering of others.

Scholar Patricia Zimmermann insisted I read Frantz Fanon. That year's programmer, Ruth Bradley, told me she missed Kathy High, the other co-programmer who'd had to leave because, I think, her father had passed away. Ellen Spiro sat on the dock talking about Buffalo. George Kuchar passed me in a hallway. With fingers in his mouth, he muttered, "I have something stuck between my teeth," and walked on.

I fell asleep during films and liked that. After all, film is dream. I slept well during James Benning's *North on Evers* (1991), an experimental film about the desert that featured impossible-to-read writing. Somehow, the desert landscape more deeply entered my soul.

I remember thinking that films are like onions whose layers of meanings get peeled away, a process that takes time.

The first layer was the films and how I felt watching them.

The second layer included the formal discussions and my voyeuristic listening. The discussions were like watching another film. Some people could stand up in front of the large group and make incredibly articulate, eye-opening, passionate, and print-ready statements. Sometimes they disagreed with other verbally adroit participants. I kept thinking, "I wish I had a camera to film these people."

The third layer centered on the talking about talking about talking about films, as well as the gossip. Whispered conversations asked why did they program *that* film? Why is that film a documentary? Why is this slick commercial filmmaker here?

The most intense discussions took place during these private sessions. Alcohol helped. At night, some of us went swimming and talked even more.

Intense camps formed. One camp advocated an expanded view that saw documentary as a big tent housing many forms. The other camp held a much narrower view. Documentary should not be self-reflexive. It should probe social issues. It should be ethical. The filmmaker should not be an outsider.

Although I immediately placed myself in the big tent camp, the passion exhibited in the more purist camp deeply impressed me. I remember thinking that documentary must be the greatest art form of all because it's so fully alive and elicits such passion.

At that Flaherty, we screamed at each other, and that was very beautiful. I wanted to make a documentary about *that*: all of us screaming at each other because we all loved documentary film.

After George Kuchar's screening of *Weather Diary 1* (1986), the built-up tension boiled over into a nasty fight. The very hot theater felt even hotter. Someone proclaimed George Kuchar's film made fun of the Oklahoma locals.

I had a different opinion. I thought George Kuchar made fun of himself. His embarrassing tasks, such as hanging up his underwear on a clothesline in his motel room while chasing hurricanes in Oklahoma, had a beautiful authenticity. They make us, as spectators, uncomfortable. (Too wimpy to make myself uncomfortable, I think I voiced that opinion after a couple glasses of wine to a small group of select friends.)

At one point, George Kuchar exclaimed, "What is wrong with you people?" I think he stormed out. But I'm not sure.

Another upheaval erupted. Loretta Todd, part of the programming team, screened her own film, *The Learning Path* (1991). Some seminarians thought her action was more unethical than George taking advantage of Oklahomans.

The fights made me realize how much I loved film. The relentless schedule made me understand that screenings are an important part of filmmaking.

After I left Wells College, I thought about this Flaherty experience many times. When I started dating my future husband, Carl, our first lengthy talk was about the Flaherty.

The seminar expanded my perspectives about documentary film as complex, nuanced, and relevant, a living art form that evolves, is contested, and arouses passionate opinions. It encouraged me to take risks and to trust my own voice.

At that Flaherty, I met a fun group from Squeaky Wheel, a media arts center in Buffalo, New York. In a strange coincidence, I became the executive director of Squeaky Wheel in 2003. I attended my second Flaherty with my Squeaky Wheel coworker Tammy McGovern. During my ten years there, I often referenced the Flaherty.

At Squeaky Wheel, I found a strong experimental film community doing small unique screenings with engaged audiences that seemed like performances. I realized screenings were not simply vehicles for exhibition but were integral to filmmaking, an idea that first came to me when I attended that Flaherty in 1996.

43

RECOVERING LOST MEMORIES

Ulises A. Mejias

ULISES A. MEJIAS is Professor in the Communication Studies Department and Director of the Institute for Global Engagement at SUNY Oswego. His research interests include critical internet studies, network theory and science, philosophy and sociology of technology, and political economy of new media. His book *Off the Network: Disrupting the Digital World* (2013) looks at the politics of inclusion and exclusion in digital networks, examining how new media broadens participation yet also exacerbates disparity. His book with Nick Couldry is *The Costs of Connection: How Data Is Colonizing Human Life and Appropriating It for Capitalism* (2019). More information is available at http://ulisesmejias.com.

Perhaps the struggle to recover fading memories, what St. Augustine would call *remembering forgetfulness*, is more useful than having access to perfect memories.

Or so I thought as I sat to write this remembrance of events from two decades ago. The truth is, at first I remembered little about my involvement with the Flaherty seminar in 1997, which is ironic given that the theme was Exploration in Memory and Modernity.

There is a somewhat valid excuse for my forgetfulness. At the time, I was holding down a full-time job producing video advertisements for a cable company, studying full-time in a master's program at Ithaca College,

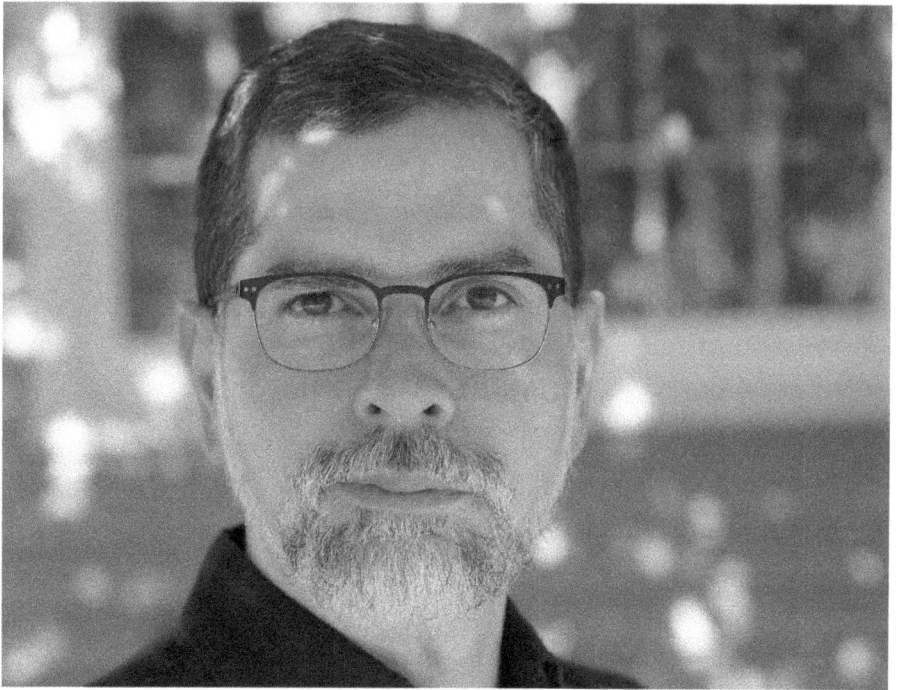

Figure 43.1.

and working as research/project assistant for Patricia Zimmermann, an Ithaca College screen studies professor who was one of the programmers for a mini-Flaherty seminar—Michelle Materre was the other.

I remember getting up at 4:30 a.m. on weekdays to do schoolwork before going to my job, then attending graduate classes in the evening. I often share this tale with my students struggling to balance work and school, which I am sure they find annoying.

In any event, the point is that I was busy, probably too busy to fully appreciate the impact of what I was involved in.

So it is only now, as I collect the isolated memories floating around my head and "curate" them into a meaningful experience, that I realize the impact that the Flaherty had on my development as a scholar.

What I *actually* remember from that October are little snippets of life as a student assistant.

I remember stuffing envelopes with invitations (this was before evites). I remember running to and fro making sure programs were distributed, chairs were available, signs were posted, and speakers were escorted to the right classrooms. I remember helping to fix projectors and setting up snacks; in short, getting done the things everyone just expects should be done when putting together an event. I do remember the artists and scholars—Anne-Marie Duguet, Daniel Reeves, Reginald Woolery—or rather, I definitely remember the names and some of the work, even if I don't always remember the faces.

I remember the parties and get-togethers and being a bit intimidated about interacting with the kind of folks whose work I previously encountered only in the classroom and who were now standing in front of me.

Most of all, I remember the Digital Salon, a room full of computers featuring websites and CD-ROM content by artists like Antoni Muntadas.

I provided technical assistance in putting the room together. I remember getting the sense even then that this was something new and exciting that redefined modes of spectatorship and interaction.

Of course, by today's standards it seems quaint that we would have to get all this digital content into one room in order for people to experience it. But it is precisely because consumption of digital content has become so atomized and individualistic that the idea of the salon seems endowed with a sense of collectivity that is now missing.

As I put all these memories together, I realize that the Flaherty was a key moment in my education as a scholar.

Yes, I was taking graduate classes at the time, reading and writing and working on research projects.

But the experience of helping to organize that weekend Flaherty gave me a sense—for the first time, I think—of belonging to an intellectual community, of being able not just to watch or read thought-provoking work, but to interact with the people who created it and be able to have a discussion about it. In other words, as a student I had done *scholarship*, but now I started to feel like a *scholar*.

I eventually went on to do my doctorate at Columbia University and have been teaching at SUNY Oswego for over a decade.

Many years from now, I know my students will probably not remember the details of everything they are learning. They are just as busy as I was.

But hopefully some of them will have similar opportunities to reflect on and organize their memories, to realize that they did find a community and a purpose in the midst of all that activity.

And hopefully they will also remember the sense of excitement about their discovery, as I do when I think about my involvement with the Flaherty in 1997.

44

I NEVER MET ROBERT FLAHERTY

Thomas W. Bohn

THOMAS W. BOHN is the retired Dean of the Roy H. Park School of Communications at Ithaca College. He is author of numerous scholarly articles and coauthor of two highly acclaimed and widely used basic textbooks, *Mass Media* (six editions) and *Light and Shadows* (three editions). His research has focused primarily on media history. He has served as a higher education consultant to many colleges and universities and continues to be active in various scholarly organizations. He enjoys teaching part-time in mass communication and film history, valiantly trying to stay one step ahead of his students.

Although I never met or knew Robert Flaherty, he has always been one of my professional and academic heroes.

I cut my teeth on *Nanook of the North* (1922) and *Louisiana Story* (1948) at the University of Wisconsin, which in turn inspired my dissertation on the *Why We Fight* (1943–1945) series.

So, when the opportunity came to host the renowned Flaherty seminar for a long weekend at Ithaca College in the fall of 1997, as dean of the Roy H. Park School of Communications at the time, I jumped at the opportunity.

Accepting the invitation was easy, but the logistics of hosting so many eminent scholars and artists was daunting. Fortunately, Professor Patricia

Figure 44.1.

Zimmermann was on the Park faculty, and the process was delightful and successful.

That seminar was entitled Explorations in Memory and Modernity. Patricia programmed it with Michelle Materre, who at the time was executive director of the Flaherty seminar in New York City.

The coming together of internationally acclaimed academics and artists to engage in thoughtful and critical discourse about the discipline of documentary practice and study was a natural fit for the Park School. I saw the school's mission as covering three domains: advancing the discipline of communications (in this case, the specific field of documentary practice and study); probing the intellectual foundations of the documentary discipline; and expanding the discipline through thoughtful and critical discourse.

Thankfully, we had the financial resources necessary to host the seminar, primarily through the James B. Pendleton Endowment, established by a longtime friend of the Park School.

Because of this resource, we were able to bring to campus such renowned figures in documentary and experimental film as Erik Barnouw, Scott MacDonald, Branda Miller, Timothy Murray, and Barbara Van Dyke, as well as our distinguished alumnus, video and installation artist Daniel Reeves (class of 1977). We were particularly happy to have Reeves serve as a role model for our students.

We screened Daniel's monumental and moving single-channel video on war, family, memory, and reconciliation, *Obsessive Becoming* (1995), a distinguished work that combines documentary and experimental modes. The seminar enabled us to honor him for his superb work and career at the vanguard of experimental video.

As with any enterprise of this nature, the devil is in the details. Thankfully, Dr. Zimmermann and I shared a passion for "getting it right." So no task was too small or insignificant. I distinctly remember us working well into the evening alongside Daniel, putting rocks on the floor and on monitors, to build his installation, *Eingang: The Way In*, in the College's Handwerker Gallery.

The seminar was one of the first media arts events in the United States to feature CD-ROMs as documentary and experimental work. It also mounted a new media salon in a classroom where seminarians could explore these works on computers.

This programming fit precisely with the stated premise of that weekend seminar, which was to "probe the dialectic between historical and new formations of independent media and how each navigates memory and modernity."

There were many highlights that weekend, but the one that stands out for me was the four Daniel Reeves installations, projects that filled the gallery and even spread across the windows. It was a groundbreaking and breathtaking exhibition about history; images, old and new; technology; memory; and modernity.

As I reflect on my twenty-three years as dean of the Park School, hosting the Robert Flaherty Film Seminar ranks at the top of a very short list.

To bring distinguished academics and artists to the college and to the Park School for thoughtful and sustained dialogue about the most important questions facing the discipline was a reflection of the Park School's central mission. To be able to show off the school and its students, faculty, staff, alumni, and facilities to these scholars, artists, and programmers was truly special.

I only wish Robert Flaherty had been there!

45

TENDON STRETCHES

Jacqueline Goss

JACQUELINE GOSS is a filmmaker. Her work includes *The Observers* (2011), a nearly feature-length portrait of a weather observatory on the windiest mountain in the world, and *The Measures* (2014), an essay film made with artist Jenny Perlin about the history of the metric system and so-called invention of the meter. A native of New Hampshire, Goss is a 2008 Tribeca Film Institute Media Arts Fellow and the 2007 recipient of the Herb Alpert Award in Film and Video. She teaches in the Film and Electronic Arts program at Bard College in the Hudson Valley of New York.

My first encounter with a Flaherty seminar must have been in 1997 at Ithaca College.

I was enrolled in an MFA program in Electronic Arts at Rensselaer Polytechnic Institute (RPI). Along with my teacher, media artist Branda Miller, and fellow grad student Julia Meltzer, I drove over for the weekend-long Digital Flaherty seminar co-programmed by Michelle Materre, then executive director of the Flaherty seminar, and Patricia Zimmermann, a documentary historian, theorist, and writer—and a professor of screen studies at Ithaca College.

I remember that I saw *Measures of Distance* by Mona Hatoum for the first time there. This formally simple but beautifully complex work

Figure 45.1.

based on images, letters, and audio recordings made by the artist and her mother became a staple in my media production teaching at Bard College.

At that intense and compressed seminar, Patricia Zimmermann's rapid-fire lecture on *Nanook of the North* (1922) served up a revelation. She staged a series of curtain draws: the fake igloo, the casting of Robert Flaherty's Inuit lover as the wife of Nanook, the reenactment of a walrus hunt on the ice, the fox hunt with the dead fox.

Patricia's post-screening discussion with Erik Barnouw, the author of *Documentary: A History of the Non-Fiction Film* and one of the key figures in the history of the seminar, applied a strange kind of sealant to the seminar's proceedings. She fired out a takedown of the eponymous white male "master"—and I loved it. How great it was for me to transform this complicated, flawed, but profoundly inspiring film into fuel for serious and meaningful discussions about the complexity of making moving images.

Two years later, RPI hosted another weekend Digital Flaherty. At this seminar, my revelation was Kevin and Jenn McCoy's work and its connection to and deconstruction of traditional storytelling. Their reworking of a pivotal scene from Jean-Luc Godard's *Weekend* (1967) as looped media in an installation environment sparked so many ideas about ways in which narrative can unfold. Their references to Vladimir Propp's writings on folklore and fairytale became crucial to my thinking, teaching, and creative work.

In 2006, almost ten years after that Ithaca College seminar, programmers Ariella Ben-Dov and Steve Seid invited me to show my video pieces *Stranger Comes To Town* (2007) and *How to Fix the World* (2004) at the seminar at Vassar College. These two works use animated characters to illustrate interviews with real people. Knowing the Flaherty conventions of close scrutiny and straight-up criticism, the invitation pushed me to make my work as strong as it could be.

I realized that the two central New York weekend seminars I'd experienced operated as very small tendon stretches for the annual weeklong seminar.

My very first encounter there was Adele Horne, the director of the powerful documentary *Tailenders* (2005). We were in an elevator. We eyed each other. We tried to figure out if the other was slated to present work or not. Later, Adele screened an untitled 16mm film that was later to be called *15 Experiments on Peripheral Vision* (2008).

The mystery about *What will we be seeing in this program?* seems deeply embedded in the seminar's history. It is fundamentally so cool. Think about some of your all-time best film viewing experiences. I bet at least one of them was a blind date where you knew nothing at all about what you were going to watch. It's the same for movie watching on airplanes: you do not arrive with the usual set of critical lenses. You're open in different ways to what you might watch.

Many revelations materialized for me in 2006: Ashim Ahluwalia's *John and Jane Toll-Free* (2005), a documentary about Indian telemarketers for American companies in Bombay; Ben Coonley's killer PowerPoint and karaoke videos; Mercedes Alvarez's inspiring film *El Cielo Gira* (*The Sky Turns*, 2004); Nancy Andrews's perfect blend of live action, puppetry, and animation in the films *The Haunted Camera* (2006) and *Monkey and Lumps* (2003). Andrews remains one of my favorite filmmakers ever—a witty, multitalented craftsperson with an uncanny ability to make the best sound/image combos you'll encounter. She is totally underappreciated and under-recognized.

We watched Vittorio De Seta's beautiful films about fishermen in Italy, *Fescherecci* (*Fishing*, 1958) and *Contadini del mare* (*Peasant of the Sea*, 1955), in a dark theater while construction workers loudly labored outside. This juxtaposition prompted a lively discussion about the romanticization of labor on the screen but the complete dismissal of it off-screen.

These discussions, where people feel safe to passionately argue and to disagree, constitute the heart of the Flaherty seminars for me. Sadly, I think these kinds of honest, intense conversations are becoming a rarity. We still need them, even more now, in the Trump era and what feels like the shutting down of debate.

At the Flaherty seminar, you can quarrel with another viewer and may walk away to grouse, but you will see the same person the next morning at breakfast. The conversation *will* move forward, because you will be there for several more days. And there will be more movies to weave into it.

Oddly, these other screenings and discussions billow as much more salient to me now than the screening of my own work. Only one memory remains: Sally Berger, then assistant curator of video at the Museum of Modern Art, skipped my screening. I was crushed.

At Vassar, we watched films for seven days from 10:00 in the morning until midnight. How did we do that?

What a tendon stretch! What a gift.

46

UP ALL NIGHT

Dan Streible

DAN STREIBLE teaches cinema studies at New York University. Since 1999, he has organized the Orphan Film Symposium, a biennial gathering of scholars, archivists, and artists devoted to screening, saving, and studying neglected audiovisual material. His publications include *Fight Pictures: A History of Boxing and Early Cinema* (2008), *Learning with the Lights Off: Educational Film in the United States* (edited with Devin Orgeron and Marsha Orgeron, 2012), and *Emile de Antonio: A Reader* (edited with Douglas Kellner, 2000). An Academy Film Scholar, he is writing a book about the orphan film movement. See http://orphan.film.

In transit to my first Robert Flaherty Film Seminar in 1999, I read the organization's description of what to expect during the weeklong immersive retreat. I wondered, is this a cult? A closed circle of devotees of a venerated figure restricted to a liminal space during an annual ritual of intense discussion of ideas and beliefs, with all meals taken together, sleep deprivation, separation from family, and complete secrecy about the esoteric content to be revealed in a darkened room by a curate selected by the elders?

Well . . . yes. But I found that beneath the cultlike veneer, the event was defined by more liberatory experiences: exposure to new and rare screen works; personal encounters with interesting people from diverse

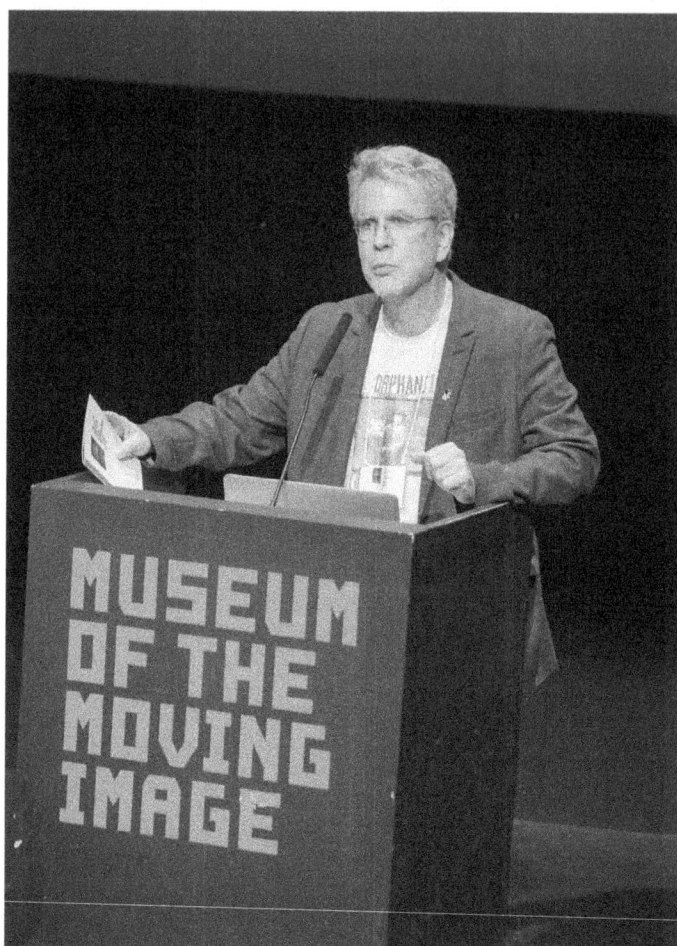

Figure 46.1. Photograph courtesy of NYU Orphan
Film Symposium (Creative Commons license:
Attribution-NonCommercial-ShareAlike).

places; long talks with like-minded souls; plenty of laughter amid the
debates; the pleasures that come with food, drink, music, and dance; and
hours of film discovery.

I've returned to seven more seminars, including the one I was fortunate to program in 2011.

The bonds formed are often lasting. Many friendships and meaningful professional collaborations began for me at a Flaherty seminar.

The best example of what the seminar can do at its most utopian
came at the end of my first. Two of the guest artists were avant-garde film
programmers Mark McElhatten and Scott Stark. One of their planned
screenings got bumped, but they, abetted by Tom Whiteside, set up a
16mm projector and screen on the lawn and improvised a set of shorts

that lasted literally till dawn. Unidentified home movies, TV news out-takes, Warhol's *Soap Opera* (1964), a soft-core film that looked like a Warhol, an indelible 1968 medical training film called *The Inner World of Aphasia,* and inscrutable pieces of found footage—a thrilling end to a derangement (as Mekas famously called for) of the cinematic senses.

The experience encouraged me later that year as I co-organized the first Orphan Film Symposium along similar lines: eclectic, unconventional programming of short archival, documentary, and experimental films packed into an intense several days and nights with a hundred enthusiasts.

I returned the following year for a Flaherty designated Essays, Experiments, and Excavations, ingeniously programmed by Kathy Geritz, which took the eclecticism of that lawn-till-dawn screening and expanded it for the entire week. The screenings were particularly enriched by historical films selected by both the curator and her guest artists.

Filmmaker Peggy Ahwesh picked *Little Tich and His Big Boots* (1900) to accompany her own works. Geritz put three versions of the Lumières' *Workers Leaving the Factory* (1895) before Harun Farocki's 1995 video of the same name, and, for new filmmaker Travis Wilkerson, *79 Springtimes of Ho Chi Minh* (1969) and *Now!* (1964) by Santiago Álvarez, the Cuban filmmaker who inspired him. We also saw uncanny films by surrealist scientist Jean Painlevé and F. Percy Smith's *The Acrobatic Fly* (1910).

As a heritage organization, the Flaherty has always dealt with the tension inherent in its mission: keeping the films, legacy, and name of the Flahertys alive while also supporting independent media makers and showcasing new work. I was always puzzled by the event's maintenance of a reverence for Robert J. Flaherty amid its well-earned reputation for discussions that sharply critique the colonialist roots and practices of the Western documentary tradition.

My first seminar experience certainly included heated exchanges about representations of race, but also playful uses of the iconic Nanook character. What I didn't hear was negative critique of Flaherty films. In 1999, we screened George Amberg's *Louisiana Story Study Film* (1962), two hours of cinematographer Richard Leacock and Frances Flaherty narrating outtakes from the 1948 documentary. Having legendary Ricky Leacock's booming voice at that seminar gave the week a charge. Yet, as in his 1962 narration, he spoke of "Bob" only in hagiographic terms. This was curiously removed from the prevailing critical discourses on documentary film history, even in 1999.

Nearly twenty years later, the Flaherty continues to thrive as a platform for independent work, but the devotion to its namesake has recently waned. The 2017 seminar showed no films by Robert Flaherty, and 2018 brought the official phasing out of the Nanook logo.

A Flaherty seminar conception I find problematic is the devotion to Frances Flaherty's neologism *non-preconception*: open your mind to experience new work with fresh eyes and ears. Yet every person comes to a film with sets of conceptions and experiences. When an audience takes in an unfamiliar screening with no introduction (a seminar tradition), the potential for misconception is ripe. Follow that immediately with a group discussion (before reading the notes distributed after), and misunderstandings can get amplified.

Another tension exists between the non-preconception ideal and the seminar's commissioning programmers to identify a central theme and a title advertising it. Suggesting to an audience that a film is about x (play, scent, sound, work, etc.) sets expectations, which may or may not focus on the strengths of the work shown.

When invited to program the 2011 seminar, I had in mind Geritz's 2000 admixture of a century of shorts. I was able to assemble a wide-ranging variety of films, many relevant to the Flaherty legacy. These included rare archival pieces: Leacock and Flaherty's 1947 color "survey film" of locations shot in preparation for *Louisiana Story* (owned by the Flaherty Study Center but never shown at the seminar); a 1960 Kodachrome film shot during the sixth seminar; and two silent films brought by Paula Félix-Didier from the Museo del Cine in Buenos Aires, both made to capitalize on *Nanook*'s commercial success: *Kivalina of the Ice Lands* (a 1925 fairytale shot in Arctic Alaska with an Inuit cast) and *Entre los Hielos de las Islas Orcadas* (1927, shot on Antarctic islands by an Argentine scientist).

However, feedback from the organization, throughout the selection process, encouraged me to keep a thematic core, which in the end became sound and the title Sonic Truth. In 2014, the executive director convened an informal Flaherty "programmers circle" to brainstorm about future directions. One point of consensus among those who had curated for the series was that a singular theme was an unnecessary limitation on creating an optimal program.

This said, we also agreed that the seminar continues to reward those who attend. Further, the spring and fall Flaherty NYC series allow for more curatorial voices, ever-new cinematic forms, and local audiences unable to attend the traditional seven-day immersion.

When I returned in 2017 after six years away, I found the formula still stimulating, and the desire to stay up all night every night had not subsided. The energy was independent of the film viewings per se. It came from a multisensational social experience that was too pleasurable and liberating to be a cult.

47

THE ART OF ASKING QUESTIONS

Tan Pin Pin

TAN PIN PIN's films question gaps in history, memory, and documentation. Her documentaries include *Singapore GaGa* (2005), *Invisible City* (2007), *To Singapore, With Love* (2013), and *In Time to Come* (2017). Her work has screened at the Berlinale, Busan, Cinéma du Réel, the Flaherty Film Seminar, Hot Docs, SXSW, and Visions du Réel. She has won or been nominated for more than twenty awards. She cofounded filmcommunitysg, a community of independent filmmakers. She is currently a board member of the Singapore International Film Festival, as well as a former board member of The Substation and the National Archives of Singapore. More information is available at http://tanpinpin.com.

Before I left Singapore in the 1990s for graduate school in the United States, my film diet was mainstream, linear, and fictional.

Although we had the excellent Singapore International Film Festival, many kinds of film could not be seen due to our nascent film culture. Though the country was economically prosperous, the arts were looked upon as a hobby. For example, our local universities did not have film, fine art, or music degree programs. I had a burgeoning interest in film and longed to see films I had read about in magazines like *Sight and Sound* that circulated at the British Council Library. Going to "the West"

Figure 47.1.

seemed to offer me the best chance to see these titles and learn the craft of filmmaking.

While in the MFA program at Northwestern University, my course mate Laura Kissel told me about the Flaherty seminar. She had heard about it from her former professor at Ithaca College, Patricia Zimmermann. With the help of grants from International Film Seminars (the nonprofit entity that produces the annual Flaherty seminar) and Northwestern, I was able to attend.

I arrived at the 1999 Flaherty seminar bright-eyed and eager to watch films. The seminar's policy to not announce what was to be screened was perfect for me—I was the perfect blank slate.

I attended two seminars back-to-back: the 1999 edition programmed by Richard Herskowitz and Orlando Bagwell with the title Outtakes Are History and the 2000 edition programmed by Kathy Geritz, Essays, Experiments, and Excavations.

Those two short weeks at the Flaherty showed a young Singaporean filmmaker what was possible. My worldview widened, and the ground softened.

Twenty years later, I vividly remember the programming, the directors, and my awe of their post-screening Q and As. I remember the mental and physical exhaustion that endured for weeks after the seminars ended. I suppose these feelings and memories reflect what the seminar's public relations mean by *the Flaherty experience*.

Many films at the Flaherty influenced my work. In Singapore, I'd wanted to make fiction films. I returned from the United States as a director taking on an essay approach, a style I continue to work in.

The 1999 Duke University edition screened Martin Arnold, Bruce Conner, Arthur Lipsett, and Scott Stark. All worked with found footage. I remember the shock of seeing Martin Arnold's *Alone: Life Wastes Andy Hardy* (1998) for the first time. Unsettled, I thought if such high-order work can be mined from found footage, most film shoots are redundant— a scary idea for someone just starting out.

Documentary giant Ricky Leacock, who shot for Robert Flaherty, D. A. Pennebaker, and Robert Drew, was among the 1999 guests. He stood up and protested the experimental works. Big divides tore through even the margins of film culture at the Flaherty. Leacock may have found more comfort in the epic, humanistic works of Armenian Artavazd Peleshyan (*Seasons*, 1975, and *We*, 1969) and Johan van der Keuken (*Amsterdam Global Village*, 1996).

At the 2000 seminar, I was introduced to Harun Farocki's oeuvre with *Images of the World and the Inscription of War* (1989) and *Workers Leaving the Factory* (1995). His films are intelligent, precise, and painfully ironic. During the seminar, a few of us transformed into Farocki groupies. We hung out together at his presentations. We still keep in touch.

We saw films by Peggy Ahwesh, Santiago Álvarez, Jean Painlevé, and Chris Sullivan. It is a testament to the thoughtful framing of the Flaherty seminar experience that I still remember these very different films. From the agitprop of Alvarez, the liminal works of Ahwesh, and the jittery hand-drawn animation of Sullivan, the films flowed from the makers' personalities and curiosities. One could feel the sustained focus of each director.

At that edition, I decided to skip the discussion with Paper Tiger Television, a public access TV organization that challenges corporate control over the broadcast medium. Back then, I didn't understand the organization's politics. I wondered why their projects were not more polished and why they'd been included in the seminar.

In retrospect, I realize their works were grassroots efforts produced with volunteers who wanted to reclaim the media for themselves. Their productions reflected a democratic perspective: it wasn't about the films as objects as much as it was about access to the mass media. I should have given Paper Tiger a chance, even if I didn't understand the context.

In 2011, programmer Dan Streible invited me to present my films at the Flaherty. I'd met him at the 2000 Flaherty, and I was happy to make contact again. I showed *Moving House* (2001), *Singapore GaGa* (2005), and *Invisible City* (2007), as well as *The Impossibility of Knowing* (2010). These films question and probe the idea of Singapore as a contested terrain.

In a lovely coincidence, Laura Kissel was also a guest, presenting her work from the *Cotton Road* series. This series followed the journey of a commodity—cotton—from South Carolina to China, exposing the global labor behind our cotton clothing.

At this Flaherty, my circumstances were different. I was no longer a graduate student. I'd moved back to Singapore. I now worked in the trenches of independent film. And I could now appreciate the robust DIY ethos of Helen Hill, Jodie Mack, Lillian Schwartz, and Melinda Stone.

My goal was to be as generous a guest as previous guests had been to me.

Across the three seminars I attended, the eloquence of some filmmakers struck me deeply. They avoided being defensive or pretentious. They were knowledgeable. I came to understand their attempts to connect with their own visions and also with the communities they sought to find through their work. I learned so much from them and wanted to find out more. They've made me a more thoughtful and conscientious filmmaker.

At my three Flaherty seminars, I learned the art of asking questions.

Generosity binds all my Flaherty experiences together. The audience listens and watches with open hearts and minds. The guest filmmakers and programmers share ideas and stories. Generosity impels the best questions from the audience.

48

INDELIBLE MARKS

Alyce Myatt

ALYCE MYATT has been Director of Media Arts for the National Endowment for the Arts and founding Executive Director of Grantmakers in Film + Electronic Media. She has served as Program Officer for Media at the John D. and Catherine T. MacArthur Foundation and Director of Children's Programming and later Vice President of Programming at PBS. She has consulted with the Annie E. Casey and Skillman Foundations, Center for Digital Democracy, Council on Foundations, Heinz Endowments, WGBH, WNET, WNYC Radio, Robert W. Deutsch Foundation, and Working Films. She has produced for *3-2-1 Contact!*, ABC's *20/20*, Nickelodeon, and the Smithsonian Institution.

It's rare that I'm "impressed" by art.

I put that word in quotes because I mean impressed in its deepest sense: when something strikes you so hard it leaves an indelible mark.

The Flaherty seminar impressed me, permanently imprinted my very being.

I first heard about the Flaherty as the program officer for media at the John D. and Catherine T. MacArthur Foundation. Various filmmakers we funded asked if I had ever attended. Discovering my cluelessness, they described the seminar with what seemed to me a rather odd reverence.

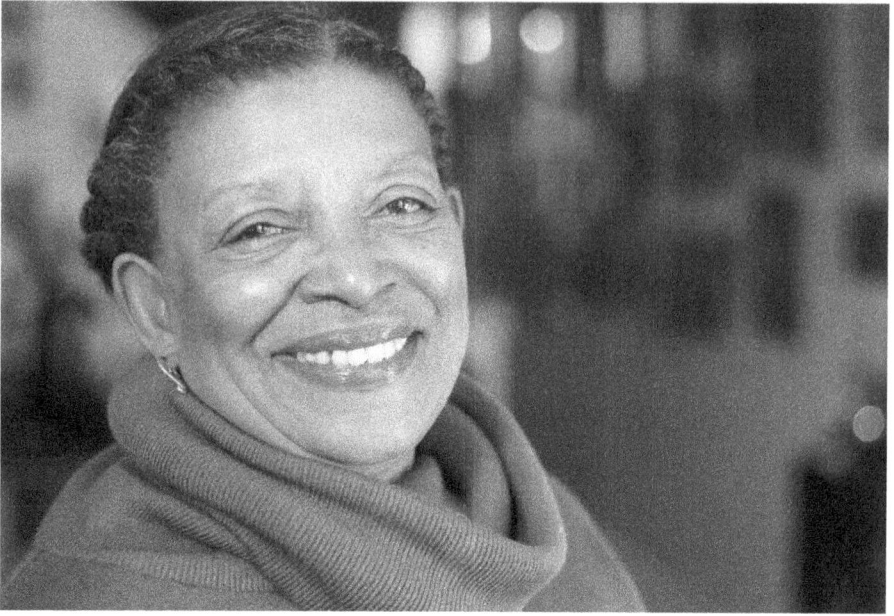

Figure 48.1.

I had a background in television. Although that world includes independent film as a small part of its complex ecology, my knowledge of independent media was limited. I began to ask myself, what *is* this thing called the Flaherty?

I attended my first seminar in 2000. Kathy Geritz from the Pacific Film Archive programmed.

Experiencing film through Geritz's careful curation and experiencing the intensive group discussions affected me in a way that was beyond my imagination at the time. I came away from that seminar with one simple question: What *is* documentary film?

Robert Flaherty's films raise questions. Was he a documentary filmmaker? Was his approach to filmmaking cinéma vérité where the camera records *actual* people and events without directorial control? Is there even such a thing as a *documentary* film?

Kathy programmed *Hidden and Seeking* (1971), where Frances Flaherty explains Robert's challenges in setting up shots. This film screened with multiple takes of the Lumière brothers' *Workers Leaving the Factory* (1895). Then we saw Harun Farocki's meditation on the Lumière films, also called *Workers Leaving the Factory* (1995).

Although staged, these "documentaries" depicted authenticity.

By the time I was invited to join the Flaherty Board of Trustees, I was not only experienced in philanthropy but also felt well-versed in independent film. I believed the seminars and the organization needed reframing to generate greater financial support.

In the early 2000s, funders saw the Flaherty as a very small specialized gathering. The number of seminar attendees was tiny compared to a film festival. Funders were unclear about the social return on an investment in what could be perceived as 150 people attending an elite film camp.

The Flaherty had not yet sold itself as a significant professional development experience for the independent media world, where artistic, global, and intellectual impressions move from the seminar into the field and on to the public.

I knew from experience that the Flaherty changes attendees' ideas, perspectives, and practices. It affects how they think, whether making content or programming, teaching, or distributing it. Horizons open. Perspectives broaden. Transformation reaches innumerable members of the public through the subsequent work of the seminarians.

In 2005, at the fiftieth Flaherty, I'd heard Russian filmmakers describe how seeing Marlon Riggs's *Tongues Untied* (1989) at the 1990 Flaherty seminar held in Riga, Latvia, had changed their perception of African Americans and gay men.

In 2007, at the Full Frame Documentary Festival in Durham, North Carolina, I'd seen films *about* Africa, but not made *by* Africans. That same year, Mahen Bonetti and Carlos Gutiérrez programmed a seminar called South of the Other. Mahen and Carlos brought filmmakers from Africa and Latin America to the Flaherty, a major intervention into the US media arts field.

Generally, film festival discussions center on fundraising, production, distribution deals, publicity. In contrast, the Flaherty is about intense interactions about artistic perspectives, ideas, the deeper meanings and impact of media, philosophical questioning, politics. For me, the Flaherty kept provoking that important question: What *is* documentary?

In an age of reality television, user-generated media, and fake news, truth is ever more pressing. Everything is up for redefinition. Do we need to abandon sacred terms like *documentary*?

A few years ago, I asked a group of filmmakers whether we might use the term *nonfiction film* instead of *documentary*. I came to this idea after a conversation with a stranger who was reading a great nonfiction book I had recently finished, Erik Larson's *In the Garden of Beasts* (2011). This stranger admitted never having thought of attending a documentary festival: that meant nature films, a perception shared by much of the general public.

A confession: I'm not a fan of what's generally referred to as *experimental film* or *avant-garde film*.

In 2004, the year after the United States invaded Iraq, Susan Oxtoby curated a seminar featuring experimental and avant-garde films. While I could respect those films as works of art, to me the programming felt utterly irrelevant in the global context. I soon left the Flaherty board. I no longer felt comfortable asserting that the seminar was always wonderful—as I was asked to do at the time by a few trustees.

Ultimately, I want films that help me to consider the human condition and move the audience to improve it. But although it may seem like a contradiction, I do long for films that explore new forms.

John Gianvito programmed the 2003 seminar. Fifteen years later, the films John showed stay with me; they are still indelible. For example, one of my all-time favorite works, Travis Wilkerson's *An Injury to One* (2003), tells the story of environmental disaster, labor versus corporate interests, and murder in Butte, Montana. It combines music, text-on-screen, an extraordinary cinematic eye, and a unique story structure. The reviews described it, correctly, as *avant-garde*—a useful kind of avant-garde. Although the events in Butte happened over a hundred years ago, they remain politically and environmentally relevant. I would love to see more US nonfiction films tell their stories in such unique artistic ways.

And since the 2016 US presidential election, Raoul Peck's *Profit and Nothing But! Or Impolite Thoughts on the Class Struggle* (2001), a nonfiction (and "avant-garde"?) film from John's seminar, still haunts me.

I keep thinking about a sentence the film repeats: "Okay, Capitalism, you won. Now what?"

49

AN UNRULY ENDEAVOR

Erika Mijlin

ERIKA MIJLIN is a filmmaker, producer, and editor who explores questions of media, power, technology, and the nature of looking at images. She was a founding partner of Artifact Pictures, a production company, and has produced animation, documentaries, interactive work, and short films. Her projects include *Greatest Hits* (2020), an annotated montage of YouTube videos about obsolete technologies, and *Notes on Facts* (2015), an essay film probing the shifting notion of the factual in the twenty-first century. She has taught courses on media culture, information and society, and media production at Bennington College, The New School, and Temple University.

Somehow I just knew about the Flaherty.

I am not sure if this knowledge was through post–grad school osmosis or experimental film community rumblings or some other more mundane way that I can't remember right now.

I first attended as a fellow in 2000. The seminar organization assigned us to create a document of the week in exchange for having been so generously included. The document could take any form as long as it left something behind for the archive. In effect, it was part ethnography and part rite of passage.

I had brought one of those early generation Mini DV cameras with me. Aside from fitting easily in my palm, its best feature was a recording

Figure 49.1.

mode that took a still image as six seconds of video while also recording the accompanying audio.

My plan was to immerse myself in the week by making a little film, six seconds at a time.

Then the screenings started: Peggy Ahwesh, Santiago Álvarez, Shirley Clarke, Harun Farocki, Jill Godmilow, Rea Tajiri.

My plans for a Mini DV mini essay flew out the window.

I tried to keep up. I walked through the days in a delicious fog. Midway through the week, something clicked. An entire beautifully unruly agora emerged, ready-made.

Once initiated, with a bit of attentive observation, one learns the rhythm, the labors of creating and sustaining such a thing, the persistence of its characters, and the depth of its legacy. But no one had warned me about the delirium the Flaherty seminar galvanizes.

Most of what I captured with my little camera was a loose impression of the community in its liminal states. I watched the crowd move together through brief moments of heady, buzzy intermission between sessions.

I wasn't fully able to capture my own small neural explosions. I remember the sense of imminent surprise around each screening, even when confronted with long-familiar works, and the electric, fascinating, meandering, tedious, volcanic, and endlessly quotable film discussions. "Hollywood makes the home movies of transnational capital," declared Patricia Zimmermann in one session, as I tried to write faster in my notes. "Experience and elaborate your wanderlust," advocated one commenter. "Resist the gated community of yourself," proclaimed another. Why hadn't I written down who said that? I might have stuck a hashtag on it and made a fortune on T-shirts.

During the Wednesday morning break, I escaped the seminar's magnetic pull to go on an antique jaunt to Red Hook with Jill Godmilow. I think she drove. We rummaged, lunched, and kibitzed: What is nonfiction for, anyway, if you're not posing a bigger question about the form? That's what Godmilow taught. And then we drove back to Vassar and the seminar.

This anecdote is, in the end, a romance, though I prefer not to mythologize the Flaherty or to drench my experience in rose-colored washes.

Instead, I would rather remember the real lived experience of going through the seminar's intensities and the frequent exhaustion, as well as the surprising ways in which boredom can suddenly become charged with useful readiness. I prefer reliving the elation and subsequent mystery of personal revelations illegibly scribbled down in the dark of the screening room. I prefer to recall the righteous rage about a comment from the person in the third row and the productive pleasure of mentally articulating my response even though I never said it out loud.

I have attended the seminar five times now. This may be enough times to understand how the seminar at its very best vibrates with the current zeitgeist, announces its arrival, or conducts a rigorous postmortem.

I worry that the Flaherty edges too close to operating in a vacuum, a utopian time-out of time, however pleasurable. I would hope that the world outside of this bubble could seep in whenever possible, to charge the curation and the conversation with even greater relevance and urgency.

Images are political, of course, and our politics are replete with the manufacture and deconstruction of images. The seminar and its many intersecting communities are engaged in a constructive, necessary, vital skirmish over the power of the image. Recent attempts to directly foster a more visible presence of people of color and non-Western makers in this ongoing conversation have been one heartening move toward the goal of piercing the bubble.

In a similar vein, the recent social media debate following the announcement of the removal of Nanook from the official logo at the 2018 seminar fascinated me. An online analog to the rangy post-screening sessions at the seminar, the debate was not high-minded and articulate. It was vivid, energized, and ample enough to open up some productive friction.

The questions suggested by the comments I saw posted were profound and more complex than can be summarized here. The conversation pulled at all the philosophical levers essential to filmmaking—the shifting ground of historical context, the power of making images of others, the agency of documentary subjects. In this social media meta argument about the logo representation of the seminar itself, I heard a refrain of Jill Godmilow's challenge from so long ago: What is nonfiction for, anyway, if we aren't continually confronting ourselves with the bigger questions about the nature and shape of the form?

The Flaherty seminar carves out a rough and overgrown territory that requires the attention of many gardeners, not all of whom share the same plan. This is just as well, as uniform purpose and design do not quite suit this weird endeavor.

I remember being pleased with my little video record of my first Flaherty.

Yet I sense that this confoundingly messy and rambunctious gathering is far too complex to be captured six seconds at a time.

50

FAMILIAR AND STRANGE

Vicky Funari

VICKY FUNARI is a documentary filmmaker and editor. Her films include *Alternative Conceptions* (1985), *skin•es•the•si•a* (1994), *Paulina* (1998), *Live Nude Girls UNITE!* (2000), and *Maquilápolis (city of factories)* (2006). They have screened worldwide at Locarno, Rotterdam, Sundance, and Tribeca and broadcast on PBS and the Sundance Channel. She was a Guggenheim Fellow and a MacDowell Colony Fellow. She teaches at Haverford College, where she curated the Strange Truth film series (2009–2017). She produced the collaborative web documentary *Troubled Waters: Tracing Waste in the Delaware River* (2014). She is currently developing a multi-platform project about American rivers.

It was 2000, and I was attending the Flaherty seminar for the first time.

Kathy Geritz of the Pacific Film Archive, the programmer that year, had invited me to present two of my films, *Paulina* (1998) and *Live Nude Girls UNITE!* (2000).

That seminar was a life-changing experience.

I had become a filmmaker because of a compelling need to speak through image, sound, and time. I was always clear on what I was doing with my own films. But I was so busy making them and trying to survive financially that I didn't have time to see as many films as I would have

Figure 50.1.

liked or to fully grasp the breadth of artistic practice in the documentary field.

The seminar introduced me to the work of Sergey Dvortsevoy, Harun Farocki, Geneviève Hamon, Jean Painlevé, Peggy Ahwesh, Chris Sullivan, and Tran T. Kim-Trang. Some of the work took me completely out of my comfort zone. These pieces left me aggravated and perplexed and thrilled. They expanded the way I think and create. And the post-screening discussions exposed me to a wide range of new ideas.

Harun Farocki's work stands out as indispensable. As the world spins further into dystopian realms during the era of Brexit, Putin, Trump, and climate disaster, his rigorous and clear films address the structures and phenomena that have brought us to the present moment. By midweek at the seminar, we had seen his *I Thought I Was Seeing Convicts* (2000),

Workers Leaving the Factory (1995), and *Images of the World and the Inscription of War* (1989). These works were new and strange to me at the time; now, they're familiar and strange.

Kathy programmed the Farocki film *An Image* (1983) with my film *Live Nude Girls UNITE!* (2000). I loved this curatorial choice. *An Image* floored me. It was a work of laser-sharp confidence, image—rather than language—based, and disturbingly, cuttingly funny. Although very different, the two films paired perfectly to open up a discussion about how capitalism commodifies women's bodies.

In *Live Nude Girls UNITE!*, codirector Julia Query and I argue that sex work is indeed *work*, for us a self-evident position, but one that not all people understand or accept. We told the story of a committed union struggle by nude dancers, women rarely taken seriously as laborers or as human beings with agency. The women's powerful, collective voice speaks through the film.

An Image fashions an argument about women's bodies and labor in a very different way. For Farocki, the woman's body is no different to the crew of the photo shoot than the hunks of cheese, watches, or pints of beer arranged for advertising photographs in his later film *Still Life* (1997). In *An Image*, with little dialogue, Farocki shows the labor the nude model engages in as she works to both embody an idealized image of "woman" and to disappear behind that image. Her labor is subsumed within the image-making labor: the studio crew building the set, arranging the lights, dabbing at the model with makeup brushes, and verbally poking her into twisted positions to achieve a sexy image. The nude model has no voice—and those producing the photograph have no interest in giving her one. *An Image* takes a crisp, clean, rigorous look at how consumer images are created.

I thoroughly enjoyed how my film played out in the programming mosaic Kathy had crafted and how the audience responded to the juxtaposition of these very different works.

It amuses me to think back to how little I knew when I found myself sitting on the dais with Harun Farocki for the post-screening discussion. At the time, I was a young whippersnapper of thirty-seven, too ignorant to fully understand who he was. I had been warned that these discussions at the Flaherty could be brutal.

That discussion has stayed with me. Some participants criticized me for creating false closure and constructing a Hollywood narrative in *Live Nude Girls UNITE!*. Some feminists who critiqued my film contended I was a pawn of Hollywood, patriarchy, and capitalism. They praised *An Image* as the antithesis of my film, because it refused closure and refused the comforts of narrative.

Whatever Farocki may have thought of my film, he was generous during the discussion. Later on, as I came to know his work better, it became clear to me that he had been perfectly positioned to give a full-on, scathing, Marxist critique of a younger filmmaker's work but had chosen not to.

These attacks did not offend me, but I thought that their theoretical academic approach seemed disconnected from the realities of working women's lives. I had worked as a cafeteria bus girl, a nude model for art classes, a shrimp runner at a Beefsteak Charlie's all-you-can-eat shrimp-'n'-salad bar, a painter, a waitress, a legal proofreader, a bookkeeper, and a peep show dancer at the Lusty Lady theater. I had also been working my way up through the ranks of the independent film world as a production assistant, assistant producer, assistant director, assistant editor, script supervisor, sound recordist, cameraperson, and finally editor, producer, and director. In 2000, I was beginning my third feature documentary, *Maquilápolis* (2006).

In my efforts to survive through those various jobs and to wrangle work in the film world, I'd missed out on documentary history and academic theory. After the 2000 Flaherty seminar, I knew I needed to work harder to expose myself to a broader range of nonfiction forms and to theory about them.

I continue to shape my working life to engage in this exploration. I now teach film production and theory at Haverford College in Philadelphia. I regularly teach with *An Image, Inextinguishable Fire* (1969) and other Farocki films. I'll never catch up with all I need to know about the documentary world, but I love the process.

In 2014, when I heard that Farocki had died, the first images that flashed in my mind were not from his films. They were memories of him at the Flaherty seminar: first, how generous and gracious he'd been toward me during the discussion of our films, and second, how he'd laughed as he performed an impromptu striptease at the closing party, both familiar and strange.

51

HOW I LEARNED TO STOP WORRYING AND LOVE THE FLAHERTY

Brian L. Frye

BRIAN L. FRYE is the Spears-Gilbert Associate Professor of Law at the University of Kentucky College of Law. His scholarship focuses on intellectual property, charity law, legal history, and art law, among other things. He is also a filmmaker whose films have been shown at the New York Film Festival, the Whitney Biennial, and other venues. In addition, he coproduced (with Penny Lane) the documentary *Our Nixon* (2013), which premiered at SXSW and on CNN.

The Flaherty seminar is a vitally important part of the independent cinema ecology, even if sometimes it seems a little ridiculous.

I first attended the seminar at Vassar College during the summer of 2000, when it was programmed by Kathy Geritz.

At the time, I lived in New York City, working odd jobs at Anthology Film Archives and the Film-Makers' Cooperative and co-programming the weekly Robert Beck Memorial Cinema film series with Bradley Eros.

As my professor at the University of California at Berkeley and as a programmer at the Pacific Film Archive, Geritz introduced me to avant-garde film. I deeply admired her, so I was flattered when she invited me (and my friend Luis Recoder) to attend the Flaherty seminar and show one of my films as part of a midnight screening.

Figure 51.1.

I knew very little about the Flaherty seminar, but when I realized how many filmmakers, programmers, and scholars who had influenced me would also be there, I was excited to attend.

I chose to show a rough collection of film scraps, home movies, and outtakes I called "Arcadia, or an Eclectic History of the American Century." It was inspired by Jack Chambers's *Hart of London* (1970) and a collection of films by John Ryder that I had seen at the Total Mobile Home microcinema in San Francisco.

When I arrived at Vassar, the unusual mix of attendees intrigued me. I knew many from the avant-garde film community, but I'd had limited experience of the documentary and activist film communities that were significant parts of the Flaherty audience.

I soon realized that the participants held many different ideas about the purpose of filmmaking and what makes a film valuable. Those differences led to some fruitful conversations, but also some frustrating ones.

Some participants expanded my own rather blinkered perspectives on filmmaking, programming, and scholarship. At the time, I fetishized film, to the point that I resisted video. I was deeply committed to the idea that art and activism were not compatible. Of course, I was wrong on both counts. The Flaherty seminar helped me understand why.

I also learned that some differences of opinion reflect incompatible normative premises. Some participants rejected films—including mine!—because of fundamental disagreements with the filmmaker's entire project. It taught me that not all differences can be resolved. And that's OK.

I found some aspects of the Flaherty format frustrating.

In particular, I disliked the refusal to announce the film schedule in advance or to provide any information about the films. Although I knew many of the filmmakers, could guess what I might see, and was familiar with some of the films, many other participants did not have this advantage.

In theory, I appreciated the potential value of seeing a film for the first time with an entirely open mind—that is, without preconceptions—a mantra of the Flaherty seminar. However, in practice, I found that participants brought plenty of preconceptions along with them. In fact, watching movies with no context often encouraged attendees to rely on those preconceptions.

Many people find the marathon discussion sessions that follow Flaherty seminar screenings exhilarating.

I confess that I was mostly exasperated.

In retrospect, I can see that the fault was partly my own. Although I found some of the discussions repetitive and unhelpful, other attendees found them just the opposite. Who am I to say they were wrong? People experience and come to understand films in different ways. Perhaps the longevity of the Flaherty seminar suggests that my experiences were in the minority.

I did find the more personal discussions I had with other participants immensely rewarding. I formed friendships with people like Christopher Allen, Steve Holmgren, Alison Kobayashi, Penny Lane, Jason Livingston, Rebekah Rutkoff, and Jim Supanick, who continue to inspire me in different ways for different reasons.

Like so many institutions, the Flaherty seminar consists of both the experiences that it intends to offer and those that participants actually have. I suspect that, all in all, my first Flaherty experience gave me what I needed.

Soon after that first seminar, I decided to go to law school.

After I graduated New York University Law School in 2005, I moved to Olympia, Washington, and then to Fairbanks, Alaska, to clerk for two different judges. Shortly after I returned to New York City in 2007 to begin working at Sullivan & Cromwell LLP, the Flaherty board asked me if I'd be interested in becoming a trustee of the organization.

I accepted. The Flaherty board was the first charitable board I joined after becoming a lawyer.

The board was an excellent fit. It consisted of sophisticated media professionals representing a mature organization with a strong institutional identity, and I could add the perspective of a lawyer.

I was pleased to be able to use the resources of a Wall Street law firm to benefit the Flaherty. I fear that I wasn't always optimally successful the first time out, but I hope that I brought some value to the organization, especially in contributing to a better understanding of the legal duties of trustees.

My Flaherty board experience became the impetus for my service on the boards of other film and art charities. It encouraged my scholarly interest in nonprofit organizations, a subject I now teach at the University of Kentucky College of Law.

I have helped Appalshop, Canyon Cinema, LexArts, Light Industry, National Alliance for Media Arts and Culture (NAMAC), ScreenSlate, Studio7Arts, UnionDocs, and other organizations apply for tax-exempt status, solve institutional problems, and address external crises.

Still a board member in 2008, I returned to the Flaherty seminar when Chi-hui Yang programmed and went back again in 2010, when Dennis Lim programmed.

While I was still conflicted about the format, my objections had mellowed.

I'd come to realize that it can be helpful to experience films in a variety of ways and that sometimes a touch of frustration is OK, maybe even tonic.

I found myself listening more and reflecting on perspectives others offered, whether or not I ultimately agreed. I think this more open way of experiencing the seminar made me a better teacher and a better scholar.

52

REMEMBERING

Ed Halter and Matt Wolf

ED HALTER is Critic in Residence at Bard College in Annandale-on-Hudson, New York, and a founder and director of Light Industry, a venue for film and electronic art in Brooklyn. He edited, with Lauren Cornell, the anthology *Mass Effect: Art and the Internet in the Twenty-First Century* (2015) and his writing has appeared in *4Columns*, *Artforum*, the *Village Voice*, and elsewhere. He curated the 2002 Flaherty Film Seminar and served on the International Film Seminar Board of Trustees. Matt Wolf is a filmmaker living in New York. His films include *Wild Combination: A Portrait of Arthur Russell* (2008), about the avant-garde cellist and disco producer, and *Teenage* (2014), about the birth of youth culture. His short, *Bayard & Me* (2017), is about the civil rights leader Bayard Rustin.

EH: Do you remember when exactly we met at Flaherty? I realize I don't remember. I know it was at the 2001 seminar.

MW: We met the first night. You were with Sam Green, and I introduced myself to you guys, and we started hanging out post-screenings and at night.

EH: Oh, OK! So Sam was there too. Interesting. I didn't remember that. Did you already know Sam?

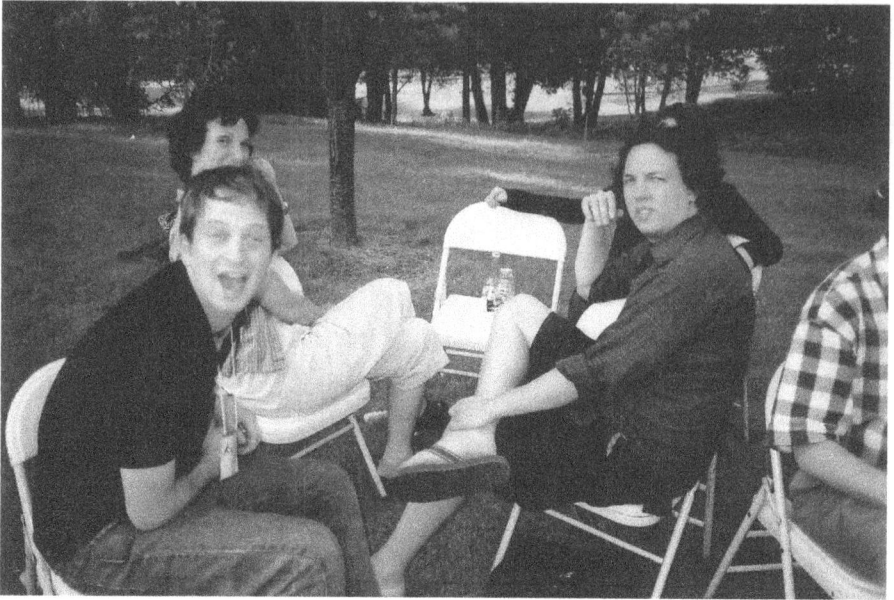

Figure 52.1. © Michael Galinsky.

MW: I didn't know anybody. I was nineteen years old. I'm not even sure how I had heard about the Flaherty seminar. Maybe my professor George Stoney at NYU had said something or through my internship with Sandi DuBowski on *Trembling Before G-D* (2001).

EH: Do you have any special memories of that year? I remember seeing a lot of movies with you.

MW: I remember the first movie we saw. It was about a blind boy, and I believe he was listening to a go-cart race, but I might be remembering it incorrectly. Sight and its relationship to sound were a big theme that year. But of course the theme wasn't sketched out in advance. It gradually revealed itself.

EH: Yes, I think that was called *Herman Slobbe/Blind Kind II* (1966) by Johan van der Keuken?

MW: Yeah, that was it. I was very young, so I had seen very little documentary or avant-garde film work. And when I saw that film, I felt like I had entered a special place where my mind would be cracked open. The other highlights of the seminar related to that theme of seeing.

EH: That's incredible. That film stuck with me as well over the years, and I think they showed an Arne Sucksdorff film about seagulls (*Trut*, "Seahawk," 1944), which also stuck with me.

MW: Derek Jarman's *Blue* (1993), the Heddy Honigmann film about military vets listening to music (*Crazy*, 1999), the blind photographers collective (the Seeing with Photography Collective gave a slide presentation with live narration entitled *Shooting Blind*)—they made me think about what it means to represent something you can't see, which is still something I think about a lot.

EH: Honigmann's work was also revelatory for me. I've loved it ever since and have watched a bootleg I have of *Crazy* many times.

MW: It's incredible to watch people's faces as they listen to a song that was meaningful to them during war, especially faces of veterans who you might expect to be fairly repressed or stoic.

EH: Yes, and especially Dutch soldiers, who are only on supposedly humanitarian missions but still have to live through wars. I'd forgotten about the Blind Photographers Collective. Derek Jarman's *Blue*—I remember I hadn't seen that film since it was brand-new; I went to a preview screening in San Francisco. I remember that seeing the film print so distressed, with scratches and specks from the intervening decade, actually made me cry. I was thinking of friends I had lost.

MW: Yeah, I remember seeing you cry, and that was a consciousness-raising thing for me, for lack of a better word. I've seen *Blue* a number of times as a digital projection, and it's so much less powerful. There's a kind of entropy to the print that seems appropriate.

EH: I've never watched *Blue* in its entirety as a digital copy.

MW: Nowadays museums loop it on video, but it's so flat that way. Remember they did a secret advanced screening of *Hedwig and the Angry Inch* (2001) too?

EH: Oh yes, that's right. That was fun. Emily Hubley's animations are the only thing I remember about that movie now.

MW: Did Emily and Faith Hubley show work that year too? It's funny, when you see so many films, they start to blur together. I can say that every film I saw there was a revelation to me.

EH: I honestly don't recall, but I think you're right. For me the big revelation was more the Flaherty world—that particularly eclectic crowd that Flaherty attracts. It wasn't exactly what I was used to in NYC film culture.

MW: At that time, my film culture was the MIX Experimental Gay and Lesbian film festival or NYU film school. Flaherty was interesting because it was this place where experimental and documentary film intersected, and the discourse there was academic, but not in the basic film-school sense. There were these ethnographic-film anthropologist types, more theory-driven film-studies professors, filmmakers, and students. And those distinctions were really flattened; it was a level playing field for everybody to discuss the films.

EH: Yes, that was super interesting. Also I remember getting a strong sense of the "old days" a lot from members. And by that, they meant the really old days, because people like George Stoney were still around and in attendance.

MW: Yes, he was my professor at the time. It was exciting for me to be in such close proximity to real filmmakers. I gained access to information and ideas that I just wasn't going to encounter at film school, particularly a traditional film school like NYU. And you were a big part of that. I remember a specific conversation we had between screenings.

EH: There was a lot of chatter about the controversies of the past too. Before I went, I recall many people in the Anthology crowd relating the story of George Kuchar getting attacked. They were like, *Those Flaherty people are crazy! Who would attack dear loveable George?*

MW: Well, attacking filmmakers is part of the culture there, and I'm not into that.

I guess people are worn down and tired and lose track of the typical decorum of speaking to a filmmaker in a Q and A setting. There's something weird about people talking about the filmmaker while he or she is sitting there. And some people don't just talk, they wax on and on about the films and the filmmaker in a way that I think is odd. There's a breaking down of boundaries, I guess you could say.

EH: Maybe that's the price of the "anything goes" discourse at the Flaherty. It's not limited in any way, really.

MW: I think good stuff comes out of that, though, and I think because it *is* such a horizontal, open forum, people get an opportunity to speak who ordinarily might not be allowed to respond openly to a film. They're not film critics or professors; they're students like me. And I probably said some stupid shit to a filmmaker.

EH: Oh yes, always there's something really amazing or fascinating. It's also just fascinating to hear everyone's different perspectives and issues and positions.

MW: Yeah, it becomes less about the film and more about the different approaches to looking at films in general. The thing that you told me that was really transformative was that you can't just analyze or interpret a film, you have to analyze it within the context of a particular historical moment. I guess on some level that idea seems basic, but it was radical to me at that time. It's interesting because so much of the present critique of young students is that they look at things ahistorically and problematize them.

EH: That's interesting. I'm not sure I would express that same sentiment in the exact same way today, but I can imagine myself saying that then.

MW: Well, in the context of Derek Jarman's *Blue*, that was really meaningful. You're not just responding to a blue screen right now, you're responding to a blue screen as a spectacle experienced by people dying of AIDS and the people around them, and the scratches on the print are artifacts of the passage of time. That's a way of representing something that can't be seen.

EH: Yes. I think it's about how all films happen in their own time, but they also happen again and again. For me, that 2001 screening of *Blue* was qualitatively different from when I saw it on its release.

MW: Yeah, that's a more nuanced way to put it. I guess what I mean is that I wasn't an adult during the height of the AIDS epidemic, and seeing how you were reacting to that film in the theater helped me understand something that I couldn't see. That was my biggest takeaway from the seminar.

53

A RADICAL OPENNESS

Chi-hui Yang

CHI-HUI YANG is a curator based in New York City. He is Program Officer on the Creativity and Free Expression team at the Ford Foundation. He served on the selection committee for Documentary Fortnight at the Museum of Modern Art (MoMA) from 2011 to 2015. He has presented programs such as The Age of Migration for the Robert Flaherty Film Seminar (2008) and Lines and Nodes: Media, Infrastructure, and Aesthetics for Anthology Film Archives (2014). From 2000 to 2010, he served as Director of the San Francisco International Asian American Film Festival.

I went to my first Flaherty in 2001, the year that Jytte Jensen and Elaine Charnov programmed, at the recommendation of Linda Blackaby. I was running the San Francisco International Asian American Film Festival at the time, and Linda was my mentor. And she was unknowingly bending my life in a new direction.

Linda had programmed a couple times before, including in 1998, when she and Barbara Abrash had brought Hirokazu Kore-eda to the seminar. This impressed and intrigued me, both because I loved his films and because his work didn't fit neatly into a nonfiction context.

In 2001, I went as a fellow and met great folks: Richard Fung, Sam Green, Ed Halter, Heddy Honigmann, so many others. We saw films and

Figure 53.1.

hung out, and looking back, I seem to mix up who was showing films and who was there to watch them.

I didn't know what to expect and remember assiduously trying to research and prepare for the seminar, which in the end didn't help much. During the week, Jytte and Elaine gave out readings, a lot of them—two or three photocopied essays after each screening. I remember staying up late each night and trying to take them in despite being completely exhausted—my continued attempt to figure out what this enterprise *was* and how best to engage it. I didn't say much during the discussions that year; maybe I didn't say anything. The experience was stimulating and intimidating, and by the time I started to understand, it was over. I took home a giant stack of paper and a lot to think about.

Over the past eighteen years, I've gone many more times and have had different relationships with the organization. I've been programmer, board member, board president, funder. And over that time, I've come to understand that what the seminar asks is for one to just be there, to be present and available for what is created. This has to do with non-preconception about the films, but also, and perhaps more importantly, collectively generating something with the 150-plus people around you in the form of social conversation.

The conversations have always been the most generative, memorable, and also inconsistent aspect of the seminar. The films, of course, have their own enormous variability. But the conversations can be totally brain-exploding stimulating or painfully frustrating and are contingent on so many things: the filmmaker, the facilitator, whether the group needs to do a documentary brawl over ethics and representation, what day of the seminar it is, and so on. It's a study in group dynamics and how people share and cocreate.

Ultimately, whether the group is able to work through the tensions shapes a lot of what one takes away. That the makeup of the seminar audience is so heterogeneous is what makes the event so special. But creating a generative conversation across such vastly different ways of thinking is hard to do when you have big-time scholars, totally nontheoretical filmmakers, grad students, experimental artists, public media folks . . . all sitting together.

I programmed the seminar in 2008 and tried out all sorts of things. I figured that creating structures could help this imperfect group exercise. I tried breaking folks into small groups and medium-sized groups; I assigned people to specific lunch tables to break up the cliques and asked folks to contribute to a comment box that would be projected on-screen before the films (this was before Twitter and backfired in a major way due to inadequate editorial oversight; Allan Sekula received the brunt of this).

In the end, I think it all added something but probably was overthought and overdesigned. And there was still an element of the group dynamic that was elusive, which is perhaps just inherent when that many people are involved.

Over the next half-dozen years, as a board member, I helped work with the programmers to build their film programs and plan how to stage the conversations. The programmers tried all sorts of things: having the audience discuss the films in the presence of the filmmakers but not with them; not giving the facilitators an advance look at the films they were guiding a conversation around, to keep things of the moment, and so on. Some of these worked, some didn't.

It wasn't until Kevin Jerome Everson and Greg de Cuir Jr.'s 2018 seminar that I had a light-bulb moment about this puzzle. The bigger question wasn't really about facilitation or how tired people were or even the films. It was about the social contract of the seminar. I think it was midway through the week when film scholar and archivist Terri Francis was facilitating a conversation with Želimir Žilnik, Beatriz Santiago Muñoz, and Karimah Ashadu.

This was a year when so many new folks came to the seminar, especially folks of color who were drawn to what Kevin and Greg had created. This was beautiful but also opened up complex tensions around some of the usual issues about authorship, about the gaze and power—and some of the lines of attack felt like they were pulling the group in circles, instead of toward clarity. In the midst of this, Terri asked the room to step up and do some hard work together to figure out how it wanted to proceed and engage. She asked for collective cocreation and accommodation and reminded us that that seminar could only be as good as the group allowed.

She had named the hardest thing to do and the thing that has been the staying power of the seminar over all these years: generous criticality when the stakes are high and a commitment to building and working through something together. This is how community is created and relationships built. And however imperfect or frustrating the results are, it's something shaped by the folks in the room. This to me is what the essence of the Flaherty is, a radical openness to what is to come and a social process of figuring out complicated ideas together.

54

FLAHERTY REFLECTIONS

Simon Tarr

SIMON TARR is Professor of Art at the University of South Carolina's School of Visual Art and Design. His films have screened in hundreds of international film festivals. He creates live video shows and immersive environments, with performances at Carnegie Hall, La MaMa, and from Tokyo to Cairo. He toured with *Blood Lust of the Wolf* (2015), a live remix of Robert Flaherty's *Nanook of the North* (1922). He is Faculty Principal of the Rhodos Fellows program, a next-generation living learning community in information, design, and computing. His work is available on his website, http://quarknova.com, and can be streamed on Amazon.

Like everyone else in graduate school for film and media, I had heard many stories and rumors about the Flaherty.

The post-screening seminar discussions with filmmakers I idolized, like Ken Jacobs, George Kuchar, and Trinh T. Minh-ha, constituted the stuff of legend. As colleagues in film and media recounted numerous Flaherty intensities and flare-ups to me, I must admit that I assumed that these oral histories had blossomed into exaggerations as they passed from person to person.

However, as I read lively discussion transcripts edited by Scott Mac-Donald in Patricia Zimmermann and Erik Barnouw's epic quadruple

Figure 54.1.

issue of *Wide Angle* (1995), it became clear these stories were *not* exaggerated. The Flaherty loomed larger than life.

Years later, in the autumn of 2001, I started my new faculty job as an assistant professor of cinema production at Ithaca College. I learned about an event happening in November at Rensselaer Polytechnic Institute (RPI) in Troy, New York, only three hours northeast of Ithaca. It was advertised as the Digital Flaherty. I was intrigued.

In that period, attaching the word *digital* to any concept, practice, or event signaled an attempt at transformation. This seminar would adhere to the long-standing Flaherty ethos—an intense, shared engagement with works, makers, and participants. But it would be shorter in duration and focus on work that was, for lack of a better term, *digital*. In this context, *digital* meant artworks existing only within a digital framework (video games, VR, code art), rather than the use of digital tools to facilitate analog workflows such as a digital editor or digital effects.

My anxiety mounted as the seminar approached.

The Digital Flaherty seemed like a great opportunity. The stories I had heard of intellectual *battle royales* invaded in my psyche. I feared that I would be discovered as a fraud—or worse, identified as Just Not That Smart.

I rode to the seminar with Patricia Zimmermann, my colleague in my then-new Department of Cinema and Photography. I was nervous about driving with her. We ended up talking so much about the upcoming event that we hardly ate the salt and vinegar potato chips we acquired for the road.

September 11 was fresh in everyone's memories. It cast a pall over nearly everything in that post-9/11 period. However, the intellectual and artistic electricity of the Digital Flaherty seemed to dissolve all those social and political uncertainties by gathering people together to explore the unknown through conversation.

The imagined combativeness of the seminar was nowhere to be found. We did not just discuss media, we talked tactics with Amy Goodman from *Democracy Now!* and Graham Harwood from the British new media collective Mongrel, which specialized in digitally based projects by artists with low income and marginalized groups. We initiated pranks and were deliberately provocative while playing Eric Zimmerman's *SiS-SYFiGHT 2000* (2000). Afterward, we spent hours discussing and arguing in small groups, trying to figure out why.

My transformative moments came from two guests at that Flaherty: video artist and activist Alex Rivera, who was in a residency at RPI that coincided with the seminar, and VJ and activist Art Jones.

One evening at the seminar, Rivera's class had taken over a large open space in downtown Troy. They transformed it into a chaotic maze of surveillance with huge movable projection surfaces that continually destroyed and rebuilt while impossibly loud drum and bass vibrated the building.

As I navigated the show (Or was it an installation? Or an immersive experience?), trying to establish my bearings, I entered an ad hoc atrium built into the art space. A ring of data projectors aimed at the surrounding temporary white walls, pointing out like spokes on a wheel.

I recognized the projected images from Flaherty's *Louisiana Story* (1948). A bank of computers and projectors distorted and recontextualized the images. At the center of this technological confluence stood Jones, manipulating madly on a couple of laptops like a wizard or a shaman. It took me a few moments to understand that everything I was experiencing was being made and remade live in the moment—the space, the sound, the video, myself, everything.

When I returned to Ithaca, I started experimenting with live VJ performance. I even had the good fortune to perform with Art Jones a few times at special music and projection events mounted in the Roy H. Park School of Communications at Ithaca College: *Within Our Gates Revisited* (2005) and *Tet Vu Lan: Dismantling Empire* (2006).

I ended up mostly leaving experimental analog filmmaking. As an artist, I transitioned almost completely into expanded cinema and live performative media, using computers with mobile and haptic interfaces to create immersive visual experiences in real time in front of audiences.

This new work led to collaborations that I could not have foreseen in my previous artistic life. I designed and performed media for plays at 3LD Art and Technology Center with the Talking Band Theater Company, the American Composers Orchestra, and composer Dan Visconti at Carnegie Hall. I created solo live cinema experiences, such as my touring show, *Blood Lust of the Wolf* (2015). For this show, I take Flaherty's *Nanook of the North* (1922) and remix it into a fugue state about ethnicity, exploitation, and race. While performing the show live, I detect audience reactions, sensing their level of engagement and even their resistance. I modulate my performance to enter into conversation with the audience, provoke them, and generate more substantive dialogue.

Before the Digital Flaherty, I gave only cursory lip service to moving between and across disciplines. Afterward, I realized that connections across different ideas, modes, and technologies galvanize everything I make, think, and do. The spark from a few days in Troy, New York, ignited fundamental changes in my thinking. In some ways, my unusual mid-career-acquired PhD in information science traces back to those explosive cross-disciplinary connections started at the Digital Flaherty.

Revelations are hard to come by. Those artists and thinkers I interacted with at the Digital Flaherty long ago in Troy afforded me a privilege beyond a mere technological awakening. They redirected my artistic practice and opened up a new space of epiphany.

55

FLAHERTY REPLACES CANNES

Lucius Barre

LUCIUS BARRE promotes worldwide distribution of films from many cultures. He was the first international crossover publicist for Pedro Almodóvar (*Women on the Verge of a Nervous Breakdown*, 1988), Luc and Jean-Pierre Dardenne (*La Promesse*, 1996), Tom Tykwer (*Run Lola Run*, 1998), and Shinji Aoyama (*Eureka*, 2000). He has promoted work by such well-established filmmakers as Errol Morris (Hiroshi Teshigahara (*Rikyu*, 1989), *A Brief History of Time*, 1991), Johnnie To (*Election*, 2005), Carlos Saura (*Fados*, 2007), and Alain Resnais (*Wild Grass*, 2009). His industry career began with an eight-year term as English-language press officer at Cannes. He currently serves on the organizing teams of the Locarno, Rotterdam, and Torino film festivals.

As marketing consultant for Zacharias Kunuk's *Atanarjuat: The Fast Runner* (2001), I attended my first Flaherty in 2001. Elaine Charnov and Sally Berger, both New York–based film and media curators, co-programmed that seminar held at C.W. Post.

The production team considered both women family friends, as Elaine had programmed Igloolik Isuma films at the Margaret Mead Festival, and Sally, an early friend and champion, had even visited Igloolik, Canada, which lies about as far north of New York as Las Vegas is west, so accepting the invitation to the Flaherty felt like coming home.

Figure 55.1. Photograph by Sandro Baebler.

Igloolik Isuma Productions was Canada's first independent Inuit production company, founded in 1990 by Zacharias Kunuk, Paul Apak
Angilirq, Pauloosie Qulitalik, and Norman Cohn. Producer and cinematographer Norman Cohn represented the film. Zach and the others were
unable to attend.

At its Cannes Film Festival premiere in May 2001, the film won the
Camera d'Or for best first feature. Although it had been programmed in
prime position on opening Saturday night, that placement turned out to
be a liability. A daylong press junket and big party outside Cannes for
Peter Jackson's *Lord of the Rings: The Fellowship of the Ring* (2001)
spirited all key press and a number of interested distributors away from
both morning and evening screenings.

This perfect storm left us high and dry. As the first Inuktitut-language
film ever to appear at Cannes, *Atanarjuat: The Fast Runner* remained

the subject of considerable anticipation, but we came away with limited press and industry word-of-mouth.

Although winning the prize was a great boost to our spirits, the festival was over by then, and everyone we wanted to talk to had gone home.

Over the years, the pace of industry life at Cannes had become so frenetic that business meetings were compressed to thirty minutes. It normally had taken buyers and sellers a month or more to unpack and follow up on all the threads of conversation that had been unspooled at the festival. Then we'd all break for the summer. After Cannes these days, it's rare that anyone in the film business has the time or inclination to undertake new business until the Toronto International Film Festival in September.

By the end of Cannes, we had agreed to one sale, to the Netherlands. Seven Paris-based distributors expressed interest in borrowing the print. I spent the following week there trying to identify three viable candidates for the producers to consider. Our aim was to partner with a distributor who could treat the film as a major cultural monument and position it as an entertaining experience.

Igloolik Isuma Productions made *Atanarjuat: The Fast Runner* to tell a story from their land mainly so that they could see people who looked like themselves on television. In the late 1970s, the Canadian Broadcasting Corporation frontier coverage package to the north consisted of pretaped programs and classic series programs like *Bonanza* and *The Man from U.N.C.L.E.* Until the 1981 formation of the Inuit Broadcasting Corporation (IBC), no northern content was included. IBC produced programming for children and teenagers, cooking shows, call-in shows, and mini documentaries about inspiring people of the region. No feature films had been undertaken.

One of my favorite selling points about *Atanarjuat: The Fast Runner* was that the story had been in development for approximately four thousand years. It is set in Igloolik a thousand years ago. The script-writing team began by reviewing the legend recounted by seven elders, whose approval was sought before the work was finalized.

Our first strategy in putting the film on the market was to affirm its authenticity. The *New York Times* later gave kudos to the scriptwriters, who'd given the characters and situations great depth of feeling. This was neither true nor accurate. The filmmakers sought only to depict the inherent feelings that gave the legend its power.

By rendering an authentic reading of the legend, we were unclear on just how much fun it would be for audiences to engage with it. So the Flaherty seminar served as our first test audience and focus group.

Seminar participants recognized that the film combined the monumental broad strokes of a Homerian return legend with the insouciance of a high school rival comedy. In the rush of Cannes and the private screening rooms where the film had been screened, no such close reading had emerged.

No matter what producers and promoters might say about a new film, the best way a film can validate its place in the market is to be road tested with audiences. The last grace note on our Flaherty experience was that Jeff Lipsky and two colleagues from the US independent distributor Lot 47 came out from New York to see the picture. Before they left the seminar, we opened talks about Lot 47 taking on US distribution. By validating the social value of the experience and putting the film on track for sale, the seminar provided results that we had initially expected to achieve at Cannes.

One last note about family.

After I first viewed *Atanarjuat: The Fast Runner* in March and joined the team, I sent the cassettes to experimental animator Faith Hubley, who was preparing her fall semester Picture Writing course at Yale University. Of all things, the course was to focus on the subject of Inuit storytelling.

Three months later, Faith, who had also been invited to present her work at the seminar, set out from New York with Norman Cohn at the wheel, me as navigator, and the print of *Atanarjuat: The Fast Runner* in the trunk. The conversation turned to the early days of children's television. Faith and Norman compared notes about the ways each faced the challenge of delivering consistently good work through the years. It seems their success and happiness were rooted in an unwavering commitment to do good work. They recognized that by simply putting their noses to the grindstone and working diligently, everything else in their careers would fall into place. They had never met before, but it was clear that Faith and Norman had always been birds of a feather.

Through that first and during subsequent seminars, the Faith-Norman paradigm seemed to pop up everywhere. The Flaherty method of putting laser-sharp focus on craftsmanship prompted participants to recognize kindred spirits who entered the discourse by first and foremost celebrating good work for its own sake.

And a good time was had by all.

56

FILM VS. TV: FLAHERTY & INPUT

Howard Weinberg

HOWARD WEINBERG is a documentary director and producer. His documentaries have won Emmy, DuPont, and other awards, have been translated into foreign languages for festivals, and are preserved in the moving image collection of the Library of Congress. His television magazine work has been shown on CBS *Sunday Morning* and *60 Minutes*. His *Nam June Paik & TV Lab: License to Create* was completed in 2014.

When I was at Columbia Journalism School, Willard Van Dyke, then curator of film at MoMA, told me to stay connected to the independent film community by joining the New York Film/Video Council—I was headed toward a career in television. Why hadn't he suggested that I attend the Flaherty Film Seminars? I don't know, but he was involved with both.

So were others I came to know, like Bill Sloan (Bill's Bar is still a Flaherty mainstay) and George Stoney, whose *All My Babies* (1953) had been shown at the first Flaherty seminar.

I'd seen *All My Babies* in a documentary course that George had taught before he went to Canada, then came back to become a legendary professor at NYU. Both Bill and George were past presidents of the New York Film/Video Council, of which I was a board member for seventeen years and president for eight.

Figure 56.1.

The NYFVC was a nonprofit that had been serving the independent media community since 1946. It programmed all forms of visual media. I never thought of TV and film as separate pursuits, but many did. Other distinctions abounded: narrative vs. documentary; film vs. video; and one that always disturbed me, journalism vs. documentary. Often at Flaherty, I heard filmmakers say, "I'm not a journalist."

The first informal continuing professional education I experienced before Flaherty was at INPUT, the International Public Television Producers Conference, in 1992 in Baltimore when I was executive producer of *Listening to America with Bill Moyers* (1992, twenty-six-part TV series) on PBS. I would go on to other INPUTS in Aarhus, Barcelona, Fort Worth, Halifax, Lugano, Rotterdam, and San Francisco.

Law, medicine, and many other professions have continuing education requirements; journalism and documentary filmmaking have none, though within each area, nonprofit organizations like the Flaherty informally make continuing education possible.

For me, the Flaherty seminar has been a condensed form of graduate school with a diverse group of students who share similar interests. Lifelong friendships are formed.

In 2003, the year I went to INPUT in Aarhus, Denmark, I attended my first Flaherty seminar at Vassar College. It was curated brilliantly by John Gianvito. Lucy Kostelanetz, a neighbor and member of the NYFVC and the Flaherty board, had recommended that I go because the topic was Witnessing the World.

Two films by Canadian filmmakers fascinated me: *Zyklon Portrait* (1999) by Elida Schogt and *Seeing Is Believing: Handicams, Human Rights, and the News* (2002) by Peter Wintonick and Katerina Cizek.

Avi Mograbi's Israeli films were incisive and humorous, especially *Happy Birthday, Mr. Mograbi* (1998). The entire audience at Vassar seemed appalled by Holly Fisher's *Kalama Sutta* (2002) because she'd made an experimental, artistic film in Burma—a place and subject that cried out for documentary reporting. I'd never before seen an audience erupt in such disapproval.

Trần Văn Thủy's Vietnam documentaries were a special gift. The British filmmaker Franny Armstrong showed *McLibel: Two Worlds Collide* (1998); it was critical of McDonald's before Morgan Spurlock's *Super Size Me* (2004).

Franny also showed an impressive film she'd made in India, *Drowned Out* (2002). I recommended it to Thirteen/WNET'S new international series *Wide Angle*, which commissioned her to make a shorter, more journalistic version for broadcast. Marlo Poras's *Mai's America* (2002) stayed with me, and I screened it for documentary students years later at Columbia.

It was at my first Flaherty that Marcia Rock, who runs the NYU documentary program, asked me if I'd like to teach a course called Documentary History and Strategy. For the next three spring semesters, I taught at NYU, and then, after raising enough money to complete production on my work in progress, *Nam June Paik & TV Lab: License to Create,* I co-taught and mentored students at Columbia Journalism School. A student filmmaker I met at Flaherty, Alana Kakoyiannis, shot second camera when I interviewed Paik's widow, Shigeko Kubota, a video artist in her own right.

In 2007, I saw two versions of Natalia Almada's *Al Otro Lado* (*To the Other Side*) (2005), one at INPUT in Lugano, the other at the fifty-third Flaherty seminar, South of the Other, at Vassar. Almada's film focuses on drug trafficking and illegal migration between Mexico and the United States and highlights *narcocorrido* music.

My last seminar was in 2011: Sonic Truth, curated by Dan Streible, of Orphan Film Symposium fame. George Stoney showed *A Reunion of All My Babies* (2010), and we saw the 1906 film *A Trip Down Market Street Before the Fire*. Most powerful for me was Tan Pin Pin's *Singapore Gaga* (2010). I've followed her films since.

Caroline Martel's *Wavemakers* (2012) was an intriguing work in progress, and I later went to the Museum of the Moving Image to see a completed version.

Sam Pollard showed some of his work with Spike Lee, and I was introduced to the animated films of Jodie Mack, whom I later ran into on Main Street in Hanover, New Hampshire, during a fall mini-reunion at Dartmouth.

I met Lillian Schwartz and learned that she had worked at the TV LAB at Thirteen/WNET, the subject of my nearly finished documentary. Dan showed her earlier experimental work at Bell Labs.

For me, the highlight of Sonic Truth was my friend Jane Weiner, who came from Paris to show her documentary *On Being There with Richard Leacock* (2010). I later drove her to interview Robert Drew in Sharon, Connecticut.

When organized well, there's no better introduction to remarkable films and significant filmmakers than the Flaherty seminar.

57

I REMEMBER BEING PROFOUNDLY MOVED AND INSPIRED

John Gianvito

JOHN GIANVITO is a filmmaker, curator, and critic. He is Professor in the Department of Visual & Media Arts at Emerson College. His films include *The Flower of Pain* (1983), *Address Unknown* (1985), *The Mad Songs of Fernanda Hussein* (2001), *Profit Motive and the Whispering Wind* (2007), *Wake (Subic),* (2015), and the collectively made *Far from Afghanistan* (2012). Retrospectives of his films have been held at the Viennale International Film Festival Vienna, the I Mille Occhi Festival (Trieste, Italy), and the Cinéma du Réel Festival (Paris, France). He is editor of the book *Andrei Tarkovsky: Interviews* (2006). He also served for five years as Curator of the Harvard Film Archive.

When I think back on the experience of programming the 2003 Flaherty Film Seminar, now fourteen years later, many memories surface.

I'd found myself unexpectedly unemployed in the year leading up to the seminar.

My efforts to research and review what had to have been literally hundreds of films in the lead-up to the program consumed me.

I recall the regular spirited conversations and stalwart support I received from Flaherty Executive Director Margarita De La Vega Hurtado and her assistant, Brian Coffey.

Figure 57.1.

I recall countless email exchanges with curatorial colleagues around the country.

I recall the challenges of securing travel commitments from filmmakers whose production schedules were tentative at best.

As the program began to take shape, I remember actually sleeping with the schedule blueprint alongside me. I often awoke to jot down new ways to best orchestrate the sequencing.

I also remember the setbacks.

There was the filmmaker whose film I had hoped to showcase on opening night but who informed me two months before the seminar that he was likely going to be in Afghanistan working on a new film. He was unable to secure manageable transportation back and forth to the United States for that week. So there was a push to quickly identify an equally strong and appropriate opening night film.

Hours after arriving at Vassar College, the site of the 2003 seminar, I learned that one of my guests, Travis Wilkerson, was unable to attend.

And the board had decided to reduce the length of the seminar by one full day. I'd been informed of this late in the process. The reduced length led to some memorable, though hardly ideal, late-night Flaherty screenings. But for many seminarians, the midnight screening of Glauber

Rocha's two-and-a-half-hour hallucinatory final masterwork, *The Age of the Earth* (1980), was intensified by the lateness of the hour.

I harbor many behind-the-scenes stories about the preliminaries leading up to that Flaherty, but for me, recollections of the ideas and the camaraderie exchanged throughout that special week are far more consequential.

From Argentina, Brazil, Canada, Israel, Japan, the Philippines, the United States, the United Kingdom, and Vietnam, that week's guests possessed a core commitment to confronting social and political injustice across many arenas and in many forms.

Some had produced a lifetime's body of work. Some had only made one or two films. Despite our differences in age, culture, experience, and language. I suspect many of us felt that we were among our tribe. None of us needed to be convinced that mighty problems everywhere needed to be faced. Our concern was how to face these problems with our cameras.

One central thread of discussion focused on the eternal debate over the role that form and aesthetics play in engendering political efficacy.

During one discussion, I remember a remark by filmmaker Franny Armstrong, whose workmanlike journalistic approach to documentary stood far afield from the overtly impressionistic approach of Holly Fisher, or the DIY, in-your-face aesthetics of Matt McDaniel, or the hallucinatory epic didactic poetics of Glauber Rocha.

Franny contended that it doesn't matter what happens during a film, it only matters what happens once it's over. Armstrong claimed that results, not reviews, count. Her own first film, *McLibel: Two Worlds Collide* (1998), seen by an estimated twenty-five million viewers on television and the internet, contributed to the global crusade against McDonalds' business practices.

I remember being profoundly moved and inspired by the sheer courage and tenacity of the filmmakers.

Raymundo Gleyzer and Joey Lozano openly risked their lives to make their work.

Despite experiencing the personal hardships caused by his previous film, *Hanoi in One's Eyes* (1982), which the Vietnamese government had banned for five years, Trần Văn Thủy persevered to produce *The Story of Kindness* (1985) an essay film propelled into being by a dying friend's request that he make a film on the subject of *tu-te*, a Vietnamese term that roughly translates as human relations, fraternity, or simply kindness. Thủy recounted how his own family turned against his making *The Story of Kindness*. Thủy's wife claimed that he was possessed by spirits! Again, Thủy found his film banned, but following the personal intervention of

Communist Party leader Nguyen van Linh, his film was not only released but rapidly became a popular and influential work.

The practice and person of Noriaki Tsuchimoto occupied the heart of the week's dialogue. At seventy-four years of age, Tsuchimoto wrote to me in advance that while genuinely honored and excited about the prospect of attending the Flaherty, he was concerned that complications from diabetes might slow his participation and his ability to sit through the weeklong program. I assured Tsuchimoto that he and his wife and collaborator, Motoko, need only attend their own programs.

Once the seminar was underway, it was clear that Tsuchimoto was drawn in by the experience. He attended every program.

Widely regarded as one of the preeminent documentarians of Japanese cinema, Tsuchimoto is most renowned for a series of eighteen-plus documentary films made over a thirty-five-year period on the impacts of toxic poisoning on residents of the fishing community of Minamata.

Among the earlier and later works of Tsuchimoto that were screened, the highlights were *Minamata—The Victims and Their World* (1971) and *Shiranui Sea* (1975).

Tsuchimoto offered deep lessons about what being a committed filmmaker means.

He discussed his ongoing autocriticism in the pursuit of pushing his work further.

Tsuchimoto described how, before home video or digital downloads, he circumvented the traditional avenues of art house and television exhibition by traveling widely in Japan and elsewhere, screening his films in nontraditional venues, often in community centers in small villages. Periodically, he would stop the films and discuss them with audiences, much as Argentinians Octavio Getino and Fernando Solanas did with their *Hour of the Furnaces* (1968).

Tsuchimoto explained how much he had learned from the spiritual values of the Minamata victims, and he shared the difficulties and challenges of depicting their story. He gave the seminarians the powerful maxim *Remembrance is Strength*, which he contended is the fundamental belief of the documentary filmmaker.

The ongoing sustenance I draw from that single week in June of 2003 continues, I suspect, to prove Tsuchimoto's point.

58

FIVE REFLECTIONS IN SEARCH OF THE FLAHERTY'S ZEITGEIST

Ilisa Barbash

ILISA BARBASH is Peabody Museum Curator of Visual Anthropology at Harvard University, where she writes, makes films, and curates photographic exhibitions. She directed/produced *In and Out of Africa* (1992) and *Sweetgrass* (2009) with Lucien Castaing-Taylor. She cowrote with Castaing-Taylor *Cross-Cultural Filmmaking: A Handbook for Making Documentary and Ethnographic Films and Video* (1997) and *The Cinema of Robert Gardner* (2007). Her book, *Where the Roads All End: Photography and Anthropology in the Kalahari* (2016), was awarded the 2017 Society for Visual Anthropology prize for best book about anthropology and photography.

Since 2003, I have attended eleven Flaherty seminars!

I have moderated my share of discussions. I was a featured filmmaker in 2009. I served as a board member from 2006 to 2008. At this point, I see the seminar as a well-oiled machine with a schedule we can count on.

Yet each seminar has been profoundly different. How to sum that up in five points? I keep coming back to the films and the five ideas that return to me year after year as key constituents of the Flaherty's unique *zeitgeist*.

Figure 58.1. Photograph by Michael Spieldenner.

Surprise

What is cinema? What constitutes a cinematic experience? I have seen the gamut at the Flaherty, from essay films, expository films, experimental, nonfiction, fiction, and musicals to installations, video games, and a Benshi performance. And each Flaherty shows work that expands my notions of cinema in wonderfully surprising ways.

Craft

Years before the GoPro and drone cameras, Leonard Retel Helmrich filmed a man walking over a narrow railroad trestle a thousand feet above an Indonesian Valley in *Stand van de Maan* (*Shape of the Moon*, 2004). The view was from above via a homemade bamboo pole mount, and it was terrifying. Helmrich filmed other scenes in the film with his own invention called *Steadiwings*. He calls his filmmaking process "one-shot cinema," because he edits more for camera movement than framing or photography.

Another example of craft at the seminar was Laura Poitras's *Risk* (2017). Through her camerawork looking up at Julian Assange, she shows the egotistical anarchist to be as self-conscious as a *People Magazine* star, even as he functions as an important historical figure in our time.

Community

I have started wonderful and enduring friendships at the Flaherty. I met longtime heroes and heroines—Scott MacDonald and Trinh T. Minh-ha—and found them incredibly down-to-earth.

Beyond these moments of connecting with people you admire, there are also those more awkward moments reminiscent of junior high school, when you emerge from the cafeteria food line with your tray, scouring the dining room for a seat. My most wonderful meals have been those when I've plunked myself down with people I've not met before: critics, established filmmakers, students.

At the 2012 Open Wounds seminar, curated by Josetxo Cerdán, I remember a great meal with Susana de Sousa Dias from Portugal and Laila Pakalniņa from Latvia. Their work had not shown yet, so I'd had no idea they were featured filmmakers. We talked about traveling, family, and the films screened at the seminar.

Later, I was completely blown away by de Sousa Dias's beautiful and horrific *48* (2010), featuring an incredibly adept use of archival mug shots woven with interviews with ordinary citizens arrested under the forty-eight-year dictatorship of António de Oliveira Salazar in Portugal.

I was mesmerized by Pakalniņa's gorgeous cinematography, measured pace, and dry humor portraying men and nature—especially riparian birds—in *Three Men and a Fish Pond* (2008). I also loved fellow seminar attendee and filmmaker Robb Todd's jilting imitation of the film-star birds during the discussion.

Pleasure

I confess that at times the quantity of images and ideas truly overwhelms. I feel the need to remind myself what I love about film. Of course, it is the ideas, but it is also the sheer pleasure I get from seeing truly beautiful images that transport me out of the room and under water in the Caribbean Sea in *Alamar* (2009) by Mexican Pedro González-Rubio and into the air in Argentine Teddy Williams's *The Human Surge* (2016) in 2017.

Humor

I loved the crazy, playful, imaginative Rube Goldberg creations of Israeli artist/filmmaker Mika Rottenberg in *Squeeze* (2010), as well as in *Cheese* (2007), where seven ethnically diverse sisters/maidens prattle and poke about an enormous wooden contraption, part farmhouse, part animal barn, part milking machine, part cheese churn, making cheese, yes, but also washing, combing, and styling each other's impossibly long, Rapunzel-like hair. The experience was mesmerizing and hilarious.

Even the most wrenching of Flaherty seminars have moments of intense humor. In the midst of films about the tragedies of Minamata disease caused by environmentally induced mercury poisoning, revealed by the Japanese documentarian Tsuchimoto Noriaki at the 2003 Flaherty, we saw Israeli Avi Mograbi's hilarious and ominous films, *Happy Birthday, Mr. Mograbi* (1999), *August: A Moment Before the Eruption* (2002), and *Wait It's the Soldiers, I'll Hang Up Now* (2003), which provided scathing views of the Israeli-Palestinian conflict. When programmed together, they traced people's reactions to Mograbi's camera and the mounting distrust in the streets, leading into the Second Intifada.

Outrage

Ah, the moments of outrage.

I have been guilty of sharing in some of the politically correct indignation over who gets to represent whom and how. And I have also been mildly piqued at the tremendous amount of time we devote to such debates, seminar after seminar. One memorable debate happened at my first seminar, Witnessing the World, curated by John Gianvito in 2003. In the post-screening discussion of Holly Fisher's faux travelogue about Myanmar, *Kalama Sutta: Seeing Is Believing* (2001), participants questioned Fisher's right to represent the Burmese. At the seminar in the summer of 2017, the debate was over Dominic Gagnon's depiction of Inuit people in *of the North* (2015). But the issues were different: if Inuit post images of themselves on the web that some feel reinforce negative stereotypes, what responsibility does a filmmaker bear if he uses them?

Of course, if we don't keep asking ourselves those difficult questions, if we don't demand that filmmakers create their work with a sense of purpose and responsibility, then there isn't much to talk about. It's why I go to the Flaherty—to see those noncommercial films I cannot see elsewhere and to talk about them with people whose varied perspectives provoke, enlighten, delight, and yes, sometimes outrage me!

59

"WITNESSING" AND WITNESSING AT THE FLAHERTY

Sam Gregory

SAM GREGORY builds the skills, tools, and collaborations to help everyone be a witness for human rights and to use the power of the moving image and participatory technologies for change. An award-winning human rights advocate, video producer, and technologist, he is Program Director of WITNESS (http://www.witness .org), the leading organization supporting anyone, anywhere to use video for human rights. He also teaches at Harvard's Kennedy School. Sam has worked on campaigns worldwide and on prize-winning tools like ObscuraCam and CameraV. In 2012, he cofounded the Video4Change network of organizations using video for human rights and social justice.

My recollections of the Flaherty are closely tied to one courageous friend and witness and to one revolution witnessed through social media.

I first came to the Flaherty in 2003 as a guest for the Witnessing the World seminar, programmed by John Gianvito. My dear friend and comrade-in-arms, Joey Lozano, attended in conjunction with the screening of Peter Wintonick and Kat Cizek's *Seeing Is Believing: Handicams, Human Rights, And The News* (2002), a prescient feature documenting the impact of video on the world.

Seeing Is Believing surveyed the use of video for human rights. It featured the organization I work for, WITNESS, which focuses on how

Figure 59.1.

to enable anyone anywhere to use video technology to advance human rights, and works closely with citizens and human rights movements around the world. One of the film's central characters is Joey Lozano, a pint-size activist who with zest and tremendous moral and physical courage documented the resistance of indigenous rights activists on his home island of Mindanao in the Philippines.

In *Seeing is Believing*, Kat and Peter's exploration of the question of who gets to tell the story of witnessed reality ranged from the members of Nakamata, an indigenous land rights movement that Joey taught to film for themselves, to anti-extremist activists in Europe and people fighting human trafficking.

Because I attended only that one session of the 2003 seminar, my memories are tied up with the emotion of seeing my dear friend Joey and celebrating him on the big screen. The subsequent loss of both Joey and Peter to early deaths from illness tinges that memory, particularly poignant for me since I believe this screening was the only time we were ever all together in the same place.

My next opportunity to come to the seminar was June 20–26, 2009, for Witnesses, Monuments, Ruins, programmed by Irina Leimbacher (hmm, I spot a magnet-like attraction to *witness* in Flaherty seminar titles). It was during this seminar that I witnessed a revolution on social media.

Some of my memories of the 2009 seminar are the classic Flaherty kind: kindred spirits meeting across a lunch table or after a discussion, amazing audiovisual experiences watched without regard for the time and in blissful ignorance of what would come next. I recall some manic dancing late at night to Michael Jackson music following the news of his death on June 25 during the seminar.

As someone who lives and works in the constant crisis mode of global activism and often watches videos as evidentiary material, sometimes on double-speed, the experience of the seminar's screenings and gatherings embodied a refreshing change of pace.

The films that most powerfully spoke to me were the works of Syrian filmmaker Omar Amiralay, as well as Lisa Barbash and Lucien Castaing-Taylor's *Sweetgrass* (2009) and Amar Kanwar's multichannel video installation, *The Lightning Testimonies* (2007). I had recently returned from Syria, which at that time was caught in the artificial passivity of an ossified authoritarian state whose prehistory Omar caught in his courageous, subtle films. Omar's *Film-Essay on the Euphrates Dam* (1970) and *The Chickens* (1977) spoke simply, directly, and powerfully to human rights issues.

Sweetgrass offered an amazing sensory experience quite different from my usual filmmaking tastes. Together with Sensory Ethnography Lab films I was to see later, this film set my mind thinking about what immersive experience could mean in a film and how one can really feel an alternate reality.

Shortly after the seminar, I began exploring how storytelling arcs of immersive livestreaming and virtual reality experiences can capture both the mundane moments and the crisis moments in frontline activism. This can help engage viewers to move from being passive spectators to immersed, engaged witnesses. This process has now evolved into a livestreaming-and-action project at WITNESS, called Mobil-Eyes Us.

However, frustration also infuses my memories of the 2009 seminar.

I was powerfully aware that a new form of witnessing was being enacted in Iran at the very moment we were enjoying the seminar. The events known as the Green Movement were entering their second week of massive global attention.

This political struggle mobilized images on social media to engage Iranian and global publics. On the first day of the seminar, Neda Agha-Soltan, a student protesting the Iranian election, was murdered on the streets of Tehran. Her death, captured horribly yet cinematically on camera, was then shared on YouTube for so many to see.

Nevertheless, the structure of the seminar, which insisted on privileging the program that had been curated, seemed to exclude this on-the-ground, amateur-produced witnessing. I remember a powerful sense that we seminarians were staying *inside* our box, *talking about* witnessing, while the world *outside* the seminar was changing and being witnessed in real time.

Of course, after eight years of continued work with movements and activists using digital media to witness so many variants of opportunity, failure, frustration, and success, the revelatory sense of that particular moment has dulled for me.

But I still remember that those of us engaged in human rights media practices occupied a moment of discovery in 2009. Yet, paradoxically, in the midst of a Flaherty seminar exploring the act of witnessing, we chose *not* to witness in real time.

I'm waiting for my next Flaherty. Surely, now is the time for a curator to include witnessing not only within another seminar title, but in real time as part of the seminar.

60

I DRANK THE KOOL-AID

Carlos A. Gutiérrez

CARLOS A. GUTIÉRREZ is Cofounder and Executive Director of Cinema Tropical, the New York–based nonprofit organization that has become the leading presenter of Latin American cinema in the United States. As a guest curator, he has presented several film/video series at different cultural institutions, including MoMA, the New York Guggenheim Museum, BAMcinématek, and the Film Society of Lincoln Center. He is a contributing editor to *BOMB* magazine. He has served as a member of the jury and panelist for various international film festivals and funds, including the Morelia International Film Festival (Mexico), Seattle International Film Festival, Santiago International Film Festival (Chile), DocsMX (Festival de Cine documental de la Ciudad de México), the Sundance Documentary Fund, and the Tribeca Film Institute's Latin American Media Arts Fund.

Based on my very first experience attending the Flaherty Film Seminar in the summer of 2003, I never would have thought I'd become part of the Flaherty family.

My first experience at the seminar, which probably was not that different from many other people's, was overall frustrating and discouraging, even though I saw some amazing work and met some great people, including filmmakers Ernesto Ardito, Virna Molina, and Eryk Rocha.

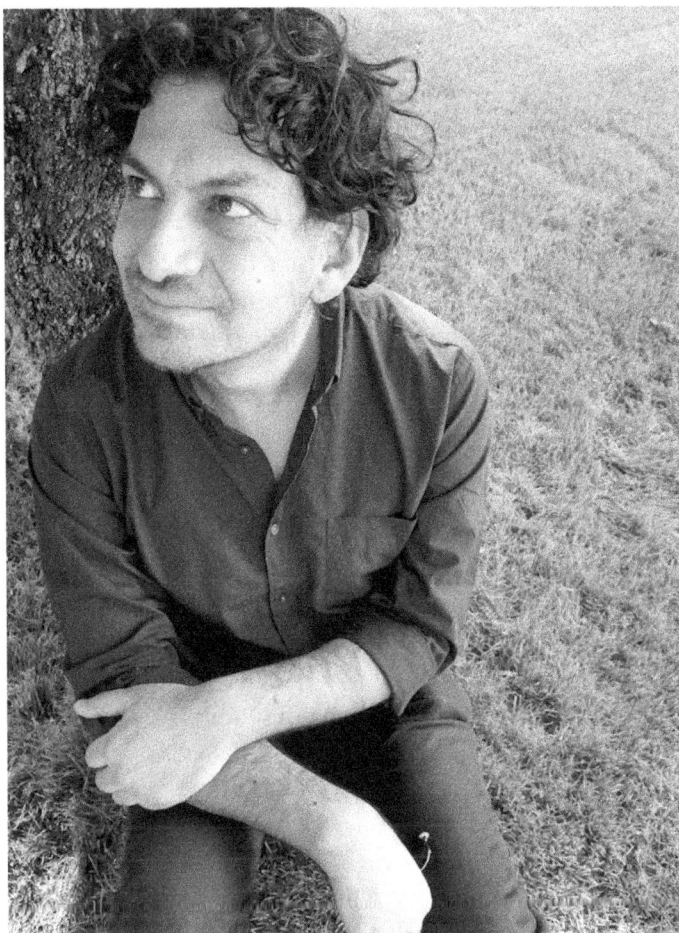

Figure 60.1. Photograph by Henny Garfunkel.

For me, having recently graduated with an MA in Cinema Studies, it seemed redundant to return to an environment where academic discourse and personal interpretations predominated over the interests of the cinephile.

However, Margarita De La Vega Hurtado, then executive director, insisted that I return, so I did in 2004 for the seminar marking the Flaherty's fiftieth anniversary and again a couple of years later. I was not conscious at the time that I was slowly sipping the Flaherty Kool-Aid.

To my surprise, I was then selected to program the 2007 seminar, along with my friend and colleague Mahen Bonetti. We had previously partnered to produce an outdoor screening of Marcel Camus's *Black Orpheus* (1959) at Brooklyn's Fort Greene Park back in 2002, drawing a wonderful crowd.

One of the biggest assets of the Flaherty seminar is its placement of curatorial practices at the forefront of the organization. With over sixty years of history, the Flaherty is one of the limited number of film organizations that do this. Sure, film festival programmers abound, but for the most part they fail at creating conversations and larger discussions with their film selections.

I'm surely not the first one and won't be the last one to say it, but curating the Flaherty seminar is a programmer's dream come true. Having a captive audience for one week, not having to announce the program in advance, and having complete freedom to mix aesthetics, formats, genres, narratives, and nationalities is an idyllic experience.

For many of us who have had the privilege to program the seminar, the experience has served as a sort of postgraduate degree that has made us reflect and improve our curatorial practices.

I have to confess that some of my favorite moments at the seminar have been non-cinematic. The recent and unexpected passing of director Eugenio Polgovsky brought to mind the times we mischievously sneaked out of screenings to catch some of the World Cup Games.

Watching the Argentina, Mexico, and Spain games at the 2010 seminar with Eugenio, Lisandro Alonso, Josetxo Cerdán, Pedro González Rubio, Sofía Gallisá, and others or watching the Brazil-Mexico game at the bar of the Colgate Inn with Cao Guimarães, Chris Gude, Daniella Alatorre, Jorge Caballero, and others created a very special camaraderie that I deeply treasure.

61

FOUR FLAHERTY SEMINARS

Joanna Raczyńska

JOANNA RACZYŃSKA programs films for the National Gallery of Art, Washington, DC. She has worked at Hallwalls Contemporary Arts Center (Buffalo, NY), the Smithsonian Institute's Hirshhorn Museum and Sculpture Garden, and the Baltimore Museum of Art. She has served as a juror for several international film festivals, including the Berwick Film and Media Arts Festival, Toronto's Images Festival, and the International Short Film Festival Oberhausen. She has also participated as a panelist for numerous individual artist award programs.

How does one extract the highlights of a cultural phenomenon that meets, exceeds, undermines, and sometimes thwarts expectations?

How does one parse an intensely subjective experience that defies easy description and begs for critique?

How does one describe the ways in which the polemical and the personal intertwine in inextricable, indistinguishable, and sometimes identical ways?

The Flaherty seminar touches all these questions and invites many more. I think of it as a complex system, somewhat like a knitted thing constructed of varying stitches: a platform, a retreat, a conference, a school, a cult, a family, a haven, a coven, a privilege, a vestige of the past, a beacon of the future, a happy holiday.

Figure 61.1.

So far, I've experienced four iterations of the Flaherty seminar.

Of course, I feel the ever-pressing obligations to write about the incredible films presented, the moderated conversations with the creators, and the conversations with esteemed academics in documentary film studies. Many others have written about the films, the people, the programs. I want to dive into a different pool.

In my heart, the Flaherty seminar feels like an intuitive and subjective experience. It unfolds with many sets of lived revelations, almost unbearable shudders, and shining moments.

Thanks to the advice and encouragement of my friend, archivist and historian Carolyn Tennant, I attended my first seminar in 2004 at Vassar College. I was fairly new to the job of film programmer. I was living in Buffalo, New York, working as media arts director at Hallwalls, the nonprofit arts center. This provided me with a magnificent and substantial hands-on education in arts management, arts funding, fundraising, curating, criticism, archiving.

The year 2004 celebrated the fiftieth anniversary of the seminar. Susan Oxtoby curated. Perhaps because it served as an introduction to generations of makers whom I encountered in person, I remember this seminar the most clearly.

At that seminar, I hung out with filmmakers Janie Geiser, Eve Heller, Louis Klahr, Julia Meltzer, Phil Solomon, and David Thorne. I was as inspired by their work as I was by their warmth. A month or two before, my father had died, and in sharing that loss with them, I felt both comforted and bolstered.

As I staggered across a field with my head spinning from excitement and agoraphobia, Ricky Leacock, the legend of direct cinema, steadied me. Scholar Erik Barnouw's widow, Betty Barnouw, told me that she would always knit in movie theaters, occasionally slipping stitches in the dark. I frequently found myself sitting alongside fellow knitter Ruth Bradley, who ran the Athens International Film and Video Festival (Ohio) and edited the journal *Wide Angle* at Ohio University.

In 2006, I returned to Vassar for Steve Seid and Ariella Ben Dov's program entitled Creative Demolition. The Buffalo contingent (Stefani Bardin, Caroline Koebel, Carolyn Tennant, and me) was in full force that year. Many people remarked at how much we seemed to like each other—a surprising observation. Of course we did!

Zoe Beloff, Patty Chang, Jacqueline Goss, Adele Horne, Sharon Lockhart, and Vittorio De Seta screened films and videos. Fridolin Schönwiese's moderated conversation with Kathy Geritz about *It Works* (1998) stays with me. The conversation was a revelation because it is so difficult to find adequate words to describe the workings and meanings of sound in film. Here were two brilliant people doing exactly that with inspiring generosity.

And at the 2006 seminar, I knit a fine-gauged, green gossamer cardigan—my "Flaherty sweater." On the last night, I finished it in my single dorm room, enjoying the self-imposed isolation. In contrast to its intense camaraderie, the seminar also affords moments of solitude, even while it does not openly encourage them.

In 2010, Dennis Lim was the programmer, exploring the theme of Work. I attended on a professional development grant and worked for the seminar. I poured wine at Bill's Bar. I attended workshops. I communed with other fellows. There was no time to knit.

The late Austrian documentarian Michael Glawogger relentlessly put himself in harm's way for films like *Workingman's Death* (2005) and *Whore's Glory* (2010). Experimental filmmaker Naomi Uman, a dear friend from the 2004 Hallwalls Artists' Residency Project, shared her *Ukrainian Time Machine* (2008). During a post-screening discussion, she spoke with the Mexican filmmaker Eugenio Polgovsky, who died in 2017, another premature loss.

As I look back on these experiences, I realize the key wonder of the seminar resides in the post-screening discussions. Their intensities and reflections compound the seminar's great wealth of screening experiences and opportunities for connection. Listening and choosing to be involved in the discussions (or not) and remembering that they are only one of the opportunities for exchange is vital. Some of the most valuable insights are rendered during chats with others between screenings and discussions, colliding in the dorms, sharing meals, or raising a glass at the bar.

My most recent seminar was in 2013. I went to take in colleague Pablo De Ocampo's program, History Is What's Happening. Of all the seminars I've attended, this was the most overtly political. Sadly, my detailed notes are illegible today, the handwriting not keeping pace with the hand knitting.

The films of Sara Maldoror—the brilliant Guadeloupian director of African descent—still resonate with me. A cameo from one of her films appeared in Chris Marker's *San Soleil* (1983), an overt yet accidental, unmistakable connection across time, lives, makers, and states of being. This concept of cinematic excavation also reverberated across the films of Basma Alsharif, Sirah Foighel Brutmann, Eitan Efrat, and Eyal Sivan, as well as the Otolith Group, all makers invested in the fine gauges of historic memory.

Complexity. There is no one Flaherty seminar experience. Each seminar is distinct. The other attendees and one's own stage of life inform each experience as much as the films programmed. One's willingness to open up and remain present might be most important in navigating the somewhat unusual experience of not choosing the films you experience.

To exhaust the knitting metaphor: the common thread to my four seminars so far, unraveled and reworked, remains this maxim—*only connect.*

62

CRITICAL HUMILITY

Roger Hallas

ROGER HALLAS is Associate Professor of English at Syracuse University, where he teaches film, visual culture, and LGBT studies. He is author of *Reframing Bodies: AIDS, Bearing Witness and the Queer Moving Image* (2009), coeditor of *The Image and the Witness: Trauma, Memory and Visual Culture* (2007), and editor of *Documenting the Visual Arts* (2019). He is Codirector of the Syracuse University Human Rights Film Festival.

I've procrastinated writing this piece for months.

Raking through my memories of attending the Flaherty, I've been looking for a compelling story that will illuminate the essence of the seminar or recount some transcendent experience that changed the way I see cinema or the world. However, rather than a glowing core, only glimmers, shards, and flashes that reflect facets of the experience come to mind.

I participated in three seminars (2005, 2009, and 2016). But it feels like so many more, partly because I had registered for two others but family emergencies pulled me away at the last moment. Both times, I guiltily hoped that they hadn't been the best seminars.

My first seminar in 2005, Cinema and History: Piling Wreckage Upon Wreckage (programmed by Michael Renov and Jesse Lerner), was a classic Flaherty initiate experience of excitement, wonder, and exhaustion. Excitement at the thrill of what we would see next and sharing extended

Figure 62.1.

time with great filmmakers. Wonder at the sheer aesthetic and thematic scope of both the works and the discussions about them. Exhaustion after staying up into the wee hours engrossed in conversation at Bill's Bar and trying to be ready for the morning screenings (and feeling guilty about dozing off during a couple of those screenings).

That first seminar exposed me to some films that have since become linchpins of my teaching documentary: Jean-Marie Teno's *Africa, I Will Fleece You* (1992), Patricio Guzmán's *Chile, Obstinate Memory* (1997), Dennis Tupicoff's *His Mother's Voice* (1996), and the work of Péter Forgács.

One memory that has really stuck with me is the anticipation us newbies felt for the "big fight" that Flaherty mythology told us would inevitably erupt during a post-screening discussion at some point during the week, exposing the fault lines of the gathered community.

But it never materialized.

I remember leaving on Saturday with a mild sense of disappointment at having missed out on a Flaherty rite of passage. Certainly, there had been localized skirmishes in the discussions and some heated personal conversations, but no big fight.

I do recall feeling incensed right after the screening of William Greaves's masterful mockumentary *Symbiopsychotaxiplasm: Take One* (1972). I got caught up in an uptight righteousness about the film's queer representation, which blinded me to its anarchic satirical bite. I just couldn't understand why everyone else was so in awe of it. But I listened to the discussion, then pursued more conversations about it in the bar and over meals. My flush reaction tempered, and eventually I cracked a smile.

By contrast, during the 2016 seminar, PLAY, programmed by the late great David Pendleton, I was immediately blown away by the beauty and tenderness of Naomi Kawase's *Genpin* (2010), about natural childbirth in Japan. Yet, during the full-seminar discussion, when several people questioned its gender politics, my exuberant reaction felt the sting of sharp—and reasoned—ideological critique. Subsequent conversations during the rest of the day enhanced and deepened my experience of the film, not into a clear-cut take on it, but into an understanding of my own ambivalence toward its complexity.

That is what I appreciate most about the durational quality of the Flaherty: it forces you to interrogate your immediate response to a film—whether that be exuberance, anger, or indifference—and allows you to continue reconsidering it in all variety of conversations that may follow.

The ritual structure of the coffee break, the seminar discussion, and then a meal or the bar provides the security of a familiar structure tempered by an aleatory dynamic of who happens to get to speak in the group discussion or whom you happen to be standing next to as you exit the screening on the way to grab a coffee.

Unlike film festivals and academic conferences, access to others is not hierarchical. You do not need an expensive pass or a colleague's introduction to enter into a conversation with a filmmaker. You can simply sit down next to them on the grass outside the auditorium or in the dinner hall.

In the more recent seminars that I've attended, I've often heard the complaint that the full-seminar discussions are now too academic or still too woolly liberal humanist, depending on to whom I talk.

This seems to be another manifestation of the enduring tension between aesthetics and politics that constitutes one of the core threads of the seminar's history. The discussions can certainly become frustrating, as various participants seem to speak past one another in their wildly divergent discourses. Nevertheless, the seminar is one of the few spaces in which such a dialectic can still be heard—discussions at academic conferences and film festivals tend to calcify around each end of this spectrum.

Somehow, the seminar fosters a culture of respecting the holistic integrity of its conversation. Whereas I might be tempted to panel hop at an academic conference or duck out of a post-screening discussion at a festival if it begins to lag, I always feel the need to see a Flaherty discussion to the end. Like a film screening, you respect the integrity of its duration, even if it ends up driving you up a wall.

Like most Flaherty faithful, I do proselytize the seminar regularly to the uninitiated, particularly my graduate students interested in documentary. I jokingly refer to it as "documentary boot camp," in an attempt to characterize its structure, ritual, and rigor. I also warn them about its intensity.

Ultimately, I enthuse most about the unique time and space of the Flaherty, which train us in the practice of a critical humility—one that resists certainty and singularity precisely because it embraces openness to alterity. Not a difference between one way of engaging the world or another, but an endeavor to imagine many more ways.

63

LONG WALKS

Jean-Marie Teno

JEAN-MARIE TENO, originally from Cameroon, has produced and directed social-issue films on the colonial and postcolonial history of Africa for over twenty-five years, for both international television broadcast and theatrical release. Exploring race, cultural identity, African history, and contemporary politics, his large body of films include *Afrique, je te plumerai* (*Africa, I Will Pluck You Clean*, 1992); *Le malentendu colonial* (*The Colonial Misunderstanding*, 2004); *Lieux saints* (*Sacred Places*, 2009); and *Une feuille dans le vent* (*A Leaf in the Wind*, 2013). The Berlin, Toronto, Yamagata, Cinéma du Réel, Visions du Réel, Amsterdam, Rotterdam, Leipzig, San Francisco, and London film festivals have honored his films.

A few months after I had completed my four-year-long project, *Le malentendu colonial* (*The Colonial Misunderstanding*, 2004), I traveled the world to present the film at the Ouagadougou Pan-African Festival of Film and Television (FESPACO), International Documentary Film Festival Amsterdam (IDFA), in Germany and elsewhere.

To further awareness of African situations and issues, I had accompanied my films at their screenings: an opportunity to enjoy life and discover a wider world. For a couple of decades from the mid-1980s to the late 1990s, going to festivals gave me a chance to relax and have as much fun as possible, until I finally grew tired of it.

Figure 63.1.

Festivals and screenings in Amsterdam, Berlin, London, San Francisco, Toronto, and Yamagata followed a standard pattern: the travel to the festival, the screening, followed by extended conversations with audiences who were more or less aware of the history and geography of Cameroon, where my films were set.

The Flaherty seminar was the final stop on my 2005 one-month tour of the United States. The seminar's theme was Cinema and History: Piling Wreckage Upon Wreckage. It was programmed by Jesse Lerner and Michael Renov, two film professors who taught at universities in southern California.

When I mentioned to friends that I was going to the Flaherty, the look on their faces bemused me. Some warned me that it was very expensive, while others said it was great. When I wanted to know more, no one could really offer much beyond the mysterious phrase *You will see for yourself.*

Of course, I knew about Robert Flaherty. I had watched his films at the Cinematheque Française and in venues such as the Cinema du Réel festival in Paris, accompanied by passionate debates attempting to define documentary. *Nanook of the North* (1922) always occupied the center of these arguments about reality and its representations in cinema.

My own work reflected on these very same questions. Because European ethnographers, anthropologists, journalists, and filmmakers gathered stories from around the planet, there was little space for alternative discourses from all the other Nanooks living in the world. Following in the wake of the first generation of African filmmakers, such as Youssef Chahine (Egypt), Souleymane Cissé (Mali), Med Hondo (Mauritania), Djibril Diop Mambéty (Senegal), and Ousmane Sembène (Senegal), I embraced a filmmaking process dedicated to deconstructing colonial representations that continue, unconsciously, to perpetuate a distorted image of Africans. My film *Afrique, je te plumerai* (*Africa I Will Fleece You*, 1992) was screened at the 2005 seminar.

The Flaherty was totally different from my festival experiences. Rather than film industry types or everyday festivalgoers, the "public" was comprised of academics who enjoyed gathering together to engage with the films from their different perspectives.

When I arrived at Claremont College in southern California, I realized that this was the first time I had ever set foot on an American campus. The size of the campus amazed me. The dorms, the canteen, and above all the beautiful screening facilities made a lasting impression on me.

I enjoyed the long walks between the different venues. These walks offered the time to meet other participants and to engage in interesting conversations. I was glad to converse with the American filmmaker William Greaves, whom I had met ten years earlier in 1995 in Paris, and the Chilean filmmaker Patricio Guzmán, whom I had occasionally met in France after his screenings. I bonded with the incredible Mexican filmmaker Juan Carlos Rulfo, director of *Del olvido al no me acuerdo* (*From Oblivion I do not Remember*, 1999).

It seemed as if everyone I talked to between films either taught at a university or was doing research for a film.

Breathtakingly packed with films, the program started early in the morning. Films screened all day long. Passionate debates unfurled. People seemed to know so much about these subjects. Their comments went North, South, East, and West before concluding with brilliant statements that the next speaker then picked apart!

The Flaherty seminar served as the space where longtime friends or enemies settled old scores. For me, it was a fascinating circus where filmmakers performed as peacemakers, especially when not defending themselves and their work from strange interpretations or misinterpretations.

But I also remember the fun part when the lights went down, after screenings and debates concluded at around 11:00 p.m. Some Flaherty insiders organized an informal bar with music, where you could talk and drink and dance until 4:00 or 5:00 a.m. After only a few hours' sleep, you had to be ready for the next day's screenings. The program always surprised because the films were not announced ahead of time.

After three days at this pace, we were all exhausted. However, the regular shouting and yelling of passionate film critics disagreeing on a theory sparked by a film kept us all alert!

Frankly, I was not prepared for this experience. I did not come from academia. I was more concerned about the fight for the visibility of African cinema. As a result, I was an outcast. However, in all fairness, the Flaherty was a tremendous experience.

Two years later, in 2007, Mahen Bonetti and Carlos Gutiérrez curated another edition of the seminar, South of the Other. As Mahen was preparing the seminar, we talked frequently. Alas, due to Flaherty rules and my own calendar, I was unable to attend. I felt that going to the Flaherty a second time would have allowed me to take better advantage of the opportunities that such a gathering of intellects creates, beyond the obvious networking opportunities.

African cinema needs a Flaherty seminar-like venue held on the continent to address its ongoing urgent issues. Thirty years ago, I represented the next generation of African filmmakers. Today, I am among the oldest. Yet the visibility of African cinema and the discourses surrounding it have gone almost nowhere.

64

BREAKING ALL THE ORDERED SURFACES

Andrés Di Tella

ANDRÉS DI TELLA is a filmmaker based in Buenos Aires. His films include *Television and Myself* (screened at Flaherty 2005), *Photographs* (2007), *Land of the Devil* (2008), *Blows of the Axe* (2011), *We shall Return to the Mountains!* (2013), and *327 Notebooks* (2015). He was also Founding Director of the Buenos Aires Independent Film Festival (BAFICI) and the Princeton Documentary Festival. He works across many forms, including performance (*By the Light of Oblivion*, 2012), essays (*327 Cuadernos*, 2015), installation (*Borges and I*, 2017), and feature-length documentary (*Ficción Privada/Private Fiction*, 2019).

As I arrived at the jacaranda-lined footpaths of the Claremont Colleges in the outskirts of Los Angeles in June 2005, I was puzzled by the news that there was no film program. Or rather: it was a secret.

One of the many ills of current film festival culture is "the buzz." As festivalgoers, we often know more than we need to know about the films we are about to see. It was a relief to walk into the dark of a movie theater in total ignorance of what was about to unfold.

The screening may turn out to be a contemporary film from an unknown director from Cameroon (or Argentina!—my *La Television y Yo*, 2003, was shown at the 2005 seminar) or a selection of experimental shorts from Hungary. Or it may offer an unexpected revelation

Figure 64.1.

from the past, such as *Symbiopsychotaxiplasm: Take One* (1972), William Greaves's unbelievable film-statement that seemed to come out of nowhere. It was a unique time capsule of the sixties and oddly relevant today.

During the week, whether it was nine in the morning after a rushed breakfast at the college cafeteria or near midnight after a few drinks at the bar, you never knew what to expect.

My experience at the Flaherty reminded me of the effect Michel Foucault evokes upon reading a text by Jorge Luis Borges, which describes a Chinese encyclopedia called *Celestial Emporium of Benevolent Knowledge*. This encyclopedia divides animals into: "a) those that belong to the Emperor, b) embalmed ones, c) those that are trained, d) suckling pigs, e) mermaids, f) fabulous ones, g) stray dogs, h) those included in the present classification, i) those that tremble as if they were mad, j) innumerable ones, k) those drawn with a very fine camelhair brush, l) etcetera, m) those that have just broken a flower vase, n) those that from a long way off look like flies."

In his preface to *The Order of Things*, Foucault explains, "This book first arose out of a passage in Borges, out of the laughter that shattered, as I read the passage, all the familiar landmarks of thought—*our* thought, the thought that bears the stamp of our age and our geography—breaking up all the ordered surfaces and all the planes with which we are accustomed to tame the wild profusion of existing things and continuing long afterward to disturb and threaten with collapse our age-old definitions between the Same and the Other."

The Flaherty too seemed to break all the ordered surfaces and the familiar landmarks that constitute how we think about a film festival program and perhaps even cinema itself. Our expectations and assumptions were taken away. We were somehow freed to think again.

My most significant moments at the seminar did not take place in the movie theater or during the post-screening discussions. Instead, they occurred while pacing unhurriedly along the footpaths with someone I often didn't know as we tried to dodge the sprinklers that kept the grass so California-green.

One such "unknown" to me was Patricio Guzmán, who was screening *Chile, Obstinate Memory* (1997) and *Salvador Allende* (2003), two further episodes in his long meditation on the pervasive effects of the 1973 military coup in his native Chile.

We quickly formed a *Latin ghetto* along with other unlikely Latin American filmmakers, such as Leandro Katz (born into a typical Buenos Aires Jewish family but living in New York for most of his life), Olivier Debroise (born in Jerusalem of French parents, he died in Mexico and was the epitome of the Mexican intellectual), and Juan Carlos Rulfo (son and heir to Juan Rulfo, one of the great Latin American cultural heroes, always at war with any hackneyed sense of "national" identity).

My own ethnic and cultural background—my mother was a Hindu from Madras—is also very unusual for Argentina. I spent my formative years in England, returning to Argentina when the Falklands/Malvinas war made the two countries bitter enemies.

In our own way, our Latin ghetto at the seminar served as a Latin American version of Borges's Chinese menagerie. Guzmán himself has by now lived many more years away from his native Chile than at "home," although he has rarely, if ever, made a film that does not deal with his long-lost homeland.

I'd thought the jacaranda trees we walked under were unique to Buenos Aires, but Guzmán remembered them from Santiago. I told him about a screening of *The Battle of Chile* (1978) I had recently organized at Princeton University, where I was running the Princeton Documentary Festival. It played to a full house of young students who had no recollection or even the dimmest notion of the 1973 coup that ousted Salvador Allende. The documentary came alive in a very surprising way, as if the historical outcome of three decades ago remained uncertain until the very end of the film.

In response, Guzmán confided something that startled me.

After his miraculous release from prison, he had managed to smuggle the cans of film out of Chile. He mulled over the footage for more than five years, initially unable to make a single cut. The long, flowing shots that characterize *The Battle of Chile*'s it's-happening-now approach often included the slate or the flash of white as the roll of film runs out. These apparent imperfections, which now seem magical, were perhaps an unexpected result of his reticence to cut.

But what surprised me was Guzmán explaining that he was not even aware he had left Chile until he finished putting together the three-hour-long final cut, started in Havana and finished in Paris.

So long as he kept watching the black-and-white, 16mm footage over and over on the Moviola, he did not have to fully acknowledge that Allende's experiment in democratic socialism had ended and that he himself was no longer living in Chile.

He said that once he had finished the task he had set out for himself, he "entered into exile" and a long depression. He has subsequently returned to Chile to make new films, but in many ways, he is now a foreigner in his own homeland.

This story begs a question on which I shall end: Should we see the French-produced films of Patricio Guzmán, who has now lived in Paris for decades, as the work of a French or a Chilean filmmaker? What does our awareness of this geographical detail bring to our expectation of the films?

My own experience in the United States and in Europe is that even sophisticated audiences, like those who show up at the Flaherty, sometimes expect a very distinct set of concerns from a Latin American film. These are often clichés that center around a presumed Latin American identity composed of extreme politics, local color, misery, and violence. Many Latin American filmmakers respond to those projected assumptions, serving up the prescribed measure of what Colombian filmmaker Luis Ospina has dubbed *pornomiseria*.

I end my story with a final question.

Wouldn't it be interesting if the Flaherty seminar's *secret formula* of "shattering the familiar landmarks of thought" were applied to seriously shaking up those latent assumptions and scenarios many hold about Latin American film?

Wouldn't it be interesting if we expected nothing?

65

UN BANQUETE AT CLAREMONT

Leandro Katz

LEANDRO KATZ is an Argentine/American artist, writer, and film-maker. His films and photographic installations deal with Latin American subjects, incorporating historical research, anthropology, and visual arts. These long-term works include *The Catherwood Project* a photographic reconstruction of two 1850s expeditions to Central American and Mexican Maya areas (1985–1995, 2001); *Paradox*, which explores Central American archaeology and Maya region banana plantations (2001); *Vortex*, which addresses the social and literary history of the Amazon region of the Putumayo River rubber industry (2004–ongoing); and *Project for the Day You'll Love Me*, an investigation into the 1967 capture and execution of Che Guevara in Bolivia (2010). His work has been widely exhibited internationally. He has received grants and fellowships from the Solomon R. Guggenheim Foundation, the National Endowment for the Arts, the New York State Council on the Arts, The Jerome Foundation, and The Rockefeller Foundation.

By the year 2005, the Robert Flaherty Film Seminar had acquired the reputation of being a whipping post where avant-garde filmmakers were subjected to rigorous criticism. So, after being invited, I attended the seminar with my claws out, expecting crucl and unusual punishment. But that was not what I found there.

Figure 65.1.

Offered on the beautiful campus of the Claremont Colleges, the 2005 experience was a real treat. I was showing some of my Central American films: *Los Angeles Station* (1970), a short made in the banana plantation train station of Quiriguá, Guatemala, and *Paradox* (2001), a documentary essay made in the same location thirty years later.

My recollections, however, are not only about my experience attending the seminar under Margarita de la Vega Hurtado's enthusiastic and delightful leadership, but mostly about Olivier Debroise, a French and Mexican writer, curator, and filmmaker who was also invited to the seminar.

I had met Olivier a few years earlier in Mexico, together with other members of the group Curare—Karen Cordero and Cuauhtémoc Medina—but this time, through the bond of the Flaherty experience, we became good friends: an unusual surprise when you are older and have decided that you love every living being except people!

We were housed in a four-unit graduate apartment with shared bathroom and showers. Every morning, a neighbor, possibly a participant, would spend extended periods of time naked in front of the mirrors applying talcum powder and admiring his rather unsightly body. Olivier and I regarded this narcissistic ritual as "an American experience," a comical and trivial attempt at sexual liberation.

In small groups of participants, we marched across the Claremont campus toward distant buildings for different events. In these walks, under the strong maternal leadership of Margarita, Olivier and I would engage in strangely passionate conversations, jumping from art to politics to filmmaking in weirdly intelligent somersault associations.

Olivier was presenting his *Un banquete en Tetlapayac* (2000), one of my favorite films—an extraordinarily audacious failure conceived on an assumption many of us make, that intelligent people may also be good actors.

Un banquete en Tetlapayac is a reconstruction of the time Sergei Eisenstein spent making *Qué Viva México*. For his film, shot in the hacienda where most of the filming had taken place sixty-seven years before, Olivier gathered a group of contemporary artists, filmmakers, and intellectuals to recreate the conversations Eisenstein may have had during a famous banquet.

Between screenings and discussions, Olivier and I would cross the drought-tolerant Claremont gardens, observing a large hawk piercing the field from a tall tree in search of his next meal, and in the process, we'd discuss Eisenstein's persecuted sexuality, Latin American contemporary art, and the vain, decades-long attempts to define it.

I saw Olivier many more times in Buenos Aires. He would stay in my studio, burn the edge of tables with abandoned cigarettes, and have sips of The Famous Grouse scotch for breakfast (I still have the bottle), while we engaged in unforgettable talks about art and social change. Olivier died on the eve of his next Buenos Aires trip, on May 7, 2008, at age fifty-six. What a loss! His presence and his voice over the course of a decade that defines global culture persist through his essays, curatorial work, and books.

The 2005 Flaherty—with the amazing collection of works assembled by Jesse Lerner and Michael Renov—became what must have been one of the most interesting among the fifty-one held to that date. And the reasons are simple: Olivier + Margarita + Claremont desert gardens + Jesse Lerner + Michael Renov + the great Péter Forgács and *El Perro Negro* (2005) + Juan Carlos Rulfo + Jean-Marie Teno and the discussions about the options between armed struggle and Christian philanthropy—OMG!

The films, the discussions, and the unusual West Coast surroundings all contributed to a splendid gathering of souls.

Thank you, Margarita, Jesse, Michael, for including me in such a fantastic seminar!

66

THE SOUND OF WHITE PEOPLE TALKING

Amir Muhammad

AMIR MUHAMMAD is a Malaysian book publisher, writer, and occasional moviemaker. His films are usually documentaries, the latest being *Kisah Pelayaran ke Terengganu (Voyage to Terengganu,* 2016). In 2011, he founded Buku Fixi, a pulp-fiction publisher that has since produced over two hundred books. He has also helped to produce shorts by new filmmakers, including those based on the stories he has published.

I was in the Flaherty of 2006. I have not been back to America since.

I don't mean to say that my experience at the Flaherty was so traumatic that I vowed never to set foot on US soil again. It wasn't like that at all!

I remember Flaherty as a mostly pleasant blur. But it also made me feel I should visit other places too.

There was so much whiteness around at the Flaherty.

Several times while listening to the discussion, it occurred to me that I had been taught to believe that when white people talk, they must be talking from a position of authority or knowledge or, at the very least, wit.

Malaysia is a former British colony (or protectorate, if you prefer), where anything associated with England (the other parts of Britain didn't seem to feature much) is thought to be the bee's knees.

Figure 66.1.

People of my generation and those who are older grew up reading the books of Enid Blyton, even though we mostly had no idea how much fried rice a half crown or a shilling would actually get us in real life. Thankfully, we were sensible enough not to crave English food.

Among the mostly Anglophilic chattering classes, life would grind to a half whenever a new Windsor royal wedding was in the offing.

Every dodgy upper-middle-class Malaysian seeking to evade media and legal scrutiny back home will invariably be revealed as "holidaying in London."

Younger Malaysians don't have an automatic link to the former empire, but this situation is simply because the juggernaut of American soft power overwhelmed us. To be American was to be not only young and restless, but also bold and beautiful, and then fast and furious and all sorts of sugar-rush adjectives.

When watching a movie where a white guy trains his guns or knife on a nonwhite antagonist, the association is clear: whiteness is not only mightier but right.

And this situation explains why white people who work in Malaysia are dubbed by employers as *expatriates*, while nonwhites are designated as *migrant workers*.

Back to the Flaherty seminar. After I screened my docu-fiction film *The Big Durian* (2003), which references the Petronas Twin Towers of Kuala Lumpur, a white American woman asked me if I had been thinking of the New York City Twin Towers. I was gobsmacked. *The Big Durian* was about Malaysian politics during the first premiership of Dr. Mahathir Mohamad (1981–2003). The Petronas Twin Towers, fully completed in 1998, were indeed emblematic of that era.

When I replied no, she pressed on. She posited rather confidently that the image of the World Trade Center must have been playing in my mind. I considered retorting "I was thinking of the KL ones, as they are still standing," but my attempt at black humor may have been #TooSoon. So I just repeated, "No."

The other title I screened, *Lelaki Komunis Terakhir* (*The Last Communist*, 2006), a road movie sort-of-biopic about the exiled leader of the banned Communist Party in Malaya, was thankfully greeted with less befuddlement. This is because it had a few cheesy songs. Cheesy songs are always good to disarm people.

There was another white comment about *John and Jane* (2005), Ashim Ahluwalia's film about a Mumbai call center. The speaker uttered something about Ashim's film along the lines that *it was like Bollywood*. This was a documentary that was consciously stylized to look like a sparse science-fiction film. Hard to imagine a less Bollywood production, no?

If I were to ever visit America again, I would need to apply for a new ten-year visa and explain to the embassy officer why I want to go. People far more qualified than me have been turned down.

One factor the embassy officers consider is the countries the applicant has visited in the past few years and the purpose of the travel. Some of the countries I have visited or plan to visit are those that may not seem friendly to the current American political establishment (insert joke about Russia and North Korea here). Do I really feel like justifying myself to these officers? No, I do not.

I want to visit places I've never been to before.

In the dozen years since that Flaherty, I have visited at least a dozen countries for the first time—including those that are geographically close, such as Cambodia, Laos, and Myanmar, but so remote in terms of contemporary cultural influence they may as well be on Mars. Although I travel mainly as a tourist and sometimes with a film-festival or book-fair badge, I am humbled to realize there are so many languages I will never be able to learn (I am slow).

My favorite line from that 2006 Flaherty was when Vittorio De Seta, the Italian film director and screenwriter known for his poetic short documentaries about everyday people in Sicily and Sardinia, replied to a questioner in the post-screening discussion. He referred to an actor (whose name I can't recall, but who was really handsome) with the observation, "Like most actors, he was not very bright."

I have quoted this line of Vittorio's a few times, sometimes to people who, by virtue of their profession, didn't take too kindly to it. (I just googled De Seta and found out he died five years after that seminar. But the utterly bland Sharon Lockhart is unfortunately still alive and creating those white-bread art pieces.)

However, my favorite moment from my entire stay in America came when I conversed with a homeless Filipino man in a New York City park.

I can't remember what led to our exchange, but he told me the Tagalog word for butterfly was *paru-paro*. This word was beautiful because the Malay word *paru-paru* means lungs. And lungs are shaped like a butterfly. Perhaps this was not a case of *faux amis*, as the two languages are related.

In fact, the Philippines and Malaysia have much in common (with the cultural imperialism of Catholicism in the first and Islam in the other). I had spent maybe ten times the number of my life's days in the United States compared to this neighboring Southeast Asian country.

I am typing this story in Korea. In September, I will be going to the Philippines. When they talk among themselves, I don't understand Koreans or Filipinos. But it's great to listen to other people talking.

67

THE FLAHERTY FINDS A NEW HOME AT COLGATE UNIVERSITY

John Knecht

JOHN KNECHT has been a practicing film and video artist since 1973. His films, videos, and multiple-channel installations have been shown widely. His recent exhibitions include *Fragments from the Wheels of Ezekiel* (2011), a fifteen-channel installation at the Everson Museum in Syracuse, New York; *Animating Destiny: Electric Paintings and Other Works* (2015) at the Esther Massry Gallery of the College of Saint Rose in Albany, New York; and *after math* (2017), Alexander/Heath Contemporary, Roanoke, Virginia. Knecht holds the Russell Colgate Distinguished Professor of Art and Art History and Film and Media Studies Chair Emeritus at Colgate University. He lives and works in Hubbardsville, New York.

Little Hall opened on the Colgate University campus in January of 2001. It was the result of a ten-year project in which I was deeply involved. Little Hall is a clean, gray-and-white space made for making and displaying images. At the center of the complex is the Golden Auditorium screening room; the Clifford Gallery is directly across the lobby. Early in the planning stages, during a conversation with Chad Floyd, the principal architect, I told him, "As you're designing, think about the inside of a camera."

Both the projection booth in Golden Auditorium and the Clifford Gallery are equipped with analog and digital technology. New 16mm

Figure 67.1.

equipment was installed to replace the earlier 16mm equipment and to complement Golden's excellent 35mm and digital projection. Golden Auditorium can show most any film from anywhere in the world. And Colgate's excellent technical staff can install video and audio installations in the Clifford Gallery.

Having the new facility to offer the Flaherty board when I went down to Vassar in 2006 made Colgate a relatively easy sell. Since the Flaherty has relocated to Colgate, the seminar has been able to show films in a more comfortable space and expand its programming by extending work into the gallery and elsewhere within the Little Hall facility. Multiple projections, installations, and works in other nontheatrical formats are now a regular part of Flaherty seminars.

I had met Scott MacDonald soon after arriving at Colgate in 1981. Almost immediately, Scott and I began collaborating on bringing visiting artists to our respective weekly film series at Utica College of Syracuse University and Colgate. Occasionally, that collaboration would include Mary Fessenden from Cornell Cinema, Laura Marks from Rochester, Bob Doyle from the Visual Studies Workshop in Rochester, Cheryl Jackson of Squeaky Wheel Media Works in Buffalo, and others.

In 1986, I had the idea of contacting the people who were programming film and video in central and western New York State to invite them to Colgate for a daylong gathering, so we could to get to know each other better and exchange programming ideas. This initial gathering was the first of a continued series of visits, in those pre-email days, to each other's institutions for daylong meetings in the fall and/or spring of each academic year to select artists who would tour the area during the following semester.

We programmers became friends, shared and learned from each other, and accomplished what no individual institution alone could have. The result was the formation of the Central New York Programmers Group (CNYPG), as it came to be known. CNYPG organized tours for experimental and nonfiction film and video artists from around the world.

Credit goes to the New York State Council on the Arts for their support not only of our individual weekly film series, but of our efforts to organize and collaborate. NYSCA funded the salary for a part-time coordinator of our efforts, and Cornell University donated an office. CNYPG facilitated programming in central and western New York State for twenty years, from 1986 to 2006.

There are many stories to tell about the history of CNYPG. I mention it here only because it is at the heart of the community that has been engaged in the history of film and media in and around Colgate for decades. It is through friends in CNYPG that I originally learned about the Flaherty's interest in finding a new place to hold their annual seminar. I heard about this very informally from both Patricia Zimmermann, who I'd met and worked with as a NYSCA panelist during the 1980s, and Scott MacDonald, both of whom were major players in CNYPG.

In 2006, I made the trip to Vassar to meet with the Flaherty board during what was the fifty-second annual Flaherty seminar. I arrived in a bad mood, since this meeting meant having to miss one of my son's Little League games, as well as Father's Day. What happened on that Vassar visit, however, was the beginning of new friendships, originating with the members of the Flaherty board and, later, with seminar attendees.

I am so glad to be part of the Flaherty family as it continues to evolve. I'm proud to have been involved in the design and implementation of Little Hall and very happy to have the Flaherty International Film Seminar using the facility as it was intended to be used. Each year the Flaherty is the capstone event for Little Hall and Golden Auditorium.

Having the Flaherty International Film Seminar at Colgate University for over a decade has been a great addition to the intellectual and cultural discourse that Colgate University continues to provide within the larger and ever-active community of central and western New York. I am happy to have been a part of what has become an ongoing relationship.

68

STRANGER COMES TO TOWN

Jim Supanick

JIM SUPANICK is a video maker and writer born in Cleveland, Ohio. His essays have appeared in *Film Comment, Millennium Film Journal, The Wire, Cineaste,* and *The Brooklyn Rail.* He has written for numerous exhibition catalogs and DVD releases. He has received a Creative Capital Arts Writers Grant and a New York Foundation for the Arts Grant for Nonfiction Literature. He is a member of Synthhumpers, a quasi-musical collaboration with Josh Solondz. He teaches at City College of New York.

They say there are only two stories in the world: man goes on a journey, and stranger comes to town.

That sentence is from a description of Jacqueline Goss's *Stranger Comes to Town* (2007), previewed as a work in progress at the 2006 Flaherty seminar.

I pondered that useful if tantalizing provocation: two separate narrative archetypes or dual aspects of one? Whatever the answer might be, I consider the sentence the meta-narrative for that first Flaherty experience.

Man goes on a journey.

Annie Howell, my friend and then-department chair at The New School, offered me and one of her grad students a lift to Vassar College.

As we were first-time attendees, our conversation up the Palisades Parkway was laced with anticipation and rumors of past seminar debacles.

Figure 68.1.

Which filmmakers would be featured this year? When would the arguments
begin? Who would storm out under real or perceived attack? I wondered
how the mix of filmmakers, scholars, archivists, and curious outsiders the
seminar attracted might come together for productive dialogue. Would
we speak the same language? If not, could an adequate pidgin be devised?

At that time, a desire to traverse aesthetic and ideological divisions
within the moving-image world had emerged as a subtheme in my film
writing.

It thrilled me to learn that the seminar's complex history contained
some of those same impulses, with works like *Culloden* (1964), *Portrait
of Jason* (1967), and *David Holzman's Diary* (1967), which redefined the
very notions of nonfiction film. It also disproved the common misconception that the Flaherty only dealt with humanist documentary forms.
I sensed affirmation of my own instincts through the programmers'
intensive self-questioning.

Stranger comes to town.

My social circle in film culture overlapped with many I was about to meet. Yet I still didn't feel plugged into the nonfiction film world or this mystique-laden gathering.

The summer of 2006 was just prior to Facebook's launch beyond campuses to the general public. This event signified a big shift in everyday social interaction and what it meant to *know* a person or event.

At the seminar's opening reception, I saw a sea of unfamiliar faces. The desire to flee was strong. What had I gotten myself into? Everyone seemed effusive. Their easy rapport with one another compounded my anxiety.

I plunged into the social swim with memories of belly flops past. I tuned into the name-tag dynamic, following the gaze of the person I was speaking to as they strained to discern my pedigree. This process was funny, like a page from *Bourdieu for Dummies*. It was even funnier when credentials were flipped inward, exposing only a pass code for the dorm. Was this then our first taste of Frances Flaherty's idea of non-preconception?

Man goes on a journey, though he knows not where.

A novel concept, a willing abduction, a cinematic journey premised on absolute trust. What other examples can you think of, aside from health insurance, where expensive goods or services are purchased sight unseen?

Say hello to the elephant in the room. In truth, the Flaherty is financially prohibitive for many. If it didn't cost so damned much, the Flaherty might promote itself as a bargain for the budget traveler (I see the seminar as a strange brand of virtual travel we do while our neighbors are on their so-called real vacations). The hefty price tag contributes to what sometimes feels like an institutionally embedded discourse.

Nothing against the good folks at Harvard or Duke, but I would love to see this fact acknowledged by some needs-based selection criteria for future seminar fellows.

Steve Seid and Ariella Ben-Dov's inspired seminar programming went a long way toward mitigating the pain of the cost. So, if you somehow manage to scrape together the funds, something my archival job at the time afforded me, you end up logging quite a lot of mental mileage.

Themes of risk and betrayal recurred throughout the week. The 2006 itinerary included an unforgettable swordfishing excursion in southern Italy by the too-secretly great Vittorio De Seta; Stanley Nelson's sensitive treatment of Jonestown's utopia-turned-catastrophe; Vit Klusak and Filip Remunda's *Czech Dream* (2004), best described as the climactic scene from the novel *The Day of the Locust* (Nathaniel West, 1939), reimagined as consumerist hoax in an empty lot outside of Prague.

Another personal favorite was Adele Horne's *The Tailenders* (2005), an excursion through her own family history. It also traced the origins of Gospel Recordings, a company founded by evangelical Christians that had developed a cheap record player that ran without electricity. As an unintended consequence, it assisted in the preservation of endangered languages. The film was quite a juggling act: part media-archaeological dig and part thoughtful meditation on the hidden connections between missionary recruitment and documentary film.

Speaking during the after-screening discussions was like an initiation ritual.

I'd had several years of teaching experience, but the risk of speaking at the Flaherty seemed much greater. As the week went on, there was a leveling effect brought about by astute analysis or the quiet sigh from a neighbor at another's attempt to shoehorn Gilles Deleuze into the discussion. At such moments, friendships were formed, and in some cases, something more.

While getting lost on a dark winding campus path, I had my first conversation with Nancy Andrews, a featured filmmaker from Maine whose work that week was revelatory. I don't think I've ever told her, but her films became an indirect, yet decisive influence on my dissertation.

One morning, I stumbled early to breakfast to see Paul Arthur, the film critic whose work I so admired, dining alone. We'd met nearly ten years before, but circumstances too tedious to recount had led to a mutual misapprehension. But there he was, so I asked to join him. That long conversation about the films we were seeing, the challenges of teaching, and dreams for the future remains a vivid memory—intensified by Paul's untimely departure less than two years later. When the seminar was over, I rode back to Ithaca with Jason Livingston to visit with old friends. That giddy debriefing solidified our friendship.

As I write this story, Jason and I have just embarked on a new collaboration. It's a film about truckers in the twenty-first century, romantic figures hounded by satellite tracking. They are faced with the paradox of constant movement while confined within a small space and haunted by the threat of driverless technologies.

We have already logged several hundred miles through the Midwest, shooting and brainstorming on the hot summer highway.

69

PATTY SENT ME

Dale Hudson

DALE HUDSON teaches in the Film and New Media Program at New York University Abu Dhabi (NYUAD), where his research and teaching focus on globalization and culture to frame questions on transnational/postcolonial migrations, environmentalisms, and structural inequalities. He is author of *Vampires, Race, and Transnational Hollywoods* (2017) and author with Patricia R. Zimmermann of *Thinking through Digital Media: Transnational Environments and Locative Places* (2015).

At my first Flaherty seminar in 2006, I was asked to sit in a circle with the other participants to introduce ourselves. Each person opened with a numerical inventory of how many seminars they had attended.

I had just returned from India. I wasn't sure whether jet lag distorted what I was hearing or if these statements were really being uttered in public.

Rumors swirled in screen studies circles that the seminar was cultish and debates vitriolic. But I remember feeling an approximation of a twelve-step program.

The seminar progressed.

I found myself addicted to the ritual of awaking each morning for three screenings of unannounced films and videos. When I attended the seminar again in 2007 and 2008, I remember feeling emboldened that I

Figure 69.1.

could announce to newcomers that it was my second or third Flaherty. I now understood how the seminar worked.

My colleague and now coauthor Patricia Zimmermann had encouraged me to attend. She'd even found a way for me to get funding from Ithaca College. She also shared that the design of the seminar owes more to Frances Flaherty than to her husband, Robert. I mused, *how typical, a woman does the work and a man gets the attention.*

I thought about how Alice Guy-Blaché films are not taught as widely as Georges Méliès films. I recalled that her role in developing film as a narrative medium had been largely forgotten until feminist scholars (all women in this instance) recovered this repressed history.

Patricia revealed that in the film studies courses at Ithaca College, she and Gina Marchetti had adapted Frances Flaherty's strategy of eliciting responses as free from preconceptions as possible.

I was part of the film studies team at Ithaca College with Patricia. We distributed syllabi that included only the titles of what would be screened. No place of production. No year of production. No running time. No language or format. And certainly no director's name.

Although the first-year film students in this large lecture class could search online to learn more about the films, few did. They all seemed to find it more fun to arrive without expectations, mesmerized by the provocations to see and to hear and to think and to immerse in the unknown.

My experiences at my first Flaherty rewired my own lingering preconceptions.

I bonded over discussions with Mahen Bonetti, Carlos Gutiérrez, Roger Hallas, Anna Siomopoulos, Sharon Lin Tay, Chi-hui Yang, and others. No matter what was screened or what was said at the large group discussions, the seminar solidified our commitment to voices academia and film culture marginalized, discredited, or ignored.

The seminar disrupts standardized histories of narrative film, documentary, and experimental media, as well as standardized programming at art houses and museums. It made me realize how much has been excluded.

I met extraordinary artist intellectuals, including Ashim Ahluwalia, Natalia Almada, Rebecca Baron, Ximena Cuevas, Theo Eshetu, Jacqueline Goss, Leonard Retel Helmrich, Oliver Husain, Khalo Matabane, Christina McPhee, Amir Muhammad, Jenny Perlin, João Moreira Salles, Eddo Stern, and Renee Tajima-Peña. Since then, their films, videos, and installations have ended up on my syllabi, and I've analyzed these works in my scholarly publications.

I also met artist intellectuals whose work I studied in graduate school or had taught in classes, such as Ursula Biemann, Vittorio De Seta, Mahamat-Saleh Haroun, and Moussa Sene Absa. I "met" Bahman Ghobadi live via Skype. He had not been able to secure a visa to enter the United States.

For me, the smaller discussions were fortifying. The big discussions were sometimes intimidating, often frustrating, and occasionally even pointless. But they were always part of something larger that was unequivocally inspiring.

Although I have not been able to attend my fourth Flaherty, I look forward to doing so. I hope that a Flaherty might be held a little closer to where I live in Abu Dhabi. Anywhere in the Middle East, Africa, South Asia, or even East Asia would be closer than central New York. I have not found another event that rivals it.

After three seminars, I am addicted to screening media in classes and public programs without advance framing. I am addicted to having my assumptions proven incomplete and my preconceptions rendered incorrect.

I give thanks to the brave women (and men) in the history of the Flaherty seminar, partisans for an international independent cinema who made this way of knowing the world possible for so many generations of seminar participants.

The Flaherty seminar pushed me to think in unanticipated and unexpected ways. I am so grateful to Patricia for encouraging me to attend my first seminar and eagerly read the seminar's history that she and Scott MacDonald painstakingly assembled after a decade of research (*The Flaherty: Decades in the Cause of Independent Cinema*, 2017).

The Flaherty is a productively disunified and unruly experience.

Note: The Flaherty seminar's international scope is evident in the array of home countries for the participants mentioned above: India (Ashim Ahluwalia), Mexico, United States (Natalia Almada), United States (Rebecca Baron), Switzerland (Ursula Biemann), Mexico (Ximena Cuevas), Italy (Vittorio de Seta), United Kingdom/Italy with family from Ethiopia (Theo Eshetu), Kurdish Iran (Bahman Ghobadi), United States (Jacqueline Goss), Netherlands/Indonesia (Leonard Retel Helmrich), Canada/Germany with family from India (Oliver Husain), Chad/France (Mahamat-Saleh Haroun), South Africa (Khalo Matabane), United States (Christina McPhee), Senegal (Moussa Sene Absa), Malaysia (Amir Muhammad), United States (Jenny Perlin), Brazil (João Moreira Salles), Israel/United States (Eddo Stern), and United States with family from Japan (Renee Tajima-Peña).

70

TILTING, TORQUING, AND SHUFFLING BETWEEN DIMENSIONS

Shannon Kelley

SHANNON KELLEY is a freelance consultant to independent film-makers. He is the former Head of Public Programs for UCLA Film & Television Archive. He previously served as Director of Programming for the Morelia International Film Festival in Mexico, Associate Director of the Documentary Film Program of the Sundance Institute, and Director of Programming for Outfest: The Los Angeles Gay & Lesbian Film Festival. He has contributed film criticism to various national publications and has served as a panelist or juror at film festivals in North America, Europe, and the Middle East.

Many years before I decided to attend, I was aware of the Flaherty Film Seminar. I first went as an observer in 2007 and then, in 2008, as a panel moderator. By that time, I had found a groove, both active and contemplative, within film culture. I had worked as a programmer at Outfest Los Angeles and as a programming consultant and documentary funder at the Sundance Institute. And in 2007, I was director of programming at the Morelia International Film Festival in Mexico.

I had experienced many international festivals, but not the Flaherty, which sported a reputation as a sustained, concentrated intellectual environment where cinema could be approached in the company of passionate colleagues committed to spading around in the fertile ground of moving-image culture.

Figure 70.1.

(My first mind-blowing encounter with Robert Flaherty's *films* and his impact on documentary had occurred years before, in a class at Ithaca College taught by Patricia Zimmermann. That class posed many questions: Why should there be films? Who are *we* to make them? What illusions do they create? Which of them are revealing and worthwhile?)

Back to the Flaherty seminar. More than once, I'd heard that besides analytical tools, I should bring along some boxing gloves. Contentious debate loomed as a seminar hallmark. Voices would be raised. Participants would divide into ideological camps. Filmmakers would depart with bruised egos and psyches.

At my first Flaherty, at Vassar College, and the next year at Colgate University, I met luminaries of my field: specialty exhibitors, museum curators, university professors, industry representatives, authors of books and monographs, and media practitioners.

And I got my first chance to consider the famous post-screening discussions between new and veteran attendees. The discourse here differed from behind-the-scenes conversations at film festivals about how a programmer ought to burnish the reputation and career of a guest filmmaker, and it differed from the typical festival-audience questions of how to raise money, attract name talent, market films, and get a foot in the door of the industry.

Guest filmmakers at the Flaherty were asked discomfiting questions. One guest was challenged about the content of his film with the opening proclamation, "How dare you!" Another guest terminated a conversation that seemed to him like a pointless exercise. Many of those present felt collateral damage.

But this experience was more than theater. The Flaherty seminar participants' comments tended toward the theoretical and the cultural and often tilted into the ethical and the moral. Why cinema? Who are we to participate in it? Which of our illusions is useful? Or perhaps less than useful?

The no-holds-barred debates gradually awakened another possibility: that the moving- image artifacts we were seeing needn't be framed only as filmmakers' accomplishments or as genre embellishments. Individual works and their makers were subjected to ideological torques and abrasions that produced meaning through sometimes uncomfortable encounters among diverse participants with a shared mission. The Flaherty experience modeled a critical engagement with media that film festivals, publicity launches, awards shows, and even some academic conferences deliberately purge.

At the screenings there were moments of discovery, exhilaration, and humanistic thrall. The works of Ximena Cuevas, Oliver Husain, Khalo Matabane, and Renee Tajima-Peña displayed widely divergent but potent formal strategies for communicating cultural discomforts and dislocations.

A special moment in 2008 was the archival screening of *The Exiles* (1961) by Kent MacKenzie, which depicted late-twentieth-century Native Americans eking out a living in urban Los Angeles. Then unknown to most Flaherty attendees, the film wowed the audience and has become a repertory standard.

An intimate, emotional Q and A session via Skype with Kurdish-Iranian director Bahman Ghobadi at the 2008 seminar, following a screening of his *A Time for Drunken Horses* (1999), stays with me even now. Due to the difficulties in traveling to the United States from Iran, he was unable to attend in person. Ghobadi's commentary on the film's microcosm of Kurdish experience enacted by orphaned children overwhelmed me, and his candid conversation with the audience ended by bringing us to our feet.

After both seminars I attended, I found myself caught up in the headiness of the experience. Leaving the seminar felt as strange as arriving—a shuffling between dimensions.

The Flaherty had generated a unique dialectic between the rarefied experience of being removed from the outside world *and* immersed within the seminar's traditional routines.

The unrelenting immediacy of going head-to-head with colleagues and new friends created exciting opportunities to bring the rapid pace of ephemeral media culture into sharper focus.

Both times, I left the Flaherty without lasting intellectual or psychic bruises. The experience presented a rare chance to consider film and media art outside the parochial concerns of professionalism and commodification.

71

RETURNING TO THE SCENE OF THE CRIME

Jason Fox

JASON FOX is a filmmaker based in New York. He has taught at NYU, Vassar College, Cooper Union, and Hunter College. He has worked as a director, cinematographer, and editor on award-winning films that have screened internationally in film festivals, on broadcast television, and in gallery settings. He has worked as a film programmer in conjunction with the American Museum of Natural History, the Flaherty Film Seminar, and the Museum of Modern Art. He is founding editor of *World Records*, the peer-reviewed journal of documentary studies published by UnionDocs in Brooklyn, New York.

I first heard about the Flaherty seminar from an avant-garde filmmaker friend (who will go unnamed here) who had been an invited artist a few years prior.

"It was the most frustrating experience of my life," he said. "But you should go. You'll love it."

He was right.

Six months after attending my first Flaherty seminar, The Age of Migration, programmed by Chi-hui Yang in 2008, I sent a note to the Flaherty office to see if I could listen to the audio recording from the opening night's post-screening discussion.

Figure 71.1.

I wanted to try to make sense of a series of exchanges between the audience and Laura Waddington, a Britain-born video maker invited to share her short works *Border* (2004) and *CARGO* (2001) [editor's note: only *CARGO* was shown on that opening evening].

I wondered if my recollection had yielded to hyperbole. Or if my very first Flaherty discussion experience truly had been as hostile and rancorous as I remembered.

I listened to the recording, quickly jotting down the withering rebukes. A few:

· "I wonder if there is a contradiction between
  reality and art in your work?"
· "What came up today is a tension because you don't hear
  from these men [in the video]. I don't need to hear what
  it is like to be another privileged white woman . . . what
  I'm coming away with is the tension of your gaze."
· "The last thing we need to hear is you and your goddamned
  Jane Austen voice-over. Let the people speak!"

Here is the context. In both of Laura's videos, she trains her consumer digital video camera on people suspended in states of exception. In *Border*, night scenes of migrants moving furtively through the fields near Calais, hunted by the French police. In *CARGO*, Romanian and Filipino sailors trapped for lack of papers on the freighters that employ them.

In both, she records at night with a slow shutter speed and very high gain, rendering painterly streaks of imagery whose subjects are often made distant and illegible. In both, her Cambridge elocution speaks over the silent images in a tone at once testimonial and plaintive, alternately romantic and repulsed by her subjects' conditions. In both, we hear the arrestingly minimalist scores of Simon Fisher Turner.

From where I sat in the theater that night, I thought there was an explicit intent in her videos to register an incommensurability of positions between filmmaker and subjects.

Images were nearly opaque, and individuals remained anonymous, most immediately for reasons of safety but also in order to reflect the failure of political vision and will that continues to allow the perpetuation of such abject conditions.

Intentionally and provocatively Eurocentric in their outlook, each video renders the space of Western liberal concern into an aesthetic, transforming viewers into the real subject of her work and undermining the *if we only knew* logic of so much humanitarian documentary.

But many others disagreed.

It would have been much easier to retreat into my own self-satisfaction, convinced that my view was the proper view, if only those hostile assertions toward Laura had not stemmed from what I perceived to be many audience members' deeply felt and long-standing commitments to social justice, a relationship I too was trying to sort out through documentary images.

So there I was, frozen, unable to decide if I wanted my position to be validated or dismissed. And it wouldn't be hyperbolic to say that I've spent the better part of the last decade attempting to sort through the tectonic collisions I encountered on that first Flaherty night.

The antagonisms that I was suddenly immersed in reflect much longer-standing tensions between the politics of form and content, ethics and aesthetics, and between the (still) predominantly white and institutionally supported seminar attendees and the often neither/nor subjects on screen.

And so, in the following years, I kept returning to the original scene of the crime whenever I could in order to reengage these questions.

What I learned from Chi-hui and what I witnessed in subsequent seminar programmers such as Josetxo Cerdán, Dennis Lim, Gabriela Monroy, and Caspar Stracke, who took their seminar programs in very different directions, were strong political commitments wedded with adventurous curatorial approaches.

Our politics are always also a question of form.

In short, it's at the Flaherty that I learned that thinking historically and politically is always a project of thinking formally. Form enables our political imaginations. It can also constrain us.

How to tell the difference?

I'm still not sure. But I recently started a new, critical journal of documentary, *World Records*, to assemble voices to interrogate these questions.

Five years after my first encounter with Laura's work, I was asked to moderate a post-screening discussion following a program that *Border* was featured in.

Outside the auditorium, I asked Laura about her current video projects.

"I don't make videos anymore," she replied. When I asked her why, she answered, matter-of-factly, that she never made a video again after her Flaherty experience.

Laura Waddington: "It's my belief in a world full of people claiming to 'represent' everyone but themselves, my small, fragile, searching, unfinished voice—which some may call useless—is a kind of resistance."

72

INDIGENOUS MEDIA DETONATIONS

Amalia Córdova

AMALIA CÓRDOVA is Latino Curator for Digital and Emerging Media, the Center for Folklife and Cultural Heritage, Smithsonian Institution. She was Latin American Program Specialist for the Film + Video Center, National Museum of the American Indian, Smithsonian Institution, New York City. She also served as Assistant Director of the Center for Latin American and Caribbean Studies at New York University. Her essays appear in *In the Balance: Indigeneity, Performance, Globalization* (2017); *From Filmmaker Warriors to Flash Drive Shamans: Indigenous Media Production and Engagement in Latin America* (2018); and *The Routledge Companion to Latin American Cinema* (2018).

At a time when indigenous film was bursting with new expressions yet circulating mainly outside mainstream circuits, I was thrilled to be asked to present indigenous films from Mexico at the 2007 Flaherty seminar, South of the Other. Mahen Bonetti and Carlos Gutiérrez thoughtfully curated the program.

It was my first Flaherty seminar. As a film programmer and scholar, I appreciated the seminar's somewhat insider yet dialogical dynamic. I looked forward to how indigenous video might reverberate within the context of a panorama of major works from a global cinema infused with a critical decolonizing spirit.

Figure 72.1.

At the time of debates about Third, imperfect, revolutionary, and exilic film theories, the cinematic production of the Fourth World, now more widely known as *Indigenous Film*, was still incipient. Within the countries of origin as well as internationally, this work was insufficiently screened.

As a result, it seemed auspicious to bring indigenous perspectives into the scrutinizing yet respectful documentary "safe space" of the Flaherty. The programming strategy implied by the seminar title seemed to reject the ethnographic and anthropological boxes that had typically contained indigenous work.

As the days went on and the films I presented were screened and debated, what transpired surprised even me. Although I was originally slated to serve as a discussion moderator, I'd had little idea about what would be screened.

The first surprise, however, unfurled as soon as I arrived. Mahen and Carlos explained that the director of the films I was to present, Dante Cerano, had had to cancel his trip. This situation left me as his sole representative at the post-screening sessions, shifting my role from moderator to participant.

Because Dante's visual style was complex and experimental, I surmised it would be challenging to represent his work. Although I had helped to subtitle his videos, translating from Spanish and Purépecha to

English and editing the English subtitles to screen more seamlessly in the anglophone world, I knew I could not speak for the absent director, even though I had presented the videos widely.

I was put into an unusual surrogate role, where the only indigenous director's voice that had been programmed would be absent from the conversation. There were no other indigenous guests or attendees, usually not the case in the indigenous film festivals and community gatherings where I've tended to show this work.

After screening Dante's *Xanini/Corn Stalks* (1999) and *Día 2/Day 2* (2003), I fielded questions I'd never heard in public presentations before. These comments ranged from the on-screen elements of the videos' aesthetics to deeper issues of authenticity and storytelling. In *Xanini /Corn Stalks*, the corn serves as the protagonist and literally "speaks" in the Purépecha language of the Mexican state of Michoacán.

In *Día 2/Day 2*, a traditional wedding includes sweeping the yard at dawn, processing across town carrying the dowry, dancing with your elder auntie (shown in dizzying split screen), eating a death-defying chili soup, and interviewing a semi-passed-out uncle. During the procession, a relative of the groom taps on the camera lens in greeting, shattering the illusion of fly-on-the-wall filming. Unconstrained by more traditional structures of documentary narration, this wedding video came out of left field for some participants.

While the Flaherty audience tends to be versed in a rich range of cinematic traditions and theories, even this sophisticated group was unprepared for Dante's imaginative video renderings shot on humble formats such as Super VHS and Mini DV. His work helped attendees realize that emergent and savvy explorations coming from very rooted (or *embedded*, to use Faye Ginsburg's term) contexts inspired by traditional practices and told in indigenous languages could be surprising, refreshing, and challenging.

I was gratified when guest filmmakers' comments resonated with the process of indigenous media. "Filmmaking is like cooking," explained Chadian director Mahamet-Saleh Haroun. "You make what you can with what you have." He was referring to the "imperfect" aesthetics of some of the films screened. He did not call them out for their lack but celebrated what they offered.

In the context of this seminar, I felt the indigenous films helped shift the debate from the deficit model, traditionally applied to so-called *southern* or *third* cinemas, and returned the emphasis back to human creativity.

In this vein, Indonesian-Dutch filmmaker Leonard Retel Helmrich, also a guest at that seminar, proposed innovative, lo-fi solutions to achieve candid interviews in intimate spaces, as we saw in his films *The Eye of the*

Day (2001), *Shape of the Moon* (2004), and *Promised Paradise* (2006). Shot in the slums, streets, and prisons of Jakarta, often in cramped quarters, these films offer the first-person voice with no buffer and no shame and characters with nothing to lose or gain. While some scenes could scan as overly intrusive and perhaps even miserabilist, in Leonard's case, who holds the camera and how made all the difference.

In indigenous spaces, listening constitutes a foundational rule of engagement. Because Flaherty audiences knew how *to listen* and how *to see*, screening indigenous films at the seminar was a natural fit. It offered a dignified experience not always achieved when indigenous films cross over into purely cinematic spaces, removed from indigenous and advocacy contexts.

Through their exhibition at the Flaherty seminar, indigenous films gained important allies, including programmers and scholars of color who had never seen these works before.

After the seminar, I stayed in touch with various directors, curators, and scholars. I received calls to bring indigenous films to university campuses. I joined the Flaherty board. While life events made me leave the board too soon, I enjoyed being a part of the inner circle. I have never worked with a better organized and more good-spirited nonprofit organization.

The Flaherty seminar validated some of my more intuitive working methodologies, such as the importance of always striving to have the first-person voice represented, the value of interdisciplinary dialogue, and the ability to discuss complicated issues respectfully.

My Flaherty circle of colleagues and friends is unconditional. Although separated by great distances, languages, and sometimes long absences, I make an effort to stay in the loop with the Flaherty. When I can, I show up at the annual Leo Dratfield Brunch in Manhattan. And of course, I harbor many curatorial dreams about the Flaherty's future editions.

A lot has happened since my debut at Flaherty in 2007, and I think the seminar was very influential in my decision to go back and get my PhD in film.

73

FORGETTING FLAHERTY

John Muse

JOHN MUSE is Visual Media Scholar at Haverford College. His projects include conference papers on Roland Barthes, Omer Fast, Roni Horn, Alvin Lucier, and Ruben Pater exploring object-oriented aesthetics, drone culture, and reenactment. In September of 2017, he and longtime collaborator Jeanne C. Finley screened their new experimental film, *Book Report*, at the Aesthetica Short Film Festival. He occasionally collaborates with Philadelphia-based performance artist Mason Rosenthal and continues to document small cairns built at the corner of Ardmore and Lancaster Avenues in Ardmore, Pennsylvania, and elsewhere.

I have been asked to tell my Flaherty story, to recover a few impressions from my first time at the seminar.

But my first-person voice, particularly when narrative and recollection are involved, tends to be weirdly "away" and about itself. I rarely remember much. At least, nothing in continuity.

Away and yet *a way*. Because I talk about forgetting. So, here we go.

Irina Leimbacher, who championed our work in the 1990s as a programmer for the San Francisco Cinematheque, invited my longtime collaborator, Jeanne C. Finley, and me to present at her 2009 Flaherty seminar, entitled Witnesses, Monuments, Ruins.

Figure 73.1. Photograph by Ryan Gooding/Haverford College.

We screened our single-channel works: *At the Museum: A Pilgrimage of Vanquished Objects* (1989), *Based on a Story* (1997), and *The Adventures of Blacky* (1998). We also installed a two-channel installation entitled *Guarded* (2003) and presented an artist's talk about other installation works.

I do remember *Guarded*, or rather I remember what it looked like, having consulted my photographs, but not the single-channel works. Fortunately, the screening notes tell me what else we showed, otherwise I would have to guess.

That is to say, I cannot remember a single story, a specific conversation, or a telling word from that seminar. Instead, there are a few images.

I remember standing next to Jeanne at the podium at the front of the packed Golden Auditorium, waiting to present our artist talk.

I remember chatting at the bar with Roger Hallas, a documentary scholar, writer, and professor from Syracuse University, though these descriptors do not form part of my recollection. And was that chat before or after our talk? I forget.

In subsequent years, I've tended to greet Roger as "Bruce." Sorry, Roger!

I remember that John Knecht, professor of Art and Art History and Film and Media Studies at Colgate—I just looked up his title online—greeted us the first evening.

Wearing jeans and sporting a gray ponytail and a mustache, Knecht was affable, warm, positive, encouraging. He must have oriented us to the space where *Guarded* was to be mounted and to the equipment available. We must have arrived early to set up.

One final image: after one of our post-screening panels, I know I talked to someone; maybe it was Lucien Castaing-Taylor, a documentary filmmaker from the Sensory Ethnography Lab at Harvard. But maybe I'm just wishing it had been him. Irina doubts my recollection. I trust her.

My Lucien said he was irritated because we handled the Iraq War so flippantly in our installation *Flat Land* (2009), a work we described during our artist talk but did not install.

He didn't say *flippant*. That is the impression that persists though. I remember Jeanne and I saying to each other afterward, "We will never present that piece in a talk again." Of course, we did subsequently, because we learned to trust our own ironies and handle them more delicately.

Over the years, I've shared many of my Flaherty photographs with friends and seminarians via social media. Yes, I photograph everything. As mentioned before, I documented *Guarded*. These pictures include me, Jeanne, and Warren Wheeler, but there are a few that someone else must have taken. Who? Strangely, aside from these, I took only three pictures.

All three are of Jeanne and my wife, Vicky Funari, the documentary filmmaker featured at the 2000 Flaherty, at dinner in the Colgate cafeteria. Jeanne talks. Vicky listens and smiles. I know it is dinner. The metadata tells me it is 7:15 p.m.

(Kafka's line in Roland Barthes's *Camera Lucida* [1980] rings true and false. Yes, I photograph things to forget them, but I cannot forget the things I have not photographed. It is as though these latter things never existed and so cannot even be forgotten.)

As I look at these three photographs now, they seem strong documents because they're filled with particulars and with people I love.

But they are also weak. They give me nothing to help me frame events that I know I lived through but cannot recall.

Fortunately, I have other ways to remember.

In a June 24, 2009, Facebook reply to a friend who wanted to know more about the 2009 seminar, I posted the following: "It was grueling. And amazing. Irina Leimbacher curated this year; and she's wicked smart and has wide-ranging and eclectic tastes. For the first time, there are installation works at Flaherty. I didn't know how huge and intense this event was; now I do . . . The schedule produces just enough exhaustion that folks finally say all the things they shouldn't, which makes for lively conversations. I like the secrecy and the saturation. The inevitable tension:

academics versus makers versus nonprofit denizens versus representatives of NGOs versus cinephiles."

And let me combine two emails I sent to Irina soon after the seminar:

Irina, thanks so much for the adventure. The week was a feast, both intellectual and sensual; and we're grateful that you thought and think enough of us to put us in the same league with the filmmakers and artists on the program . . .

It was really exciting and strangely fulfilling: *Guarded* looked great, and I feel better about the work, even *At the Museum* (and I take back my own objection: the work doesn't dictate the destruction of all museological habits, otherwise the interviews would make no sense.) I and we feel better about the work for having shown it there and survived.

The "enchiladas" (Vicky's word for academic intellectuals) were lukewarm but warm. Which, given the power of most of the work, is good enough for me.

For me, remembering is simply the process I'm undertaking right now as I write this piece.

I scour social media. I talk to friends. I fill in a few gaps and leave others to their enigmas. I talk about how I do this "remembering" while I do it.

The *I* that narrates its labors and the *I* found in memory and lost in forgetting coincide nowhere but here. And here is the place of recollection.

74

BREATHING THROUGH THE SCREEN

Marit Kathryn Corneil

MARIT KATHRYN CORNEIL is a Canadian scholar and filmmaker teaching film studies and documentary at the Department for Art and Media Studies at the Norwegian University of Science and Technology (NTNU) in Trondheim, Norway. She has published chapters in *Beyond the Visual* (2010), *Challenge for Change: Activist Documentary at the National Film Board of Canada* (2010), and *Hvor Går Dokumentaren?* (2014). Her research examines contemporary documentary film theory and practice, tracing genealogies of various approaches, epistemologies, and traditions.

I first heard about the Flaherty Film Seminar when I was an undergraduate in Cinema Studies at the University of Toronto back in the mid-1980s.

In filmmaker Kay Armitage's documentary class, I watched Robert Flaherty's films. As a child, I'd seen *Nanook of the North* (1922) and *Man of Aran* (1934) many times as a result of the National Film Board of Canada's 16mm public library distribution system. At the time, Erik Barnouw's *Documentary* (1974) and Bill Nichols's *Ideology and the Image* (1981) were the only textbooks.

I can't exactly remember when I became aware of the Flaherty seminar. Maybe it was watching Jonas Mekas's *Lost Lost Lost* (1976), where

Figure 74.1.

filmmakers Mekas and Ken Jacobs shoot freewheeling 16mm images in a field of flowers. In 1963, these monks of cinema, not welcomed at the seminar, slept in the back of their truck parked on the farm where the seminar was held.

Many assume the Flaherty seminar is a closed cult with a mystique of inaccessibility and elitism. I overheard this critique in film studies department hallways on two continents.

I was surprised to discover that anyone could sign up, as long as you were quick enough to secure a spot on the first-come, first-served registration list. So in 2009, I signed up.

At the time, I was working through a research project on the effects of digital culture on documentary. I needed inspiration. I needed to breathe.

I had observed the rise of new performative and political documentary forms in films by Nick Broomfield, Michael Moore, Errol Morris, and Laura Poitras, as well as the turn to the more personal autobiographical and essayistic documentaries of Jonathan Caouette, Werner Herzog, Hubert Sauper, and Agnès Varda.

However, Irina Leimbacher's powerful international program in 2009 consolidated a new world and a new way of thinking about cinema and documentary for me. Her expanded understanding of documentary, ethnographic, and experimental work (what Scott MacDonald calls *avant-doc*) included video art installations and multiple modalities of single-stream cinema exemplified in the work of filmmakers like Kamal Aljafari, Ilisa Barbash, Lucien Castaing-Taylor, Susanna Helke, and Amar Kanwar.

In subsequent years at the seminar, I realized that this new, ever-expanding experimental documentary arena featured a plethora of approaches and forms ranging from witness and testimony, single- and multichannel, animation, reenactment, mockumentary, observational, sensorial, ethnographic, hybrid, diasporic, abstract, and exploratory.

Each year, I saw films that stayed with me:

In 2010, Uruphong Raksasad's *Agrarian Utopia* (2011), Michael Glawogger's *Workingman's Death* (2004), Kazuhira Soda's *Campaign* (2007), and Lisandro Alonso's *Libertad* (2001).

In 2011, Les Blank's *A Poem is a Naked Person* (1974) and Caroline Martel's *Wavemakers* (2012).

In 2012, Minda Martin's *Freeland* (2009), Ben Rivers's *Ah Liberty!* (2008), Sylvain George's *Qu'ils reposent en révolte* (2010), and Susana de Sousa Dias's *48* (2008).

In 2013, Deborah Stratman's *O'er the Land* (2008), The Otolith Group's *The Radiant* (2012), and Sarah Maldoror's *Sambizanga* (1972).

In 2014, Eric Baudelaire's *The Anabasis of May* (2011), Hito Steyerl's *How Not to be Seen* (2013), CAMP collective's *From Gulf to Gulf to Gulf* (2013).

In 2015, Steve Reinke's *Squeezing Sorrow from an Ashtray* (1992), Tariq Teguia's *Inland* (2008), and Hala Lotfy's *Coming Forth by Day* (2012).

In 2016, Joaquim Pinto's *What Now? Remind Me*(2013), Saul Levine's *On the Spot* (1973), Naomi Kawase's *Katatsumori* (1994), Luis Ospina's *It All Started at the End* (2015).

Of course, there are many more. And after a while, the films blend together within the ritual experience of watching them in the theater.

The discussions flow out from the theater into the discussion room, the dining hall, and into Bill's Bar, a makeshift setup of a folding table, wine, beer, and a jar for donations. I usually manage to speak with nearly all the participants—graduate students, Flaherty fellows, seasoned academics, or invited filmmakers.

I've gotten a chance to discuss my passion for documentary with scholar Deirdre Boyle, one of my heroes, as we enjoyed the shade together. She later introduced me to her friends at the National Film Board of Canada (NFB) and to filmmaker George Stoney, who told me stories about working with Judith Helfand and the NFB's indigenous film unit.

Bill Brand shared his work restoring the films of Helen Hill after Hurricane Katrina left them stained. Lourdes Portillo saw through my hesitancy and gave me purpose. Patricia Zimmermann gave me invaluable career advice.

At my third or fourth Flaherty, I discovered such hidden rituals as playing four square, dancing in Bill's Bar until 3:00 a.m., and sneaking off to swim in a nearby pond. By the end of the week, the highly skilled deejays, Flaherty regulars, manage to get everyone dancing, even stiff Northerners like me.

The seminar's morning-to-night schedule deprives me of sleep. I start to wake and breathe through the screen.

The inevitable, intense, frustrating, sometimes enraged discussions around questions of representation, rights to the image, and ethics usually feel to me like circular debates that may never be reconciled—though sometimes they remain with me for months afterward.

Programmed by Nuno Lisboa, the 2017 seminar crystalized the debate around these issues. The controversy over Dominic Gagnon's *of the North* (2015) apparently spurred the cancellation of the annual screening of a Flaherty film, a seminar tradition.

Nuno's European festival circuit programming crashed against the young, politically agitated North American audience comprised of many more fellows than in other years. This clash felt politically volatile.

I have gone on to write about and teach the works of many Flaherty filmmakers. I've also incorporated Frances Flaherty's ideas about non-preconception into my teaching. It opens up my students to film experiences they would otherwise never encounter.

In the middle of each seminar, I declare, "This will be the last!"

Every year, I come back, to breathe through the screen once again.

75

THE ACT OF SEEING ATTENTIVELY

Richard Shpuntoff

RICHARD SHPUNTOFF is a filmmaker and photographer from Queens, New York, residing in Buenos Aires, Argentina, since 2002. His first feature-length documentary, *Julio of Jackson Heights* (2016), is a portrait of the neighborhood where he was born and raised as it responded to the 1990 gay-bashing murder of Julio Rivera. His intimate essay film on language, history, and identity is entitled *Buenos Aires para vos* (2018). Together with Kelly Cogswell, author of *Eating Fire: My Life as a Lesbian Avenger* (2014), he directed a film about the seduction of hate politics called *Tales from the Rainbow Wars* (2019).

I first met Margarita De La Vega Hurtado in 2008 in Caracas, Venezuela, at what had been dubbed *the first meeting of Latin American documentary filmmakers of the twenty-first century.*

The meeting had two purposes.

Developed by Mexican filmmaker Oscar Menendez along with Argentine filmmakers Humberto Rios and Dolores Miconi, the original idea for the meeting was to recover the memory of the historic 1968 Merida Film Festival. That festival was a culminating event for the Latin American film movement of the 1960s.

But this seed of an idea planted by Oscar Menendez at the end of the Film Festival of Memory in Tepoztlan, Mexico, in 2007, grew in the hands and minds of Rios and Miconi.

Figure 75.1. Photograph by LuluSolei Photography.

Working from their offices at the documentary image archive in Argentina's national film school, they pushed the idea of an international meeting that would not only remember and celebrate the Merida festival and its historic importance, but that also might build a bridge between that past and the present reality: a revisiting of the issues and ideas of Merida to recover what is and should be relevant today.

After I interviewed Humberto for an article I had written on the history of Argentine documentary film, he invited me to cover the event. Humberto, who has since passed on, was the camera person on *México, la Revolución congelada* (*Mexico, the Frozen Revolution*, 1973), directed by Raymundo Gleyzer, who was disappeared by the Argentine military in 1976. Some of Humberto's work is featured in the landmark film *La hora de los hornos* (*The Hour of the Furnaces*, 1968) by Fernando Solanas and Octavio Getino.

I sat down for an interview with Margarita, who had attended the 1968 festival. It was the most important interview I did at the event.

Margarita gave me enormous insight into the meaning of Merida and what filmmaking was like at that time. We also hit it off.

We spoke about the particular nature of living bicultural lives: Margarita, a Colombian from Medellin who had lived all over the United States, and me, a Queens Jew living in Buenos Aires. I talked with her about my checkered history as a documentary photographer and filmmaker.

Somewhere in the middle of this conversation, she paused and said, "You need to attend the Flaherty seminar. Do you know the Flaherty?" And then she added, "And you should cover it for a film magazine."

At this point, I was so impressed by Margarita that had she said, "You should spend a hot, sweaty summer in Boca Raton," I probably would have gone. Fortunately, she'd suggested the Flaherty seminar.

I pitched the idea to Tom White of the International Documentary Association, which publishes the magazine *Documentary*. He said yes. I got to work and learned about the Flaherty.

If I had been true to the spirit of the Flaherty and its idea of non-preconception (an idea much more seriously developed by Frances than by Robert), I would not have read a thing. I would have gone and experienced the event. But that's not me.

Maybe that is precisely why the Flaherty had such a great impact on me.

Committing to watching hours of film—even a few films that were mind-numbing experiences for me—without any idea what would appear next on the screen, in order to participate in group conversations and to try to understand and accept that a film that said nothing to me spoke mountains to someone else, was a difficult but rewarding experience.

More important to me than any individual film was the overall Flaherty experience, the way the week of films and conversations melted into one large experience of reflection.

The Flaherty seminar is a massive collaborative effort. People like then–program director Mary Kerr and manager Farihah Zaman, as well as Steve Holmgren and Laura Major, made the seminar real. I still remember drunkenly spinning Mary Kerr in my arms to a Jackson Five song the night we learned that Michael Jackson had died!

Fortunately, the year I was there (2009), Irina Leimbacher was the seminar curator. Film after film washed over me. Conversations from one day seemed to creep into conversations from another day. I slowly gave up on the idea of trying to find some solid logical idea behind her selection and structure. I did, however, believe that there was an evil genius behind all of this.

When I interviewed Irina for the article after the seminar was over, I asked her about the decision to start the festival with no introduction. She'd just turned off the lights and hit the button to project Chick Strand's *Kristallnacht* (1979). The film contrasted a powerful title—especially for an Ashkenazi Jew—with a rapturous, visual beauty.

Irina explained: "*Kristallnacht* was presented opening night, before any introductions were made, as a way of bringing attention to the act of seeing attentively. It was my attempt to get the participants to let go of the anxiety of needing to understand everything and instead give themselves over to the multifaceted and sensuous experience of film."

At that moment, she confirmed that the Flaherty had become a before-and-after moment for me.

76

FROM COLGATE UNIVERSITY TO THE CENTRAL AFRICAN REPUBLIC

Frances Guerin

FRANCES GUERIN teaches film at the University of Kent in Paris. She is author of *A Culture of Light: Cinema and Modernity in 1920s Germany* (2005); *Through Amateur Eyes: Film and Photography in Nazi Germany* (2011); and *The Truth is Always Grey: A History of Modernist Painting* (2018). She is coeditor of *The Image and the Witness: Trauma, Memory and Visual Culture* (2007, with Roger Hallas) and editor of *On Not Looking: The Paradox of Contemporary Visual Culture* (2015) and *European Photography Today* (2017).

In early winter 2008, my friend and colleague Roger Hallas insisted that I attend the Flaherty seminar at Colgate University in central New York the following summer.

Roger assured me it would be life-changing—especially because the theme, Witnesses, Monuments, Ruins, was the focus of our recently published anthology, *The Image and the Witness* (2007).

Even though the films to be screened were not announced in advance, Roger assured me not to worry about the programming. Our mutual friend, Irina Leimbacher, former artistic director of the San Francisco Cinémathèque, was the programmer for the 2009 seminar.

I could never have imagined the central place some of the films would take in my future thinking and writing about the relations between film,

Figure 76.1.

trauma, and witnessing. Irina's packed schedule of screenings, talks, discussions, interviews, and special events opened door after door.

Seeing the films Irina had chosen, I realized I had only just begun to scrape the surface of film's relationship to witnessing the tensions between traumatic historical and personal events and the unique challenges to monumentalization enabled by film as a medium.

The week began with a screening of Chick Strand's *Kristallnacht* (1979), a complex and provocative film that set the tone for a week of surprises and revelations. Irina announced that her one regret about showing this film was that Strand was too ill to be present for the occasion. I had heard of Strand (through her work with Bruce Baillie at Canyon Cinema), but I had never seen her films.

Admitting this, I feel somewhat inadequate as a film scholar. When I studied cinema at New York University in the 1990s, most books on the American avant-garde focused on New York filmmakers. If it weren't for figures such as Bruce Baillie and Jordan Belson, I might have believed that postwar experimental film was the exclusive purview of the East Coast while Hollywood entirely dominated the West Coast.

I was mesmerized by Strand's images of water, its reflections and movement in *Kristallnacht* . . . until images of women enjoying a night swim were violently interrupted by sounds of a gong and a train bursting into the idyllic scene. The sonic invasion was physically disturbing.

Together with the soundtrack, the film's title reminded me that something devastating lurked around the edges of the water and the film. A text at the beginning of *Kristallnacht*—"White chrysanthemum/before that perfect flower/scissors hesitate"—and one at the end—"For Anne Frank"—clarified why *Kristallnacht* was a disturbing, yet perfect film to open the week.

Kristallnacht suggests that devastating historical events leave their imprint on the private lives and bodies of women. The sensuality of water, the violent incursion of the train and of the gong generate emotional and intellectual effects resonating all the way from the night of broken glass in 1938 to the present moment of watching.

The representation of a direct line between past and present set the scene for the week to come.

If Strand's *Kristallnacht* demonstrated the capacity of cinema to record what we know but cannot see, a film shown at 9:00 a.m. on Wednesday morning showed the opposite: documentary cinema's responsibility to make explicit what *can* be seen, as a way of inciting change in the world.

I dragged myself out of bed to see *Clean Thursday* (2004), a Russian film about military forces occupying Chechnya in the aftermath of war. The film demonstrated the chilling capacity of documentary cinema to make visible what otherwise might never be known.

Clean Thursday is a strange mosaic of scratched leader tape overlaid with the sound of distant guns, black-and-white stock footage from the Chechen conflict, and color footage of young occupation forces posted at a military outpost at the war's end. The young soldiers live in a retrofitted train, complete with laundry, showers, sleeping bunks, kitchen, and mess room.

While Strand's camera in *Kristallnacht* expresses the sensuality of women's experiences and how war in the twentieth century impacts them, *Clean Thursday* conveys the hidden vulnerability of young Russian men as they fight one of the bloodiest conflicts of the twenty-first century.

In a scene that begins with wastewater spilling onto the mud underneath the shower carriage of the train, the camera slowly pans to reveal the men's naked bodies as they recount with bravado their stories of sexual prowess, rape, blasphemy, and murder. The men tenderly wash each other's backs. In a later scene, one carefully shaves the others' heads.

These touching representations of young men who are no more than boys abut the repulsive battlefield behavior they boast about under the showers. The film left me reflecting on the irreconcilability of the public and the private sides of war.

The director, Aleksandr Rastorguev, was apparently fired from his position at the state regional Don TV in Rostov-on-Don shortly after making *Clean Thursday*.

In July 2018, while filming a documentary about Russian mercenaries operating in the Central African Republic, Rastorguev was assassinated.

While the thread between past and present is kept alive in *Kristallnacht*, *Clean Thursday* and the fate of its director remind me that in some parts of the world, the connections between past and present have been broken.

It's hard to believe that the same country that produced pioneering documentary films during the postrevolutionary period, pushing the cinema beyond its limits and challenging the relationship between cinema and the world, is now killing people for making documentary films.

The makers of two of my favorite films at that 2009 Flaherty are now dead: one from the spread of cancer invading her body, the other from a politically motivated violent attack on his.

Both deaths remind me that the need for film to find its way among the ruins, to continue as a witness to the trauma created by historical and personal events, and to challenge the monumentalization so coveted by repressive regimes has never been more urgent.

77

A VIRUS AND A MISSION

Dagmar Kamlah

DAGMAR KAMLAH is a filmmaker and curator from Germany. In 1996, her feature narrative about money, *Heidengeld* (*Unbelievable Money*, 1996), received a Hessian Film award. Her short *Schöne Alte Welt* (*Brave Old World*, 2000) was in the Kinodot online festival. In Boston, she produced *Blue Jay Territory* (2009). Her feature documentary about eight collectors from Boston and Germany is entitled *Von Dingen* (*Of Things*, 2019). Since 2001, she has curated programs at Kommunales Kino Freiburg, International Film Festival Braunschweig, and Kino für Moabit Berlin. Since 2013, she has been a member of the festival programming team of the Freiburger Film Forum.

In Germany, the Flaherty isn't well-known.

But I had lived in Boston from 2006 to 2012 and spent my weekends at the Harvard Film Archive (HFA). Through the Boston filmmaking grapevine, I heard about the Robert Flaherty Film Seminar.

Another regular HFA patron mentioned the seminar to me with great respect. She said that everybody who returned from the Flaherty raved about it. Since I was a foreign filmmaker seeking contacts and insights, the seminar seemed to be *the* place to go.

So, in 2009, I went to the Flaherty. I'd imagined a seminar of maybe fifty participants. When I got there, I was shocked to realize that I was one of 180!

Figure 77.1.

I had trouble following the large group discussions, partly because I speak German and partly because I could not hear everything that was said. For me, these huge discussions neither added much to the films nor opened up the programming concept.

However, I enjoyed the programming itself. I discovered filmmakers I'd never heard of, including Omar Amiralay, Pavel Medvedev, and Chick Strand. I also liked that year's program curator, Irina Leimbacher.

I was lucky to take part in some lively late-night talks at Bill's Bar. I made a few friends. And I became more familiar with the Boston film-making community. Ilisa Barbash and Lucien Castaing-Taylor's *Sweet-grass* (2009) was screened with many Bostonians present.

I would have loved to return to the seminar the following year, because the theme was WORK. In 2007, I had curated a little film series in Germany, as part of a big project supported with national cultural funding, entitled "Work in Progress." I applied for a LEF fellowship to attend the seminar but wasn't lucky enough to receive one. Since my financial situation was less than stable, I could not afford to pay my own way.

In 2014, an ethnic German filmmaker named Caspar Stracke cocurated the seminar together with his Mexican partner, Gabriela Monroy. Although I had returned to Germany, I could not resist going to this Flaherty.

Also, I had a mission.

I had joined the programming team of a small ethnographic film festival, the Freiburger Film Forum. Since 1985, it has run biannually in an old university town in the south of Germany.

I hoped to start a collaboration between the Freiburger Film Forum and the Flaherty. Our forum and the seminar share a similar structure of continuous screenings with only one film shown at a time and a focus on dialogue and discussion between the filmmakers and participants.

I recruited a filmmaker friend from Germany who was planning a US trip. We both enjoyed the seminar. We loved some of the programming and especially the chance to listen to the great experimental documentarian Jill Godmilow.

I'd contacted the seminar director and some board members concerning my idea of a collaboration. They were friendly and interested. I departed from that seminar with a clear intention to develop a Flaherty homage for the Freiburger Film Forum.

In 2016, I returned to the seminar to arrange a mutual project. I studied the history of the seminar in order to develop a programming proposal, which evolved from a retrospective of ethnographic work to a focus on contemporary political documentary with some historical works: *Eloge du Chiac* (1969), *Los Sures* (1984), *An Injury to One* (2002), *Free Land* (2009).

Our collaborative program eventually happened in May 2017.

We invited former Flaherty curator and board member John Gianvito to serve as a special guest. He discussed the films in a most delightful way. This well-received program made a strong statement about the committed cinema of resistance in the United States.

I wanted to introduce the long-standing institution of the Flaherty Film Seminar to the German film community. Because our Freiburg venue belongs to the nationwide association of community theaters, the programmers who belong to this organization are stimulated by our careful curation. They learn about our programming through articles published in the association's magazine.

My hope is that the collaboration between the Freiburger Film Forum and the Flaherty Film Seminar will inspire others to provide access to the immense archive of films that have been shown at the seminar over the decades. For me, these programs signal love for the documentary genre and the treasures of reality one can discover in these films.

My Flaherty story underscores that one important aspect of the seminar is to facilitate networking among those who care deeply about accomplished filmmaking. I am happy to be a small part of this community. Though I would not call myself a seminar devotee, the virus of the Flaherty has touched me.

Nevertheless, I would suggest that downsizing might be something for the seminar to consider.

It is also true that the Flaherty is not exempt from the self-aggrandizement that often characterizes public cultural environments. Instead of a true dialogue between different kinds of participants, the large group discussions tend to become a chain of overly elaborate scholarly statements. I would like some of the scholars in attendance to behave in a less "scholarly" way.

Nevertheless, compared to other film gatherings I have attended, the Flaherty is the best at providing a democratic and open platform.

78

I DIDN'T KNOW WHAT I WAS DOING

Paweł Wojtasik

PAWEŁ WOJTASIK is a filmmaker and video artist born in Łódź, Poland, and living in Brooklyn, New York. He trained as a painter. From 1998 until 2000, he was a resident at Dai Bosatsu Zendo Buddhist monastery. Wojtasik's work has been exhibited at MoMA PS1, the Whitney Museum, the Museum of the Moving Image, the Reina Sofia Museum (Madrid), and the Martos Gallery, New York. It has also screened at the Locarno, Berlin, and New York film festivals and other international venues. Wojtasik codirected *End of Life* (2017) with John Bruce. His *Every Pulse of the Heart Is Work* (2019), a feature-length film shot in Varanasi, India, was included in 2020 Doc Fortnight at MoMA.

I was asked by Mary Kerr to film a trailer for the seminar, something that could be used for "propaganda" purposes.

The filming was to take place during the 2010 seminar, WORK, programmed by Dennis Lim. The idea was to give viewers the visceral sensation of being in the thick of it, as if they were taking part in the screenings, discussions, and extracurricular activities.

I'd been a Flaherty filmmaker the year before. The 2009 seminar, Monuments, Witnesses, Ruins, programmed by Irina Leimbacher, was my first, and it was love at first sight. I was happy to help promote the cult of Flaherty.

Figure 78.1.

I was delighted to find out that my friend Josh Solondz would be participating in the project as assistant director. Josh and I were born on the same day (December 11). The stars were definitely aligning in our favor.

Our producer was Mary Kerr herself; Lucila Moctezuma was associate producer. We enlisted the help of Gerry Hooper, a frequent Flaherty participant and an experienced DP who had worked in Bollywood on the breakthrough gangster film *Satya* (1998).

From the start, the idea was to conduct interviews with the seminar filmmakers. This would be a way for us to get to know them, learn from them, poke fun at them, and, perhaps, abuse them a bit. Our team got a boost from Daniela Alatorre, who helped with the interviews.

Our dual role made the seminar experience exhilarating for me—and a constant challenge. But because of our special situation, we could see more than an average participant, and we could enjoy the comic aspect of this gathering of film lovers who brought their various preconceived notions and prejudices to a place where non-preconception was the official rule.

We'd been asked to make a trailer, something on the level of a brief commercial, but somehow we were inspired to approach the task as a serious film project. Surrounded by brilliant seminar filmmakers, academics, and other outstanding participants, I felt we had to try for the highest level of excellence.

The problem was, I didn't know what I was doing. I'd hardly ever filmed human beings, except for dead ones (in *Nascentes Morimur*, 2009)! I'd filmed pigs and naked mole rats and sewage!

I tried to place the interviewed filmmakers in environments corresponding to the atmosphere of their films. Michael Glawogger's *Megacities* (1998) and *Workingman's Death* (2004) put viewers in the midst of perilous workplaces—a slaughterhouse in Nigeria, a do-it-yourself coal mine in the Ukraine, sulfur collection inside an Indonesian volcano—so we interviewed Michael in the Flaherty kitchen, in the midst of the clamor, with workers passing in front of the camera.

I would start each interview asking about the idea of non-preconception. Michael asserted that there was no such thing but that it was a nice idea to entertain.

We shot two great Mexican filmmakers, friends and rivals Eugenio Polgovsky and Pedro Gonzalez Rubio, in the swimming pool, a location suggested by Pedro's *Alamar* (2009).

For Lisandro Alonso, we tried a Hitchcockian *Vertigo* zoom—suggested by Lisandro's film *Los Muertos* (2004). As Lisandro and Dennis Lim walked up a ramp toward the camera, which had been placed on a rug, we attempted, at first without success, to pull the rug and camera backward as I zoomed in. Lisandro was amused and said that our clumsiness reminded him of shooting *Los Muertos* in the midst of the jungle. We enlisted the filmmaker Uruphong Raksasad to help us, and the rug began to move.

We filmed the artist Mika Rottenberg at the local gym, using exercise machines and lifting weights as she spoke—a fabulous location full of reflections in the mirrors and different types of bodies in motion. At some point, my conversation with Mika veered toward sex. That part was later excised from the online interview. Flaherty censorship!

We also interviewed Uruphong, Lucy Raven, Benj Gerdes and Jennifer Hayashida, Akosua Adoma Owusu, Alex Rivera, Kazuhiro Soda, Dayong Zhao, and Naomi Uman. The interviews were exhaustive. We'd set no limit to how long the conversations should be.

We began to spread the word that this would be a feature film about the seminar. We quickly produced a meta-trailer for that fictitious feature while working on the trailer proper. In our meta-trailer, Bill Brand, using the small, waterproof Kodak camera Mary Kerr had loaned us, filmed underwater shots of Lucy Raven doing laps in the pool. Dennis agreed to show the meta-trailer as part of a regular screening. I wonder if this was the first time that a film made during the seminar was shown at the seminar?

After the seminar was finished, Josh and I began editing our many hours of footage. We loved the material and had endless fun with it. During particularly hot summer days, we'd strip and edit au naturel. Many versions were created, representing the various modes of experimental filmmaking. Six months later, we had a two-and-a-half-hour feature.

We'd have continued had Mary not come by to bring us back to reality; the Flaherty, she reminded us, had requested only a two-minute piece.

Josh and I are still entertaining the idea of making the feature. After all, there's an entire archive of interview footage and discussion tapes that could be tapped. The feature could be endless—a Flaherty film that continues to grow longer, like the Flaherty experience itself, which feeds us and through which we continue to grow.

https://vimeo.com/18136767

Thanks to Josh Solondz and Jim Supanick for reviewing and adding valuable points to this piece.

79

SCENTS

Dayong Zhao

Translated by Elizabeth Wijaya

DAYONG ZHAO was born in 1970 in Fushun, People's Republic of China. He is a Chinese artist, a sometime entrepreneur and publicist, and more recently a film director. In 1997, he founded the design agency Guangzhou Dake, and in 1998, he began working as a director for commercials. He was founding editor of the now discontinued magazine *Culture & Morals* on contemporary art in China. He is director of the documentaries *Street Life* (2006), *Ghost Town* (2008), *Rough Poetry* (2009), *My Father's House* (2011), *The High Life* (2010), *Shadow Days* (2014), and *The Nailhouse: One Says No* (2016).

Though I have been living in New York for over a year, at this very moment I am on the high mountains of Yunnan shooting my new film and using my rest time to write this recollection.

More than eight years have passed since the 2010 Flaherty. There are many details I cannot remember clearly.

The car is driving along the narrow, windy, mountainous road in central New York state. It is four o'clock in the afternoon. The setting sun casts a layer of pale yellow on the hills.

A colleague who works with images drives. Two other media types are also in the car. I do not speak English, so I cannot communicate with them. I am wearing a light blue T-shirt with the image of a sewer worker

Figure 79.1.

lifting the manhole cover—for me, a visual metaphor for documentary filmmakers.

Outside the window, farms pass by. Horses leisurely graze. A gentle wind is blowing.

Sitting against the window, I sense the fragrance of the plants and the earth, bringing to mind the Changbai Mountain area in Northeast China, the hometown I left more than twenty years ago.

Every year after the long winter, I'd bring my dog to the open country to lie on the grass and bask in the sun. Looking up at the blue sky, I'd imagine myself growing up. The scent on this drive reminds me that I once had a homeland.

In the distance, a black horse-drawn carriage driven by two women in long dresses approaches us in the other lane. I have only seen this before in films. I suddenly become excited and use Mandarin to ask my companions, "Are there still people like these!" It seems like they understand me, and they use English to give me an explanation, and I seem to understand too.

When we arrive at Colgate University, the Taiwanese American film critic/programmer Chi-hui Yang helps me register. For the next few days, he translates for me. I am grateful to him.

The entire university, quiet and beautiful, is built against the hills. Each building has a history of nearly a hundred years. From time to time, a groundhog stands to look at us across the grass.

More than a hundred people have come for this event. We all stay in the student dormitory. On the first floor, there is a bar. Meals are served at the school's canteen. It is summer vacation, and other than us image workers, no one is around.

One night, programmer Dennis Lim brings a few of us to an Italian restaurant in the small town. Chi-hui Yang urges us to not let others know when our works will screen, so that everyone will have a surprise.

Each day divides into morning, afternoon, and evening screenings of features and shorts. Discussions follow each screening. Every day ends very late in the evening, and then it is time for the bar. Drinking goes on until nearly morning. But I go to bed early—I've come from China for this and am still dealing with the time difference.

The films are screened in the school's small cinema. At the screenings, a lot of people turn up. Some sit in the aisles. Having everyone crowd together every day to watch films creates a warm feeling.

The post-screening discussions are fierce. My film, *Ghost Town* (2008), is scheduled to be screened on Wednesday evening. The organizing committee has hired a translator for me, an anthropologist named Kevin (his Chinese name is Kai Da Xiong). His live translation is great! Later, he would come to Guangzhou, China; we've become good friends,

My deepest memories from that week are of Michael Glawogger's films.

In Glawogger's *Haiku* (1987), a short film about a Ukrainian steel mill worker, the first shot is a huge pneumatic hammer smashing down on a burning red iron block. The clang is deafening, shattering. Then a worker hoists this iron block back up, repeating the process. It feels like the theater is being demolished.

Suddenly the man is at home with a woman. The two of them face a simple meal; there is only the pleasant sound of eating. There is not one line of dialogue in the film—only that clang of the pneumatic hammer smashing on the iron and the sound of eating.

Workingman's Death (2005) shows the working conditions of laborers from a few different countries. It's a "big film"; you can tell a lot of money was spent on it.

A powerful segment is shot in the open-air slaughter market in Nigeria. Extremely bloody and disgusting. Butchers carry and drag the freshly cut cow legs and heads, placing them on a burning tire to roast. Thick smoke shrouds the huge space. This is the cow's hell, and humanity is the devil in this hell.

There are also segments about Ukrainian workers crouched low in caves to mine coal in the severe cold, about a sulfur mine in Indonesia, about a ship-breaking operation in Pakistan, about an old man who writes with a brush and water on the ground of a square in Anshan, China, and about Germany's abandoned-factory parks.

Glawogger's work is full of strength, just as he was. It made a deep impression on me.

During the last two days of passionate post-screening discussions, some feminists complain about the programmer. Why are so many of the films about men? This was the first time I had ever encountered such a question. In mainland China today, a totalitarian state and a feudal society, it is rare for someone to care about the status and rights of women.

The screening of *Ghost Town*, about a remote village in China, appears to satisfy the feminists because there is a section that tells the tale of a young mother who was swindled into a marriage in Shandong province.

The last night, everyone gathers at the bar to drink and dance. Dennis Lim opens a skull-shaped bottle of alcohol. Each person takes turns to drink a mouthful.

The days of many questions have filled my brain to the brim. I'm exhausted, but it's a fatigue that feels good.

On the morning of my departure, I wake up very early. Alone, I follow a mountain road until I reach a forest. I find a log to sit on while the morning sun shines through the tree branches and warms my body. A layer of mist drapes the mountain slope. I close my eyes and deeply inhale.

The scent around me is just like the scent of my childhood hometown.

80

MY OWN PRIVATE *RAYUELA*

Josetxo Cerdán

JOSETXO CERDÁN LOS ARCOS is a professor at the Universidad Carlos III de Madrid as well as Director of the Spanish Film Archive (Filmoteca Española). He has written on documentary, transnational film, the Atlantic Hispanic, and mobility. He has published articles in *Screen, Studies in Spanish & Latin American Cinemas*, and *Transnational Cinemas.* He has collaborated on collective books such as *The Routledge Companion to Latin American Cinema* (Marvin D'Lugo, Ana M. López, Laura Podalsky, 2017) and *Transnational Cinema at the Borders: Borderscapes and Cinematic Imaginary* (edited by Ana Cristina Mendes and John Sundholm, 2018). He was Artistic Director at Punto de Vista International Documentary Film Festival (2010–2013) and Programmer of the Flaherty seminar in 2012.

#1

Yes! I programmed the Flaherty seminar in 2012. We were young and wild. Well, more wild than young.

(From here on, you can read the whole text in a linear way, paragraph after paragraph, or choose your own way. I'll try to help you with some indications. If you're just interested in my Open Wounds seminar, you can read #3, #5, #10, and #12, and skip the rest.)

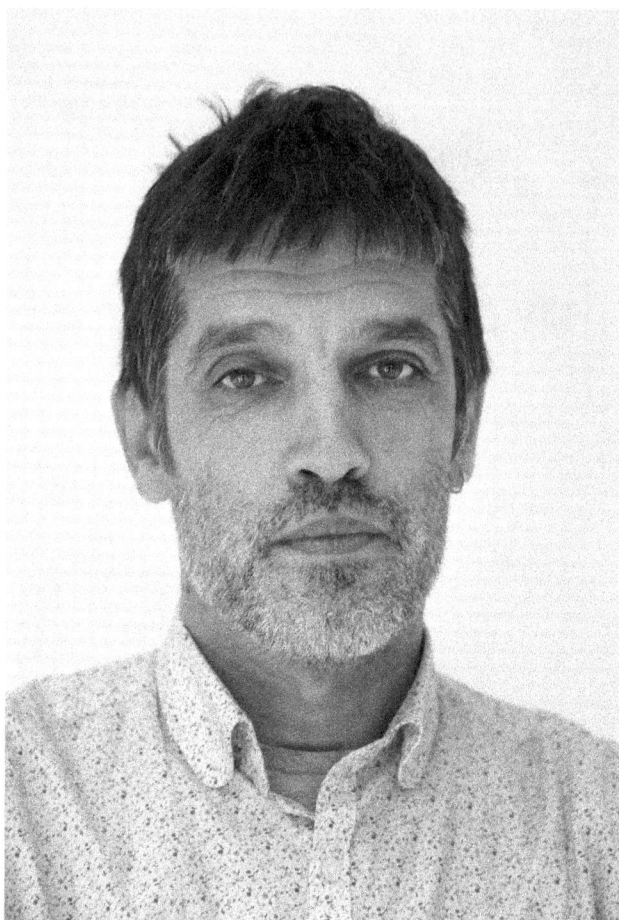

Figure 80.1.

#2

Since then, I've been wanting to return. I didn't try to come back in 2013—I needed a rest after attending three seminars in a row and being in the center of the storm during the last one. Anyway for one reason or another, I haven't been back. And yes, I miss you, Flaherty seminar.

(More about the earlier seminars I attended in #4, #5.)

#3

I think 2012 was a good year for the seminar. At least, people looked happy at the end, and most of the anonymous surveys confirmed this. Don't worry, I won't bore you with the nice comments I received; I read them to myself when I'm feeling down.

(If you think this is too corny, you can find some wilder anecdotes in #5, but if you're really enjoying it, you might want to jump to #10.)

#4

I participated in my first seminar in 2010. I'd arrived in New York that year on a grant from NYU's Department of Spanish and Portuguese Literature. The year before, I had agreed to be artistic director of the Punto de Vista. Former executive director of the Flaherty, Margarita De La Vega Hurtado, was my contact in America for Punto de Vista, so, being in New York and given my new programming position, there was no excuse: I had to go.

(If you would like to program the Flaherty, you'll find more about how I was selected to program in #6 and #7.)

#5

The 2010 seminar, WORK, was programmed by Denis Lim. I remember meeting Dennis the day before the seminar. He looked extremely nervous. I have great memories of that year. Carlos Gutiérrez has also shared this in his Flaherty story: 2010 was the year of the World Cup in South Africa (yes, the one won by Spain!). Most of the Latinos at the Flaherty, including Lisandro Alonso, Eugenio Polgovsky, and Pedro González Rubio, were soccer fans, so when there was a match (and there were matches all the time), we skipped screenings. I remember Lisandro saying to us in a low voice, "Hey guys, the next film is one of mine; let's watch the game!" The problem was that Lisandro's films are short, and we couldn't see the whole match before the discussion.

In 2012, there was no World Cup, but someone knew about a lake near Colgate University where people could swim. At the end of the seminar, there were two kinds of participants: those who had gone to the lake and those who hadn't.

(Is this too frivolous? Maybe you can find something more transcendental in #7 or #11.)

#6

If Margarita De La Vega Hurtado was the one to bring me to my first seminar, Lucila Moctezuma, then a Flaherty trustee, first made me think about the possibility of programming a Flaherty. I have a clear memory of her innocent smile when she asked me, during the 2010 seminar, "Would you like to program a seminar?" During my holidays, I drew up a proposal, and at the end of 2011, when my Flaherty experience was a distant midsummer night's dream, I received a call from Mary Kerr.

(You'll learn about the curatorial process in #7 and #9.)

#7

I learned a lot working on my Flaherty for almost a year and a half. I remember a crisis with Mary Kerr. It happened eight or ten weeks before the seminar. I sent Mary a first draft of the program and then, after a long, sleepless night, changed everything. She was really mad, and Lucila needed to mediate. Finally, Mary accepted my changes, and I agreed not to work during sleepless nights. My seminar was the last one for Mary as executive producer—no connection, I hope! By the end of the seminar, Mary and I were like two old pals after a dangerous mission. The title for my seminar (Open Wounds) was Mary's idea. I'd wanted it to be Bleeding Wounds. Dennis suggested There Will Be Blood. I liked them all.

(Now I need to summarize; if you feel you didn't read anything remarkable in the previous paragraphs, maybe you'd better stop reading, because you won't in the next five either!)

#8

Steve Holmgren was, at least for me, another key person during those years; he ran the bar my year and was the one who introduced me to the Flaherty Skull Ceremony. If you haven't heard about this, either you know little about the Flaherty or you're not interested in nightlife!

(A lot of partying goes on during the Flaherty. There are some other words about sleepless nights in #12.)

#9

I do have bittersweet memories, too. Debating my ideas with the advisory board on the phone was sometimes painful. I thought *I* was the programmer, but everybody had something to critique or something to propose.

On the good side, I remember the conversation with Kathy Geritz about Sun Xun and how she opened my mind—and Sun became part of the program. I have a special memory of a couple of conversations about seminar dynamics with John Gianvito at the Yamagata Documentary Film Festival. And Maria Campaña, a Flaherty fellow my year, helped me after the seminar: she made possible our having Eduardo Coutinho at Punto de Vista in 2013. I also remember Mar Cabra, a young Spanish woman who didn't enjoy the experimental part of my program. Now she's a well-known investigative journalist in Spain.

(In #11, I try to develop some controversial thoughts on the seminar dynamics.)

#10

I loved having Lourdes Portillo and Su Friedrich heading my filmmaker team. Now, almost six years later, I think even the collisions between filmmakers during the discussions allowed us to go further into how we think about film, history, and humanity.

(Do not read the next one if you haven't read #3, #5, and #9.)

#11

There is always something repetitive about the Flaherty. Not because of the regular structure of the event, but because of the dynamics of the discussions. It doesn't matter what the topic of the seminar is; at a certain point, particular issues will arise again and again. I was astonished during the WORK seminar that there was no discussion about class struggle at all. I mentioned it at some point, but the discussion went back to gender issues right away.

And in between discussions, there is always an underground battle going between two groups: the academics on one hand (too pretentious and theoretical for the others) and the filmmakers and people from the industry on the other (often identified as the old-timers). Of course, neither group believes in the principle of non-preconception, and part of the programmer's work is to deal with the preconceptions of both groups. I faced it in a confrontational way by playing a song before every screening to create a particular mood.

(Last paragraph: I hope your journey through my text has been worthy of your time.)

#12

The morning after my seminar, I remember a small group of sleepless people crossing the campus, heading down into the town of Hamilton to have breakfast. I was walking with a Flaherty newcomer, David Pendleton, the programmer at the Harvard Film Archive. He was completely enthusiastic about the seminar. Later, he had his own (PLAY, 2016). David is one of the three now-dead friends I've mentioned in my text, along with Eugenio and Eduardo. If documentary is about something, it's human beings, and the passing of these loved ones has left us all with bleeding wounds.

81

REVERBERATIONS AND AMPLIFICATIONS

Karin Chien

KARIN CHIEN has produced ten feature-length independent films, receiving the Cinereach Producers Award and the Independent Spirit Producer's Award. Her films have won over one hundred festival awards, premiered at the Sundance and Berlin Film Festivals, and been distributed in twenty countries. She is Founder/President of dGenerate Films, the leading distributor of independent cinema from mainland China. She cocreated the Cinema on the Edge screening series, celebrating contemporary Chinese cinema, and cofounded the boutique production company i love 2, which specializes in socially conscious short-format content. She consults for the Sundance Institute, *The New York Times*, Film Independent, Independent Television Service (ITVS), and Cinereach.

My Flaherty story really begins at the end of my first Flaherty seminar. But let's start at the beginning.

In 2010, Dennis Lim curated a Flaherty seminar on the theme of work. He included films by Dayong Zhao, an indie filmmaker from mainland China. My company, dGenerate Films, distributes Dayong's documentaries. We helped facilitate his visa to the United States so he could attend.

Dayong returned filled with passion and joy about his Flaherty experience. His enthusiasm inspired us to think about mounting a Flaherty seminar in China. Independent cinema was in a sense flourishing in

Figure 81.1. © Josh Telles.

mainland China at the time. Several independent Chinese film festivals were showcasing groundbreaking Chinese documentary work that would also premiere at Berlin, Cannes, Rotterdam, and Venice. A Flaherty seminar seemed an essential next step to further deepen documentary discourse in China.

Mary Kerr, then executive director of the Flaherty, and I started brainstorming. We talked about a smaller-scale Flaherty seminar to test the waters, maybe a three-day event. Excited, we thought about how the Chinese public, the independent filmmaking milieu, and men and women in academic circles might accept a Flaherty-type event. We discussed whether we would allow international attendees or limit it to Chinese participants.

In 2011, I was invited to the seminar as a Leo Dratfield Fellow, a special award to get a programmer and mid-career filmmaker to the event. This was my chance to see how the seminar worked and to determine which elements of it we could feasibly bring to China.

I had another reason for attending. I wanted to meet the other Leo Dratfield Fellow, independent filmmaker Matthew Porterfield. Matt makes microbudget films set in Baltimore, his hometown, with nonprofessional actors. I had recently seen and loved Matt's *Putty Hill* (2010). I felt his work was reshaping American independent cinema.

When I arrived on the Colgate University campus on a summer day in 2011, I was reverberating with excitement and passion for cinema.

However, the Flaherty's rigorous eating, screening, and discussion schedule soon caused me to fall behind in my producing and distributing work. Producers are essentially on call twenty-four seven. We spend our days negotiating and renegotiating deals, listening to grievances, resolving conflicts, hiring, and firing. In the midst of this chaos, we offer creative feedback and guidance. Distribution, on the other hand, requires sustained attention to licensing agreements, marketing assets, bookings, DVD covers, and print traffic logistics.

I ran back and forth to my dorm room in between screenings and discussions, trying to keep up with the work. When Monday morning rolled around, emails, texts, and calls overwhelmed me. I walked around campus muttering, "Who has time to watch and discuss movies all day!" It felt like a faraway ideal I couldn't reach. I gave up making time to eat.

By day three, I was exhausted and needed to return to reality. Former Flaherty executive director and Museum of Modern Art curator Sally Berger and her partner offered me a seat back to Brooklyn in their car. In 2010, Sally and I had traveled to Beijing and Nanjing to visit China's then-thriving independent film scene. In 2013, at MoMA, Sally Berger curated a groundbreaking twenty-five-year retrospective called "Chinese Realities/Documentary Visions," cocurated with dGenerate Films programmer Kevin Lee. As I write this in 2018, the film festivals Sally and I attended have been shut down or forced out of the public sphere. Many of China's best independent documentary makers, including Dayong Zhao, have left mainland China.

Though I left that first seminar early, filled with guilt, it turned out that my Flaherty experience was just beginning; it would continue to reverberate.

Against the odds, in 2012, with the help of curator Ou Ning (*Meishi Street*, 2006) and leading Chinese independent film figure/curator/professor/producer Zhang Xianmin, plans for a mini-Flaherty in China started to come together.

But with the transfer of power to Xi Jinping, the environment in China had become more conservative. Mary Kerr and two Flaherty filmmakers, Ilisa Barbash and Laura Kissel, flew to China to present their work at the Bishan Harvest Festival in Anhui. When they landed in Shanghai, they learned that the authorities had shut down the festival.

However, private screenings continued, and Laura was also able to arrange university screenings in Hangzhou and Shanghai.

Later, during his first US visit, Zhang Xianmin presented a paper called "How to Kill a Festival" at New York University, which analyzed the death of independent film festivals in China, including plans for a Chinese Flaherty Film Seminar experience.

Nevertheless, the Flaherty experience continued to amplify. The films we had proposed for the Chinese Flaherty found their way to a new screening series, ISAAS (Indie Screening Alliance of Art Spaces), curated by Zhang Xianmin. ISAAS and other screening series offered decentralized networks of alternative screening spaces in mainland China, providing a way for curators to screen films for localized audiences. Zhang Xianmin sent four Flaherty-selected titles to be included in this 2015 screening tour.

The Flaherty continues to reverberate for me. When I lived in Lisbon in 2016, I spent time with Nuno Lisboa and guest taught in his film class at the Escola Superior de Artes e Design de Caldas da Rainha. Nuno curated the 2017 Flaherty and runs Doc's Kingdom in Portugal, another Flaherty-inspired global gathering.

Matt Porterfield and I have stayed in touch and are supporters of each other's work. A few months ago, Matt asked me to mentor one of his promising film students in the Johns Hopkins University Film and Media Studies program.

Through these past ten years and the ongoing amplifications of my original, truncated Flaherty experience, my first impression of the seminar hasn't changed much. The Flaherty is both an imagined ideal and a real space. It's where gathering together all day and all night to watch and discuss movies embodies not only a privilege, but a freedom worth fighting for.

82

DANS MON IMAGINAIRE

Caroline Martel

CAROLINE MARTEL is a documentary filmmaker/artist/researcher interested in archives, invisible histories, and audio/visual technologies and heritage. Her critically acclaimed work includes the montage essay; *The Phantom of the Operator* (2004); *Wavemakers* (2012); the solo show at the Museum of the Moving Image, *Industry/Cinema* (2012); and a thirty-five-screen archival installation on Expo 67's expanded cinema commissioned by the Musée d'art contemporain de Montréal, *Spectacles du monde* (2017). She works in audiovisual and oral history research with the city of Montreal.

The Flaherty occupies a spot in my memory. Or is it in *mon imaginaire*? *Imaginaire* doesn't have an exact equivalent in English. In French it means something like "the territory of imagination."

The seminar is a place I had tried to picture in my mind for a long time after being told—with no further explanation—that I should definitely attend.

In the cinema milieu I come from, the Flaherty also strikes a chord in the historical imagination. It is where, in 1959 at the University of California, Santa Barbara, mythical pioneer cameraman Michel Brault met Jean Rouch, who invited Brault to experiment abroad with his approach to filming *cinéma vérité*. Emerging French-Canadian filmmakers didn't get much chance of feeling part of the world of cinema back then, but

Figure 82.1. Photograph by Nathanael Corre.

somehow the Flaherty had made that happen. Also, Maya Deren became one of the great influences on this so-called father of Québec cinema, and I like to think that the Flaherty may have instigated his interest in her work.

In June 2011, I had the privilege of being included in the mostly female cast of Dan Streible's Sonic Truth program at Colgate University. I showed *The Phantom of the Operator* (2004), the first cut of my feature-length documentary on the mystery of the Ondes Martenot musical instrument (*Wavemakers,* 2012), and my double-screen/double-soundtrack installation *Industry/Cinema* (2011). Although I believe that the exploration of the intersections between sound/music/voice and the documentary could have been taken much further, the seminar continued its traditional magic to provoke some important encounters that summer.

Image-memories still resonate:

Upon my arrival, the sight of my bunk bed bringing me back to my Girl Guide summer camp years and the thought *Be Prepared.*

The 1950s-style cafeteria and the thrill of wondering *who will I get to sit next to this time?*

The very moment when, seconds after the dark screen lights up, the man beside me asks, "Whose film is this?"—and I answer, "Mine!"

Frank Scheffer—who confessed later that he would have shit his pants if he had dared, like I had, to show an unfinished documentary—suggesting that we should say "work in process" rather than "work in progress." I have been faithful to his insight ever since.

Pioneer computer animator Lillian Schwartz sharing her recent epiphany that the films she created decades earlier at the Bell Labs were in three dimensions or, minimally, enhanced by the 3D glasses we wore happily for the 2011 Flaherty group portrait.

Fellow Québécoise musician Kareya Audet getting invited by Schwartz to score some of her work.

A Famous Movie Person (the otherwise quite charming Samuel D. Pollard, editor and coconspirator of Spike Lee) making me a bit grumpy for not playing by the rules of the seminar and just showing up for his part—in other words, not enduring the experience/experiment from beginning to end, like everyone else.

The discovery of the oeuvre of free spirit Les Blank documenting, among gap-toothed women and other wildly beautiful humans, the life of some French-from-the-Americas descendants like me making music in Louisiana. We talked about showing a retrospective of his work in Montréal, which he was keen to do, but unfortunately he left us all before that could happen. Since then, whenever I hear *Less is More*, I think of Les.

Jodie Mack igniting conversations about giving more space to experimental cinema in the Flaherty programming.

By the campfire, encountering a meeting of the minds with professor Winifred Wood, who later brought me to Wellesley ("Hillary's college"!) to present my work and mentor her students.

George Stoney sharing his insights about the direct-cinema tradition I come from in Francophone Canada, which is rarely acknowledged in documentary anthology books (mostly written by Americans or French), and *moi* realizing he likely became the public access television pioneer he was in the United States thanks in part to his involvement with the National Film Board of Canada's (NFB) *Challenge for Change* program at the end of the 1960s.

The time I saw *Phantom of the Operator* as a pinkish black-and-white Betacam video instead of as the multicolor archival film it is—perhaps the worst screening it has had, but with an audience who wouldn't blink. The projectionist, West Coast filmmaker Gibbs Chapman, taught me that I could have put the show on pause to switch to DVD. A few days later, at UnionDocs in Brooklyn, I would scream "Stop!" at the bad start of the screening of another work.

And last, the feeling of returning home, solidified by a sort of never-alone-now feeling when I have to face the well-meaning NFB production and distribution civil servants/bureaucrats and festival moguls around the world.

The Flaherty also got me a gig as a visiting scholar teaching film at Virginia Commonwealth University, through some mysterious references. I suspect one was from the spectator whose Southern accent I could barely understand in the conversations following the screening of my work in process but who somehow offered the boldest comments. James Parish became my beloved colleague. He eventually cofounded The Bijou, a micro-cinema in Richmond, Virginia, where I'm certain the spirit of the seminar thrives during post-screening Q and As.

One of the takeaways of the seminar was experimenting with Frances Flaherty's radical notion of non-preconception to assume a bare and raw position before the big screen, to take "life as is" as it was projected by filmmakers—and projected back by spectators. More than ever now, I take to heart being a spectator, and watching films well has become for me something to revere as much as *making* films well.

The Flaherty remains an ideal documentary think tank and an event I always want to go back to. Since the summer of 2011, every spring I believe this time I will return for real—my *imaginaire* embodied.

83

FROM DOC'S KINGDOM TO THE BROTHERHOOD OF THE CRYSTAL SKULL

Susana de Sousa Dias

Susana de Sousa Dias's films have been exhibited internationally at festivals, art exhibitions, and venues such as Documenta 14, PhotoEspaña, Viennale (Vienna International Film Festival), Sarajevo International Film Festival, Cinéma du Réel, Pacific Film Archive, Harvard Film Archive, Arsenal Institut für Film und Videokunst, Museum of Contemporary Art of Ceará (Brazil), Centre Pompidou, and Institute of Contemporary Arts (ICA) London. Her film *48* (2009) received the Grand Prix Cinéma du Réel and the FIPRESCI (Fédération Internationale de la Presse Cinématographique) award. In 2012 and 2013, she codirected the International Film Festival Doclisboa, opening up new sections such as Cinema of Urgency and Passages (Documentary and Contemporary Art). She is on the Fine Arts Faculty of the University of Lisbon.

My history with the Flaherty seminar began in 2001, years before I went to the event in person. It began when I first went to the Doc's Kingdom, the international seminar on documentary film, held in Serpa, a little village in the south of Portugal.

The Doc's Kingdom sessions were organized around films made by filmmakers from different parts of the world, shown within an atmosphere circumscribed by the small town. Discussions were motivated by

Figure 83.1.

the "clash" of films shown during each session. These clashes made the discussions fascinating.

At that 2001 Doc's Kingdom seminar, I learned that the primary model for Doc's Kingdom was the Flaherty Film Seminar. The Portuguese seminar was organized by Apordoc, the association of documentary film founded in 1996 by a group of enthusiastic Portuguese documentary filmmakers and programmers.

In the following years, I continued to follow Doc's Kingdom—sometimes participating as guest director and intervening in discussions at Apordoc

From Doc's Kingdom to the Brotherhood of the Crystal Skull | 333 around the seminar format, which underwent adjustments and modifications every year, some more successful than others.

Always on the horizon lay the Flaherty seminar, so close to our thinking and yet so distant.

Exactly ten years after my first visit to Serpa, I received an invitation to be a guest artist at the Flaherty. I have no words to describe the enthusiasm I felt when I realized that I would have the privilege of showing my work in a context I was sure would be highly stimulating. It was Josetxo Cerdán, programmer of the 2012 Flaherty, who reached out and invited me to participate in Open Wounds.

Writing this text almost six years later, I can evoke my Flaherty experience with two words: *thought* and *community*.

Thought was instigated by the confrontation of visions. In the context of the seminar, films are presented in such a way that they directly interact with each other, harmonizing or clashing, often in dazzling encounters/collisions.

In a certain sense, I'd encountered a similar sensation when I first went to the Staatsgalerie in Stuttgart many years ago. There, as in most museums, artworks are arranged either chronologically or thematically. However, in a room full of depictions of medieval angels, there was a smaller depiction of an angel dating back only to the early twentieth century: an *angelus* (in this case, the *militans*) of Paul Klee—a disturbing intrusion into the medieval system of representation. Klee's vision of an angel was so powerful in this context that it created a fracture in that space, which quickly sent me beyond the physical.

I felt the presence of Walter Benjamin's angel of history, and suddenly the angels ceased to be in the past and, in a dialectic flash, the past became *now*—throwing into question the temporality of artworks and of history and its images.

At the Flaherty, we see films coming together under the same general topic but interacting and opening up, coming into dialogue, colliding or entering into consonance with one another. We confront different understandings of what documentary *is*; we participate in ardent and sometimes almost incendiary discussions around particular films. And we take a stand. Not just against or in favor, not just around A or B, but regarding what goes on in the world.

And maybe because of this, one of the strongest impressions I had during Open Wounds was the sense of community. Vibration, strength, energy. Discussion, controversy, irritations, elective affinities. All of this is part of the Flaherty. Even moments of seclusion are part of the seminar—if we want to stay in our rooms to think about what we have seen and heard or if we want to wander reflexively through the expansive Colgate University campus.

Our meetings can be around a small table or in a wide circle facing each other in a big room or under a tree. These meetings can be both organized and informal. They can be both serious and playful.

I remember when someone brought a ball. It was already late at night, but I found myself playing a game reminiscent of my childhood, with Sylvian George, John Gianvito, and some really tough guys who held out until dawn. Later, someone was looking at a picture of this event and asked, incredulously, "Do you play games at Flaherty?" Yes, we play at Flaherty. We allow ourselves to be open to the *now*, even to the pleasurable and childlike time of a game.

We intertwine in small connecting threads, in a community that is constantly widening. There are people I met at the Flaherty who I've never spoken to again—but I feel I can go back to them if the right situation comes along. And there are many others with whom I've maintained regular contact.

From the profusion of people I met at the seminar in 2012, a few were re-encounters, such as Patricia Zimmermann and Scott MacDonald, whom I already knew from the Visible Evidence conference. Others who I met for the first time allowed me to expand my American experience, including Kathy Geritz and the much-missed David Pendleton, who I later met up with at Harvard, then in Lisbon.

Others I've met again recently: Ruth Somalo and Aily Nash—at the time Flaherty fellows, part of the scholarship program then coordinated by Jason Livingston. Another fellow was Nuno Lisboa, who later that same year would become director of Doc's Kingdom and, later, the first organizer of the Portuguese seminar to have programmed the Flaherty—an experience that would prove to be transformative for Doc's Kingdom, which acquired a new dynamic from then on.

It's amazing how many Flaherty veterans I've met as I've crisscrossed countless countries and several continents during the last six years.

This sense of community was, for me, symbolically sealed on the day of the last session, when Ben Russell's energetic performance was followed by a nocturnal party where we all, dancing frantically to the sound of vibrant music and illuminated by psychedelic lighting, drank vodka from the same crystal skull—as if we were celebrating a vast, eclectic brotherhood, united by the creative and transforming need to work with moving images.

84

HOMECOMING

David Gracon

DAVID GRACON, a native of Buffalo, New York, has been engaged
in post-punk, experimental music, zines, college radio, and activist
experimental film, video, and documentary communities since the
mid-1990s. His work has screened at the Chicago Underground
Film Festival and the Mexican Centre for Music and Sonic Art. In
the 2017–2018 academic year, David was a US Fulbright Scholar
teaching media studies in Ukraine. He is currently Assistant Professor of Integrated Media at Gonzaga University.

The Flaherty seminar is a homecoming.

But home isn't always the most pleasant of places.

At the Flaherty, I leave behind my life as a professor, media maker,
and programmer in the Midwest, a place I've never really considered
home.

I make the long drive to Colgate University. Along the way, I visit family and friends in the Buffalo area. The vast rolling hills of central New
York amaze me. Photos never do them justice. Zigzagging on rollercoaster
roads, I manage to remember how to find Hamilton, New York, where
the Flaherty seminar happens. I have gone four times.

When I went to college, my family couldn't afford the dorm experience. So going to the Flaherty offers a chance to live the youth I never

Figure 84.1.

had. While many participants don't like the dorms, I think it's fun living there for a week. I often joke I should hang a Creed poster on the walls.

The rigid schedule of screenings, discussions, and meals comforts me. Perhaps it is similar to how military people appreciate routine or how prisoners eventually relish their own institutionalization. Structure provides a weird comfort: it takes care of everything.

At the Flaherty, I have conversations with the custodians and cafeteria staff, the working folks running things behind the scenes. These are sometimes my best, most unpretentious Flaherty conversations. To watch all these documentary films about ordinary people and not actually engage such people in real life would feel strange.

The seminar challenges participants to exist without preconception, a task difficult to accomplish, especially for smart academics with big egos. But can these faculty types do four square, a schoolyard game often played at the seminar?

After the last screening and discussion of the day, I like to walk quietly through the small thicket of trees to return to my dorm room. No media. Insects buzzing. Stars.

Once, late at night, seminarians packed into a van and went skinny-dipping. Like a lost scene from *Dead Poets Society* (1989), naked people from Mexico, Spain, and maybe Portugal swam in a secluded lake owned by a fancy school. As the sun rose, we returned on winding back roads flanked by foggy landscapes, feeling exhilarated.

Rubbing shoulders with others from Buffalo is another Flaherty highlight. These DIY media makers, folks from Squeaky Wheel and descendants of the radical Media Study Department at SUNY Buffalo, remind me where I am from.

A rust-belt city, Buffalo's unofficial nickname is the City of No Illusions, which for me translates as a city with a vastly under-recognized experimental and media-activist legacy. Without fail at the Flaherty, I meet New Yorkers who wear fancy glasses that cost more than my monthly rent and talk shit about Buffalo. Their disdain drives me mad.

One year, Tony Conrad, my former mentor at SUNY Buffalo, crashed the seminar. It was a pleasure to catch up. Some whispered, "I think that's Tony Conrad over there." To me, he was just Tony.

I remember his radiating smile. At a local dive bar in Hamilton, Tony playfully hopped up and down on the dance floor like an ostrich, a nod perhaps to Tony's band, The Primitives, and their famous song and dance, "The Ostrich." Tony's dancing was joyfully out of place and challenging, just like his experimental films and videos.

We chatted about the trials of my life as a professor in Illinois. We joked that the Department of Media Study is such a radical program that afterward it's hard to fit in anywhere else. I sought career advice. Tony replied cryptically, "These things take time. They can take a long time." Tony passed away the following year. This was our last conversation.

Tony's teachings, Buffalo's vanguard media scene, and the Flaherty heavily inform my ideas about underground media, radical experimentation, and challenging the status quo.

The documentary filmmaker Robert Flaherty made a career constructing dehumanizing films about other people and cultures. Now a seminar exists in his name. Yet, that seminar is very critical, even of him—a strange contradiction.

Beyond Robert Flaherty's problematic representations of others, many criticize the seminar for high cost and limited accessibility. When I enthusiastically tell others about the seminar, a common response is, "I'd love to, but it's too expensive." What about all the people who might never have a chance to attend the Flaherty?

Combined with the Buffalo scene and DIY punk culture, my Flaherty experiences galvanized me to create a microcinema in the irregular hallway in my Champaign, Illinois, apartment. I called it Hallways Microcinema, a nod to Buffalo's Hallwalls. It had a two-year run with twenty-one events, all free.

I programmed screenings drawn directly from the Flaherty, including projects by Su Friedrich, Johan Grimonprez, Jesse McLean, and Lourdes Portillo. I met up with Vanessa Renwick from the Oregon Department of Kick Ass at a Flaherty. While touring, she presented her films for us. Without Hallways, these works wouldn't have seen the light of day in Champaign.

Hallways served as a microcosm of the Flaherty seminar. We screened challenging works and opened up lively discussion. People drank, hung out, talked, and formed a community. Like any community, it could be seen as exclusionary.

At the Flaherty, you work through half-baked ideas and get advice over meals. You never know where a conversation might lead you.

In 2016, I was thinking about applying for a Fulbright Fellowship. Somehow, I got connected with screen studies scholar Patricia Zimmermann. She had recently spent time in Ukraine, delivering lectures. She encouraged me to apply to Ukraine, an emerging democracy with students voraciously consuming new ideas. Her enthusiasm sold me.

I write this Flaherty story looking at winter outside my window in Ivano-Frankivsk, Ukraine, my home for a year. I contemplate my next course of action. I think about how the Flaherty seminar supported and nurtured me. I consider how fortunate I was to be able to attend.

The problem with experiencing a mind-blowing Flaherty seminar is that the next one will most likely disappoint you. Even though this has happened to me twice, my return to Buffalo, central New York, and the Flaherty always conjures a homecoming, reminding me where I am from and where I might go.

85

MY FIRST FLAHERTY

Joel Neville Anderson

JOEL NEVILLE ANDERSON is Visiting Assistant Professor of Cinema Studies and Film at Purchase College, State University of New York. His research and teaching encompass cinema and media studies, personal documentary, community media, experimental filmmaking, environmental justice, film festival studies, and Japanese cinema. Anderson's writing appears in *Afterimage, Film on the Faultline, Hyperallergic, International Feminist Journal of Politics, Millennium Film Journal, Routledge Handbook of Japanese Cinema, Senses of Cinema,* and *Studies in Documentary Film.* He curates JAPAN CUTS: Festival of New Japanese Film, the largest festival of contemporary Japanese cinema in North America at Japan Society, New York.

Breakfast, screening, discussion, lunch, screening, discussion, dinner, screening, discussion, dancing, repeat.

The more I read about the Flaherty seminar, the more I was reminded of the description I'd heard applied to my BFA conservatory: hippie bootcamp. I applied for a graduate-student fellowship, cobbled together the remaining half of the subsidized registration fee and bus fare from my university, and found myself, in June 2013, at Colgate for the fifty-ninth Flaherty.

Figure 85.1. © Melissa Haizlip, Flaherty
Fellow 2016.

I soon learned that following the seminar organizers' egalitarian intentions, everyone was provided with the same dormitory rooms and cafeteria meals, along with an experiment in cinephilic endurance and sleep deprivation that forced a confrontation with the art and ethics of film curation.

Upon reflection, I feel fortunate to have had my first Flaherty experience at Pablo de Ocampo's History Is What's Happening. This challenging confrontation became emblematic of the struggle to talk seriously about documentary ideas as a group that I've experienced every time I've returned to the Flaherty.

From *Queen Mother Moore Speech at Greenhaven Prison* (1973) by the People's Communication Network, which opened de Ocampo's program, to its repetition at the very end, so much has stayed with me: Basma Alsharif's *Home Movies Gaza* (2013), The Otolith Group's *People to be Resembling* (2012), Deborah Stratman's *O'er the Land* (2008), and Joyce Wieland's *Solidarity* (1973).

I won't forget sitting down for the first afternoon screening with no idea it would be Eyal Sivan and Michel Khleifi's 272-minute *Route 181* (2003). The discussion of Mathieu Kleyebe Abonnenc's *Ça va, ça va, on continue* (*It is OK, it is OK, we go on,* 2012–13) led me to Édouard Glissant's life-changing book, *Poètique de la Relation* (*Poetics of Relation,* 1990). And Jean-Paul Kelly's *Service of the Goods* (2013) forever marked my thoughts on Frederick Wiseman's documentaries from the 1960s and 1970s about social safety nets and institutions.

After Sarah Maldoror's *Sambizanga* (1972), I can never see Chris Marker's *Sans Soleil* (1983) the same way again, an experience that was repeated with Sana Na N'Hada's *O Regresso de Amílcar Cabral* (*The Return of Amílcar Cabral*, 1976) at the 2017 seminar.

More retreat than a conference or festival with overlapping panels and screenings, the Flaherty's medium is the program assembled by the curator. As the week continues, the burden is on "captive" participants to take control of the seminar through discussion sessions and make it their own. Tension builds amid interstitial coffee breaks, happy hours, late-night conversations, and small-group breakout sessions, demanding some form of response in the large discussion forum. This often results in a midweek bloodletting.

In 2013, this came with a performance by the BLW collective (Roza-linda Borcila, Sarah Lewison, and Julie Wyman): *A Call to the Square* (2013). Lewison and Wyman read Queen Mother Moore's speech, then invited participants to recite Asmaa Mahfouz's January 18, 2011, call to join the January 25 protests in Tahrir Square, demanding an end to Egypt's Mubarak regime.

Participants were invited to re-perform Mahfouz's address in small groups, writing down their reactions. Intended or not, the exercise rehearsed the documentary proposition of re-presenting another's physical performance or speech and relocating its site of communication, necessitating confrontation with the space of reassembly. The discussion that followed voiced important criticisms of how the exercise reinforced me as the white colonizing subject.

The problems brought to the surface by the performance reflected a central conceit of the seminar: the principle of non-preconception, originally instituted by Frances Flaherty at the earliest seminars. Revealing the nature of each film only as the projector's light hits the screen, with titles and program notes found later in the discussion room, is a constitutive feature of the seminar. It recruits an audience based entirely on the desire to return to its cinematic well and on the qualifications/theme of the announced programmer.

The principle reveals two diverging understandings: the notion that one *can* dispose of preconceptions versus a recognition that stripping typical curatorial preconditioning necessitates a different kind of controlled environment and requires that the group deal with new ways of preconceiving. Navigating it challenges the group to deconstruct modes of preconceiving and embrace a shared yet always uneven vulnerability in imagining a more equitable space.

More often than not, the discursive spaces generated by the Flaherty remain embattled with normative power structures, defenses scraped down to blunt candor by cycles of sleeplessness, inebriation, and waking dreams in the cinema—leading to moments of generosity, embarrassment, cruelty, and epiphany from veterans and first-timers alike.

The yearly exercise is a reminder of what it takes to honestly approach an art object, others' reactions, and the ramifications of refining lines of separation and/or coalescing into general consensus.

86

EVERYONE RECOMMENDED IT

Bo Wang

Bo Wang is a Brooklyn, New York–based artist and filmmaker. His works have been exhibited at the Museum of Modern Art, the Guggenheim, CPH: DOX in Copenhagen, the Shanghai Biennale, Bi-City Biennale of Urbanism/Architecture, Asia Society Texas Center, DMZ Docs in South Korea, and DOKUARTS at the German Historical Museum in Berlin. He was a Robert Flaherty Film Seminar Fellow in 2013. He is a faculty member in the Visual and Critical Studies program at the School of Visual Arts, New York.

The 2013 Flaherty Film Seminar was my first time.

Many film friends were somehow connected with the Flaherty seminar. Everyone recommended it. So I sent in my fellowship application.

The five-hour ride from Brooklyn to the small upstate New York village of Hamilton was shorter than expected. Chi-hui Yang drove the car, with me, Kimi Takesue, and Raquel Schefer, who had flown from Paris to New York the day before, talking all the way.

We talked about the Robert Flaherty Film Seminar organization, about past films screened, and about Laura Poitras and Edward Snowden, who had flown to Hong Kong a few weeks before in order to leak thousands of classified NSA documents. I was planning a film on Hong Kong.

I was new to the New York independent film community. In 2011, I'd earned an MFA from the School of Visual Arts. In early 2013, the

Figure 86.1.

Museum of Modern Art's Doc Fortnight had screened my first film, *China Concerto* (2012). I was struggling to make work and to survive in New York. The Flaherty seminar promised both inspiration and community.

I had heard so much about the weeklong, faraway, intense film seminar, which caged film people up together so they could watch films together and fight over them. The Flaherty's reputation for intensity, the principle of non-preconception (which I later learned was Frances Flaherty's idea and not Robert's), and egalitarianism both attracted and intimidated me.

The theme for the 2013 seminar was History Is What's Happening. Pablo de Ocampo curated.

That first evening, the program opened with *Queen Mother Moore Speech at Greenhaven Prison* (1973).

The year 2013 was the time of post–Occupy Wall Street political fatigue. Trumpism was yet to appear on any horizon but his own.

Pablo's programming was a map of contested geographies: Israel and Palestine; decolonization and postcolonial struggles in Africa and Asia; Japan, post-Fukushima; and America's landscapes of racism.

As I look back from the vantage point of 2018—and Trump, Brexit, the wars, migrants, refugees, and environmental destruction—the seminar's call for historical consciousness, radicalism, and collectivity looms as pertinent and urgent.

The first post-screening discussion was an immersion, and the intensity and ruthlessness continued throughout the week. The participatory lecture performance, *A Call to the Square* (2013) by BLW, provoked criticism about how it positioned participants in its reenactment of history.

The discussions heated up quickly.

I found Eyal Sivan's *The Specialist: Portrait of a Modern Criminal* (1999) one of the most interesting films in that year's program. And it triggered one of the most intense discussions.

The Specialist focuses on the trial of Adolf Eichmann in 1961, employing archival footage, much of it never widely seen before this film. Instead of concentrating on the victims, Sivan had turned his attention to Eichmann, a perpetrator, who sat inside a bulletproof glass cage during the trial.

The human face of the perpetrator defending his actions, combined with the repetitive spectacle of a trial comprised of archival footage, provoked questions about how we perceive history through archives and about the ethical construction of Hannah Arendt's concept of the "banality of evil."

I was conflicted by Deborah Stratman's works. *O'er the Land* (2009) and *Village, Silenced* (2011) were the most enjoyable films I watched that week. However, I found *King of the Sky* (2004) problematic. The film was shot in Xinjiang, the Uyghur province in Northwest China. At the beginning of the closing credits, Deborah described its location as East Turkestan, the term used by Uyghur jihadists advocating independence. I've never been a Han nationalist, but Stratman's (Western liberal) position seemed too easy. It ignored historical complicity and complexity.

Sometimes the discussions became overly intellectual and theoretical—the discussions about the Otolith Group, for example. And the intensities of continuous viewing and extensive talking were exhausting. For most people, it's rare to experience such intellectuality and intensity in post-screening discussions.

By the fourth or the fifth day, after days of challenging films and exhausting debates, everyone was tense. We walked into the theater to discover that the movie was Chris Marker's *Sans Soleil* (1983). I have to admit that I thoroughly enjoyed this screening, compared to my previous experiences watching it in a graduate school class. With the new context that the other films in the program had provided, *Sans Soleil* released me, and others, from the heated anxieties of intensive debate.

Many questions kept coming back to me all through the seminar. One especially salient problem was how documentary and experimental films should respond to the realities of the lived world.

Pablo's programming combined conventional documentary films with many experimental works inflected with documentary qualities—blurring most boundaries.

The alleged role of documentary filmmaking—to use the camera as a way of exploring subject matter external to the filmmaker or to capture a social reality—has been questioned for more than a hundred years. The Flaherty was continuing this debate, but in new ways, with new films and new participants.

The epistemological question haunting the entire history of documentary filmmaking is actually quite simple: How, and how closely, can the camera approach the reality of the subject filmed? Can the camera, in the end, only reveal its own practice?

Self-reflexive strategies and formalist experimentation offer safe, extremely self-conscious paths to validate the work of documentary as it intersects with the world. But are self-reflexivity and formalistic avant-garde styles enough to guarantee a progressive response to changing social realities and historical urgencies? Or are they, given their limited audience, just another form of conservative politics?

I left with many questions about cinema, along with pages of handwritten notes from screenings and discussions that I looked forward to examining later: Wendelien van Oldenborgh's utilization of historical materials and spaces, Deborah Stratman's aesthetics and playfulness . . . My brain was exhausted from watching so many films and talking with so many different seminarians.

Driving home, I realized that my pre-Flaherty views on cinema needed reconstruction.

Beyond the gutting of my own preconceptions, that seminar left me with a curious and most welcome sense of empowerment and a newfound confidence that now, I could think through how *I* make films.

87

TURNING THE OUTSIDE IN AGAIN

Gabriela Monroy and Caspar Stracke

GABRIELA MONROY is a Mexican visual artist and curator working between Mexico City and Berlin. She has been awarded Mexico's FONCA Fellowship for Young Emerging Artists, a MacDowell Colony's National Endowment for the Arts Fellowship, and a New York Foundation for the Arts Fellowship in Digital and Electronic Arts. Gabriela has participated in exhibitions in Europe, Korea, Mexico, and the United States. Her work is in the collection of Museo Nacional de Arte, INBA (Mexico). She has collaborated with Caspar Stracke since 2002. CASPAR STRACKE is a filmmaker, visual artist, and curator from Germany, living and working in New York City since 1993 and Helsinki since 2012. His work investigates sociopolitical and aesthetic potentialities in architecture, urbanism, and media archaeology as well as the poetics and time-based mechanisms of cinema itself. His films and installation work have been shown in numerous exhibitions and festivals worldwide. From 2012 to 2017, he taught as a professor for Contemporary Art and Moving Image at the Finnish Academy of Fine Arts (Kuva) in Helsinki. He is editor of *GodardBoomerang* (2020).

How many times have we had imaginary debates after animated discussions, when the issues discussed have remained unresolved? There is hardly ever a satisfying time frame for discussion, which is a considerable

Figure 87.1.

frustration at mass conferences, world festivals, and other hectic public gatherings.

As a viable alternative, many of us escape from these big bustling events and move to safe havens. To outdoor screenings under the night sky of Temenos, Greece. To the mountains of Portugal. Or to the island of Harakka, Finland. For many of us, the Flaherty seminar is also an island and maybe the mother of all mind-bending film-seminar experiences. Once you've witnessed a Flaherty, an experience during which time stands still and thoughts, debate, and dialogue are carried onward from one day to the next, it is almost impossible to accept any other form of public discussion about film.

In 2014, we had the honor to be invited to program the sixtieth anniversary Flaherty.

We titled our seminar Turning the Inside Out, with the intention to start an in-depth study of the current state of the documentary form.

We began our research with the emergence of the so-called *documentary turn*—a term that emerged with the documentary works presented at Documenta10, curated by Catherine David back in 1997. One aspect that distinguished the documentary turn from conventional nonfiction filmmaking was its interdisciplinarity. Many of the documentary art projects presented at Documenta10 materialized not only as films, but also as installations, performances, public interventions, or sculptures.

The Flaherty seminar has a rich history of experimentation within the documentary genre, as well as a continuing focus on avant-garde cinema. Although the new documentary impulses emerging from the fine arts have been recognized at the Flaherty, we felt they had been under-represented. So we decided to make this the foundation of our research for the seminar.

During the curatorial process, we focused on the potential of self-reflexivity that enables a continuously shifting relationship between author and subject. This reminded us of a radical set of questions recalling Mao and Godard: "Who speaks and acts, from where, for whom, and how?" To which we added another question: How *effective* is a chosen form?

Over many decades, political engagement within artistic practice has offered filmmakers the potential of developing radical aesthetics. Yet, only in rare cases does this happen in a fine-tuned equilibrium that "neither sensationalizes aesthetics nor spectacularizes the ethical" (Okwui Enwezor).

Our research on the experimentation with form brought us to the outer limits of the documentary genre and to the insight that criticism and social awareness can also be inscribed in the formal aspects of an audiovisual work. We discovered radical accounts of political commitment in uncompromising forms. As filmmakers ourselves, we realized that our fascination with these strategies had unconsciously underpinned our own concepts, long before we could verbalize them.

The artists and collaborative groups invited to the sixtieth seminar—Eric Baudelaire (United States/France), CAMP (India), Duncan Campbell (Ireland), Jill Godmilow (United States), Cao Guimarães (Brazil), Johan Grimonprez (Belgium), Jesse McLean (United States), Karen Mirza and Brad Butler (United Kingdom), Lois Patiño (Spain), Raqs Media Collective (India), and Hito Steyerl (Germany)—revealed specific qualities of interdisciplinary experimentation with documentary.

We found that almost more challenging than selecting the artists was programming the seven days of the Flaherty. We knew that every dialogue between two, three, or four artists was going to determine the discourse of the day and of the days that followed.

What happened at the seminar surpassed our imagination.

Our guest artists provoked thought trajectories that moved the discussion topics beyond what we had anticipated. Fundamental philosophical arguments about life, love, consciousness, biopolitics, humanism, and post-humanism emerged. A discussion on the history of airplane hijacking was itself hijacked into questions of the reconstruction of subjectivity in contemporary media. And Shuddhabrata Sengupta from Raqs elaborated on how the word *human* can etymologically be traced back to *burying bones in soil*.

By the end of the week, a well-known Flaherty phenomenon was occurring.

The intense routine of screenings and discussions was producing an experience of collapsing time and space. The seminar seemed to be taking us everywhere at once. We found ourselves in Raqs's night of the worker in an industrial New Delhi landscape and at the same time on the gushing seashores of Patiño's Galicia and Flaherty's Aran, in Baudelaire's unrecognized state of Abkhazia, in Mirza/Butler's Deep State, on CAMP's Indian trade ships in Somalia, with Guimãrae's ants after the Brazilian Carnival, and most of all, in Steyerl's free fall.

88

THE TACTILE UNCONSCIOUS

Ohad Landesman

OHAD LANDESMAN is a teaching fellow in the Steve Tisch School of Film and Television at Tel Aviv University and a faculty member in the History and Theory department at Bezalel Academy of Art and Design in Jerusalem. His publications have appeared in several anthologies, such as *Contemporary Documentary* (2015), *Vocal Projections: Sound and Documentary* (2018), and in journals: *Animation: An Interdisciplinary Journal; Projections: The Journal for Movies and Mind; Studies in Documentary Film;* and *Visual Anthropology Review.*

Cinephilia is not antithetical to *epistephilia*. The love of documentaries interlaces with the pleasures of knowing more about the real world.

I think I knew all this before I came to the Flaherty seminar. I'd read extensively in documentary studies, particularly the writings of Michael Renov, who attributed the pleasures of fiction to documentary as well. My week at the seminar in 2014, however, provided me with a lucid illustration that documentary grants us an excursion into the unconscious and the irrational and that cinephilia for art documentaries is absolutely alive and kicking.

Of all the work presented, the short films of the American artist Jesse McLean, whom I had never heard of, lingered with me the longest after the seminar was over. They provided a perfect example of how the

Figure 88.1.

Flaherty offered a site to practice collectively, as opposed to individually, the documentary gaze into the unconscious.

McLean creates hypnotic collages from found-footage materials with mysterious thought-provoking texts. Difficult to categorize, her work drifts somewhere between video, documentary film, and conceptual art. On the big screen, it was immediate, sensual, and emotional. McLean's short films, which can be viewed online, dismantle the complex relationship viewers have with mass culture and popular media. McLean explores how television, Hollywood cinema, or music can, on the one hand, unite us all almost mystically, but on the other hand, manipulate, confuse, and contribute to loneliness and alienation.

McLean never drifts easily into a critical position of the blinding power of popular media. Instead, she creates a dynamic tension between a critical standpoint and a special interest in the emotional impact of popular media. In her world, mass culture has a commercial and cynical side yet also fosters a directly affective, difficult-to-evade audience connection. McLean's oeuvre explores how a viewer responds emotionally, sensuously, cognitively, and actively to cinematic or television material. It questions what establishes an ultimate viewing experience and how individual spectatorship differs from collective viewing.

In *Magic for Beginners* (2010), McLean probes the mythologies of fan culture by interweaving personal stories. A woman tells us about her obsession with the film *Titanic* (1997). A young man speaks of a special experience he had while watching *Tron* (1982). Another describes an emotional and spiritual journey he had while attending a rock concert by Oneida.

Summoning the legacy of experimental cinema, McLean uses found-footage material modified via Photoshop to examine the impact of media. I felt a theatrical screening was the only proper way to experience *Magic for Beginners*. McLean draws the viewer in, invites a tactile reaction to the screen, and turns the viewer into a participant.

The central scene summons a trancelike state with flickering images very rapidly playing to the Oneida experimental rock band's monotone sounds. My watching this experiential homage to the avant-garde's flicker films tradition was an intense experience, both physiologically and psychologically. Collaborative viewing amplified the hypnotic impact.

Some images at the Flaherty were incredibly beautiful, sometimes in quite disturbing ways. I was not aware that Johan Grimonprez's *Dial H-I-S-T-O-R-Y* (1997), screened on the first day, was such an important art-documentary classic, first shown at Documenta X.

Grimonprez's film celebrates new possibilities for avant-garde documentary filmmaking in the digital era, obscuring boundaries between thinking and action. It outlines the genealogy of airplane hijacking by building contradictions into its use of archival material. Its strange mix of disco music and images of catastrophe and disaster results in a viewing experience oscillating between fascination and recoil, desire and rejection.

Incredibly jet-lagged after a long flight from Israel, I struggled not to fall asleep watching this enchanting film. After an hour or so, the jet lag hit hard. I dozed off for what seemed a few moments, only to wake up to the end credits, where the gripping disco music of Van McCoy accompanies images of an airplane crash, an unforgettably sublime experience of the tension between beauty and disaster.

The following day, we watched Lois Patiño's *Montaña en sombra* (*Mountain in Shadow*) (2012), a contemplative look at a snowy mountain and the skiers on it—the vastness of space contrasted with the almost invisible small people. This screening too had a dreamlike tactile quality, as the image gradually became flat, pictorial, unreal, hypnotic. Was it a tactile vision? I think so.

The opening titles of Chris Marker and Alain Resnais's *Les stat-*
ues meurent aussi (1953) led to enthusiastic applause of a kind I never
expected to hear from an audience watching a black-and-white essay film
about colonialism and African statues. I overheard participants whispering self-congratulatory remarks to their companions, such as "Hey, this
is the Resnais and Marker short, do you know it?"

The film felt remarkably fresh. While Marker's overtly poetic commentary is delivered by a voice not his own, the film's self-reflexivity becomes
increasingly layered. The audiovisual montage passionately engages in
more-relevant-than-ever anti-colonial, anti-racist, and anti-capitalist
thinking. Half a decade after its original screening, *Les statues* requires
us to ponder our complicity, not only in the events it alludes to but also
in everything that has occurred thereafter.

Loud praise ensued as the opening titles for Jill Godmilow's *What
Farocki Taught* (1997) appeared on the screen. A perfect replica in color
and in English of Harun Farocki's black-and-white German film *Inextinguishable Fire* (1969), Godmilow's homage is an agitprop challenge
emphasizing immediate and unmediated direct address.

What Farocki Taught starts with black-and-white footage from the
original and could easily be mistaken for it. Was the audience applauding
Farocki's work, a chilling gesture made only a month before his sudden
death in Berlin, or was it showing explicit approval for Godmilow, who
sat with us in the theater?

As I had spent time gazing into the historical world rather than into
fantasy, my week at the Flaherty fascinated me. Consciously, I devoured
the epistemological value of documentary images. Unconsciously, I could
never escape their delirious, ecstatic, and tactile properties.

89

SMALL VICTORIES

Alberto Zambenedetti

ALBERTO ZAMBENEDETTI is Assistant Professor in the Department
of Italian Studies and the Cinema Studies Institute at the University
of Toronto. He is editor of *World Film Locations Florence* (2014)
and *World Film Locations Cleveland* (2016) and coeditor of *Federico
Fellini: Riprese, riletture, (re)visioni* (2016). He has published
scholarly essays in *Annali D'Italianistica*, *The Italianist's* film issue,
Journal of Adaptation in Film and Performance, *Short Film Studies*, and *Studies in European Cinema*. He oversaw the Italian DVD
editions of *Home* (Yann Arthus-Bertrand, 2009), *It Seems to Hang
On* (Kevin Jerome Everson, 2015), and *Dawson City: Frozen Time*
(Bill Morrison, 2016) and contributed essays to the Kino Lorber
DVD releases of *Fire at Sea* (Gianfranco Rosi, 2016) and *Dawson
City: Frozen Time*.

"There won't be any time," said the hazel-eyed woman standing next
to me at the check-in desk.

She was smiling warmly, but I tensed up.

I had just arrived at Colgate University after a seven-hour drive in
my tiny car from Oberlin, Ohio. I was exhausted and more than a bit
anxious. I'd recently finished an intense but rewarding year as a visiting
professor at the University of Toronto. It was my first job teaching film,

Figure 89.1.

so I'd meticulously prepared every lecture, planning into the wee hours of the night.

I'd left Canada for a postdoctoral fellowship in the Cinema Studies Program at Oberlin College, but I was second-guessing my decision. I knew that Oberlin had launched some careers, sunk others. Things would eventually work themselves out for me, but back then I didn't know that.

My life felt very unstable. My spouse and I had been apart for three long years, and I was nervous about my professional choices. Still, I was about to dive into a crowd of curators, filmmakers, programmers, and scholars gathered together by their passion for experimental documentary.

I had studied documentary with the late George Stoney at New York University and had written a short article on the films of Francesco Pasinetti, a Venetian documentarian active in the first half of the twentieth century. That was the extent of my knowledge. I felt more than a bit intimidated. Impostor syndrome, they call it, commonly reported among graduate students and early career academics. No surprise there.

The group stages of the 2014 FIFA World Cup, hosted by Brazil, were in full swing. The much-favored home team was about to be humiliated by Germany with a crushing 1–7 defeat, the worst in the tournament's history. A loyal supporter of my own national team (Italy), I was apprehensive about not finding a place to watch the two matches that coincided with the seminar's opening and closing screenings. "Is there a TV on campus where I could watch the World Cup Games?" I queried at the check-in desk. Later, I learned that the woman who intercepted the question was Ruth Somalo, a Spanish filmmaker, future NYC Flaherty programmer (*Broken Senses*, 2017), and one of the nicest people on the planet. She was clearly aware that this was my first seminar. And of course, she was right. There was no time.

Luckily, I was not the only soccer fan in this erudite crowd. Filmmaker and programmer Jason Fox, who was then pursuing an MFA at Hunter College, worked his considerable charm with the projection staff. He cajoled them into beaming snippets of matches onto the same theatrical screen where, during that week, we watched works by Eric Baudelaire, Duncan Campbell, Cao Guimarães, Johan Grimonprez, and Hito Steyerl, among others.

Italy won the first match, lost the second. And then the third. *Better luck in 2018*, I thought. Things didn't work out for them; in 2018, the team didn't even make it through the qualifying rounds.

I'd become aware of the Flaherty seminar in 2010, when my then-roommate, Robert Sweeney, traveled upstate to attend what sounded like a film-nerd boot camp, programmed by Dennis Lim, a critic he had always admired. Rob and I were friends from graduate school and were beginning to shape our respective careers out of our shared passion for film. He was already working at Kino Lorber and slowly working his way up the ranks of the New York film critics circle; I was writing a PhD dissertation on migration in Italian cinema, a topic that was as vast and complex as it was personal.

Rob was always the more intellectual one, an omnivorous cinephile scurrying off to screenings of obscure films in musty basements throughout the city. He would carefully study all the schedules, organizing his week accordingly. Sometimes I would tag along, trusting his taste and hoping to learn something new. I often did.

That 2014 Flaherty felt a bit like those New York evenings watching films carefully selected by my friend. Except that the seminar took place in an air-conditioned auditorium with comfortable seating, pristine image quality, and an expert projectionist. There was even a piece projected in the campus planetarium.

I sat back and relaxed as much as I could, trying to overcome the awkwardness of forgotten names and shared bathrooms, of damp dorm rooms and sleep deprivation. The presence of my friend Ohad Landesman, a documentary film scholar I knew from graduate school, comforted me. He became my social buoy throughout the week.

I let Gabriela Monroy and Caspar Stracke, the programmers of Turning the Inside Out, take me on a journey. I learned by watching and listening, rarely taking part in the group conversations that followed the screenings. I forced myself to ask a question on the last day. I felt like the child who spends the day talking himself into finally riding the roller coaster when the park is about to close, when most of the people have already gone home.

I made my one and only comment on the last day of my second Flaherty, too: the 2016 seminar, PLAY. I suggested smugly that the morning program be renamed "The Michelangelo Antonioni Memorial Program: The Genius of David Pendleton."

Probably rather pedantically, I proceeded to compare the films we'd just viewed to different periods in the long career of the Italian maestro. It was meant to be a heartfelt compliment to both the filmmakers and to David, whose programming savvy I had quietly admired all week.

One morning at breakfast, David approached me to talk about one of his passions, Pier Paolo Pasolini, a filmmaker whose work I was never truly able to appreciate—at least not as much as David. He looked fatigued, but at the time I was not aware that he was already fighting the disease that eventually took his life in 2017. I'm grateful for that short conversation.

I felt validated by David's gesture, which he performed so gracefully. I will watch more Pasolini, who, coincidentally, was also a soccer fan, and I will think of David, who taught me so much in so little time.

The Flaherty seminar will never be a comfortable experience for me, but it will always be a deep one. It has exposed me to things I would not otherwise have had access to. It has introduced me to films I now teach regularly. And it's made me feel connected to a great community, even if only for brief moments. It is also a humbling experience. A room overflowing with talent and history can have that effect.

I will return. I will make a comment on the last day, voice quivering and palms sweating, but it will be a good moment for me. A small victory.

90

WHAT THE FLAHERTY TAUGHT

Eli Horwatt

Eli Horwatt is a scholar and film programmer. His doctoral research at York University, Toronto, examined the unwritten history of institutional critique in cinema environments and the political activism of filmmakers in relation to cultural institutions. He has programmed with the nomadic experimental microcinema Pleasure Dome, the Hot Docs International Documentary Festival, and the Wavelengths program at the Toronto International Film Festival. He was Visiting Assistant Professor in the Film and Media Studies Department at Colgate University from 2016 to 2019.

The 2014 Flaherty, Turning the Inside Out, examined "the state of documentary as it travels between the art gallery, the cinema, and the interactive screen," according to seminar marketing. At the time, this issue constituted the heart of my doctoral research and a significant part of my film-festival programming.

I was ecstatic to be awarded a fellowship to attend. I traveled from Toronto to Colgate University with film scholar Tess Takahashi and former Flaherty curator Pablo de Ocampo. Right away, the fellows met with Jill Godmilow, whose *What Farocki Taught* (1998) I had seen previously but whose larger body of work was new, thrilling, and uncompromising. Generous to us fellows yet recalcitrant in her documentary dogma, Godmilow set the stage for the Flaherty's storied conversations and arguments.

Figure 90.1.

The seminar opened with Godmilow's *Far from Poland* (1984), which provoked the audience to erupt into applause as the first frames appeared. It was a kind of nerdy nirvana to experience it.

Filmmakers I admired participated that year, including Johan Grimonprez, Jesse McLean, Raqs Media Collective, and Hito Steyerl beamed in via Skype, as her daughter was ill. A number of new-to-me films were screened that left me reeling. *The Anabasis of May and Fusako Shigenobu, Masao Adachi, and 27 Years Without Images* (2011) by Eric Baudelaire transported me so intimately that I felt the dread of the haunted subjects' lives. Duncan Campbell's *Bernadette* (2008) transformed homage into mystery. His film and others I saw at that seminar found their way into my programming and course syllabi.

An unexpected key issue emerged: a critical look at the currency of the term *essay film* and the rhetorical strategies of artists using documents, historical records, archival materials, and standard talking heads. Many attendees asserted that this format had shifted so much that some entries seemed more like lecture films. They circumvented the open, interrogative, and often surprising logical connections the essay form embodied.

Those rooted in the documentary film world exhibited anxiety toward gallery-based moving-image work. Gallery artists mounted a defensive, apologist discourse about the shortfalls of film and video installation. Many agreed a black box would need to be built inside a white cube in order to sustain a gallery screening. These debates raged on through the week of the seminar.

The seminar's format cannot ever completely fail—curation be damned.

If audiences don't like the programming, the discussions still produce generative observations and insights into strategies and approaches. When the programming is well received, the most successful qualities of a work bubble up in discussions, crystallizing. The Flaherty's intensive and immersive schedule produces a think-tank-like focus where a mutual interrogation of ideas germinates into a richer, more pronounced understanding of documentary. Still, a few more breaks in the screening schedule would be welcome.

The fellowship program introduced me to many remarkable people. I met scholars and curators, such as Sonja Bertucci, Almudena Escobar López, Laliv Melamed, Herb Shellenberger, and Josephine Shokrian. I met talented filmmakers, such as Emily Mkrtichian, Bjargey Ólafsdóttir, Arjun Shankar, Peter Snowdon, Libi Striegl, and Julia Yezbick.

The seminar came with both catharsis and a few regrets. Highs included being on a dance floor with Tony Conrad not long before he left us.

After the most intense critical discussion, I ate dinner with two filmmakers who had just experienced a less-than-jubilant reception. Their harshest critic sat next to me at the table. The filmmakers shed any defensiveness. A discussion about protest, representation, and the self-mythologization of the Left ensued. Conclusions were made, and some consensus formed. Here, I felt the generosity and openness of the Flaherty as an intellectual laboratory of artists and thinkers.

There were a few regrets, such as when I returned to my dorm room exhausted, missing a fun night gallivanting in a nearby pond with new comrades. I didn't want to bother curators Gabriela Monroy and Caspar Stracke, a lost opportunity. I later connected with them at DocPoint Helsinki. Their intelligence, curiosity, and behind-the-scenes anecdotes overwhelmed me.

In 2014, I was at a crossroads. I was simultaneously finishing my PhD with a dissertation about experimental documentary and post-minimal art and programming for film festivals in Toronto. I wasn't sure what I wanted to pursue next. In a strange way, the Flaherty impacted my decision. Three years later, I was appointed a visiting assistant professor at Colgate University to teach documentary film classes.

Epilogue: The 2014 Fellows

On the second to last day of the 2014 seminar, I collaborated with the other fellows to try to give something back to the Flaherty.

We created a list of notable quotes we'd overheard. I've pulled a few of the gems from the sheet we distributed at the end of the seminar, entitled "What the Flaherty Taught in 2014." This is what we wrote:

> Over the last week during breakout sessions, in private discourse over drinks, or otherwise, conversations between the fellows have generated many critical insights, deft observations, and valuable provocations that, so far, have been left unshared with the larger seminar.
>
> We want these comments to reach those best served by them, so here are a few morsels.
>
> How to make a film (borrowed from *Rules of the Road* driving manual):
>
> 1. Get the big picture.
>
> 2. Watch out for the other guy.
>
> 3. Make sure they see you.
>
> 4. Keep your eyes on the road.
>
> 5. Always have an out.
>
> Thesis number one for documentary practice: films need to be beautiful not just on the outside but on the inside.
>
> Every film should ask the viewer, "Who am I, standing next to this?"
>
> You can only be conscious of yourself when there is an *other*.
>
> You can't be in solidarity with yourself.
>
> Where's your labor going, baby?
>
> We're not looking at the panopticon, this is the reverse shot.
>
> Read yourself into a crisis—then make a film.
>
> Eisensteinian montage can be a Pavlovian proposition.
>
> A film should break vases.
>
> Film festivals outsource risk to independent filmmakers.
>
> The Flaherty runs on caffeine and alcohol.
>
> I think we should just stay here and never go back to where we came from.

91

CERTAIN VOICES WERE PAINFULLY MISSING

Hend F. Alawadhi

HEND F. ALAWADHI is Assistant Professor at the College of Architecture in Kuwait University. She holds a doctorate in Visual and Cultural Studies from the University of Rochester, where her dissertation, "Tracing Trauma: Gender, Memory, and Erasure in Contemporary Arab Cinema," earned the Susan B. Anthony Institute for Gender, Sexuality, and Women's Studies Dissertation Award. Her research interests center on the history of moving image in the Arab world, particularly as it relates to urban space and post-oil modernism in the Gulf. Her work also explores feminist media activism and the gendered representations of disability and illness in Arab media. Her writing has appeared in *Afterimage: The Journal of Media Arts and Cultural Criticism*; *Artslant*; *Journal of Media, Communication & Film*; and *Public Journal: Art/Culture/Ideas*.

It was a week of many firsts for me: My first film seminar. My first time staying in college dormitories. My first summer not leaving upstate New York the moment the semester at University of Rochester ended. My first time moderating in a theater (thanks to Laura U. Marks, Steve Reinke, and Khalil Joreige).

More significantly, it was the first time I saw films from the Arab world in such a context. I'm still unsure how to describe it: summer camp for sleep-deprived filmmakers and academics, having daily intense

Figure 91.1. Photograph by Julia Tulke.

conversations after multiple screenings and one too many caffeinated beverages.

I had heard of the Flaherty seminar through the Film and Media Studies program at University of Rochester, which offers two annual fellowships that allow doctoral students from different departments to attend. At that time, I had just finished my coursework, and I wasn't sure I was going to commit to film. Logistically, it seemed very unlikely that I would have access to contemporary Arab or Middle Eastern cinema.

My hesitation immediately dissipated when I saw the announcement for Laura U. Marks's program for the sixty-first seminar, The Scent of Places/عطر الأماكن. I had met Laura U. Marks in the spring of 2013. My adviser, director of the Film and Media Studies program Jason Middleton, had invited her to screen *Arab Glitch*, a film series she curated. I designed the poster for the event: an image of Suad Husni juxtaposed with the text *Hubbell Auditorium, University of Rochester*. Arab cinema—experimental Arab cinema—was coming to Rochester, New York!

Only two years later, it was back again—at the Flaherty. As a Kuwaiti student living in upstate New York, I found the idea that a whole week would be dedicated to experimental film from the Arab world less than two hours' drive away from me to be an adrenaline rush.

I was especially intrigued by Marks's program because of my own interest in Arab cinematic practices that shift away from mass-mediated trauma and politics. After spending so many years in the United States, I found myself yearning for alternatives that would cut through the homogeneity of images circulating around me.

Despite the constant influx of images from the Arab world, certain voices were painfully missing. Where were the voices of those on the peripheries? The disabled communities, the LGBT communities that fell outside the project of the homonationalist other, the brown women who needed saving but didn't want to feed into a Western savior complex: Where were they?

And what were people cooking nowadays in Syria? Who supplied medical equipment, and how much does a wheelchair cost? What kinds of pets did people in Yemen have? When will we confront anti-blackness in our communities? Are people still buying Coca-Cola in crates? What parts of the lamb were the *khalas* and *ammos* cooking these days?

What does Baghdad smell like today?

The Scent of Places answered many of these questions for me. In *Rawane's Song* (2006), Lebanese filmmaker Mounira Al Solh states that after trying—and failing—to make art about the war, she probably has "nothing to say about the war!" Though she stages a refusal to engage with geopolitics, Al Solh deftly works through her own conflicting identity politics, art clichés, gender restraints, and pregnancy woes in her films.

Similarly, in *Sometime/Somewhere Else* (2001), Egyptian filmmaker Hassan Khan refuses categorical identification through his use of irony and the absurd. Hala Lotfy's arresting *Coming Forth by Day* (2013) captures one exceedingly long day in the lives of a mother and daughter providing around-the-clock care for their disabled husband/father, who is confined to his bed; they, too, are confined. Without any governmental or social support, the women's lives are suspended.

These films left a lasting impact on me.

The program also included filmmakers who were not from the Arab world, such as Marie-Hélène Cousineau, Arthur Jafa, Ulrike Ottinger, Steve Reinke, Juan Manuel Sepúlveda, and Ramon Zürcher, and which provided an interesting array of perspectives.

The Scent of Places was a profoundly moving and thought-provoking experience. I am very grateful that I had the opportunity to go as a fellow, especially during a time when images from the Arab world continue to occupy hollowed-out binaries.

Many thanks to Patricia Zimmermann for inviting me to write this piece. *Shukran* to Laura U. Marks, Anita Reher, Sarie Horowitz, Toby Lee, and everyone whose labor contributed to such a wonderful week.

92

LEARNING THINGS, LOSING THINGS

Ekrem Serdar

EKREM SERDAR is Curator at Squeaky Wheel Film & Media Art Center, where he is responsible for the organization's exhibitions, public programming, and artist residencies. Previously, he was a programmer with Experimental Response Cinema in Austin, Texas, which he cofounded. He is a 2017 recipient of a Curatorial Fellowship from the Andy Warhol Foundation for the Visual Arts. His writing has been published in *The Brooklyn Rail*, *Millennium Film Journal*, and other publications. He is from Ankara, Turkey. More information is available at http://ekremserdar.info.

Sarah Elder sent an encouraging email about the Robert Flaherty Film Seminar to the State University at Buffalo's Media Study listserv in the early 2000s, when I was an undergraduate in the Media Study Department. It was the first time I'd heard of the Flaherty seminar.

I noticed later that Sarah would send an annual, heartfelt reminder to go to the Flaherty, each time contending that the experience would be life-changing.

Because Sarah's class on nonfiction cinema had been so influential on me, I looked up each year's seminar. The titles intrigued me: The Age of Migration; Witnesses; Monuments; Ruins; WORK.

In 2009, I finally applied for a student fellowship. I was rejected. I applied again a couple of years later. I was rejected again. Long after I

Figure 92.1.

graduated, I applied for the third time in 2015 and, finally, was accepted for a Professional Development Fellowship.

I was at the tail end of living in Austin, Texas. I was also at the end of programming with Experimental Response Cinema, at the time my most significant film programming experience. Over three years, we had presented nearly a hundred events, screening the videos of Theresa Hak Kyung Cha and Chantal Akerman's *Jeanne Dielman, 23 Commerce Quay, 1080 Brussels* (1975) . . . and hosting Jeanne Liotta, Jesse McLean, and Michael Robinson.

A friend once told me that he considered everything he had done before that day juvenilia—an annoying reflection then, but I wholeheartedly repeat it here. Three years later, as I look at my notes from that 2015 Flaherty and compare my thinking before Flaherty to my thinking now, I see the measure of the seminar's influence.

Curated by Laura Marks, the 2015 edition was called The Scent of Places. The featured guests included Mounira Al Solh, Marie-Hélène Cousineau, Arthur Jafa, Khalil Joreige, Hassan Khan, Hala Lotfy, Ulrike Ottinger, Steve Reinke, Juan Manuel Sepúlveda, Laila Shereen Sakr, Tariq Teguia (over Skype), and Ramon Zürcher.

When I arrived at the seminar, I was entirely unfamiliar with most of these makers.

I did know of the Flaherty's notion that participants should enter the seminar without preconceptions and participate in its efforts to establish a space for serious discussion. I prepared myself to be a bit more vocal than usual, but I also committed to critically attacking my own tastes and conceptions.

My hand shot up after Ulrike Ottinger's gorgeous *Unter Schnee* (2014). I asked if the filmmaker was uncritically fetishizing clichéd elements from Japanese culture. Someone from the audience exclaimed, "You're talking to Ulrike Ottinger!"

Later, I ended up feeling betrayed by the pairing of Mounira Al Solh's *Rawane's Song* (2006) and Marie-Hélène Cousineau and Madeline Ivalu's *Before Tomorrow* (2008). What seemed like an effective dialectical match also seemed to throw *Before Tomorrow* to the wolves. The film suffered from the juxtaposition. I voiced my opinion and continued to talk about this screening during the following days.

I'm glad I don't remember many public statements besides those two, and I'm glad I don't remember much of what I said to others.

As I flip through my notes from the seminar, I see four variations on the same question, scrawled quickly and illegibly.

I tried to grapple with my reaction to Laila Shereen Sakr's artworks. My scribbles seem to be trying to figure out *something* about what it means for so many of us in the world to have access to moving-image tools such as cell phones at a moment when these images are more disposable than ever and what it means for those who do not have the tools to represent themselves. I'm now properly obsessed with these thoughts, but until I began writing this, I'd forgotten that I first started scribbling about them at that 2015 Flaherty.

The names Toby Lee, Pooja Rangan, and Chi-hui Yang are in my notes; I perked up every time they spoke. *Belena* (2004), Ramon Zürcher's beautiful short film written in all caps, was shown during the same lovely screening as that year's Flaherty film, *Reflections* (1955) by Madeline Tourtelot.

"Ha! Mounira Al Solh" is written on a corner of a page. I still think about her voice in *The Sea Is A Stereo: Paris Without a Sea* (2007).

Lines and curves are on the pages with Tariq Teguia's name. Clearly, I was trying to understand the way Teguia's masterful works grapple with geography and what the land maintains and portends.

Some very personal notes were written next to Hala Lotfy's heartrending *Coming Forth by Day* (2012).

Somewhere near the end of the notebook, I wrote, "Refusals of testimony, how to grapple with them."

The notes don't include that I danced and drank every single night and that I talked so much my lungs were shot. I may have gone swimming. Also, I lost some belongings. Since that Flaherty, I've understood that there's a direct proportion between the quality of an art or film event and how many things I lose.

This is a nice little narrative about where the Flaherty took me and how attending that 2015 session impacted my life and career. However, my narrative is not as important as the artists and the artworks—and the ideas generated by that 2015 seminar, which continue to resonate.

It's a special experience—a hundred-plus folks, all gathered together, their ears and eyes focusing together. I can't wait to meet everyone again.

93

TIME TRAVELS

Jonathan Marlow

JONATHAN MARLOW is a curator, composer, cinematographer, film producer, and distributor of award-winning shorts and feature-length films. In addition to his roles at Arbelos Film Distribution and the California Film Institute, Marlow was affiliated with numerous film festivals, such as Telluride and Camera Obscura; film institutions, including Northwest Film Forum and San Francisco Cinematheque; and on-demand film distribution companies as disparate as Amazon and Fandor. He has served as Co–Vice President of the Flaherty Seminar Board of Trustees and a board member of the Canyon Cinema Foundation. He hosts screenings throughout the world, showcasing rarely seen films.

If I could ever be given the keys to a time-traveling craft, outside of the inevitable "prevent atrocities by eliminating dictators" expeditions, my ultimate inclination would be to return to periods impossible to recreate.

I would gladly give many treasures to travel back to Dan Streible's 2011 Flaherty seminar or Dennis Lim's in 2010. Or Ed Halter's in 2002, or Patricia Zimmermann's with L. Somi Roy and Erik Barnouw in 1994, or Richard Herskowitz's in 1987. Although I was in grade school at the time, I would have loved to attend Standish Lawder's seminar in 1981 or even go back to the very beginnings of the seminar, in 1955, with Frances Flaherty.

Figure 93.1.

Chi-hui Yang's phone call to me in 2013 was relatively unexpected. We'd first met shortly after I'd moved to San Francisco. Chi-hui's The Age of Migration seminar was legendary among the filmmakers and media folks with opinions that matter.

The persistent Bay Area connection to the seminar with several decades of programmers is relatively well-known: Ariella Ben-Dov, Linda Blackaby, Kathy Geritz, Irina Leimbacher, and Steve Seid. All were either residents at the time or, in the case of Richard Peterson and Susan Oxtoby, relocated to the area soon after their respective seminar involvements. Even Greg de Cuir Jr. had a Bay Area connection long before his 2018 co-programming role.

I had always wanted to attend the Flaherty seminar, yet each year, the mid-June timing and the remoteness of the event's assorted locations were problematic for me. I explained to Chi-hui that I was uncomfortable joining the board of trustees without ever having attended the seminar.

Chi-hui immediately dispelled these concerns by noting that it wouldn't be the first time it had happened.

He asked again. I accepted. I was reminded of an earlier occasion, when Sam Green invited me to join the San Francisco Cinematheque Board. When asked to serve by someone you admire, how can you decline?

Several film historians contend that the Flaherty format inspired the Telluride Film Festival. "I don't think it was an influence at all," Telluride cofounder Tom Luddy told me recently. He noted that the curatorial work of Albert Johnson at the San Francisco Film Festival was a primary inspiration for him and Bill Pence.

Debates about inspiration and causality aside, the two events share several surface similarities in their efforts to make independent works available. But perhaps most importantly, they share a collective faith in the removal of preconceptions. The audiences must trust that the programmers will take them on a worthwhile and rewarding journey.

The Scent of Places, programmed by Laura Marks in 2015, was my first seminar; it was everything I'd imagined it would be and more. There were opportunities to rescreen works by Ulrike Ottinger, Steve Reinke, and Ramon Zürcher that I had seen elsewhere but was now able to view again in an entirely new context. There were opportunities to see a handful of films by Tariq Teguia and Arthur Jafa I'd only read about. And I was able to see films I'd not known about and meet filmmakers about whom I had heard very little, such as Khalil Joreige and Juan Manuel Sepúlveda.

The "not knowing" aspect was frequently exhilarating and occasionally beguiling, admittedly for all of the reasons everyone mentions about the seminar. Much of the notoriety of the Flaherty derives from the exhaustive post-screening discussions. As expected, things were said during The Scent of Places, and discussions would occasionally boil over—quite unlike the usual platitudes and rote answers of film festival post-screening question-and-answer sessions.

I was able to invite my Fandor colleague Amanda Salazar along to the 2015 seminar. We both enjoyed its ample opportunities for cinematic assessment and appreciation.

Coincidentally, 2015 also launched a long-planned upheaval in my own life. Four months after the seminar, I packed up the archive and moved away from my neighborhood of fifteen years to settle in a more rural setting roughly one hour north of San Francisco. Due to infrequent visits and brunches in Petaluma with poet Joanna McClure and filmmaker Lawrence Jordan, I was relatively familiar with the area. Immediately after moving, I visited the Hotel Petaluma, built in 1923 and under extensive remodeling. I walked into the refurbished ballroom and conceived the nefarious plan of hosting film screenings in its enormous empty space.

When I returned to San Francisco a few days later, I spoke to Amanda about her interest in collaborating on a Flaherty-inspired event at the hotel. She did not hesitate. A mere five weeks after arriving in Petaluma, we jointly presented the First Annual Report of the reconstituted Camera Obscura, an organization originally cofounded by the aforementioned Lawrence Jordan with Bruce Conner and a handful of others in 1957.

Each Annual Report expands on a Flaherty-esque program pairing films together and featuring in-depth discussions with each of the film-makers in attendance. Everyone watches the films together and lodges in the same location, much like they do at the Flaherty seminar.

The Fifth Annual Report was held in 2019. Our Camera Obscura programming initiative has surpassed the life span of the original.

The real impact and significance of any event is reflected in the rever-berations it leaves behind. By that standard, the Flaherty seminar has no parallel.

94

A CINEMA THAT BREATHES

Roy Grundmann

ROY GRUNDMANN is Associate Professor of Film Studies at Boston University, where he teaches film and visual theory, queer theory, film history, and a curriculum of courses on avant-garde film and experimental media. He is author of *Andy Warhol's Blow Job* (2003), editor of *A Companion to Michael Haneke* (2010) and *Werner Schroeter* (2018), and coeditor of *The Wiley-Blackwell History of American Film*, Vols. 1–4 (2012) and *Michael Haneke: Interviews* (2020). He has programmed retrospectives on Andy Warhol, Matthias Müller, and Michael Haneke. He is also a contributing editor of *Cineaste* magazine.

"A cinema at play is a cinema that breathes—a cinema open to the shifting rhythms of the world."

This declaration opens the program notes of the 2016 Flaherty seminar, PLAY.

PLAY was my first Flaherty. Its invocation of the visceral dimension of life, of feeling the raw impact of encountering something unexpected, something genuinely new, would in fact turn out to be how I experienced the seminar.

I had wanted to attend for many years, because of the reputation of its programming and the rigorous schedule of screenings and intense discussions.

Figure 94.1.

The Flaherty is expensive and selective. It is invariably scheduled in mid-June, a time I usually don't want to commit to being sequestered for a whole week in an environment demanding my undivided attention, no matter the subject.

But I was also aware of the seminar's rewards, the raves from first-time participants, and the unquestioned enthusiasm of its regulars, including Roger Hallas and John Gianvito, who I know personally. For me, the Flaherty sounded like that rare kind of boot camp actually worth submitting to. But it still sounded like boot camp.

I would be proven both right and wrong about all this.

I ended up attending its 2016 edition, PLAY, on the invitation of its programmer, David Pendleton. I had met David, a good friend and colleague, when he came to the Boston/Cambridge area to join the Harvard Film Archive as programmer. David soon reached out to me at Boston University. We collaborated on Michael Haneke and Werner Schroeter retrospectives.

But despite all I had heard about the Flaherty, I had not been able to form a full picture of it. So I treated my participation as an adventure.

Colgate University is in the middle of nowhere and really hard to find. On this level, it confirmed my boot camp association.

But as soon as I was able to lay eyes on it, I realized, with some relief, that boot camps look different. This was a rather splendid-looking college campus, a serene environment. The buildings the seminar uses are at the foot of a steep hill participants climbed multiple times every day to reach the cafeteria overlooking the campus. The architecture's quaint look belied the advanced state of the facilities, especially the approximately 180-seat screening room.

I next realized that Flaherty, while smallish in comparison to conferences and film festivals, was a lot bigger than university seminars. And its almost 200 participants were not only filmmakers and programmers, but people of diverse pursuits and backgrounds ranging from critics and scholars, students of film and literature, and professionals working in film distribution to people who simply have a passion for the subject.

The seminar turned out to be rigorous but not disciplinary. The days were long, with each morning, afternoon, and evening screening followed by in-depth discussion sessions. These were free-flowing and open without being rambling or random.

The clearest sign of how the seminar implanted itself into everyone's minds was that discussion continued into and through most breaks. I had the best intentions to make regular use of the university's Olympic-size pool located in the building next to my dorm. I was able to tear myself away from the seminar exactly twice to do so.

Over the week, I truly came to cherish many participants' perceptiveness and the subtlety and pith of their reasoning, impassioned without being reductive or polemical.

There were difficult moments, for sure. One was during the post-screening discussion of Naomi Kawase's *Genpin* (2010), a film about natural childbirth. I was among those who voiced skepticism about what I felt was a somewhat idealized representation. But the Flaherty's participants' well-reasoned responses ultimately made the discussion constructive. Some female participants' eloquent, measured critiques created a climate of productive exchange that encouraged feedback from every side, including me as a male.

I now understood what constituted the Flaherty's famed rigor: discussions were to the point, rather than reflecting ideological trench wars.

Ultimately, PLAY generated precisely the experiences in me its opening description proclaimed. It really did expose me to cinema as a vital, living thing, a cinema in tune with the shifting rhythms of the world.

I was already familiar with and cherished the creative energy of Saul Levine's films. But being introduced to the works of Brigid McCaffrey and Luke Fowler immediately made me aware of all my senses, turning me into the infant at the center of Stan Brakhage's famous questions from *Metaphors of Vision* (1976): "How many colors are there in a field of grass to the crawling baby unaware of 'Green'? How many rainbows can light create for the untutored eye?" Except that Luke's films, particularly *A Grammar for Listening: Part 1* (2009), and *Depositions* (2014), also demand that we extend such metaphors to sound and listening.

A downright chiasmatic experience of a cinema breathing with such liberating, cosmic intensity that it takes one's breath away was Joaquim Pinto and Nuno Leonel's portrait of fishermen on the Azores Islands, *Fish Tail (Rabo de Peixe)* (2015). Few films use the cinema so movingly in negotiating the contradictions between a political filmmaker's passionate solidarity with and solitary erotic passion for his subjects.

This film was a deeply personal experience for me. As a queer child of ten on a rainy Sunday afternoon, I'd been initiated by German television into the cinema's all-consuming erotic force with a tale of forbidden desire on the ocean, the man-boy romance *Captains Courageous* (1937), which turned Spencer Tracy into my first love. The moment Pinto and Leonel referenced that very film in *Rabo de Peixe*, my heart almost stopped. Yet, how surprised could I really have been by having cinema's cosmic potential reconfirmed?

Billy Woodberry's *Marseille après la guerre* (2016), about the dock-workers of Marseille in the aftermath of World War II, preceded the screening of Pinto and Leonel's film. What a double bill David had created! Woodberry's film is another indelible Flaherty memory—and a precious find, as my own work is now centering on cinema's depiction of ships, the sea, and sexual and racial alterity.

When I wear my PLAY T-shirt, I think of David. Play was central to his view of the world. "Play allows cinema to be a vital, living thing," he wrote. By the time he saw those words printed in the seminar program, he was more than ever invested in them and more than ever convinced they were true. He was right.

95

GRASS, ROCKS, WATER

Lina Žigelytė

LINA ŽIGELYTĖ is an educator, curator, and audiovisual artist. She was born in Vilnius, Lithuania, and is now based in Rochester, New York. Her work explores the relationships between transnational media history and sexuality studies. In 2018, her dissertation on the transatlantic queer networks of the interwar years and their visual culture received the Susan B. Anthony Dissertation Award. Her audiovisual work has been screened at Jerk Off Festival (France) and Nida Artist Colony (Lithuania). She is a faculty member in the Media and Society program at Hobart and William Smith Colleges.

A good friend of mine who had once gone to the Flaherty seminar assured me the participants went skinny-dipping, a ritual at the event.

I'm a bad swimmer. I almost drowned twice. The first time was in a swimming pool when I was a child. The second was in the Baltic Sea at the age of eighteen. Both took place in Palanga, a popular holiday resort in my native Lithuania.

Water also reminds me of precious moments with my chosen family, such as camping in the Adirondacks with my wife and our dog or summer picnics on lakeshores with past lovers. In spite of my almost-drowning history, water intrigues me. It makes me think of a break from routine and inspires a sense of kinship.

Figure 95.1.

After the fall of Communism, Palanga became too expensive for my family's annual holidays. My parents never owned a car, and so, despite my close calls, the ability to go for a swim remains ingrained in my memory as a special occasion.

Although I greatly anticipated the skinny-dipping at the Flaherty, I also looked forward to everything the seminar seemed, at least by rumor, to be famous for: dozens of films, conversations with filmmakers, and camaraderie with scholars obsessed by documentary. In 2016, I was almost done with my doctoral studies in the Visual and Cultural Studies program at the University of Rochester. My dissertation focused on the ways queer migrants shaped transatlantic visual culture in the years between the World Wars. I secured a Flaherty fellowship to attend the seminar, and that June, off I went.

The late David Pendleton curated the program that year, called PLAY. I was familiar with David's writing on homoexoticism in the films of Sergei Eisenstein, F. W. Murnau, and Pier Paolo Pasolini through my dissertation research. David's curatorial statement for the 2016 Flaherty seminar spoke about "a cinema of curiosity," "alternative histories," and "the tug of history." As a queer immigrant, I read between the lines and was certain David's program promised films rich with multiple creative interpretations of queerness and its possibilities for world-making, kinships, speculations about the future, and memory's afterlives.

During the week at Colgate University, I grew increasingly disenchanted with the seminar. My trouble began on opening night, which kicked off with a screening of Saul Levine's flicker film *Light Licks: By the Waters of Babylon: In the Hour of Angels* (2004). The film starts with a handheld camera focusing on the moon in night sky, followed by over ten minutes of rapidly flashing lights. Then the film focuses on the New York skyline. Instead of looking at the world, Levine's camera blinks and squints. Watching the screen, I caught my eyes doing the same.

I wondered if this film foreshadowed the kind of cinema to come during the rest of the seminar. Why does a week on experimental documentary need to start with New York and the work of a white American film-maker? This was the first of a series of questions I returned to throughout the week. Why did my cohort of Flaherty fellows seem to be the youngest people at the seminar? Why do the post-screening discussions so poorly confront the generational and racial divides among the Flaherty attendees? What is the income of the many participants who struggle to remember the number of seminars they have attended (the registration fee is close to $1,500)? These questions linger as my most vivid memories.

I did see a number of memorable films and filmmakers during that week, including Kidlat Tahimik's uncompromising decolonizing wit both on and off camera. The Mojave Desert in Brigid McCaffrey's footage and the Azores in Joaquim Pinto and Nuno Leonel's *Fish Tail* (2015) reminded me about the ways queerness can be encountered in remote locations. In scholarly accounts, the focus is mostly on what city life has historically offered queer people—in bars, parks, nightclubs, and abandoned areas such as the piers along the Hudson River in New York. I frequently struggle to connect to Western urban centers and their iconic status in queer imagination. Today, many young queer people can hardly afford to live in larger cities. So in a peculiar way, I am grateful to that Flaherty experience for ultimately turning me toward grass, rocks, and water.

As the week progressed, the dissidents I found myself drawn to moved to the back rows of the screening and discussion rooms for stretching and gossip. Here emerged *sotto voce* comments confronting the seminar's issues head-on, especially the questionable selection of works by women filmmakers. Here, Ute Aurand faced criticism for colonial sentiments in her diary film on India, and Ana Vaz was confronted for unacknowledged privilege in her works on Brazil.

Contrary to the 2016 seminar's theme, the Flaherty did not at all feel like an environment dedicated to play, especially the post-screening sessions. In spite of a number of non-American seminar participants, questions and comments posed in accented English were rarely the first ones to be heard. Again and again, entitled white men raised their hands first to vocalize their thoughts. I sometimes envied their confidence.

I'd envisioned the Flaherty as an inspiring educational experience, but on many occasions, the seminar instigated flashbacks to the grad school trauma I carry as a first-generation student. At Flaherty, as in grad school, I kept experiencing the feelings of lagging behind, of struggling without a sense of progress, of not being seen. My memories of drowning are haunted by the same sensations.

I am writing this story after two historical events, one macro and one micro: a year of the #metoo movement across the globe and a number of changes in the Flaherty organization, such as the push to abandon the logo that included a silhouetted still from *Nanook of the North* (1922).

Back at the seminar I attended, most of my disenchantments with the Flaherty had less to do with curatorial decisions or logos than with the seminar's climate, which seemed to have been cultivated for decades to promote rigid higher-education frameworks and to empower the regulars accustomed to these frameworks.

If I could change one part of the Flaherty so future iterations would be less traumatizing to new participants like myself, I would dispose of these frameworks. The seminar could aspire to have more participants of lesser financial means, rather than those with the resources to pay the full fee year after year. The seminar could actively commit to moderating those voices that dominate. The seminar could have more early career professionals.

And the seminar could have rituals like swimming in nearby lakes—because collective experience of nature can be as memorable and formative as collective experience of culture.

96

NOT EXACTLY A HOUSE OF PRAYER

Jiangtao (Harry) Gu

JIANGTAO (HARRY) GU is Visiting Assistant Professor in Media and Society at Hobart and William Smith Colleges. His work on the early history of photography in China bridges the postcolonial critique of the nation-state with the nationalistic tendencies in the writing of photography's other histories. His writings have been featured by *Trans Asia Photography Review*, *Journal of Contemporary Chinese Art*, and China's *Wenhui Bao*. His dissertation research was supported by the Social Science Research Council and the Andrew W. Mellon Foundation.

I first attended the Flaherty seminar in 2017 as a University of Rochester Fellow.

One week prior to that, I'd passed the qualifying exam of my PhD program. However, I did not feel a sense of relief.

Six months into Donald Trump's presidency, I was emotionally ravaged.

The symbolic disturbance caused by the election of a tycoon as the president of the United States trickled down more violently and quickly than I had expected. The nation is divided, communities fractured, allies have turned against each other, and discourses are broken. Ever since the Democratic primary, the meanings of *identity politics* have been corrupted and foreclosed, as if the political pursuit for multiple subject positions has come to a dead end.

Figure 96.1.

In times like this, it is perhaps natural to withdraw from potential conflicts, to shut up and mind your own business, to huddle with those just like us. But silence and self-seclusion are never easy. The desire for discourse and community erupts in every solitary moment of this crisis.

For a godless person like me, I thought maybe cinema would be the place where a sense of communion could still be found.

I've always liked the feeling of walking into a theater, saying "hi" to the person next to me, settling down in my seat, and waiting for the first beam of light from the projector to hit the screen. For however long a film runs, our times are synced and our bodies connected.

Despite the Flaherty Seminar's cult reputation, I already knew that it is not exactly a house of prayer. There is no singular God bathed in light at the altar. On the contrary, I knew that antagonisms and arguments are engineered, sometimes quite heavy-handedly.

Indeed, *heavy-handed* is the word that one of the fellows used to describe Nuno Lisboa's programing at Future Remains. Canadian filmmaker Dominic Gagnon's *of the North* (2015) was a programing choice that many in attendance argued that the seminar could have done without. Composed of found footage from YouTube, the film shows Inuit people in vulnerable conditions, and many felt that the film reinforces degrading stereotypes of Canada's indigenous Northerners.

The rage ignited by the questionable ethics of Gagnon's film in the community arena of the Flaherty discussion room and the more sympathetic reactions to the film that many shared with me during private conversations afterward are especially revealing of the division that fractures today's Left.

The differing opinions about Gagnon's film did not happen in a vacuum. At the center of this division reside people's differing opinions about *identity politics*. The term originated in the social movements of the 1970s and was critically revisited in leftist discourses following the 2016 U.S. election.

While I did not like *of the North*, I'm troubled by some of the critiques of the film and Gagnon during the discussion. The audience's repeated characterization of Gagnon's work as "boy art," for instance, sounds more like a personal attack on the filmmaker's perceived failure in achieving artistic maturity or perhaps manhood than a denunciation of the deafness of his tone and subject position.

Others questioned whether the filmmaker had obtained consent from his subjects, which also seems to simplify the difficult ethical questions of representation into a straightforward procedural check. After all, Gagnon recycled YouTube postings that had been made public by the posters themselves. The ethics of a film, in my opinion, is infinitely more complicated than any consent form.

Contrary to what was suggested by many people at the 2017 Flaherty, I think the complexities of the issues at hand, both at the seminar and in today's political discourse, will not be solved by limiting documentary filmmaking to self-representation, just as hiding from the world will not solve the world's problems.

The idea that white people can only make films about white people is perhaps a symptom of the polarized and divided world that we are living in today, rather than its solution. Moreover, the naivete of a politics of self-representation is also antithetical to what the camera can do—point at and film *the Other*. Without that, we would be left with a world of selfies.

That said, the question regarding who is behind the camera filming whom is an old one.

After the election of Trump, the timing of Nuno Lisboa's programming provided an interesting conundrum. The meta question regarding documentary ethics—whether filming *the Other* is ever permissible—has once again been raised. Let's consider it from fresh angles.

97

SPEAKING NEARBY FLAHERTY

Greg de Cuir Jr.

GREG DE CUIR JR. is the selector for Alternative Film/Video and Beldocs (both in Belgrade, Serbia). He has organized moving-image programs for the National Gallery of Art in Washington, DC, the Museum of Modern Art in Warsaw, Los Angeles Filmforum, goEast Wiesbaden, and Experiments in Cinema in Albuquerque, New Mexico. His writing has been published in *Art Margins, Cineaste, Festivalists, Jump Cut, La Furia Umana, Politika,* and elsewhere. De Cuir received his PhD from the Faculty of Dramatic Arts at University of Arts Belgrade. He lives and works in Belgrade as an independent curator, writer, and translator.

My personal highlight at the sixty-third Robert Flaherty Film Seminar in 2017 was meeting the theorist and artist Trinh T. Minh-ha.

Trinh has loomed large over my writing and my conceptualizations of the moving image ever since I was introduced to her work as a graduate student some fifteen years ago. Her influence is so immense that I would have had the same feeling meeting Dziga Vertov or James Baldwin or some other titan of international arts and letters.

It seems fitting she is such a diminutive woman with a soft voice and a modest, inviting manner of speaking and relating to people.

At first it seemed a slight disappointment to see her *Reassemblage* (1982) projected in a low-quality digital version. Then again, I do not

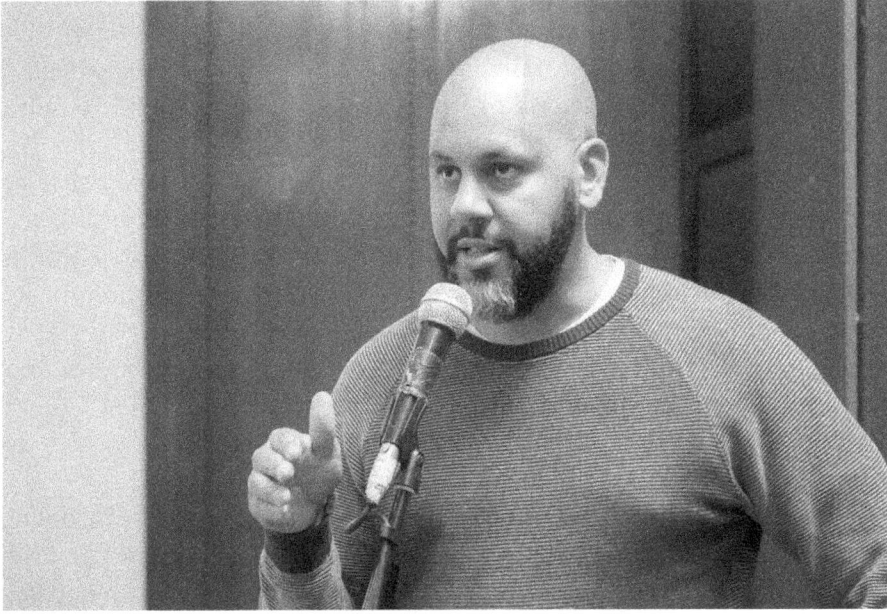

Figure 97.1.

think I've ever seen this work on celluloid. At least for me, a degraded *Reassemblage* is better than no *Reassemblage* at all. No deficiency in image quality can mask the poetic and political resonance of this film. Furthermore, hearing Minh-ha speak about *Reassemblage* was worth the sacrifice in technical quality. Perhaps that is also fitting.

As she recounted to the assembled audience, when she was invited to the Flaherty more than thirty years ago to present *Reassemblage,* she was given stiff rebukes about the technical (and by implication artistic) qualities of her work.

Seminarians attacked her use of silence, as if silence is not an essential component of music! They questioned her use of black frames, as if the cinema is not also an art of absence and as if *Reassemblage* is not embedded in black experience. They complained that "this is not a film," as if that is not among the highest compliments that can be paid to any artist who works to dismantle and decolonize "their" notions of what a film is, of what "they" stand for, and what "they" subject others to.

The grand old founding fathers of our discipline in attendance at that screening must have felt their hegemonic tradition of quality being chopped down to size, then set on fire.

As we see an image of a burning field, Minh-ha asks, "What can we expect of ethnology?" Her film answers: the charred remains of the natural world. *Reassemblage* refused to submit, refused to play by the rules, and refused to "speak about." Her film indeed *speaks nearby*. It must miss the mark of the totalizing quest of meaning, offering instead a chance to reassemble the world of ethnographic representation in a more humane and generous manner.

Cut to 2017 and the post-screening discussion of *Reassemblage*. I sit in the back of the room taking notes, curious to observe the effect of the film on new audiences in this new century. History repeats itself. The film is attacked for its representation of Africans and African culture, for its perceived incoherence, and again for its technique. All these years later, the film has not lost its avant-garde edge, its ability to stir bodies and souls, the sincere insolence of its documentary refusal.

Still, whether or not I consider it an impeccable chef d'oeuvre is beside the point.

The fires that Minh-ha lit under the false assumptions of the documentary right of representation must also lick at the edges of her own project. But like a crafty arsonist, Minh-ha knows how to get in and get out, how to pick the right spot at the right time.

I was warned that Flaherty seminarians can be ruthless and can sometimes even break careers. But Minh-ha's film is fireproof.

I was planning to present a 16mm print of *Reassemblage* in a screening I was organizing. When I discussed this idea with Minh-ha over lunch at the Colgate University café, I felt very much like that student who first encountered her monumental work.

Maybe that is the secret effect of the Flaherty. It disarms while simultaneously empowering both audience and artist. It is something like speaking both nearby and far away, from a place that is both familiar and estranged.

98

NO LONGER AN ODD VOICE
AT THE FLAHERTY

Sheafe Satterthwaite

SHEAFE SATTERTHWAITE has probably attended more Flaherty seminars than anyone. Longtime veterans of the seminar can never forget his distinctive manner of address: if you heard Satterthwaite ask a question or make a comment about a film, you never forgot his voice and his forthright but gentle and amusing way of regaling the assembled seminarians. The most recent Flaherty he attended was PLAY in 2016. Satterthwaite, now retired from teaching landscape history at Williams College, lives at Alexander McNish House (1794, National Registry of Historic Places) in Salem, New York, where he has often tutored high school and college wrestlers.

I stopped going to the Flaherty after a run of some thirty years (not including "teenage" stints of working at the seminars while they were still held at Black Mountain Farm in Dummerston, Vermont, where Robert and Frances resided late in life). My sundering was partly because of an increasing irksomeness with the unhelpfulness of Frances Flaherty's advocacy of non-preconception.

The Zen-derived principle of non-preconception is a fine stance if you can afford to shoot umpteen feet of film and spend months screening and devouring and assessing it, as with the abundant outtakes of *Louisiana Story* (1948), but it is not very helpful if a one-time screening is about a tribe in Indonesia, with a culture quite disparate from high-tech America

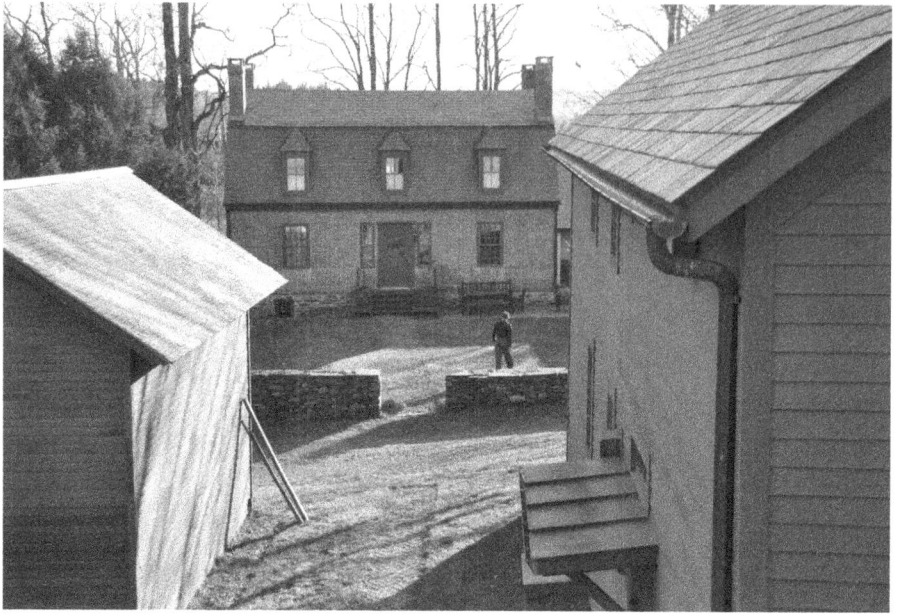

Figure 98.1. Photograph by Kenny Hersey.

and that culture being appraised by an audience armed with iPhones. With non-preconception, the single viewing can become an avenue to ignorance. Or, worse, to prejudice, with supposedly advanced, current American values and fetishisms being thrust onto the film.

But there were other issues, as well.

I remember viewing a feature-length film within the past decade and wondering where I was. The combination of an abundance of English in an obviously Islamic culture with abundant minarets caused me to assume I was in Pakistan—when, if I had realized the director was Egyptian, I would have known I was in Cairo. Deliberately placing an attendee in such ignorance is abhorrent!

The audience's primary American-ness makes discussion difficult. The nuances, say, of Persian or Sri Lankan culture are literally foreign to most all Americans and hence most all seminarians. Here is where short, pithy introductions to the works by the directors themselves, or by a critic or teacher, could be helpful. Rather than come to the film cold, espousing non-preconception, could ten minutes of knowing the relevance of Persian or Sri Lankan behaviors, ways of thinking, kinds of looking, embedded traits be explained and make the act of screening, *at the seminar*, more intelligent?

Put simply, I would like the Flaherty seminar to run like an anthology of essays or poems, with short prefaces and introductory commentaries, especially when the works are difficult or particularly non-American!

Maybe still more, my sundering was because of the pernicious dominance of programmers. I want to know where a seminar is headed. My sense at Flaherty is that the programmer is omnipresent in the sense of orchestrating the events, their sequence, and their articulation in discussions. But this person, at least at most seminars, is silent, unheard, in the shadows. Why?

I wonder how destructive it would actually be to issue a program upon the opening of the seminar and to have the programmer explicate that program—albeit with the proviso that the ordering could be modified during the week.

And just what does the branding of the seminars with keywords like *work* and *play* reveal, other than an unbecoming modishness and a commitment to marketing? When programmers feel they must adhere to these vague, useless terms, such categorizing tends to deprive, starve, segregate the richness and disparateness of film expression.

As well, the recent tendency to spread out a director's work over many days diffuses its impact and does not enable a rich-enough apprehension of the director's oeuvre. Could the ordering of films and discussion be under the aegis of the particular directors? I could envision a seminar in which, during five successive days, each of five directors had a day to herself/himself—maybe including their presenting other makers' works that have had a major influence on that filmmaker.

A precipitating event for my sundering was a morning during which a young Californian filmmaker's work, somehow occasioned by a reservoir, was screened. As a landscape historian (although for years I occasionally offered a class on experimental and nonfiction film at Williams College), I am disinclined to too personal an approach to film. I wanted to know about *the reservoir*, not about the filmmaker, and I realized, then, that the tendency of the seminars to disparage works of fact, imaginatively expressed, and to promote personal "documentaries" is not what I personally want in films.

I realize that the seminar may never have a week largely devoted to the work of (and necessary presence of) Ken Burns, because of his success (abhorrent perhaps to "independent" filmmakers) and what many might see as his formulaic approach to history or his not representing the latest or most modish thinking. Are the programmers afraid to have the seminar actually consider the values and problems of a documentary filmmaker's success?

The seminars have become demonstrations of how ideologically trendy or up-to-date the programmers are, as if they were showing a new line on a fashion runway. The Flaherty now seems more a projection of programmer prejudices, proclivities, and current political interests than a selection of the year's best and most interesting work.

When I think back through all the films I've seen at the many Flahertys I've attended (most of them now a blur to me), the ones that
have most moved me were works by filmmakers whose minds, in the
discussions, proved impressive and subtle and cultured and nuanced and
articulate—the makers sometimes even more impressive than the work.
An example: Mani Kaul, whose work included several long documentaries on classical Indian musicians. Another is the Budapest filmmaker
Péter Forgács, whose work exploited so poignantly the home movies of
Central European Jews before the Second World War calamities and
ethnic annihilations.

Within the past decade, Anita Rehrer, then Flaherty executive director, held a board meeting at my home in Salem, New York. I was at
a loss to understand the composition of this particular board, which
was comprised of a plurality of women of roughly the same age—late
thirties—other than that it appeared to have virulently feminist proclivities. The board seemed a bit more a clique than an assembly of major
film authorities, makers, aficionados, and intellects. Some of these board
members' interests seemed rather distant from film; wouldn't a board
with larger varieties of experience be more likely to produce less predict-
ably personally focused seminars?

And so far I have here neglected the worst Flaherty development: what
has become its sheer size and ungainliness. For many years, attendance
was a good deal less than one hundred; now it is verging on two hundred.
Can what happens after the screenings really be called *discussions*?

99

UNCERTAIN EXPEDITIONS

John Bruce

JOHN BRUCE is a design strategist and filmmaker. He is Assistant Professor of Strategic Design at Parsons School of Design. He was a 2015–2016 Fellow at the Graduate Institute for Design Ethnography and Social Thought at The New School. He codirected the film *End of Life* (2017) with Paweł Wojtasik, who he met at his first Flaherty seminar in 2010. John served on the Flaherty Board of Trustees, 2012–2018.

Strong opposition to and support for including Dominic Gagnon's film *of the North* (2015) at the 2017 Flaherty seminar was voiced from outside and inside the organization. This caused questions to surface around the organization's clarity about and stewardship of the core values that support its mission. The members of the board of trustees had found themselves in the position to either censor *of the North* at the seminar or to allow the screening, as per the desire of guest programmer Nuno Lisboa.

Arguments against inclusion focused on the film's content and its author's relationship to the source material. Arguments to include the film centered on the Flaherty's unique context as a space for critical discourse, thus perhaps the best setting to debate the issues surrounding the film. North American indigenous communities, along with some academics, were said to have rejected the work as enforcing negative stereotypes and

Figure 99.1.

protested its exhibition. Gagnon defended the work, citing the fact that everything in the film had been culled from online sites where the publicly posted, self-authored videos were found.

How the Flaherty organization came to find itself, during the seminar, with the decision to censor or exhibit *of the North* involves a complex narrative over time. But this moment is reflective of so many heated stalemates of recent years. The *he said, she said* accounts of events too often serve as an unproductive shell game for diverting our attention from the heart of the matter. Context and complexity are imperative to recognize while exploring possible logics, perspectives, poetics, provocations, and proposals that do not rely on simple didactic agendas.

It is easy to become seduced into promoting bandwagon-esque postures (on any side of any argument), for in noisily convoluted and infuriating times, such places seem like the only available platforms. I'd like to believe that alternatives, such as the Flaherty, are possible and preferable, especially when the going gets tough. Where else might we hash issues out with rigor, respect, and the benefit of reflective space over substantive time?

The actual value of the Flaherty is not clearly understood unless experienced firsthand. The six days of the Flaherty's durational impact can seem merely a summer-camp drive-by. However, these six days, combined with a carefully designed atmosphere and experience of engagement, can deliver an exceptionally rich opportunity for reflection and exchange. This is the fundamental role of the Flaherty.

Having had a great number of very influential and celebrated figures of cinema participate as featured artists or attendees, the Flaherty might look like a hit factory for experimental nonfiction film. But the fundamental goal of the Flaherty is not to promote, support, or celebrate films and filmmakers. The organization relies on a co-creative, open-ended scattershot of risky speculation and the spurring of an immersive exchange of ideas by participants at the event.

Through an active embrace of methods for elevating concepts of non-preconception and non-hierarchy, the Flaherty experience asks people to show up and come together—to collaborate, from a place of their humanity first, regardless of titles, roles, or expertise. The attempt, as Tony Fry expresses in his book *Design as Politics* (2010), is to allow for "difference in common." The Flaherty organization serves as the designer for a carefully choreographed gathering, with nonfiction cinema as accelerant for more expansive discourse around culture.

Can we productively talk about a film without having witnessed it ourselves? Perhaps. The danger arises when we believe we are certain and empower this certainty by a refusal to be uncomfortable. After all, being comfortable is not always the point. The value of the *polis*, as Hannah Arendt describes in *The Human Condition* (1958), arises from the spaces where people act and speak together.

These spaces can be vulnerable and fragile at times. Genuine pain and crisis might be present and can motivate decisions to dismantle the polis. Indeed, conflict can be conflated with abuse. Sarah Schulman's book *Conflict is Not Abuse: Overstating Harm, Community Responsibility, and the Duty of Repair* (2016) speaks to this idea:

> Shunning . . . is designed to maintain a unilateral position of unmovable superiority by asserting one's status as Abused and the implied consequential right to punish without terms. This concept . . . is predicated

on a need to enforce that one party is entirely righteous and without mistake, while the other is the Specter, the residual holder of all evil. If conflicted people were expected and encouraged to produce complex understandings of their relationships, then people could be expected to negotiate . . . And it is in the best interest of us all to try to consciously move to that place.

As stewards of the Flaherty, the board of trustees could not take a position of censorship and deny the screening of *of the North*. At the same time, all involved were able to recognize that conflict and pain were present in the surrounding issues. Personally, the experience caused me some sadness. Not because my job as president of the board was hard in those moments, but because I had thought we had become better than we are. By *we*, I mean those of us dedicated to the hard work it takes to build bridges, not burn them, for approaching discourse.

I remain optimistic yet am reminded that ways forward require the courage to face stretches of groundlessness. Ideally, the Flaherty will continue to rise to its mission, and not devolve into a reductive academic conference or a self-congratulatory platform for politically correct cineastes. Now, more than ever, the world needs models for active, collaborative progress. As my colleague Lisa Norton, professor of Design Leadership at The New School, likes to say: *Brave space needs to be safe, and safe space needs to be brave.* Certainly, this is what Frances Flaherty had in mind when she founded the seminar.

Of the North was screened during the 2017 Flaherty seminar. What did this mean? Ask someone who was there. Or, listen to the audio file of the post-screening discussion. For the Flaherty, this event prompted many discussions over many months and thus informed insights and subsequent actions addressing our role and responsibility for confronting systems of power and privilege.

100

IN THAT SILENCE

Anocha Suwichakornpong

ANOCHA SUWICHAKORNPONG lives and works in Bangkok, Thailand. She received the Tiger Award for her film *Mundane History* (2009) at the International Film Festival Rotterdam 2010. Her second feature-length narrative film, *By the Time It Gets Dark* (2016), premiered at the Locarno Film Festival 2016. She founded the Bangkok-based production company, Electric Eel Films, in 2007. She is Codirector of Purin Pictures, a film fund to support Southeast Asian cinema production, distribution, screenings, workshops, events, and other related activities.

The most poignant moment at the 2018 Flaherty seminar occurred during the very last post-screening discussion, after many people had spoken.

One participant took the microphone and asked everyone to not say anything. She asked us to remain silent for a moment.

Suddenly, the room fell into total silence. It lasted only a minute.

In that silence, I felt the energy circulating through the room. I could not decipher what kind of energy. I'm not sure if anyone else could either.

An ineffable energy was very much present. It felt expansive.

This moment is how I remember my first Flaherty seminar.

When Greg de Cuir Jr. invited me to be a guest artist for 2018, I gladly accepted.

Figure 100.1.

Although I had heard of the Flaherty seminar, my understanding of what kind of events it mounted was quite limited. One week prior to the seminar, I had casually mentioned to Ben Rivers that I was going. It turned out he had been a guest artist too. He smiled. He told me it was an intense experience.

That conversation was the first time someone used the word *intense* to describe the seminar to me. Since then, I have heard it repeated countless times.

My friend was right.

Spending one week with more than a hundred complete strangers was not easy, especially for an introvert like me.

Talking about my work was even more difficult. In the first few days, I struggled. I tried to navigate the space. I tried to adjust or rather reacclimate to the North American confrontational style. For a few years, I'd lived in New York. But back in Thailand for over a decade, I seem to have lost my confrontational abilities.

My short, *Nightfall* (2016), was my first screening. In the discussion afterward, I found myself unable to be articulate about the film. I felt defensive. I revealed that I didn't think my work could be understood outside of Southeast Asia.

At this point in my story, I should mention that there was another invited Southeast Asian guest filmmaker: John Torres. We've been friends for many years.

On the first day of the seminar, as we walked to the opening reception, John told me he was happy that I was also there. This sentiment was reciprocal. For the first day or two, we felt like the outsiders. We would ask ourselves *what exactly are we doing here?* We knew we were there to present our films and to talk about them. But why?

I remember saying to John that even though we did not feel totally comfortable, it was probably good we were there. I tend to get a kick out of being placed in a vulnerable position. I feel I can *experience* something and maybe out of that experience, I can *learn* something.

One particular night, something in me shifted.

The lights came on after Christopher Harris's *Still/Here* (2001), a meditative 16mm black-and-white film shot in the north side of St. Louis. People left the theater one by one.

As I watched them depart, I was unable to get up from my seat. I felt I had experienced something profound without really understanding it. A sense of irrevocable loss deeply affected me. I had to spend another few minutes before I could gather my strength to walk to the discussion room.

From that point, I didn't think about my alienation anymore. I began to absorb things. I realized that I was in a very good place to learn. Because of my experience with Christopher's film, I questioned my earlier defensive position that my work couldn't be understood outside Southeast Asia.

As the days went by, my appreciation of Kevin Jerome Everson and Greg de Cuir Jr.'s radical and political programing of films and discussions grew.

Among the ten guest artists, there was only one white man, the great Želimir Žilnik, the Serbian film director considered a major figure in the Yugoslav Black Wave film movement of the 1960s and 1970s. He lenses ordinary people with such respect and care.

The Flaherty Board of Trustees announced the discontinuation of the seminar's logo due to its misrepresentation of the Inuit. The logo is a silhouette image of Allakariallak (known as Nanook in Robert Flaherty's *Nanook of the North*, 1922) with his harpoon. For me, the decision seemed to reflect the impact of Kevin and Greg's programming.

I had managed to make some new friends. Quite a few were Asian Americans. We joked around and called ourselves "the Asian bloc" each time we gathered.

Then Beatriz Santiago Muñoz's *Oneiromancer* (2017) was screened, a film about the *memory* of the Fuerzas Armadas de Liberación Nacional, the Puerto Rican anti-colonial movement. As I watched it, a strange feeling composed simultaneously of sadness and joy overcame me. I felt connected to this work. I recognized something of myself in it.

In the post-screening discussion, Bea so spoke eloquently and sincerely about her personal story that I ended up approaching her to tell her how much I appreciated her work. Although we came from opposite sides of the world, I felt we shared similar histories.

Later that night, my feature-length narrative film *By The Time It Gets Dark* (2016) screened. It probes the impossibility of making a film about the October 6, 1976, massacre in Thailand. After that screening, when Bea and I saw each other again, we exchanged a knowing look.

That same night, Cauleen Smith, an experimental filmmaker whose work I truly admire, invited "the Asian bloc" to share a bottle of whiskey back at the dorm. Crystal Campbell, Anita Chang, Robert Chang, Michael Gillespie, Christopher Harris, Lan Thao Lam, Lana Lin, and John Torres were there. Strangely enough, a handmade sign indicating that the room was *the Harlem Renaissance Center* was affixed to the wall.

Cauleen was a super host. We finished the whiskey. Kevin and Greg joined us later. It was a beautiful gathering. In retrospect, I wish one of us had taken some photos. It's not likely that we'll have another special encounter like this one. We were so busy enjoying ourselves, no one thought of it.

The seminar ended, but these relationships do not. The conversations keep going. The work keeps expanding.

And then, we will need other moments for silence.

101

ALAS, THE LOGO!

Scott MacDonald

The image of Allakariallak—"Nanook" in *Nanook of the North*—with harpoon, demonstrating a technology long used for the sustenance of his family and community, has been a canonical image from Flaherty's film for decades. Scott MacDonald and Patricia R. Zimmermann demanded that the silhouette rendering of this image, which had become the logo for the Flaherty seminar, be on the cover of their book, *The Flaherty: Decades in the Cause of Independent Cinema* (2017)—their way of honoring Allakariallak and his community, Flaherty's film, and the seminar. The full logo, in small, is on the back cover of the book.

In the fall of 2018, I was disappointed to learn that the Flaherty board had suppressed what had been for two decades the organization's logo: the canonical image of Nanook in the act of throwing his harpoon, presumably at a walrus or a seal.

I had come to take the logo for granted. When Patricia Zimmermann and I were preparing our first Flaherty book, *The Flaherty: Decades in the Cause of Independent Cinema*, for Indiana University Press, we made clear that the logo needed to be the cover image. The designers had suggested a generic man-with-camera.

For me, the logo has always evoked the collaborative nature of *Nanook of the North* (1922) and the Flaherty seminar. Designed in the late 1990s at the suggestion of longtime Flahertyites Phred Churchill and Phil Wilde, the logo had come to symbolize the seminar's escape from the threat of

Figure 101.1. © Flaherty / International Film Seminars Inc.

economic collapse and its subsequent emergence as a crucial organization and annual event within the modern history of documentary.

By 2017–2018, the logo (and Nanook/*Nanook*) had become for some, apparently including the majority of board members, a visual emblem of colonialism and exploitive capitalism, an instance of a stereotype of the indigenous Eskimo, described in a proclamation read at the 2018 seminar (quoting Joseph E. Senungetuk, an Inupiat from Northwest Alaska), as "a people without technology, without a culture, lacking intelligence, living in igloos, and at best, a sort of simplistic 'native boy' type of subhuman arctic being" (*Give or Take a Century: An Eskimo Chronicle*, San Francisco: Indian Historian Press, 1971: 25).

Theory is at its best when it illuminates, but it can also blind. If, theoretically, any film about an indigenous group made by a person considered a descendant of a colonizing group can never be anything more than exploitive, then I suppose one might conclude that *Nanook* is an instance of the Eskimo stereotyping Senungetuk became familiar with, growing up in the 1940s and 1950s.

However, it would be an unusual viewer who could see Nanook as subhuman. Flaherty is at pains to demonstrate that the Inuit had survived as a people in what for most would be a hostile environment, specifically by developing a range of remarkably efficient technologies for hunting, fishing, and moving through the world. Certainly the depiction of Inuit culture in *Nanook* is limited, as no film about a culture can escape limitations. But Allakariallak and the other actors in the film who demonstrate aspects of traditional Inuit life remain, nearly a century after the film's release, thoroughly engaging, aware, and adept, quite the opposite of the subhuman depictions of indigenous groups so common in popular films before *Nanook*.

The complaint in the proclamation that Nanook is holding a harpoon despite the fact that "the Inuit portrayed in the film were using guns at the time" (i.e., that Flaherty ignored the realities of modern Inuit life) also seems problematic. *Nanook* begins with Nanook and other Inuit bringing the furs they've collected over the year to the trader. Clearly, the Inuit are seen as part of what was in the 1920s a major industry, the fur trade.

In fact, a gun is seen in one of the shots depicting Nanook and other men bringing a walrus to shore. We don't see them use the gun to kill the walrus, just as, later in the film, we don't see Nanook kill the small fox he has trapped. Flaherty was hoping to depict the Inuit in a way that would demonstrate their commonalities with American moviegoers. He may have felt that depicting the killing of the animals would interfere with this goal.

Over the years, much has been made of a scene at the trader's, where Nanook seems befuddled by a phonograph. But this is less a joke on Nanook than Allakariallak's reenactment of an experience most of us have on a regular basis: amused astonishment at what a new, seemingly magical technology can do.

That some Flahertyites would rebel against an image from what they believed was a retrograde film is hardly surprising. Over the decades, the seminar has seen a series of more or less progressive small rebellions. The change of the seminar from a private gathering to a more public intellectual event under the influence of Erik Barnouw and Willard Van Dyke may have been the first rebellion.

In 1968, Van Dyke and D. Marie Grieco hosted a group of avant-garde filmmakers from the West Coast who rebelled against what they saw as the Flaherty's stuffiness and its devotion to certain narrowly defined modes of documentary. They exchanged name tags to confuse the other seminarians. Filmmakers and theorists concerned with image ethics soon returned the seminar more fully to its realist documentary focus. Then came the feminist rebellion of the 1970s, 1980s, and early 1990s. After that came demands that the Flaherty expand the international and ethnic diversity of its filmmaker guests and seminarians.

In recent years, the seminar has become increasingly academic, sometimes more like a college classroom than the free-form seminars of old. Academics trained in postcolonial theories arrived in the mid-2010s to take action against the logo—as if suppressing previous generation's attempts at progressive and useful change absolves a younger generation of the weight of history.

The elimination of the logo is full of ironies. Among other things, it suggests that those who came to feel embarrassed about the image of Nanook-with-harpoon are more aware of Inuit reality than Flaherty himself, who spent much of his youth in northern Canada and lived with the group he filmed for sixteen months. It is not hard to find modern Inuit who express gratitude for Flaherty's depiction of their grandparents' ways of dealing with their environment.

To suppress Flaherty's image is to assume that the men and women who collaborated with him for so long lacked agency, implicitly rendering them into the stereotype described above.

And how does eliminating the one image of an adult Inuit known around the world create respect for the history of that cultural group or their descendants?

Ultimately, to suppress the Flaherty logo is not just to disrespect Robert Flaherty and the history of the seminar. It also patronizes Allakariallak, Maggie Nujarluktuk, and all the Inuit we see in *Nanook*, whose dignified presence/performance defies bigotry, film history, and recent social theory every time the film is screened.

102

SEEING BILL SLOAN, 1928–2017

Patricia R. Zimmermann

Longtime supporter of the Flaherty seminar Lucy Kostelanetz contacted PATRICIA ZIMMERMANN asking her to write a short tribute to
Bill Sloan to be read at his fall 2017 memorial service in New York
City. Zimmermann had met Sloan at the first Flaherty Film Seminar
she attended as a fellowship recipient in 1980. In the 2000s, when
researching the Flaherty's history for her book with Scott MacDonald, *The Flaherty: Decades in the Cause of Independent Cinema*
(2017), she interviewed him on multiple occasions, seeking his help
to understand the labyrinths of arguments, films, film movements,
and people of the Flaherty.

If you took a film studies course at a university, you've met Bill Sloan.

If you teach film at a university, you've met Bill Sloan.

If you ever have borrowed a DVD of an independent film from a
public library, you've met Bill Sloan.

For decades, Bill Sloan served as the film librarian/curator for the
Museum of Modern Art (MoMA) Circulating Film and Video Library.
He was appointed in 1980, after decades at the New York Public Library
film collection. His wide-ranging vision of independent cinema, documentary, and experimental film populates MoMA's landmark collection.

Figure 102.1. © Flaherty / International Film Seminars Inc. Photograph by Lance Bird.

He knew which films were significant and which were breakthroughs. The library collection Bill built constitutes one of the major building blocks of the discipline of cinema studies.

With his hair and beard engulfing his always-smiling face like white cumulous clouds, Bill always seemed one of those special wizards of cinema who operated in some wry meta mode that knew where you needed to go before you got there.

In 1980, very early in my scholarly career, I met Bill at the Flaherty Film Seminar. He served as president from 1974 to 1977. Until I met Bill, I suffered under the bizarre delusion that the holy trinity of films, filmmakers, and programmers defined film culture.

Bill gently opened me up to the idea that librarians at museum collections and public libraries who bought and showed films sustained the infrastructure of independent cinema. Due to his advocacy, many librarians attended the Flaherty.

Graduate school transformed me into a partisan fighter defending the form of cinema I felt mattered the most—documentary. In contrast, Bill's view of the cinematic revealed a more expansive galaxy: he was curious and open about all films, all genres, all periods. He could find something marvelous in most everything he saw.

His pluralist view of cinema materialized in his programming with Nadine Covert, another legend of the film library world, of the landmark

1972 Robert Flaherty Film Seminar. In their heterogeneous program, film combinations provoked the combustion of ideas between filmmakers such as Les Blank, St. Clair Bourne, Liane Brandon, Marcel Ophuls, Yasujiro Ozu, and Ousmane Sembène. In 1979, he programmed again, featuring radical documentary filmmaker Joris Ivens.

Many knew Bill from the Flaherty seminar's Bill's Bar, the jerry-rigged speakeasy-like bar assembled from a folding table, an ice bucket, and a glass jar for donations for libations. I realize now why he always worked the bar: literally and figuratively, he loved serving the next generation of independent cinema.

Bill's generosity impacted me profoundly as I researched Scott Mac-Donald's and my *The Flaherty: Decades in the Cause of Independent Cinema* (2017). I interviewed Bill four times. He conjured a boiling brew of films, people, debates, board decisions, and the 1960s and 1970s and beyond.

A wizard of independent cinema, Bill was the man behind the screen who coaxed us all into a wider, more exciting cinematic world we never could have imagined—or gotten to—without him.

Index

Abrash, Bobby, 35, 72, 97, 121, 212
Adventures of Blacky, The (Finley and Muse, 1998), 292
Afrique, je te plumerai (Africa I Will Fleece You) (Teno, 1992), 248, 253
Afternoon, March 22, 1999 (Reinke, 1999), 131
Agrarian Utopia (Raksasad, 2011), 297
Ah Liberty! (Rivers, 2008), 297
Ahwesh, Peggy, 62, 150, 185, 189, 196, 200
Aibel, Bob, 32
AIDS epidemic, 78, 93, 97, 211
AIDS Show, The (Adair and Epstein, 1986), 71
Akerman, Chantal, 44, 369
Alamar (Gonzalez-Rubio, 2009), 234, 313
Alambrista (Young, 1977), 33, 38
Allakariallak, image on seminar logo, 401, 403–6
All American High (Rosenfeld, 1986), 71
Allen, Austin, 141, 171
Allen, Christopher, 205
Allende, Salvador, 257–58
Almada, Natalia, 227, 277, 278
Alonso, Lisandro, 111, 242, 297, 313, 321
Al Otro Lado (To the Other Side) (Almada, 2005), 227
Al Solh, Mounira, 75, 131, 132, 366, 369, 370

America Lost and Found (Bird and Johnson, 1974), 38
American Film Institute, 18–19
Amiralay, Omar, 238, 308
Amsterdam Global Village (van der Keuken, 1996), 114, 189
Anabasis of May, The (Baudelaire, 2011), 297, 361
And One And One And One (De Michiel, 1986), 78–79
Andrade, Joaquim Pedro de, 23
And You Act Like One Too (Seidelman, 1976), 19
animation, 33, 35, 38, 85, 111, 119, 149, 181, 189, 209, 297
Anything You Want to Be (Brandon, 1971), 19
"Arcadia, or an Eclectic History of the American Century" (Frye), 204
Arendt, Hannah, 346, 397
Armstrong, Franny, 226, 230
Ashadu, Karimah, 63, 76, 214
Association of Independent Video and Filmmakers (AIVF), 20
Atanarjuat: The Fast Runner (Kunuk, 2001), 220–23
Athens International Film and Video Festival (Ohio), 38, 65, 245
Atomic Café (Rafferty, Loader, and Rafferty, 1982), 34
At the Museum: A Pilgrimage of Vanquished Objects (Finley and Muse, 1989), 292, 294

Bagwell, Orlando, 88–90, 96, 110, 114, 118, 188
Baillie, Bruce, 305
Barbash, Ilisa, 238, 297, 308, 327
Barnouw, Erik, 22, 31, 43, 55, 178, 245, 405; benediction by, 39; *Documentary: A History of the Non-Fiction Film,* 37, 113, 180, 216, 295; programmer for 1982 Flaherty Film Seminar, 29–30, 34, 36–37, 42; programmer for 1994 Flaherty Film Seminar, 149, 372
Barret, Elizabeth, 115, 171
Barrios, Jaime, 23, 71, 75
Barroco (Baroque) (Leduc, 1989), 143
Based on a Story (Finley and Muse, 1997), 292
Baudelaire, Eric, 297, 350, 351, 358, 361
Baudrillard, Jean, 57
Before Tomorrow (Avingaq and Ivalu, 2008), 131, 370
Belena (Zürcher, 2004), 370
Ben-Dov, Ariella, 181, 245, 273, 373
Benjamin, Walter, 131, 334
Benning, James, 44, 171
Benning, Sadie, 58, 135
Berger, Sally, 84, 107, 182, 326
Bernadette (Campbell, 2008), 297, 361
Bershen, Wanda, 134
Big Durian, The (Muhammad, 2003), 265
binge-watching, 135–36
Blackaby, Linda, 35, 54, 65, 70, 78, 84, 97, 212, 373
Black Mountain Farm (Dummerston, Vermont), 7–9, 391
Black Power, 69
Blank, Les, 23, 33–34, 63, 297, 330, 409
Blind Ambition (Kahn, 2012), 76
Blindness Series (Tran, 1992–2000), 62, 151
Blue (Jarman, 1993), 209
Blues Accordin' to Lightnin' Hopkins, The (Blank, 1968), 23
BLW collective, 342, 346
Bombing of Osage Avenue, The (Massiah and Bambara, 1986), 84, 103–4

Bonetti, Mahen, 193, 241, 254, 277, 287–90
Bontoc Eulogy (Fuentes, 1995), 170
"bordering on fiction," 47–48
Borges, Jorge Luis, 256, 257
Bourne, St. Clair, 23, 409
Bowling Alley (Cheang, 1995–1996), 157–58
Bowser, Pearl, 14–16, 61, 82–85, 88, 116–20
Braddock Food Bank (Buba, 1985), 71
Bradley, Ruth, 4, 38, 65, 102, 113, 141, 171, 203, 245
Brandon, Liane, 19, 23, 409
Brault, Michel, 166, 328
Brexit, 200, 346
Bruce, John, 111
Buba, Tony, 58, 71
Button, Button: A Dream of Nuclear War (Mandelbaum, 1982), 34
By The Time It Gets Dark (Suwichakornpong, 2016), 402

Camera Obscura, 375
Campaign (Soda, 2007), 297
Cannes Film Festival, 221–23, 325
Canticle of the Stones (Khleifi, 1990), 126
Cartagena International Film Festival, 112
Ça va, ça va, on continue (It is OK, it is OK, we go on) (Abonnenc, 2012–2013), 341
Center, The (Rothschild, 1970), 19
Central New York Programmers Group (CNYPG), 269
Cerdán, Josetxo, 97, 234, 242, 285, 322, 334
Charnov, Elaine, 212–13, 220
Chickens, The (Amiralay, 1977), 238
Chi-hui Yang, 206, 283, 285, 317, 344, 370, 373–74
Children of Violence (Jersey, 1982), 46
Chile, Obstinate Memory (Guzmán, 1997), 248, 257
cinéma vérité, 31, 114, 146, 166, 192, 328

cinephilia, 352
Citizen (Farley, 1982), 46
civil rights movement, 18, 34, 69, 71
Cizek, Katrina, 226, 236
Claiming Open Spaces (Allen, 1995), 171
Clarke, Shirley, 46, 196
Clean Thursday (Rastorguev, 2004), 305–6
climate change, 25, 27
Cohen, Jem, 111
Coming Forth by Day (Lotfy, 2012), 297, 370
Coming of Age (Hanig, 1982), 46
Conner, Bruce, 54, 60–61, 189, 375
Conrad, Tony, 338, 362
Consuming Hunger (Ziv, 1987), 107
Contadini del mare (*Peasant of the Sea*) (De Seta, 1955), 182
Conversations with Willard Van Dyke (Rothschild, 1981), 18, 20
Cosmic Ray (Conner, 1969), 60
Cotton Road series (Kissel), 190, 227, 329
Cousineau, Marie-Hélène, 366, 369, 370
Coutinho, Eduardo, 34, 71, 322
Covert, Nadine, 20, 42, 43, 408–9
Crazy (Honigmann, 1999), 209
"crisis of representation," 15
Crossroads (Conner, 1976), 60
Custen, George, 32
Czech Dream (Klusak and Remunda, 2004), 273

D'Aguiar, Tom, 162–63
Damned If You Don't (Friedrich, 1987), 95, 96
David, Catherine, 349
Dead Poets Society (Weir, 1989), 337–38
de Antonio, Emile, 19, 22
Debroise, Olivier, 257, 261–62
de Cuir Jr., Greg, 63, 75, 214, 401
De La Vega Hurtado, Margarita, 108, 111, 135, 143, 228, 241, 260–61, 299, 301, 321
de Ocampo, Pablo, 63, 246, 341, 346, 360

Deren, Maya, 61, 329
De Seta, Vittorio, 182, 245, 266, 273, 277
de Sousa Dias, Susana, 234, 297
dGenerate Films, 325–26
Día! (*Day!*) (Cerano, 1999), 289
Dial H-I-S-T-O-R-Y (Grimonprez, 1997), 354
Dialogue with a Woman Departed (Hurwitz, 1980), 46
Diaries (1971–1976) (Pincus, c. 1980), 33
digital, concept of, 217–18
Digital Flaherty, 179, 181, 217–19
Digital Salon, 93–94, 175
D.O.A. (Kowalski, 1980), 38
Doc's Kingdom, 327, 332–35
documentary, definition of, 58
Documentary Film Lab, 32
Door to the Sky, A (Benlyazid, 1989), 126
Double Burger and Two Metamorphoses, A (Al Solh, 2011), 131
Dreams Are Colder than Death (Jafa, 2014), 131
Drive-By Shoot (Cobb, 1992), 142
Drowned Out (Armstrong, 2002), 226
Dummerston, Vermont, 7–9, 391

Educational Film Library Association (EFLA), 20
Eichmann, Adolf, 346
Eingang: The Way In installations (Reeves), 178
El Cielo Gira (*The Sky Turns*) (Alvarez, 2004), 181
Elder, Sarah, 368
Elephant Boy (Korda and Flaherty, 1937), 119–20
Ellis Island (Monk, 1981), 53, 55
Emperor's Naked Army Marches On, The (Hara, 1987), 143
End of Summer, The (Ozu, 1961), 23, 42
epistephilia, 352
Essene (Wiseman, 1972), 22
Everson, Kevin Jerome, 63, 75, 214, 401

Eye of the Day, The (Helmrich, 2001), 289–90
Eyes on the Prize (Hampton, 1987–1990), 34, 71, 114

Faces of November (Drew, 1964), 38
Family Album, The (Berliner, 1986), 107
Family Life (Loach, 1971), 23
Fanon, Frantz, 38, 171
Far from Poland (Godmilow, 1984), 47
Farocki, Harun, 150, 185, 189, 192, 196, 200–202, 355
feminism, 38, 47, 58, 62, 93, 107, 109, 111, 167, 201, 276, 318, 394, 405
Fescherecci (*Fishing*) (De Seta, 1958), 182
50 Feet of String (Pierce, 1995), 170–71
Film-Essay on the Euphrates Dam (Amiralay, 1970), 238
Finding Christa (Billops and Hatch, 1991), 143
First International Festival of Women's Films, 19
Fisher, Holly, 226, 230, 235
Fish Tail (*Rabo de Peixe*) (Pinto and Leonel, 2015), 148, 379, 382
Flaherty, David, 9
Flaherty, Frances "Frannie," 49, 55
Flaherty, Frances H., 40–42; at Black Mountain Farm (Dummerston, Vermont), 7–9, 391; collaboration with Robert, 115; death of, 49; narration for *Louisiana Story Study Film,* 185; principles of non-preconception and exploration, 70, 115, 131, 147, 148, 167–68, 186, 273, 276, 298, 331, 342, 345; seminar founding and design, 21, 39, 49, 126, 127, 276, 372, 398
Flaherty, Monica, 152–55, 163
Flaherty, Robert J. *See individual films*
Flaherty: Decades in the Cause of Independent Cinema, The (Zimmermann and MacDonald), 42, 51, 101, 102, 127, 278, 403

Flaherty Film Seminar (1955), 372
Flaherty Film Seminar (c. 1957), 7–9
Flaherty Film Seminar (1959), 328–31
Flaherty Film Seminar (1963), 99
Flaherty Film Seminar (1964), 10–12, 42; *Flaming Creatures* (Smith, 1964), 10–12, 99, 137–39
Flaherty Film Seminar (1970), 17–20; *Woo Who? May Wilson* (Rothschild, 1970), 17
Flaherty Film Seminar (1971), 19; *Center, The* (Rothschild, 1970), 19; *Growing Up Female: As Six Become One* (Reichert and Klein, 1971), 19; *Interviews with My Lai Veterans* (Strick, 1971), 19; *Millhouse: A White Comedy* (de Antonio, 1971), 19; *Mosori Monika* (Strand, 1970), 19; *Murder of Fred Hampton, The* (Gray and Alk, 1971), 19; *One P.M.* (Pennebaker and Godard, 1971), 19; *Sad Song of Yellow Skin* (Rubbo, 1970), 19; *Selling of the Pentagon, The* (Davis, 1971), 19; *Wanda* (Loden, 1970), 19; *Woman's Film, The* (Smith, Alaimo, and Sorrin, 1971), 19
Flaherty Film Seminar (1972), 22–23, 42, 43; programmers Nadine Covert, Bill Sloan, 42; *Blues Accordin' to Lightnin' Hopkins, The* (Blank, 1968), 23; *End of Summer, The* (Ozu, 1961), 23, 42; *Essene* (Wiseman, 1972), 22; *Family Life* (Loach, 1971), 23; *Greed* (Von Stroheim, 1924), 42; *It Happens to Us* (Rothschild, 1971), 19; *Qué hacer!* (Landau, 1971), 23; *Reminiscences of a Journey to Lithuania* (Mekas, 1972), 22; *Sorrow and the Pity, The* (Ophuls, 1969), 23, 42, 43; *Spend It All* (Blank, 1971), 23; *Walking* (Larkin, 1968), 23
Flaherty Film Seminar (1976), 20; *And You Act Like One Too* (Seidelman, 1976), 19
Flaherty Film Seminar (1977), 28–31
Flaherty Film Seminar (1979), 42

Flaherty Film Seminar (1980), 32–33, 36–39, 48; programmer John Katz, 33, 37; *Alambrista* (Young, 1977), 33, 38; *America Lost and Found* (Bird and Johnson, 1974), 38; *D.O.A.* (Kowalski, 1980), 38; *Faces of November* (Drew, 1964), 38; *Gal Young 'Un* (Nuñez, 1979), 38; *Garlic is as Good as Ten Mothers* (Blank, 1980), 33, 38; *Heartland* (Pearce, 1979), 38; *Mourir à Tue-Tête* (Miller, 1979), 38; *N!ai, the Story of a !Kung Woman* (Marshall, 1980), 38; *Poto and Cabengo* (Gorin, 1980), 38; *Scenes from Childhood* (Guzzetti, 1980), 38; *Trials of Alger Hiss, The* (Lowenthal, 1980), 38; *War at Home, The* (Silber and Brown, 1979), 38

Flaherty Film Seminar (1981), 33–34, 372; programmer Standish Lawder, 33, 372; *Conversations with Willard Van Dyke* (Rothschild, 1981), 18, 20; *Diaries (1971–1976)* (Pincus, c. 1980), 33; *Werner Herzog in Peru/Burden of Dreams* (Blank, 1982), 33–34

Flaherty Film Seminar (1982), 30, 34, 41–42; programmer Erik Barnouw, 29–30, 34, 36–37, 42; *Atomic Café* (Rafferty, Loader, and Rafferty, 1982), 34; *Button, Button: A Dream of Nuclear War* (Mandelbaum, 1982), 34; *Meta Mayan II* (Velez, 1981), 30, 34; *No Place to Hide* (Johnson and Bird, 1983), 34; *Smothering Dreams* (Reeves, 1981), 30, 34

Flaherty Film Seminar (1983), 30, 46–47, 48–49; programmers Bruce Jenkins, Melinda Ward, 46–47; *Children of Violence* (Jersey, 1982), 46; *Citizen* (Farley, 1982), 46; *Coming of Age* (Hanig, 1982), 46; *Dialogue with a Woman Departed* (Hurwitz, 1980), 46; *Far from Poland* (Godmilow, 1984), 47; *Guerre et Revolution* (Marker, 1977), 46; *Who Invented the Yo-yo?/Who Invented the Moon Buggy?* (Tahimik, 1980–1981), 47; Jenkins and Ward, programmers, 46–47; *Reassemblage* (Trinh, 1982), 47; *Seeing Red* (Klein and Reichert, 1983), 46; *Seventeen* (DeMott and Kreines, 1980), 46; *Turumba* (Tahimik, 1982), 47; *What You Take for Granted* (Citron, 1983), 47

Flaherty Film Seminar (1984), 31, 52–54, 60–61; *Cosmic Ray* (Conner, 1969), 60; *Crossroads* (Conner, 1976), 60; *Ellis Island* (Monk, 1981), 53, 55; *Mongoloid* (Conner, 1978), 53; *Movie, A* (Conner, 1958), 53, 60; *Permian Strata* (Conner, 1969), 53; *Ritual in Transfigured Time* (Deren, 1946), 61; *Study in Choreography for the Camera, A* (Deren, 1945), 61; *Ten Second Film* (Conner, 1965), 53

Flaherty Film Seminar (1985), 54, 64–67; *Paul Cadmus: Enfant Terrible at 80* (Sutherland, 1984), 65–66; *We Were So Beloved* (Kirchheimer, 1985), 66

Flaherty Film Seminar (1986), 34, 54, 69–72, 74–75, 78–81, 84; programmers Linda Blackaby, Tony Gittens, 54, 70, 78, 84; *AIDS Show, The* (Adair and Epstein, 1986), 71; *All American High* (Rosenfeld, 1986), 71; *And One And One And One* (De Michiel, 1986), 78–79; *Braddock Food Bank* (Buba, 1985), 71; *Eyes on the Prize* (Hampton, 1987), 34, 71; first seminar to embrace video as equal to film, 71; *Forest of Bliss* (Gardner, 1986), 79–80; *International Sweethearts of Rhythm* (Weiss and Schiller, 1986), 71; *Kukurantumi: The Road to Accra* (Ampaw, 1983), 71; *Made in China: A Search for Roots* (Hsia, 1985), 71; *Man Marked for Death/Twenty Years Later, A* (Coutinho, 1984), 71; *Memories of*

Flaherty Film Seminar (*Cont.*)
  an Everyday War (Barrios, 1986),
  71; *Nicaragua: Hear-Say/See-Here*
  (Skoller, 1986), 74–75; *Orientations*
  (Fung, 1986), 71; *Rate It X*
  (Winer and de Koenigsberg, 1986),
  71; *Routine Pleasures* (Gorin,
  1986), 71; *Shadow of the Earth*
  (Louhichi, 1982), 71; *Sherman's
  March* (McElwee, 1986), 71; *To
  Taste a Hundred Herbs* (Hinton
  and Gordon, 1984), 71; *Troubled
  Waters* (Hansen, 1986), 71
Flaherty Film Seminar (1987), 48–50,
  54, 87–88, 95–96, 99–102, 103–4,
  106–7, 146, 372; programmer
  Richard Herskowitz, 48–51, 84,
  87–88, 95, 100, 101, 104, 106, 372;
  Bombing of Osage Avenue, The
  (Massiah and Bambara, 1986), 84,
  103–4; *Consuming Hunger* (Ziv,
  1987), 107; *Damned If You Don't*
  (Friedrich, 1987), 95; *Family Album,
  The* (Berliner, 1986), 107; *From
  the Pole to the Equator* (Gianikian
  and Ricci Lucchi, 1986), 107; *Haiti
  the Unfinished Revolution* (Howe,
  1986), 107; *Handsworth Songs*
  (Akomfrah, 1987), 107; *Journey,
  The* (Watkins, 1987), 4, 50, 87–88,
  100–102, 103–4, 107; *Moscow Does
  Not Believe in Queers* (Greyson,
  1986), 107; *Ties that Bind, The*
  (Friedrich, 1984), 95
Flaherty Film Seminar (1988),
  67, 109, 112; *Lightning Over
  Braddock: A Rustbowl Fantasy*
  (Buba, 1988), 64, 67
Flaherty Film Seminar (1989), 61–62,
  63, 84–85, 88; programmers Pearl
  Bowser, Grant Munro, 61, 82–85,
  88, 116–20; *Elephant Boy* (Korda
  and Flaherty, 1937), 119–20;
  La Ofrenda (Portillo, 1989), 85;
  Power! (Massiah and Rockefeller,
  1988), 85; *Sermons and Sacred
  Pictures* (Sachs, 1989), 61–62, 118–
  19; *In the Street* (Levitt, Loeb, and
  Agee, 1948), 118

Flaherty Film Seminar (1990),
  122–24; *Interpretation of Dreams*
  (Zagdansky, 1989), 123–24;
  Man with a Movie Camera, The
  (Vertov, 1929), 122; *Nanook of
  the North* (Flaherty, 1922), 122;
  Roger and Me (Moore, 1989), 123;
  Seasons, The (Peleshyan, 1975),
  123; *Sherman's March* (McElwee,
  1986), 123; *Thin Blue Line, The*
  (Morris, 1988), 122; *Ties that Bind,
  The* (Friedrich, 1984), 96; *Tongues
  Untied* (Riggs, 1989), 123
Flaherty Film Seminar (1991), 125–26,
  133–36; *Canticle of the Stones*
  (Khleifi, 1990), 126; *Door to the
  Sky, A* (Benlyazid, 1989), 126;
  Halfaouine: Boy of the Terraces
  (Stah, 1990), 126; *Omar Gatlato*
  (Allouache, 1977), 126
Flaherty Film Seminar (1992), 50–51,
  141–44; programmers Austin Allen,
  Ruth Bradley, Scott MacDonald, Bill
  Sloan, Jacqueline Tshaka, and Lise
  Yasui, programmers, 141; *Barroco
  (Baroque)* (Leduc, 1989), 143;
  Drive-By Shoot (Cobb, 1992), 142;
  *Emperor's Naked Army Marches
  On, The* (Hara, 1987), 143; *Finding
  Christa* (Billops and Hatch, 1991),
  143; *Janine* (Dunye, 1990), 143; *No
  Justice No Peace* (Cobb, 1992), 142;
  *Points of Departure for a Diaspora
  Dawta!* (Cobb, 1991), 142; *She
  Don't Fade* (Dunye, 1991), 143;
  Species in Danger Ed! (Cobb, 1989),
  142; *XCXHXEXRXRXIXEXSX*
  (Nervous System performance)
  (Jacobs, 1992), 50–51, 135, 139–40,
  142–43
Flaherty Film Seminar (1993), 145–47;
  Mirror Mirror (Krawitz, 1990), 127
Flaherty Film Seminar (1994), 147;
  programmers Erik Barnouw, Somi
  Roy, Patricia Zimmermann, 149,
  372; *Video Letters 1, 2 & 3* (Yau,
  1993), 127
Flaherty Film Seminar (1995,
  Camera Reframed), 152–55,

156–59, 160–63; programmers Marlina Gonzalez, Bruce Jenkins, 156–59, 161; *Bowling Alley* (Cheang, 1995–1996), 157–58; *History and Memory* (Tajiri, 1991), 157–58; *Moana with Sound* (Flaherty, 1981), 154; *Sonic Outlaws* (Baldwin, 1995), 155; *Spin* (Springer, 1995), 155; *Sweep* (Hoffman and van Ingen, 1995), 153, 154–55

Flaherty Film Seminar (1996), 165–66, 169–72; programmers Ruth Bradley, Kathy High, Loretta Todd, 4; *Bontoc Eulogy* (Fuentes, 1995), 170; *Claiming Open Spaces* (Allen, 1995), 171; *50 feet of String* (Pierce, 1995), 170–71; *If You Lived Here, You'd Be Home by Now* (McDougall, 1993), 170; *Learning Path, The* (Todd, 1991), 171; *North on Evers* (Benning, 1991), 171; *Roam Sweet Home* (Spiro, 1996), 170; *Weather Diary I* (Kuchar, 1986), 171

Flaherty Film Seminar (1997, Explorations in Memory and Modernity), 173–75, 176–78, 179–81; programmers Michelle Materre, Patricia Zimmermann, 93, 173–75, 177–78, 179; *Eingang: The Way In* (installations) (Reeves), 178; *Measures of Distance* (Hatoum), 179–80; *Nanook of the North* (Flaherty, 1922), 180–81

Flaherty Film Seminar (1998), 34–35; programmers Barbara Abrash, Linda Blackaby, 34–35, 97, 212; *Eyes on the Prize* (Hampton, 1987), 34; *Hide and Seek* (Friedrich, 1996), 97; *House in Jerusalem* (Gitai, 1998), 34; Israel seminar, 34–35

Flaherty Film Seminar (1999, Out-takes Are History), 88–90, 96, 110, 114–15, 183–85, 187–89; programmers Orlando Bagwell, Richard Herskowitz, 88–90, 96, 110, 114, 188; *Amsterdam Global Village* (van der Keuken, 1996), 114, 189; *Damned If You Don't* (Friedrich, 1987), 95, 96; *Inner World of Aphasia: The Thirteen* (Williams, 1998), 89; *Lillian* (Williams, 1993), 88, 114; *Louisiana Story Study Film* (Amberg, 1962), 114, 185; *Nina Split in Two* (Williams, 1988), 88–89; *Noblesse Oblige* (Sonbert, 1981), 147; *Seasons* (Peleshyan, 1975), 189; *Stranger with a Camera* (Barret, 1999), 115; *Thirteen* (Williams, 1997), 50, 89; *We* (Peleshyan, 1969), 189

Flaherty Film Seminar (2000, Essays, Experiments, and Excavations), 149–51, 185, 189–90, 192–93, 195–98, 199–202, 203–5; programmer Kathy Geritz, 150, 185, 186, 188, 192, 199, 201, 203, 245; "Arcadia, or an Eclectic History of the American Cen-tury" (Frye), 204; *Blindness Series* (Tran, 1992–2000), 62, 151; *Image, An* (Farocki, 1983), 201; *Images of the World and the Inscription of War* (Farocki, 1989), 189, 201; *I Thought I Was Seeing Convicts* (Farocki, 2000), 200; *Little Tich and His Big Boots* (Ahwesh, 1900), 185; *Live Nude Girls UNITE!* (Funari and Query, 2000), 201; *Workers Leaving the Factory* (Farocki, 1995), 185, 189, 192, 201; *Workers Leaving the Factory* (Lumière Brothers, 1895), 185, 192

Flaherty Film Seminar (2001), 207–11, 220–23; programmers Elaine Charnov, Jytte Jensen, 212–13; *Atanarjuat: The Fast Runner* (Kunuk, 2001), 220–23; *Blue* (Jarman, 1993), 209; *Crazy* (Honigmann, 1999), 209; *Hedwig and the Angry Inch* (Mitchell, 2001), 209; *Herman Slobbe (Blind Kind II)* (van der Keuken, 1966), 208; *Shooting Blind* (Seeing with Photography Collective), 209; *Trut (Seahawk)* (Sucksdorff, 1944), 208

Flaherty Film Seminar (2002),
110–11, 372
Flaherty Film Seminar (2003,
Witnessing the World), 226,
231, 235–37, 240; programmer
John Gianvito, 194, 226, 235,
236; *Drowned Out* (Armstrong,
2002), 226; *Happy Birthday, Mr.
Mograbi* (Mograbi, 1998), 226;
Kalama Sutta (Fisher, 2002), 226;
Mai's America (Poras, 2002),
226; *McLibel: Two Worlds
Collide* (Armstrong, 1998), 226;
*Minamata—The Victims and Their
World* (Tsuchimoto, 1971), 231;
*Seeing Is Believing: Handicams,
Human Rights, and the News*
(Wintonick and Cizek, 2002), 226,
236–37; *Shiranui Sea* (Tsuchimoto,
1975), 231; *Zyklon Portrait*
(Schogt, 1999), 226
Flaherty Film Seminar (2004,
50 Years of Flaherty), 244–45;
programmer Susan Oxtoby, 194,
245; *Arctic Requiem*, 166–68;
Killer of Sheep (Burnett, 1978),
166; *Pour la suite du monde (For
Those Who Will Follow)* (Brault,
1963), 166; *Self Portrait Post
Mortem* (Bourque, 2002), 127
Flaherty Film Seminar (2005, Cinema
and History: Piling Wreckage
Upon Wreckage), 247–49, 252–54,
255–58, 259–62; programmers Jesse
Lerner, Michael Renov, 247, 252,
262; *Afrique, je te plumerai (Africa
I Will Fleece You)* (Teno, 1992),
248, 253; *Chile, Obstinate Memory*
(Guzmán, 1997), 248, 257; *His
Mother's Voice* (Tupicoff, 1996),
248; *La Television y Yo* (Di Tella,
2003), 255; *Los Angeles Station*
(Katz, 1970), 260; *Mutual Analysis*
(Forgács, 2004), 127; *Nanook
of the North* (Flaherty, 1922),
166–67; *Paradox* (Katz, 2001), 260;
Salvador Allende (Guzmán, 2003),
257; *Symbiopsychotaxiplasm: Take
One* (Greaves, 1972), 127, 135, 249,
256; *Tongues Untied* (Riggs, 1989),
193; *Un banquete en Tetlapayac*
(Debroise, 2000), 261
Flaherty Film Seminar (2006,
Creative Demolition), 181–82,
245, 263–66, 273–74, 275–78;
programmers Ariella Ben-Dov,
Steve Seid, 181, 245, 273; *Big
Durian, The* (Muhammad, 2003),
265; *Contadini del mare (Peasant
of the Sea)* (De Seta, 1955),
182; *Czech Dream* (Klusak and
Remunda, 2004), 273; *El Cielo
Gira (The Sky Turns)* (Alvarez,
2004), 181; *Fescherecci (Fishing)*
(De Seta, 1958), 182; *Haunted
Camera, The* (Andrews, 2006),
181; *How to Fix the World* (Goss,
2004), 181; *John and Jane Toll-
Free* (Ahluwalia, 2005), 181, 265;
*Lelaki Komunis Terakhir (The
Last Communist)* (Muhammad,
2006), 265; *Monkey and Lumps*
(Andrews, 2006), 181; *Stranger
Comes To Town* (Goss, 2007),
181; *Tailenders, The* (Horne,
2005), 274
Flaherty Film Seminar (2007,
South of the Other), 193, 287–90;
programmers Mahen Bonetti,
Carlos Gutiérrez, 193, 241, 254,
287–90; *Al Otro Lado (To the
Other Side)* (Almada, 2005), 227;
Día! (Day!) (Cerano, 1999), 289;
Eye of the Day, The (Helmrich,
2001), 289–90; *Promised Paradise*
(Helmrich, 2006), 290; *Stand van
de Maan (Shape of the Moon)*
(Helmrich, 2006), 233–34, 290;
Xanini (Corn Stalks) (Cerano,
1999), 289
Flaherty Film Seminar (2008,
The Age of Migration), 281–82,
283–86, 368; programmer Chi-hui
Yang, 206, 283, 285, 317, 373–74;
CARGO (Waddington, 2001),
284–85; *Exiles, The* (MacKenzie,
1961), 281; *Time for Drunken
Horses, A* (Ghobadi, 1999), 281–82

Flaherty Film Seminar (2009, Witnesses, Monuments, Ruins), 232, 237–39, 291–94, 296–97, 301–2, 303–6, 307–10, 311, 368; programmer Irina Leimbacher, 31, 237, 291, 293, 296–97, 301–2, 303, 308, 311; *Adventures of Blacky, The* (Finley and Muse, 1998), 292; *Based on a Story* (Finley and Muse, 1997), 292; *Chickens, The* (Amiralay, 1977), 238; *Clean Thursday* (Rastorguev, 2004), 305–6; *Film-Essay on the Euphrates Dam* (Amiralay, 1970), 238; *Flat Land* (Finley and Muse, 2009), 293; *Guarded* (Finley and Muse, 2003), 292, 293, 294; *Kristallnacht* (Strand, 1979), 302, 304–6; *Lightning Testimonies, The* (Kanwar, 2007), 238; *At the Museum: A Pilgrimage of Vanquished Objects* (Finley and Muse, 1989), 292, 294; *Sweetgrass* (Barbash and Castaing-Taylor, 2009), 208, 238

Flaherty Film Seminar (2010, WORK), 35, 245–46, 297, 308, 311–14, 315–18, 321–22, 323, 324, 368, 372; programmer Dennis Lim, 206, 245, 285, 311, 313, 317, 318, 321, 324, 358, 372; *Agrarian Utopia* (Raksasad, 2011), 297; *Alamar* (Gonzalez-Rubio, 2009), 234, 313; *Campaign* (Soda, 2007), 297; *Ghost Town* (Zhao, 2008), 317, 318; *Haiku* (Glawogger, 1987), 317–18; *Libertad* (Alonso, 2001), 297; *Los Muertos* (Alonso, 2004), 313; *Megacities* (Glawogger, 1998), 313; *Ukranian Time Machine* (Uman, 2008), 245–46; *Whore's Glory* (Glawogger, 2010), 245; *Workingman's Death* (Glawogger, 1998), 108, 245, 297, 313, 318

Flaherty Film Seminar (2011, Sonic Truth), 63, 184, 186, 190, 227, 297, 325, 334–35, 372; programmer Dan Streible, 63, 190, 329, 372; *Cotton Road* series (Kissel), 190, 227, 329; *Impossibility of Knowing, The* (Tan, 2010), 190; *Industry/Cinema* (Martel, 2011), 329; *Invisible City* (Tan, 2007), 190; *Moving House* (Tan, 2001), 190; *Phantom of the Operator, The* (Martel, 2004), 329, 330; *Poem is a Naked Person, A* (Blank, 1974), 297; *Reunion of All My Babies, A* (Stoney, 2010), 227; *Singapore GaGa* (Tan, 2010), 190, 227; *Trip Down Market Street Before the Fire, A* (Miles brothers, 1906), 227; *Wavemakers* (Martel, 2012), 227, 297, 329

Flaherty Film Seminar (2012, Open Wounds), 97, 234, 326–27; programmer Josetxo Cerdán, 97, 234, 319–22, 334; *Ah Liberty!* (Rivers, 2008), 297; *48* (de Sousa Dias, 2008), 234, 297; *Freeland* (Martin, 2012), 297; *Qu'ils Reposent en Revolte* (George, 2010), 297; *Three Men and a Fish Pond* (Pakalniņa, 2008), 234

Flaherty Film Seminar (2013, History Is What's Happening), 63, 322, 340–43, 344–47; programmer Pablo de Ocampo, 63, 246, 341, 346; *Ça va, ça va, on continue* (*It is OK, it is OK, we go on*) (Abonnenc, 2012–13), 341; *Home Movies Gaza* (Alsharif, 2013), 341; *O'er the Land* (Stratman, 2008), 297, 341, 346; *O Regresso de Amílcar Cabral* (*The Return of Amílcar Cabral*) (Na N'Hada, 1976), 342; *People to be Resembling* (Otolith Group, 2012), 341; *Queen Mother Moore Speech at Greenhaven Prison* (People's Communication Network, 1973), 341; *Radiant, The* (Otolith Group, 2012), 297; *Route 181* (Sivan and Khleifi, 2003), 341; *Sambizanga* (Maldoror, 1972), 297, 342; *San Soleil* (Marker, 1983), 246, 342; *Services of the Goods* (Kelly, 2013), 341–42

Flaherty Film Seminar (2014, Turning the Inside Out), 130, 348–51, 352–55, 356–59, 360–63; programmers Gabriela Monroy, Caspar Stracke, 309, 348–51, 359, 362; *Anabasis of May, The* (Baudelaire, 2011), 297, 361; *Bernadette* (Campbell, 2008), 297, 361; *Dial H-I-S-T-O-R-Y* (Grimonprez, 1997), 354; *From Gulf to Gulf to Gulf* (CAMP collective, 2013), 297; *How Not to be Seen* (Steyerl, 2013), 297; informal "programmers circle," 186; *Les statues meurent aussi* (Marker and Resnais, 1953), 355; *Magic for Beginners* (McLean, 2010), 354; *Montaña en sombra* (*Mountain in Shadow*) (Patiño, 2012), 354; *What Farocki Taught* (Godmilow, 1997), 355; "What the Flaherty Taught in 2014," 363

Flaherty Film Seminar (2015, The Scent of Places), 43, 130–32, 364–67, 369–71, 374–75; programmer Laura U. Marks, 75, 129–34, 365–67, 369, 374; *Afternoon, March 22, 1999* (Reinke, 1999), 131; *Belena* (Zürcher, 2004), 370; *Blind Ambition* (Kahn, 2012), 76; *Coming Forth by Day* (Lotfy, 2012), 297, 370; *Double Burger and Two Metamorphoses, A* (Al Solh, 2011), 131; *Dreams Are Colder than Death* (Jafa, 2014), 131; *Hacla* (*The Fence*) (Teguia, 2003), 131; *Inland* (Teguia, 2008), 297; *Night of Storytelling, A* (Flaherty, 1935), 131; *Qulliq* (*Oil Lamp*) (Arnait Video Collective, 1989), 131; *Ramad/Ashes* (Hadjithomas and Joreige, 2003), 132; *Rawane's Song* (Al Solh, 2006), 370; *Reflections* (Tourtelot, 1955), 370; *Squeezing Sorrow from an Ashtray* (Reinke, 1992), 297; *Before Tomorrow* (Avingaq and Ivalu, 2008), 131, 370; *Unter Schnee* (*Under Snow*) (Ottinger, 2014), 131, 370

Flaherty Film Seminar (2016, PLAY), 377–79, 380–82; programmer David Pendleton, 148, 249, 323, 377–79, 381; *Fish Tail* (*Rabo de Peixe*) (Pinto and Leonel, 2015), 148, 379, 382; *Genpin* (Kawase, 2010), 249, 378; *It All Started at the End* (Ospina, 2015), 297; *Katatsumori* (Kawase, 1994), 297; *Light Licks: By the Waters of Babylon: In the Hour of Angels* (Levine, 2004), 381–82; *Marseille après la guerre* (Woodberry, 2016), 379; *Now What? Remind Me* (Pinto, 2013), 297; program notes, 376; *On the Spot* (Levine, 1973), 297

Flaherty Film Seminar (2017, Future Remains), 384–87, 388–90, 395–98; programmer Nuno Lisboa, 75, 148, 298, 327, 335, 386, 387, 395; *Human Surge, The* (Williams, 2016), 234; *of the North* (Gagnon, 2015), 76, 235, 298, 386, 395–96, 398; *Reassemblage* (Trinh, 1982), 388–90

Flaherty Film Seminar (2018, The Necessary Image), 75–76, 214, 399–402; programmers Kevin Jerome Everson, Greg de Cuir Jr., 63, 214, 399, 401; *Nightfall* (Suwichakornpong, 2016), 400; *Oneiromancer* (Santiago Muñoz, 2017), 401; removal of Nanook from official seminar logo, 185, 198, 383, 401, 403–6; *Still/Here* (Harris, 2001), 76, 401; *By The Time It Gets Dark* (Suwichakornpong, 2016), 402

Flaming Creatures (Smith, 1964), 10–12, 99, 137–39

Flat Land (Finley and Muse, 2009), 293

Forest of Bliss (Gardner, 1986), 79–80

48 (de Sousa Dias, 2008), 234, 297

Foucault, Michel, 38, 57, 256

Fox, Jason, 358

Francis, Terri, 214

Freeland (Martin, 2012), 297
Freiburger Film Forum, 309
Friedrich, Su, 58, 93, 101, 323, 339
From Gulf to Gulf to Gulf (CAMP collective, 2013), 297
From the Pole to the Equator (Gianikian and Ricci Lucchi, 1986), 107
Fry, Tony, 397

Gabriel, Teshome, 62, 85, 118
Gagnon, Dominic, 76, 235, 298, 386, 395–96, 398
Gal Young 'Un (Nuñez, 1979), 38
Garcia, Jerry, 157, 158
Gardner, Robert, 75, 79–80
Garlic Is as Good as Ten Mothers (Blank, 1980), 33, 38
gender politics, 28, 249
Genpin (Kawase, 2010), 249, 378
Geritz, Kathy, 62, 75, 108, 111, 322, 335, 373; programmer for 2000 Flaherty Film Seminar (Essays, Experiments, and Excavations), 150, 185, 186, 188, 192, 199, 203, 245
Ghost Town (Zhao, 2008), 317, 318
Gianikian, Yervant, 101, 107
Gianvito, John, 194, 226, 235, 236, 309, 322, 335, 377
Ginsburg, Faye, 13–16, 289
Gittens, Tony, 54, 84
Glawogger, Michael, 108, 111, 245, 297, 313, 317, 318
Gleyzer, Raymundo, 230, 300–301
Glissant, Édouard, 341
Godmilow, Jill, 47, 196, 197, 198, 309, 350, 355, 360–61
Gonzalez, Marlina, 156–59, 161
González-Rubio, Pedro, 234, 242, 313, 321
Gordon, Richard, 34, 71
Greaves, William, 22, 83, 118, 127, 135, 249, 253, 256
Greed (Von Stroheim, 1924), 42
Greyson, John, 84, 101, 107
Grieco, D. Marie, 21, 30, 39, 49, 54, 60, 405
Grillo, Michael, 54, 147

Grimonprez, Johan, 339, 350, 354, 358, 361
Growing Up Female: As Six Become One (Reichert and Klein, 1971), 19
Guarded (Finley and Muse, 2003), 292, 293, 294
Guerre et révolution (Marker, 1977), 46
Gutiérrez, Carlos, 193, 241, 254, 287–90, 321
Guzmán, Patricio, 248, 253, 257–58

Hacla (The Fence) (Teguia, 2003), 131
Haiku (Glawogger, 1987), 317–18
Halfaouine: Boy of the Terraces (Stah, 1990), 126
Hallas, Roger, 277, 292, 303, 377
Halter, Ed, 75, 110–11, 212, 372
Hampton, Henry, 34, 71, 83, 85, 114
Handsworth Songs (Akomfrah, 1987), 107
Happy Birthday, Mr. Mograbi (Mograbi, 1998), 226
Hara, Kazuo, 135, 143
Harvard Film Archive (HFA), 131, 307, 323, 377
Hatoum, Mona, 179–80
Haunted Camera, The (Andrews, 2006), 181
Heartland (Pearce, 1979), 38
Hedwig and the Angry Inch (Mitchell, 2001), 209
Heller, Eve, 164, 245
Helmrich, Leonard Retel, 233, 277, 278, 289
Herbert F. Johnson Museum of Art (Ithaca, New York), 145
Herman Slobbe (Blind Kind II) (van der Keuken, 1966), 208
Herskowitz, Richard, 107, 111; director of Cornell Cinema, 52, 54, 100, 145; president of Flaherty Film Seminar, 34; programmer for 1987 Flaherty Film Seminar, 48–51, 84, 87–88, 95, 100, 101, 104, 106, 372; programmer for 1990 Flaherty Film Seminar, 96–97; programmer for 1999 Flaherty Film Seminar (Out-takes Are History), 88–90, 96, 110, 114, 188

Hide and Seek (Friedrich, 1996), 97
High, Kathy, 4, 93, 171
Hinton, Carma, 34, 71
His Mother's Voice (Tupicoff, 1996),
    248
History and Memory (Tajiri, 1991),
    157–58
Holmgren, Steven, 205, 301, 322
Home Movies Gaza (Alsharif, 2013),
    341
Horne, Adele, 181, 245, 274
Horrigan, Bill, 46
House in Jerusalem (Gitai, 1998), 34
How Not to be Seen (Steyerl, 2013),
    297
How to Fix the World (Goss, 2004),
    181
Hubley, Emily, 33, 38, 209
Human Surge, The (Williams, 2016),
    234

identity politics, 70, 130, 366, 384,
    386
*If You Lived Here, You'd Be Home
    by Now* (McDougall, 1993), 170
Igloolik Isuma Productions, 220–22
Image, An (Farocki, 1983), 201
*Images of the World and the
    Inscription of War* (Farocki, 1989),
    189, 201
Impossibility of Knowing, The (Tan,
    2010), 190
indigenous film and filmmakers,
    13–16, 71, 171, 220–22, 237, 281,
    287–90, 404
Industry/Cinema (Martel, 2011), 329
Inland (Teguia, 2008), 297
*Inner World of Aphasia: The
    Thirteen* (Williams, 1998), 89
International Film Festival
    (Washington, DC), 72
International Film Seminars (IFS), 13,
    15, 20, 30, 31, 70, 188, 270
International Sweethearts of Rhythm
    (Weiss and Schiller, 1986), 71
Interpretation of Dreams
    (Zagdansky, 1989), 123–24
Interviews with My Lai Veterans
    (Strick, 1971), 19

In the Street (Levitt, Loeb, and Agee,
    1948), 118
Invisible City (Tan, 2007), 190
ISAAS (Indie Screening Alliance of
    Art Spaces), 327
It All Started at the End (Ospina,
    2015), 297
It Happens to Us (Rothschild, 1971), 19
I Thought I Was Seeing Convicts
    (Farocki, 2000), 200
Ivens, Joris, 22, 146, 409

Jacobs, Flo, 10–11
Jacobs, Ken, 10–11, 12, 51, 99, 135,
    142, 216, 296
Jafa, Arthur, 132, 366, 374
Janine (Dunye, 1990), 143
Jenkins, Bruce, 156–59, 161
Jensen, Jytte, 212–13
John and Jane Toll-Free (Ahluwalia,
    2005), 181, 265
Johnson, Albert, 374
Johnson, Tom, 13, 34, 43
Jones, Jacquie, 115, 143–44
Jordan, Jeanne, 115
Jordan, Lawrence, 374–75
Joreige, Khalil, 132, 364, 369, 374
Journey, The (Watkins, 1987), 4, 50,
    87–88, 100–102, 103–4, 107

Kalama Sutta (Fisher, 2002), 226
Kanwar, Amar, 31, 238, 297
Katatsumori (Kawase, 1994), 297
Katz, John, 33, 37
Kawase, Naomi, 249, 297, 378
Kerr, Mary, 301, 311, 312, 314, 322,
    325, 327
Khan, Hassan, 75, 366, 369
Killer of Sheep (Burnett, 1978), 166
Kissel, Laura, 188, 190, 327
Klee, Paul, 334
Klein, Jim, 19, 46
Korda, Alexander, 119
Kristallnacht (Strand, 1979), 302,
    304–6
Kuchar, George, 171–72, 210, 216
Kukurantumi: The Road to Accra
    (Ampaw, 1983), 71
Kunuk, Zacharias, 220–23

La Ofrenda (Portillo, 1989), 85
La Television y Yo (Di Tella, 2003),
  255
Lathan, Stan, 23
Lawder, Standish, 33, 372
Leacock, Richard, 9, 35, 44, 89, 114,
  147, 166, 171, 185, 186, 189, 245
Learning Path, The (Todd, 1991), 171
Leduc, Paul, 135, 143
Lee, Spike, 114, 227, 330
Lee, Toby, 367, 370
Leimbacher, Irina, 31, 75, 237, 291,
  293–94, 296–97, 301–2, 303, 308,
  311, 373
Lelaki Komunis Terakhir (The Last
  Communist) (Muhammad, 2006),
  265
Leonel, Nuno, 379, 382
Lerner, Jesse, 247, 252, 262
Les statues meurent aussi (Marker
  and Resnais, 1953), 355
Let's Talk About Water project
  (Lilienfeld), 25, 27
Levine, Saul, 297, 378, 381–82
Levinson, Julie, 112
LGBTQ issues, 70–71, 154, 158, 163,
  193, 209, 366
Libertad (Alonso, 2001), 297
Light Licks: By the Waters of
  Babylon: In the Hour of Angels
  (Levine, 2004), 381–82
Lightning Over Braddock: A
  Rustbowl Fantasy (Buba, 1988),
  64, 67
Lightning Testimonies, The (Kanwar,
  2007), 238
Lillian (Williams, 1993), 88, 114
Lim, Dennis, 206, 245, 285, 311, 313,
  317, 318, 321, 324, 358, 372
Lisboa, Nuno, 75, 148, 298, 327, 335,
  386, 387, 395
Littin, Miguel, 23
Littlebird, Larry, 15
Little Tich and His Big Boots
  (Ahwesh, 1900), 185
Live Nude Girls UNITE! (Funari
  and Query, 2000), 201
Livingston, Jason, 54, 205, 274, 335
Los Angeles Station (Katz, 1970), 260

Los Muertos (Alonso, 2004), 313
Lotfy, Hala, 297, 366, 369, 370
Louisiana Story (Flaherty, 1948), 40,
  41, 114, 176, 186, 218, 391
Louisiana Story Study Film, 9, 114,
  185
Lozano, Joey, 230, 236, 237

MacDonald, Scott, 107, 108, 166,
  178, 234, 269, 335; on "avant-doc,"
  297; first Flaherty Film Seminar,
  48, 50; programmer for 1992
  Flaherty Film Seminar, 51, 104,
  141. See also Flaherty: Decades
  in the Cause of Independent
  Cinema, The (Zimmermann and
  MacDonald)
Mack, Jodie, 190, 227, 330
Made in China: A Search for Roots
  (Hsia, 1985), 71
Magic for Beginners (McLean, 2010),
  354
Mahfouz, Asmaa, 342
Mai's America (Poras, 2002), 226
Maldoror, Sara, 246, 297, 342
Man Marked for Death/Twenty Years
  Later, A (Coutinho, 1984), 71
Man of Aran (Flaherty, 1934), 41, 295
Man with a Movie Camera, The
  (Vertov, 1929), 122
Marcorelles, Louis, 12
Margaret Mead Festival, 220
Marker, Chris, 39, 46, 166, 246, 342,
  347, 355
Marks, Laura U., 75, 129–34, 269,
  364, 365–67, 369, 374
Marseille après la guerre (Woodberry,
  2016), 379
Martel, Caroline, 227, 297
Massiah, Louis, 14–16, 65, 103, 114
McCoy, Kevin and Jenn, 181
McElwee, Ross, 34, 71, 123
McLean, Jesse, 339, 350, 352–54, 361,
  369
McLibel: Two Worlds Collide
  (Armstrong, 1998), 226
Measures of Distance (Hatoum),
  179–80
Media Study/Buffalo, 44, 338, 368

Medvedev, Pavel, 108, 308
Megacities (Glawogger, 1998), 313
Mekas, Jonas, 4, 23, 46, 99, 137, 185, 295–96
Memories of an Everyday War (Barrios, 1986), 71
Menendez, Oscar, 299
Meta Mayan II (Velez, 1981), 30, 34
México, la Revolución congelada (*Mexico, the Frozen Revolution*) (Gleyzer, 1973), 300–301
Miconi, Dolores, 299
Millhouse: A White Comedy (de Antonio, 1971), 19
Minamata—The Victims and Their World (Tsuchimoto, 1971), 231
Mirror Mirror (Krawitz, 1990), 127
Moana (Flaherty, 1926), 163
Moana of the South Seas (Flaherty, 1926), 154, 163
Moana with Sound (Flaherty,1981), 154
Mograbi, Avi, 226, 235
Mongoloid (Conner, 1978), 53
Monk, Meredith, 53, 55
Monkey and Lumps (Andrews, 2006), 181
Monroy, Gabriela, 309, 348–51, 359, 362
Montaña en sombra (*Mountain in Shadow*) (Patiño, 2012), 354
Moore, Michael, 123, 296
Morelia International Film Festival, 279
Morris, Errol, 122–23, 296
Moscow Does Not Believe in Queers (Greyson, 1986), 107
Mosori Monika (Strand, 1970), 19
Mourir à tue-tête (Poirier, 1979), 38
Movie, A (Conner, 1958), 53, 60
Moving House (Tan, 2001), 190
Muhammad, Amir, 277, 278
Munro, Grant, 20, 84, 88, 119
Murder of Fred Hampton, The (Gray and Alk, 1971), 19
Museum of Modern Art, 37, 39, 47, 65, 84, 88, 182, 224, 326, 344–45, 407–8

Museum of Natural History, 25
Mutual Analysis (Forgács, 2004), 127

N!ai, the Story of a !Kung Woman (Marshall, 1980), 38
Nair, Mira, 35, 71, 79
Nanook of the North (Flaherty, 1922), 122, 166–67, 176, 180–81, 295; *Blood Lust of the Wolf* (Tarr, 2015) and, 219; commercial success of, 186; criticism and controversy, 39, 119–20, 158–59, 185, 252–53; filming of, 153; Flaherty Film Seminars, 122, 166–67; seminar logo and, 185, 198, 383, 401, 403–6; Zimmermann, Patricia, lecture on, 180
National Endowment for the Arts, 18, 46
National Endowment for the Humanities, 18
National Film Board of Canada, 38, 295, 297, 330
National Gallery of Art, 25
New Day Films, 19, 20
New School, The, 40, 271, 398
New York Film Festival, 1970, 17
New York Film/Video Council, 135, 224
New York State Council on the Arts (NYSCA), 41, 84, 94, 269
Nicaragua: Hear-Say/See-Here (Skoller, 1986), 74–75
Nightfall (Suwichakornpong, 2016), 400
Night of Storytelling, A (Flaherty, 1935), 131
Nina Split in Two (Williams, 1988), 88–89
Noblesse Oblige (Sonbert, 1981), 147
No Justice No Peace: Young, Black, Immediate (Cobb, 1992), 142
non-preconception, principle of, 70, 115, 131, 147, 148, 167–68, 186, 273, 276, 298, 331, 342, 345
No Place to Hide (Johnson and Bird, 1983), 34
North on Evers (Benning, 1991), 171

O'er the Land (Stratman, 2008), 297, 341, 346

of the North (Gagnon, 2015), 76, 235, 298, 386, 395–96, 398

Olson, Dorothy, 34, 43

Olson, Paul, 34, 43

Omar Gatlato (Allouache, 1977), 126

On Being There with Richard Leacock (Weiner, 2010), 227

Oneiromancer (Santiago Muñoz, 2017), 401

One P.M. (Pennebaker and Godard, 1971), 19

On the Spot (Levine, 1973), 297

Ophuls, Marcel, 23, 42, 44, 409

O Regresso de Amílcar Cabral (The Return of Amílcar Cabral) (Na N'Hada, 1976), 342

Orientations (Fung, 1986), 71

Other, the, 28, 31, 107, 120, 159, 193, 227, 254, 257, 387

Otolith Group, 63, 246, 297, 341, 346

Ottinger, Ulrike, 35, 131, 167, 366, 369, 370, 374

Oxtoby, Susan, 75, 194, 245, 373

Ozu, Yasujirō, 23, 42, 409

Pakalniņa, Laila, 97, 234

Paper Tiger Television, 30, 46, 49, 71, 189, 190

Paradox (Katz, 2001), 260

Parsons, Peggy, 25

Pather Panchali (Ray, 1955), 9

Paul Cadmus: Enfant Terrible at 80 (Sutherland, 1984), 65–66

Pearl, Daniel, 108

Peck, Raoul, 35, 127, 135, 147, 194

Peleshyan, Artavazd, 114, 115, 123, 189

Pendleton, David, 323, 335; death of, 132; E agora? Lembra-me (What Now? Remind Me) (Pinto, 2013), 148, 297; programmer for 2016 Flaherty Film Seminar (PLAY), 249, 323, 377–79, 381; "Reasons to Believe in This World: The Responsibilities of a Film Programmer," 131

Pennebaker, D. A., 19, 22, 44, 189

People's Communication Network, 341

People to be Resembling (Otolith Group, 2012), 341

Permian Strata (Conner, 1969), 53

Phantom of the Operator, The (Martel, 2004), 329, 330

Pincus, Ed, 33, 65

Pinto, Joaquim, 148, 297, 379, 382

Poem is a Naked Person, A (Blank, 1974), 297

Points of Departure for a Diaspora Dawta! (Cobb, 1991), 142

Poirier, Anne-Clair, 33, 38

Pollard, Samuel D., 114, 227, 330

Porterfield, Matthew, 326–27

Post, Marjorie Merriweather, 29–30, 34, 42

Poto and Cabengo (Gorin, 1980), 38

Pour la suite du monde (For Those Who Will Follow) (Brault, 1963), 166

Power! (Massiah and Rockefeller, 1988), 85

Prelinger, Rick, 161–62

"programmers circle," 186

projectors, film and video, 9, 50, 54–55, 57, 67, 79, 147, 162, 184

Promised Paradise (Helmrich, 2006), 290

Queen Mother Moore Speech at Greenhaven Prison (People's Communication Network, 1973), 341

Qué hacer! (Landau, 1971), 23

Qu'ils reposent en révolte (George, 2010), 297

Qulliq (Oil Lamp) (Arnait Video Collective, 1989), 131

Radiant, The (Otolith Group, 2012), 297

Ramad (Ashes) (Hadjithomas and Joreige, 2003), 131

Rastorguev, Aleksandr, 306

Rate It X (Winer and de Koenigsberg, 1986), 71

Rawane's Song (Al Solh, 2006), 131, 370

Ray, Satyajit, 9

Reagan, Ronald, 33, 78, 122

Reassemblage (Trinh, 1982), 47, 76, 388–90

Reeves, Daniel, 30, 34, 71, 175, 178

Reeves, Jennifer, 166

Reflections (Tourtelot, 1955), 370

Rehrer, Anita, 394

Reichert, Julia, 19, 46, 49

Reinke, Steve, 132, 364, 366, 369, 374

Reminiscences of a Journey to Lithuania (Mekas, 1972), 22

Renov, Michael, 247, 252, 262, 352

Resnais, Alain, 166, 355

Reunion of All My Babies, A (Stoney, 2010), 227

Ricci Lucchi, Angela, 101, 107

Riggs, Marlon, 35, 58, 62, 85, 93, 97, 107, 123, 141, 193

Rios, Humberto, 299–301

Ritual in Transfigured Time (Deren, 1946), 61

Rivera, Alex, 93, 218, 313

Roam Sweet Home (Spiro, 1996), 170

Robert Flaherty Film Seminar. *See* Flaherty Film Seminar

Rocky Mountain Film Center, 105–6

Roger and Me (Moore, 1989), 123

Rossell, Deac, 54

Rossi, Giancarlo, 35

Rothschild, Amalie, 19, 23

Rottenberg, Mika, 235, 313

Rouch, Jean, 146, 328

Route 181 (Sivan and Khleifi, 2003), 341

Routine Pleasures (Gorin, 1986), 71

Roy, L. Somi, 149, 372

Rubin, Barbara, 10

Ruby, Jay, 39

Rulfo, Juan Carlos, 253, 257, 262

Sachs, Lynne, 118, 119

Sad Song of Yellow Skin (Rubbo, 1970), 19

Sakr, Laila Shereen, 7, 369, 370

Salvador Allende (Guzmán, 2003), 257

Sambizanga (Maldoror, 1972), 297, 342

San Soleil (Marker, 1983), 246, 342

Santiago Muñoz, Beatriz, 76, 214, 401

Scenes from Childhood (Guzzetti, 1980), 38

Schulman, Sarah, 397–98

Schwartz, Lillian, 190, 227, 330

Seasons, The (Peleshyan, 1975), 123, 189

Seeing Is Believing: Handicams, Human Rights, and the News (Wintonick and Cizek, 2002), 226, 236–37

Seeing Red (Klein and Reichert, 1983), 46

Seid, Steve, 181, 245, 273, 373

Self Portrait Post Mortem (Bourque, 2002), 127

Selling of the Pentagon, The (Davis, 1971), 19

Sembène, Ousmane, 23, 253, 409

seminars. *See under* Flaherty Film Seminar

Sepúlveda, Juan Manuel, 366, 369, 374

Serkin, Rudolf, 9

Sermons and Sacred Pictures (Sachs, 1989), 61–62, 118–19

Services of the Goods (Kelly, 2013), 341–42

Seventeen (DeMott and Kreines, 1980), 46

Shadow of the Earth (Louhichi, 1982), 71

She Don't Fade (Dunye, 1991), 143

Sherman's March (McElwee, 1986), 71, 123

Shiranui Sea (Tsuchimoto, 1975), 231

Shooting Blind (Seeing with Photography Collective), 209

Singapore GaGa (Tan, 2010), 190, 227

Singapore International Film Festival, 187

Sivan, Eyal, 246, 341, 346

Sloan, William "Bill," 20, 43, 135, 407–9; "Bill's Bar," 55, 66, 88, 224,

409; at Donnell Film Library (New York Public Library), 21–22, 407; at Museum of Modern Art, 34, 39, 65, 88, 407; programmer for 1972 Flaherty Film Seminar, 22, 23, 42, 408–9; programmer for 1992 Flaherty Film Seminar, 141; on programming as an art, 84

Smith, Jack, 10

Smothering Dreams (Reeves, 1981), 30, 34

Solondz, Josh, 312, 314

Sonic Outlaws (Baldwin, 1995), 155

Sorrow and the Pity, The (Ophuls, 1969), 23, 42, 43

Species in Danger Ed! (Cobb, 1989), 142

Spend It All (Blank, 1971), 23

Spin (Springer, 1995), 155

Squeezing Sorrow from an Ashtray (Reinke, 1992), 297

Stand van de Maan (*Shape of the Moon*) (Helmrich, 2006), 233–34, 290

Still/Here (Harris, 2001), 76, 401

Stoney, George, 23, 31, 35, 36, 43, 55, 63, 65, 90, 208, 210, 224, 227, 297, 330, 357

Stracke, Casper, 75, 285, 309, 348–51, 359, 362

Strand, Chick, 19, 302, 304–6, 308

Stranger Comes To Town (Goss, 2007), 181

Stranger with a Camera (Barret, 1999), 115

Stratman, Deborah, 297, 341, 346, 347

Streible, Dan, 63, 190, 329, 372

Study in Choreography for the Camera, A (Deren, 1945), 61

Sundance Film Festival, 45, 114

Sweep (Hoffman and van Ingen, 1995), 153, 154–55

Sweetgrass (Barbash and Castaing-Taylor, 2009), 208, 238

Symbiopsychotaxiplasm: Take One (Greaves, 1972), 127, 135, 249, 256

Tahimik, Kidlat, 46, 49, 382

Tailenders, The (Horne, 2005), 274

Tanner, Alain, 28–29

Teguia, Tariq, 75, 132, 297, 369, 370, 374

Telluride Film Festival, 374

Tennant, Carolyn, 244, 245

Ten Second Film (Conner, 1965), 53

Thin Blue Line, The (Morris, 1988), 122

Thirteen (Williams, 1997), 50, 89

Three Men and a Fish Pond (Pakalniņa, 2008), 234

Ties that Bind, The (Friedrich, 1984), 95, 96

Todd, Loretta, 4, 172

Todd, Robb, 234

Tongues Untied (Riggs, 1989), 123, 193

Toronto International Film Festival, 67, 222

Torres, John, 400–401, 402

To Taste a Hundred Herbs (Hinton and Gordon, 1984), 71

Tran T. Kim-Trang, 62, 150, 151, 200

Trần Văn Thủ, 226, 230

Trials of Alger Hiss, The (Lowenthal, 1980), 38

Trinh T. Minh-ha, 47, 49, 62, 71, 74, 75, 76, 84, 118, 216, 234, 388–89

Trip Down Market Street Before the Fire, A (Miles brothers, 1906), 227

Troubled Waters (Hansen, 1986), 71

Trump, Donald, 182, 200, 346, 384, 387

Trut (*Seahawk*) (Sucksdorff, 1944), 208

Tshaka, Jackie, 141, 143

Tsuchimoto, Noriaki, 231

Turumba (Tahimik, 1982), 47

Ukranian Time Machine (Uman, 2008), 245–46

Un banquete en Tetlapayac (Debroise, 2000), 261

Unfinished Revolution (Howe, 1986), 107

Unter Schnee (*Under Snow*) (Ottinger, 2014), 131, 370

van der Keuken, Johann, 35, 101, 107, 114, 146, 147, 189, 208
Van Dyke, Barbara, 20, 37, 42, 43, 49, 178
Van Dyke, Murray, 42
Van Dyke, Willard, 18, 19–20, 22, 37, 39, 224, 405
van Ingen, Barbara (Flaherty), 163
van Ingen, Sami, 163
Vasulka, Steina, 55, 114
Vélez, Edin, 30, 34
Vertov, Dziga, 31, 122, 388
Video Letters 1, 2 & 3 (Yau, 1993), 127
Vietnam War, 18, 69

Waddington, Laura, 284–86
Walking (Larkin, 1968), 23
Wanda (Loden, 1970), 19
War at Home, The (Silber and Brown, 1979), 38
Ward, Melinda, 45–46, 47
Watkins, Peter, 50, 87, 88, 100–102, 103–4, 107
Wavemakers (Martel, 2012), 227, 297, 329
Waxman, Dani, 35
We (Peleshyan, 1969), 189
Weather Diary I (Kuchar, 1986), 171
Weill, Claudia, 23, 42
Weiner, Jane, 227
Werner Herzog in Peru/Burden of Dreams (Blank, 1982), 33–34
We Were So Beloved (Kirchheimer, 1985), 66
What Farocki Taught (Godmilow, 1997), 355
What You Take for Granted (Citron, 1983), 47
Who Invented the Yo-yo?/Who Invented the Moon Buggy? (Tahimik, 1980–1981), 47
Whore's Glory (Glawogger, 2010), 245
Wide Angle (journal), 38, 102, 217, 226, 245
Williams, David, 50, 88–89, 114–15
Williams, Teddy, 234
Wintonick, Peter, 226, 236
Wiseman, Frederick, 23, 342
WITNESS, 236–37, 238

Woman's Film, The (Smith, Alaimo, and Sorrin, 1971), 19
Women's Film Festival, 19
women's movement, 18, 28
Woodberry, Billy, 379
Woo Who? May Wilson (Rothschild, 1970), 17
Workers Leaving the Factory (Farocki, 1995), 185, 189, 192, 201
Workers Leaving the Factory (Lumière Brothers, 1895), 185, 192
Workingman's Death (Glawogger, 1998), 108, 245, 297, 313, 318
World Cup, 35, 242, 321, 357–58
Worth, Sol, 20, 28, 32

Xanini (Corn Stalks) (Cerano, 1999), 289
XCXHXEXRXRXIXEXSX (Nervous System performance) (Jacobs, 1992), 50–51, 135, 139–40, 142–43
Xi Jinping, 327

Yang, Chi-hui, 206, 277, 283, 285, 317, 344, 370, 373–74
Yasui, Lise, 141
Young, Robert M., 33

Zhang Xianmin, 326–27
Zhao, Dayong, 313, 324, 326
Žilnik, Želimir, 214, 401
Zimmermann, Patricia, 48, 84, 91, 101, 106, 113, 131, 165, 171, 180, 218, 269, 276, 280; first Flaherty Film Seminar, 36–39; on Hollywood, 197; programmer for 1994 Flaherty Film Seminar, 149, 372; programmer for 1997 Flaherty Film Seminar (Explorations in Memory and Modernity), 93, 173–75, 177–78, 179. *See also Flaherty: Decades in the Cause of Independent Cinema, The* (Zimmermann and MacDonald)
Ziv, Ilan, 101, 107
Zornow, Edith, 17
Zürcher, Ramon, 366, 369, 370, 374
Zyklon Portrait (Schogt, 1999), 226

www.ingramcontent.com/pod-product-compliance
Lightning Source LLC
Chambersburg PA
CBHW080922100426
42812CB00007B/2344

SCOTT MACDONALD is Professor of Art History and Director of Cinema and Media Studies at Hamilton College. He is author (with Patricia R. Zimmermann) of *The Flaherty: Decades in the Cause of Independent Cinema* (IUP, 2017). Other recent books include *American Ethnographic Film and Personal Documentary: The Cambridge Turn*; *Avant-Doc: Intersections of Documentary and Avant-Garde Film*; *Binghamton Babylon: Voices from the Cinema Department, 1967–1977* (a nonfiction novel); and *The Sublimity of Document: Cinema as Diorama*. He curates the F.I.L.M. series at Hamilton College.

PATRICIA R. ZIMMERMANN is Professor of Media Arts, Sciences, and Studies at Ithaca College and Director (with Thomas Shevory) of the Finger Lakes Environmental Film Festival. She is author (with Scott MacDonald) of *The Flaherty: Decades in the Cause of Independent Cinema* (IUP, 2017). Other recent books include *Documentary Across Platforms: Reverse Engineering Media, Place, and Politics* (IUP, 2019); (with Helen De Michiel) *Open Space New Media Documentary: A Toolkit for Theory and Practice*; and *Open Spaces: Openings, Closings, and Thresholds of Independent Public Media*.